The People of the Book, ahl al-kitāb

STUDIES IN THEOLOGY
SOCIETY AND CULTURE

Series Editors:

Dr Judith Gruber
Dr Norbert Hintersteiner
Dr Declan Marmion
Dr Gesa Thiessen

Volume 14

PETER LANG
Oxford • Bern • Berlin • Bruxelles • New York • Wien

Richard Lawrence Kimball

The People of the Book, ahl al-kitāb

A Comparative Theological Exploration

PETER LANG
Oxford • Bern • Berlin • Bruxelles • New York • Wien

Bibliographic information published by Die Deutsche Nationalbibliothek.
Die Deutsche Nationalbibliothek lists this publication in the Deutsche National-
bibliografie; detailed bibliographic data is available on the Internet at
http://dnb.d-nb.de.

A catalogue record for this book is available from the British Library.

Library of Congress Control Number:

Names: Kimball, Richard Lawrence (kimballr@tcd.ie), 1962- author.
Title: The people of the book, ahl al-kitab : a comparative theological exploration /
   Richard Lawrence Kimball.
Description: New York ; Bern : Peter Lang, 2019. | Series: Studies in theology,
   society and culture ; v. 14 | Includes bibliographical references and index.
Identifiers: LCCN 2018024742 | ISBN 9781788742689 (alk. paper)
Subjects: LCSH: Islam--Relations--Christianity. | Islam--Relations--Judaism.
   | Christianity and other religions--Islam. | Judaism--Relations--Islam. |
   Islam--Doctrines.
Classification: LCC BP171 .K585 2018 | DDC 297.2/83--dc23 LC record available at
   https://lccn.loc.gov/2018024742

Cover image: 'New Jerusalem' by Marija Kovać.

ISSN 1662-9930
ISBN 978-1-78874-268-9 (print)   ISBN 978-1-78874-269-6 (ePDF)
ISBN 978-1-78874-270-2 (eBook)   ISBN 978-1-78874-271-9 (Mobi)

© Peter Lang AG

Published by Peter Lang Ltd, International Academic Publishers,
52 St Giles, Oxford, OX1 3LU, United Kingdom
oxford@peterlang.com, www.peterlang.com

All rights reserved.
All parts of this publication are protected by copyright.
Any utilisation outside the strict limits of the copyright law, without
the permission of the publisher, is forbidden and liable to prosecution.
This applies in particular to reproductions, translations, microfilming,
and storage and processing in electronic retrieval systems.

This publication has been peer reviewed.

Printed in Germany

Contents

Acknowledgements	vii
Introduction	1
PART I A Critical Study of Qur'ānic Christians in Islamic *Tafsīr*	9

CHAPTER 1
Ahl al-Kitāb: The Qur'ānic People of the Book	11

PART II Challenging the Constructs: Expanding *Tafsīr* of the Qur'ānic People of the Book	71

CHAPTER 2
Beyond *Al-jāhiliyya*: The Social and Historical Context of the People of the Book in Pre-Islamic Arabia	73

CHAPTER 3
Resisting the Construct: Post-Conquest Christian Theological Responses to Islam	143

PART III Contemporary Refiguring of the People of the Book	207

CHAPTER 4
Contemporary Islamic Use of the Term "People of the Book"	209

CHAPTER 5
Contemporary Muslim-Christian Engagement with
the People of the Book										237

Conclusions: Challenges and Opportunities						279

Glossary											287

Bibliography										297

Index											313

Acknowledgements

I would like to thank God for the courage and strength to complete this research. May God be pleased with the results and allow it to help provide a bridge between religious divisions and misunderstandings towards a more just and peaceful world.

Many people helped and encouraged me to persevere over the course of this project. First and foremost, I would like to express my sincere gratitude to Prof. Dr Norbert Hintersteiner who supervised my PhD research. Over the course of his supervision he introduced me to some of the most respected minds in the field of Muslim-Christian relations. I am especially grateful to have made the acquaintance of Sidney H. Griffith, Shawqi N. Talia, David Thomas, Ataullah Siddiqui and Fadi Daou. I would especially like to thank Sidney H. Griffith for his tutorage with the translation of a text by the tenth-century Bishop of Gaza, Sulaymān ibn Hasan al-Ghazzī, and Shawqi Talia for showing me just how small the world really is. I would like to thank Dr Nayla Tabbara for providing constructive insights that helped shape the final outcome of this book.

The Religious Society of Friends has been a great source of support to me throughout the course of this exploration. On a number of occasions, the Robert and Kezia Stanley Chapman Trust provided timely financial support for which I am grateful. My friends in the Galway Preparative Meeting afforded me a nurturing environment and the opportunity to share snippets of my research. I would like to especially thank Joe Fenwick and Rachel Cave for proofreading the many drafts.

I would like to thank my wife Anne, sons, Liam and Tomás, as well as my mother Susan and brother David. Their patience, sacrifice and encouragement have been a constant source of inspiration to me.

I would also like to thank my friends for their moral support and encouragement. In particular I would like to thank my dearest sister, Mai Abu Marasa, my colleagues Marija Kovač and Vicki Crowley and brothers Tareq Natsheh, Ali Selim, Mohamed Altawil, Eugene Duffy, Billy

Hamilton, Khalid Sallabi and Sami Abo Akle. In the same spirit, I would like to thank Marie Salaün for her assistance with the French-language material, Sumia Sallabi and Abdul Haseeb for their support with Arabic material, as well as Greg Sheaf and Eoghan Mac Cormaic for their support in laying out this research.

Enfin, je voudrais revenir à la source de mon inspiration pour ce project. Je tiens à remercier la communauté chrétienne de la Tunisie de sud, et plus particulièrement Père Dominique Tommy-Martin, pour avoir démontré pendant mon travail avec le Peace Corps qu'il est possible d'être chrétien et d'aimer et de respecter l'islam. Finally, I would like to return to the source of my inspiration for this project. I would like to thank the Christian community of southern Tunisia, and in particular Fr Dominique Tommy-Martin for having demonstrated during my work with the Peace Corps that it is possible to be a Christian and to love and respect Islam.

I would also like to thank the staff at Peter Lang for the opportunity to present my research and for all their encouragement and patience.

Introduction

In today's post-modern, interdependent world where Muslims and Christians are increasingly living and working side-by-side there is a greater need to understand the faith of the religious other better. This is necessary so that Muslims and Christians can appreciate the commitment each makes to serve God in a manner in which their conscience dictates, without diminution of their own faith and its role in God's universal design. Therefore, it is necessary for Christians and Muslims to take sincere steps towards each other with a view of serving God by serving humanity, not as adversaries with conflicting truth claims, but as fellow believers, united in faith, seeking answers to the theological questions that divide us, leaving to God those differences we cannot reconcile. Through this interaction one might hope that each may learn from and be transformed by the experience and knowledge of the other. Through this research, and as a Christian, this author hopes to embark upon such an exploration.

The questions posed in this research are questions that many others more capable than this author have considered before. Yet, the theological differences that divide Islam and Christianity remain unresolved. There appears to be a need to investigate the foundations of dialogue between Muslims and Christians based on a re-examination of the origins of their relationship and following through the formative centuries, when Christians were a sizeable proportion of the population in the Middle East. It is this author's opinion that by returning to the beginning we may find valuable lessons for the present. To this end this book is divided into three parts.

Part I examines the representation of Christians and Christianity in light of their membership in the Qur'ānic collective *ahl al-kitāb* [the People of the Book]. Examining the Islamic concept of *ahl al-kitāb* through Qur'ānic *tafsīr* [traditional commentary], unveils many profound insights regarding how Islam views Christians and Christianity. It is a frequently overlooked fact that the Qur'ān uniquely discusses the strengths and weaknesses of several religions, offering Muslims an authoritative synopsis of the religious other. The Qur'ān discusses Christians and Christianity by a number of appellations.¹ Sometimes the religion and virtues of Christians are held in esteem, as people nearest in faith, while on other occasions the Qur'ān portrays Christians as following false doctrines, or as people not worthy of friendship. Consequently, what the Qur'ān has to say can appear quite contradictory and is therefore in need of greater exploration in order to avoid facile interpretations and needless misunderstandings.

Through the Qur'ānic commentary tradition it is possible to appreciate the individual merit of any particular verse and contemplate the verse's more universal applications. This research examines the commentary of four renown Islamic scholars whose work spans more than a thousand years. These scholars are Mujahid ibn Jabr (*c.* 722), author of the oldest complete *tafsīr*; Muhammad ibn Jarir Al-Tabari (d. 923), one of the most respected scholars in Islam; Ismail Ibn Kathir (d. 1373), whose easily accessible commentary is cited by scholars and laymen alike, and Muhammad Rashid Rida (d. 1935) whose *tafsīr* with its political overtones inspires many modern Salafi movements.

Their commentaries demonstrate that what the Qur'ān has to say about Christians and Christianity is highly contextual regarding the salvific merits of Christianity, what it means to be a believer, and the opposite, *kāfir* [an unbeliever]. The research examines the four key verse groups. *Sūrat al-baqarah* (2):62 names the different religious communities of the People of the Book that the Qur'ān accepts as following divinely revealed texts. *Sūrat an-Nisā* (4):171 warns Christians not to go to excess in their religion, especially in relation to the position of Jesus. *Sūrat al-mā'idah* (5):48 encourages Christians and Muslims to strive in good works with people of other faiths. The final verses examined are *sūrat al- mā'idah* (5):82–3.

---

1   Jane Dammen McAuliffe, *Qur'ānic Christians: An Analysis of Classical and Modern Exegesis* (New York: Cambridge University Press, 1991), 3. Other variant appellations acknowledge reception of divine revelations such as, *"those to whom We gave the Book"*, *"those who were given a portion of the Book"*, *"those who read the Book before you"*, *"Those who follow you"* (referring to followers of Jesus), *"Those who follow him"*, and on occasion, *"a balanced people"*.

Introduction

These verses encourage Muslims to expect the best from Christians in spite of theological and periodic political differences.

The commentary tradition offers profound insights, but there are also serious limitations. It is this author's opinion that understanding Christians and Christianity through the traditional commentary alone is insufficient for comparative theological purposes.[2] Since the traditional commentary does not adequately describe the nuanced Christian self-understanding, the study requires expansion into the nascent socio-cultural, historical and interreligious terrains. This expansion is necessary in order to more comprehensively elaborate the concept of the People of the Book and recognize the possible challenges and opportunities it contains for contemporary Muslim-Christian currents of encounter.

The traditional commentary suggests a *theoretical construct* of the character of Christians and their beliefs that is authoritative for Muslims, and for good reason. The theoretical construct is based on different historical encounters with Christians throughout the revelation of the Qur'ān. The theoretical construct does not represent the particular beliefs of any one denomination of Christianity, but rather acts as a general description of all Christians.[3] Subsequently, a Christian reader from a particular denomination, then and now, could easily take issue with this theoretical construct as unrepresentative of "their" Christian beliefs. This research therefore seeks to understand how *tafsīr* may be employed to gain a greater understanding of how Islam views Christians and Christianity and the reasons why and when the Qur'ān takes a particular view. In this way a Christian who wishes to engage meaningfully with Muslims may better understand Islam and engage in more fruitful dialogue.

Through the lens of *tafsīr* problems emerge concerning the social-cultural character of pre-Islamic society and the self-understanding of Christian creedal formulations that require further investigation. This period of time is frequently referred to as *al-jāhiliyya*, or the *Time of*

---

2   The hermeneutic of tafsīr is explained in further detail below, in the section entitled "A Brief History of the Qur'ān and the Islamic Science of Tafsīr".
3   Jane Dammen McAuliffe, *Qur'ānic Christians: an analysis of classical and modern exegesis* (Cambridge: Cambridge University Press, 1991), 288.

Ignorance. Use of this term creates a colourful generalization, a historical construct, that unfortunately neglects some very important details concerning the communities encountered by Muhammad. Although the *tafsīr* literature provides some background information regarding the *asbāb an-nuzūl* [occasions of revelation], of the verses of the Qur'ān, the social-cultural and historical context of the revelation of the Qur'ān is not an area that is well understood. Many important aspects of Arabian society at the dawn of Islam that might have been familiar to the companions of the prophet and their followers are now long forgotten.

Part II of this book examines further areas identified in the *tafsīr* literature as requiring closer examination. The research focus is on the social-cultural and historical character of pre-Islamic Arabia. How the various communities described as the People of the Book arrived in Arabia and spread from there is of seminal importance. The research explores the different Christian and Jewish communities from Arabia, as well as the neighbouring peoples of Abyssinia and Yemen with which Muhammad came into contact. The research examines possible historical, religious and social baggage that might have influenced these communities' relationship with one another and how Islam was initially received. The research contends that this period is where the Qur'ān needs to be understood, before postulating interpretations into future contexts. Most importantly, a greater understanding of the period of *al-jāhiliyya* and the context of the revelation of the Qur'ān will contribute to the ability of scholars to engage in authoritative development of the traditional commentary.[4]

The next area of inquiry concerns the spread of Islam beyond the Arabian Peninsula following the death of Muhammad in 632 CE. By now many in the ranks of the Army of Islam had never met Muhammad. These Muslims relied on the developing commentary tradition for their understanding of Qur'ān, while applying its teachings in completely new contexts. Here, in the eastern Mediterranean region, or Levant, Islam came into contact with new audiences unconnected with the occasions of revelation in both culture and language. These new communities of the People of

---

4 McAuliffe, *Qur'ānic Christians*, 289.

the Book also questioned the Qur'ānic representation of their faith. This research examines the effects of the Islamic conquest on the centuries-long historical conflicts taking place between the Byzantine and Persian Empires. This conflict often aggravated the sectarian tensions between Jews and Christians, as well as differing Christian communities emerging into their various creedal formulations. While the conquest is often depicted as a negative event, there is a case for suggesting that the results are actually more nuanced, especially as evidenced by the capture of Jerusalem?[5]

The research further queries how Christians living in the region began to formulate their liturgical and theological response to the accusations of excess discussed in *tafsīr* literature, as Arabic becomes the common language and Islam the dominant culture. The research examines the many ways Christians writing in Arabic use Islamic idiom, including use of *asmā allāh al-husnā* [the Beautiful Names of God], as an apologetic tool of *kalām* [the interfaith dialogue] of the time.

Coincidently, but with surprising significance, the Islamization of the Levant takes place as scholars from both Jewish and Christian backgrounds engage in the translation of Greek literature, including Aristotelian philosophy, into their respective languages thus inspiring the great Graeco-Arabic translation movement.[6] This research reflects on the effect this translation movement may have had on levels of co-operation across the Islamic world and on the quality of dialogue. The scholars examined here include Theodore Abū Qurrah (*c.* 820 CE), the first Christian scholar writing in Arabic known by name and one-time Bishop of Harrān; Sulaymān ibn Hasan al-Ghazzī (*c.* 940 CE), a poet and former Bishop of Gaza, who wrote during a difficult period of political upheaval and persecution; and Paul of Antioch (*c.* 1200 CE), the Bishop of Antioch, who is remembered for composing a particularly contentious response to Islam. The research inquires if there is any evidence to suggest that Christians are responsive to Islamic criticisms, or adopt the use of *tafsīr*, in defence of their own tenets

---

5   E. Gibbon, *The History of the Decline & Fall of the Roman Empire* (Penguin, 1994), 65.
6   Dimitri Gutas, *Greek Thought, Arabic Culture: The Graeco-Arabic Translation Movement in Baghdad and Early 'Abbāsid Society (2nd–4th/8th–10th Centuries)* (London: Routledge, 1998), 7–8.

of faith against Muslim interlocutors and in order to bolster the faith of their own community. In addition, the research asks what regard is given by Christian scholars to the Qur'ān and the prophethood of Muhammad.

Part III of this book examines how a selection of modern Muslims and Christian scholars employ the term People of the Book. The first scholar examined is Yusuf Qaradawi. He is based in Qatar and represents a very traditional voice that acts as a sort of control group for the other Muslim scholars. Other scholars include Ataullah Siddiqui, a British Muslim academic and Reader at the Markfield Institute for Higher Education; Tariq Ramadan a French-Swiss scholar and political commentator, who describes himself as a Salafi reformist; Daniel A. Madigan an Australian Jesuit based in Georgetown University where he teaches Islamic studies and religious pluralism; Paolo Dall'Oglio an Italian Jesuit, who until the civil war in Syria, was the director of Mar Moussa monastery, that served as an interfaith centre.[7] Then there are Fadi Daou and Nayla Tabbara, two scholars who promote better understanding of citizenship and religious and cultural plurality in Lebanon. The research inquires whether the challenges and opportunities identified in earlier chapters configure in today's secularized societies, or have new concepts like citizenship, social democracy and human rights become more important for defining relations? The research taps into the shift in authority taking place among Muslims scholars, more confident than previous generations, in their own ability to interpret the requirements of Islam for themselves in their own contexts. As for the Christian scholars, there seems to be a growing willingness to acknowledge the Qur'ān as divinely inspired and Muhammad as a prophet.

The book concludes with the author's personal perspective of the challenges and opportunities that exist today for interfaith dialogue and religious plurality based on an Islamic concept that acknowledges the common unity of the origins of the People of the Book and Islam. Through this process of comparative theological research, it is hoped that Muslims and Christians may come to a greater appreciation of each other's beliefs

---

7   It appears that Fr Dall'Oglio is a casualty of the civil war. <https://aawsat.com/english/home/article/1069241/moroccan-isis-commander-we-killed-italian-father-paolo-dalloglio> accessed 3 March 2018.

Introduction

and from this progress towards a more fruitful dialogue in the spirit of fostering mutual respect and harmonious coexistence.

On a technical note, throughout the book this author has attempted to faithfully transliterate Arabic names and Islamic terms in a manner conducive to the academic reader, while keeping in mind that several renown academics employ differing transliterations for the same names and terms. In these instances, I have chosen to follow the transliteration suggested by Dr. Nayla Tabbara and in consultation with the online version of *The Encyclopaedia Islam*. The glossary at the back of the book contains the Arabic form of many terms in order to allay any possible confusion.

PART I

A Critical Study of Qur'ānic Christians in Islamic *Tafsīr*

CHAPTER 1

Ahl al-Kitāb: The Qur'ānic People of the Book

> May the curse of Allah be upon those who provoke animosity and hatred among the servants of Allah in utter self-interest or to please their masters.
> — RASHID RIDA

Introduction

This chapter begins the exploration of Christianity through the lens of Qur'ānic traditional commentary in light of their membership in the Qur'ānic collective *ahl al-kitāb*, the People of the Book. The primary objective is to examine a selection of verses from the Qur'ān that contribute to the formation of the Qur'ānic image of Christianity. Of seminal importance is the affirmation of the existence of the *theoretical construct* and understanding how the construct works.

Historically, Christian scholars have viewed the term *"ahl al-kitāb"* as both a demeaning label that equates Christianity with other religions that Christians regard as following false doctrines and as a useful tool, that lends a certain degree of status to their position in Islamic society.[1] Equally, the traditional commentary provides challenges and opportunities for Christians that requires fresh analysis for modern society.

---

[1] Sidney H. Griffith, *The Church in the Shadow of the Mosque: Christians and Muslims in the World of Islam* (Princeton, NJ: Princeton University Press, 2008), 71, 160.

CHAPTER 1

A Brief History of the Qur'ān and the Islamic Science of *Tafsīr*

In order for Christians to appreciate what the Qur'ān has to say about them it is necessary to have some understanding of how the Qur'ān came into being and how it is revered and interpreted by Muslims. This brief synopsis of the history of the text of the Qur'ān attempts to encapsulate a very complex period of Islamic history that is an area of research in its own right.

To begin, for Muslims the Qur'ān is God's word revealed to Muhammad through the angel Gabriel.[2] The full contents of the Qur'ān were not written down during the life of Muhammad. At this time the Muslim community relied on the memorization skills of devoted followers to recite the chapters/*sūrat* that had been revealed. Following the death of Muhammad, a series of uprisings began across the peninsula known as *riddah* [the Wars of Apostasy]. At the Battle of Yamamah, many of those capable of reciting the Qur'ān died and Muslims feared that parts of the Qur'ān could be lost. Hence, the process of recording and organising the Qur'ān commenced in earnest.[3]

Zaid b. Thabit (d. 665–6), one of the secretaries of Muhammad, oversaw the first transcription of the *suhuf* [oral tradition] of reciting the Qur'ān, in a process commissioned by the first caliph, Abu Bakr (d. 634).[4] This process continued under the guidance of the second caliph, 'Umar b. al-Kittab (d. 644), with the assistance of 'Umar's daughter and a former wife of Muhammad, Hafsah.[5] After a few years slight variations in the recitation

---

[2] Claude Gilliot, "Creation of a Fixed Text", in *The Cambridge Companion to the Qur'an*, ed. Jane Dammen McAuliffe (New York: Cambridge University Press, 2008), 41. M. M. Al-Azami, *The History of the Qur'anic Text: A Comparative Study with the Old and New Testaments* (Leicester: UK Islamic Academy, 2003), 25.

[3] McAuliffe, *Qur'ānic Christians*, 14. Gilliot, "The Cambridge Companion", 45. Al-Azami, *The History of the Qur'anic Text: A Comparative Study with the Old and New Testaments*, 78, 86, 88.

[4] *The History of the Qur'anic Text: A Comparative Study with the Old and New Testaments*, 78–86.

[5] McAuliffe, *Qur'ānic Christians*, 14.

Ahl al-Kitāb: *The Qur'ānic People of the Book* 13

developed that were dealt with by the third caliph Uthman b. Affan.⁶ Uthman established a commission headed again by Zaid Ibn Thābit that adjudicated over the available material and decided the definitive rendition. Copies of this rendition, *mushaf*, were distributed to the major Islamic centres along with orders to destroy all other previous copies.⁷ Uthman's Codex was written in bare consonant form in Quraysh Arabic, the dialect spoken by Muhammad, without diacritical points to distinguish consonants or pronunciation marks.⁸ The *scripta defectiva* [incomplete script], was more of a mnemonic tool to aid the memorization, *hifz*, of the Qur'ān and to support the oral recitation, which has always been central to the teaching of Islam. Inevitably, minor regional variations developed in the pronunciation of the Qur'ān primarily due to the lack of *tashkīl* [vowel and diacritical markings].⁹

Abu Bakr b. Mujahid (d. 936), oversaw the final stage of the Qur'ānic textual development.¹⁰ Seven recitations that did not contradict the Uthmanic codex gained acceptance. Over time these [recitations] *ikhtiyār*, formed the complete scripture [*scripta plena*] of the Qur'ān. This position seems to be supported by a *hadīth* in which Muhammad said, "the Qur'ān was sent down according to the *ahruf* [seven letters]".¹¹ From this brief synopsis it is possible to appreciate that the Qur'ān, with just one prophetic

---

6   Ali Muhammad As-Sallabi, *The Biography of Uthman Ibn Affan Dhun-Noorayn*, trans. Nasir Khattab (Riyadh: Maktaba Dar-us-Salam, 2007), 319–28.
7   McAuliffe, *Qur'ānic Christians*, 15. Gilliot, "The Cambridge Companion", 45. Al-Azami, *The History of the Qur'anic Text: A Comparative Study with the Old and New Testaments*, 90–1, 93, 94. A few variant codices compiled by Muhammad's closest companions like Abdallah Ibn Mas'ud, Ubayy b. Ka'b, and Abu Musa al-Ash'ari survived. They are mentioned in many early commentaries.
8   McAuliffe, *Qur'ānic Christians*, 14–5. Gilliot, "The Cambridge Companion", 47. Al-Azami, *The History of the Qur'anic Text: A Comparative Study with the Old and New Testaments*, 95, 135–50, 51–64.
9   *The History of the Qur'anic Text: A Comparative Study with the Old and New Testaments*, 87. Here it is reported that Muhammad taught the Qur'ān to people in their variant dialects, which became a problem as the communities merged together.
10 Gilliot, "The Cambridge Companion", 49–50. McAuliffe, *Qur'ānic Christians*, 16.
11 *Qur'ānic Christians*, 15–16. The extra canonical readings of the Qur'ān number around fourteen. Gilliot, "The Cambridge Companion", 51. Al-Azami, *The History*

source and while possessing a continuous line of editorial scrutiny, is for Muslims a sacred unerring text. In addition, because the Qur'ān's authoritative rendition remains in its original Arabic language, readers can be confident that what they are reading today is as close to the original text as any historical document.

From the very beginning of the revelation of the Qur'ān there has been a need to explain its meaning. During his lifetime Muhammad was of course the undisputed authoritative source of interpretation. After his death the science of exegesis, *tafsīr*, developed rules to guide subsequent generations. In the introduction to Ibn Kathir's great work *Tafsīr al-Qur'ān Al-Azim*, he explains the process that developed in early Qur'ānic exegesis. He states that what is discussed in general terms in one place in the Qur'ān is usually discussed in more detail somewhere else in the Qur'ān.[12] That is, the first step of *tafsīr* is to look to the Qur'ān for explanation of the Qur'ān. When an explanation is not readily found then the *sunnah an-nabi* may be consulted.[13] The *sunnah an-nabi*, or *sunnah*, are the normative sayings and practices of the prophet Muhammad.[14] The purposes of the *sunnah* are to help explain the Qur'ān and the faith of Islam. This belief is based on various verses of the Qur'ān including *sūrat an-Nisā'* 4:105: "Surely, We have sent down to you (O Muhammad) the Book (this Qur'ān) in truth that you might judge between men by that which Allah has shown you, so be not a pleader for the treacherous". And another *hadīth* (traditions of the Prophet narrated by his companions) conveys the message, "I was given the Qur'ān and its equal with it" referring to the *sunnah*.[15]

---

    of the Qur'anic Text: A Comparative Study with the Old and New Testaments, 153. A similar story is quoted from a *hadīth* transmitted by Muslim.

12 Al Hafiz Ibn Kathīr, *Tafsīr Al-Qur'ān Al-Azim* [Al-Misbah Al-Munir fi Tahdhib Tafsir Ibn Kathir], ed. Shaykh Safi Ur Rahman Al-Mubarakpuri, trans. Jalal Abualrub, 10 vols, Tafsīr Ibn Kathīr (Abridged) (Riyadh: Darussalam, 2003), Vol. 1:29.

13 G. H. A. Juynbol, *Studies on the Origins and Uses of Islamic Hadih* (Aldershot, Hampshire: Variorum, 1996), Vol. V. 97–9, 101.

14 Deeb Al-Khudrawi, *A Dictionary of Islamic Terms, Arabic-English*, trans. Diane Humaidh Deeb Al-Khudrawi (Damascus-Beirut: Al Yamamah, 1995), 204. Juynbol, *Studies on the Origins and Uses of Islamic Hadih*, V, 98.

15 Ibn Kathīr, *Tafsīr Al-Qur'ān Al-Azim*, Vol. 1:29.

Ahl al-Kitāb: *The Qur'ānic People of the Book*   15

Following the death of Muhammad, his *sahabah* [companions] became involved in the exegesis of the Qur'ān. Prior to his death their involvement would have been unthinkable. Jane Dammen McAuliffe quoting Subhi al-Salih sums up the reasoning in simple terms, "They would not dare explain the Qur'ān while he (Muhammad) was still among them".[16] However, among the *sahabah* there were people recognized as possessing a clear understanding of the Qur'ān and *sunnah* of Muhammad. One of the greatest scholars from among the *sahabah* was Ibn Abbas. His authority is vouchsafed by Muhammad in a *hadīth* that comes down through Al-Bukharī in Fath Al-Bari, 1:205: "O Allah teach him *fiqh* [understanding of the fundamentals of Islam] in religion and interpretation". In support of this *hadīth* Al-Tabari reported that Ibn Mas'ud, another famous scholar and *companion* of Muhammad, confirmed, "yes, Ibn Abbas is the interpreter of the Qur'ān".[17]

The religious science of Ilm al-Hadīth was established in the early centuries of Islam to guard the authenticity of *sunnah* and *hadīth* against *awda* [fabrication].[18] The use of *hadīth* in exegetical work varies from scholar to scholar. Traditionally, when *hadīth*s are quoted, they are accompanied by the relevant *isnād* (chain of transmission) to support the authenticity of the relevant *hadīth*. There have been many studies concerning the authenticity of extra-scriptural sources of authority dating back to the time of Muhammad.[19]

In the second century following the death of Muhammad, discrepancies in the authenticity of many *hadīth*s led six Persian Muslim scholars to research and validate the thousands of *hadīth* extant. The product of their endeavour became known as the *al-kutub al-sittah*. The collection is highly regarded by Muslims as being an authoritative and extensive collection of *hadīth*.[20] Within this collection two scholars rank supreme. These are the

16   McAuliffe, *Qur'ānic Christians*, 17.
17   Ibn Kathīr, *Tafsir Al-Qur'ān Al-Azim*, Vol. 1:30.
18   McAuliffe, *Qur'ānic Christians*, 22.
19   Ibid., 22–3. Cf. Herbert Berg, *The Development of Exegesis in Early Islam* (Richmond, Surrey: Curzon Press, 2000).
20   Al-Khudrawi, *Dictionary of Islamic Terms*, 361. Berg, *Early Islam*, 6, 11. The collection is also sometimes referred to as the *al-Sihah al-Sittah*, the authentic six.

text of Muhammad b. Isma'il al-Bukharī (*c.* 869–70), with his work, *Sahih Bukharī*, and *Sahih Muslim*, the work of Muslim b. Hajjaj al-Naishapuri (*c.* 874–5).[21]

When one is unable to find a suitable explanation through use of the Qur'ān, the *sunnah* or from the *hadīth* of the *sahabah*, it is permissible to examine the *tafsīr* of the *tābi'ūn* [the second generation of Islamic scholars and students of the companions].[22] Mujahid ibn Jabr is one such *tābi'ūn*. His *tafsīr* forms part of the focus of this chapter. Mujahid's quest for knowledge of the Qur'ān and its meaning is immense. He was a dedicated student of Ibn Abbas. So great was his knowledge of the *tafsīr* of Ibn Abbas that the renowned scholar Sufyan Ath-Thawri remarked, "If the *tafsīr* reaches you from Mujahid it is sufficient for you".[23]

Interpreting the Qur'ān has always been a very serious undertaking, even for devout Muslims. Christian scholars would do well to keep in mind that *tafsīr* by mere personal opinion (*ra'y*) is strictly prohibited. A succinct *sunnah* traced back to the prophet Muhammad through Ibn Abbas warns, "Whoever explains the Qur'ān with his opinion or what he has no knowledge of, then let him assume his seat in the fire".[24] Accordingly, the *salaf* [the righteous ancestors] would never have discussed theological issues of which they had no knowledge. The *hadīth* are replete with stories of the *salaf* going to great lengths to avoid venturing opinions that veered close to breaching this command. In one such *hadīth*, Abu Bakr, the first companion of Muhammad says, "Which land will carry me and which heaven will shade me if I said about Allah's book that which I have no knowledge".[25] Where one has no certain knowledge silence is surely the best policy. Little wonder later generations of scholars are reluctant to venture opinions where the *salaf*

---

21 *Early Islam*, 6. Berg also includes to a lesser extent the work of Ahmad ibn Hanbal. Other contributors to the collection are Abu Dawood Sulaiman b. Ash'ath al-Sijistani (*c.* 888–9), Muhammad b. 'Isa al-Tirmidhi (279/892–3), Abu 'Abd al-Rahman al-Nasa'i (915–6), and Ibn Majah al-Qazwini (*c.* 886–7).
22 Ibn Kathīr, *Tafsir Al-Qur'ān Al-Azim*, Vol. 1:32.
23 Ibid., Vol. 1:32.
24 Ibid., Vol. 1:33. McAuliffe, *Qur'ānic Christians*, 20.
25 Ibn Kathīr, *Tafsir Al-Qur'ān Al-Azim*, Vol. 1:33.

Ahl al-Kitāb: *The Qur'ānic People of the Book*

feared to tread. On the other hand, there is a balancing obligation on everyone to convey and explain issues relating to exegesis instructed by the Qur'ān, *sūrat Āl-'Imrān* (3):187: "To make it known and clear to mankind and not to hide it". There is also a *hadīth* reflecting the seriousness of the command, "Whoever is asked about knowledge that he knows but hid it will be tied with a muzzle made of fire on the day of Resurrection".[26] This is not to say that there is no place for the use of rational faculties, but that the use of reason must be based on proper respect and understanding of *taqlīd* [following, or imitating a tradition] the solid foundations of the application of the means of exegesis described above.[27] Only a few scholars have ever been trusted to offer their own independent opinions. Those who were trusted were given the title *mujtihid* [a Muslim scholar of the highest degree of learning] and were allowed to give *ijtihād* [independent legal ruling].[28] Whether or not the gates of *ijtihād* are closed to scholars is debated.

Another tool in the arsenal of exegesis is the use of evidence in support of an opinion drawn from the above sources that are found in "Israelite" Scripture, but this scripture may not be used as evidence on its own.[29] There are early *hadīth* that caution Muslims to be very careful in their use of Israelite Scripture. The concern of Muhammad is very well depicted in a story that comes to us by Ahmad: "O! Ibn al-Khattab, are we going to play in religion? By Allah, I have come to you with a pure religion. Do not ask them about anything, for that they may say something true and you do not believe what they say or they may say something false and you believe it. By Allah, if Musa (Moses) was alive he would not have done anything but follow me".[30]

---

26 Ibid., Vol. 1:34–5.
27 McAuliffe, *Qur'ānic Christians*, 291. It should be noted that the great Muslim theologian was very much opposed to the prevailing trend of blind obedience to *taqlīd* because of the political implications *taqlīd* came to acquire in his lifetime.
28 Al-Khudrawi, *Dictionary of Islamic Terms*, 71–2, 75. Abdal Hakim Murad, "Understanding the Four Madhhabs: The Facts About Ijtihad and Taqlid", in *The Muslim Academic Trust*, ed. The Muslim Academic Trust (London: The Muslim Academic Trust, 2012), 8–10.
29 Ibn Kathīr, *Tafsir Al-Qur'ān Al-Azim*, Vol. 1:31.
30 Rashid Rida, *Al Manar*, trans. Abdul Haseeb, 1990 edn, 7 vols, Tafsir Al-Manar (The General Egyptian Foundation of the Book, 1990), Vol. 5 & 6:341.

Lukewarm support for the use of "Israelite" Scripture is given in a later *hadīth* transmitted by Al-Bukhārī in *Fath Al-Bari* 6:572, "Convey on my behalf, even if it is one *ayah* [sentence], and narrate from the Children of Israel, as there is no sin in this".[31] There are three types of Israelite Scripture accounts and stories to be found: those that are certainly authentic because they are supported by the Qur'ān, those considered false because they are contradicted by the Qur'ān and those neither supported nor denied by the Qur'ān.[32]

The criteria outlined above comprise the considerations employed when Muslim scholars formulate their commentary on the Qur'ān. Appreciation for this process is very helpful for Christians wishing to engage meaningfully in dialogue with Muslims.[33] The story concerning Muhammad and Ibn al-Khattab, and the exhortations against speculation help to illustrate the conditioned conservatism within Islam that is reluctant to engage in intertextual exploration. This conservative bias is understandable, especially if one factors into consideration the need for Islam, during its nascent stage, to come to grips with its own revelation. The warning of Muhammad is ever present: "Do not ask them about anything, for that they may say something true and you do not believe what they say or they may say something false and you believe it".[34]

On the one hand, valid as the warning may be in its proper context, out of context the same warning severely inhibits the willingness of all but a few Muslim scholars to engage with the Christian theology for fear of being out of step with mainstream Islamic thinking. Ironically, this practice also inhibits the ability of Muslims to convey the message of Islam, which is in part, to encourage the People of the Book to re-examine the veracity of the very faith claims with which Islam takes issue, expressed in *sūrat al-mā'idah* (5):19 and *sūrat al-ahqāf* (46):12. As unnerving an exercise as it possibly may be, to lay bare for scrutiny the basis for Christian faith claims cannot but help,

---

31   Ibn Kathīr, *Tafsir Al-Qur'ān Al-Azim*, Vol. 1:31.
32   Ibid. Usually the third type does not have daily or religious significance.
33   For a modern variation see, Ayatullah Ja'far Subhani, *Introduction to the Science of Tafseer of the Qur'an* [Tafsir-e-Sahih-e-Ayat-e-Mushkile-Qur'an], trans. Saleem Bhimji (Middlesex, England: The Islamic Education Board of the Federation of KSIMC, 2006).
34   Rida, *Tafsir Al-Manar*, Vol. 5 & 6:341.

in the end, to strengthen the faith of all believers. Without a mutual appreciation and understanding of each other's text and historical development, Muslims and Christians will, by and large, speak at each other rather than to each other, in the manner intended by God in *sūrat al-ʿankabūt* (29):46: "And dispute ye not with the People of the Book, except in the best way".[35]

The verses chosen for discussion represent a selection of suitable verses from the Qurʾān sufficient to present a Qurʾānic image of Christians and Christianity. According to the research of Jane Dammen McAuliffe there are three categories by which Christians are discussed.[36] The first is through criticism. Some of the criticism is directed against Christians directly, on other occasions the criticism is in conjunction with other communities from the People of the Book. These verses criticize Christians for stubbornly rejecting Muhammad as prophet, preferring their own misguided beliefs, *sūrat al-māʾidah* (5):75, and for wishing to convert Muslims away from their faith, *sūrat al-baqarah* (2):120. In fidelity to the New Testament the Qurʾān warns Christians, as part of the People of the Book, that they themselves are responsible for altering the true message of Jesus, as in *sūrat Āl-ʿImrān* (3):71, and affording undue respect to their monks and priests as lords as in *sūrat at-tawbah* (9):31. One *hadīth* warns, "Do not believe the People of the Book, nor reject what they say. Rather, say, 'we believe in Allah and in what was sent down to us and that which has come down to you'".[37]

A second category identified by McAuliffe, but not touched upon in this chapter, refers to the treatment of Christians by Muslims as in the collection of the *jizyah* [tax], *sūrat at-tawbah* (9):29, levied against the protected communities of the *ahl al-kitāb* in post-conquest times, inter-marriage, *sūrat al-māʾidah* (5):5 and respect for religious structures, *sūrat al-hajj* (22):40.

The third category of verses praises Christians for their piousness and as a "balanced people" (*ummatun muqasidatun*), *sūrat al-māʾidah*

---

35   The Presidency of the Islamic Researches and IFTA, *The Holy Qurʾān: English Translation of the Meanings and Commentary*, trans. Ustadh Abdullah Yusuf Ali (Al-Madinah Al-Munawarah, Saudi Arabia: King Fahd Holy Qurʾan Printing Complex, 1989), 1164.
36   McAuliffe, *Qurʾānic Christians*, 4.
37   Ibn Kathīr, *Tafsir Al-Qurʾān Al-Azim*, Vol. 1:411.

(5):66.³⁸ These verses appear to accept Christians for their sincerity and their faith, but as this exploration will show, context is everything. There are limits to acceptance and tolerance that are exemplified through the *tafsīr*. Whether a verse appears to promote acceptance and co-operation, or whether a verse warns against taking non-Muslims as friends, depends on the context of the revelation and careful study of the relevant *hadīth*. Otherwise one could very easily lose sight of the universal principle of a verse in favour of an interpretation highly dependent on a specific context.

From the more than forty verses of the Qur'ān that discuss Christians and their beliefs the verses chosen below for examination have been selected for the following reasons. First the literal interpretation of each verse has the potential to describe a balanced view of Christians and their beliefs. Second, and most importantly, the traditional commentary of Islamic scholars bears witness to the *theoretical construct*. The primary English translations of the text under discussion are from the Abdullah Yusuf Ali's translation, endorsed by the King Fahd Holy Qur'ān Complex.³⁹ Slight variations with the translation may be noted when quoting from the exegete's own material. The following verses are examined: *sūrat al-baqarah* (2):62, *sūrat an- Nisā* (4):171, *sūrat al-mā'idah* (5):48 and *sūrat al-mā'idah* (5):82.

The Boundaries of the People of the Book: *Surat Al-Baqarah* (2):62

Sūrat al-baqarah (2):62 is a Medinan *sūrat*.⁴⁰ This *sūrat* is one of the most influential *sūrat* in the Qur'ān, because it was revealed in Medina to the early Muslim community. According to Ibn Kathir, scholars say that the *sūrat* contains "a

---

38   McAuliffe, *Qur'ānic Christians*, 192–200. This is in reference to a delegation from Abyssinia who converted to Islam, or People of the Book that do not dispute with Muhammad.
39   The Presidency of the Islamic Researches and IFTA, *The Holy Qur'ān*, 456.
40   Abū Ja'far Muhammad B Jarīr Al-Tabarī, "L'exégèse Du Saint Coran", in *L'Exégèse* (Dar Al-Kotob Al-Limiyah, 2009).

Ahl al-Kitāb: *The Qur'ānic People of the Book*

thousand news incidents, a thousand commands and a thousand prohibitions".[41] Therefore the *sūrat* provides a structure for the early community, encompassing all aspects of life. At the time of its revelation the community began to suffer persecution. Several of Muhammad's followers fled to the Christian Kingdom of Abyssinia to escape from the polytheists of Mecca.[42] Later, Muhammad's community sought refuge in Medina making the great migration, *hijra* in 622 CE.

Several themes are introduced through the commentary of this verse. These are: the identity of the People of the Book, the understanding of "belief" in light of the arrival of Muhammad as well as the Qur'ān, the importance of living one's faith with examples of righteous deeds, and the highly debatable area of abrogation.

Preceding this *sūrat* there are three letters: *alif, lam*, & *mim*. These letters form part of the *Muqatta'āt* letters [fourteen mysterious letters] that appear on occasion to introduce twenty-nine of the 114 *sūrat* found in the Qur'ān. Their significance is disputed, but according to Ibn Kathir "there is no doubt that Allah did not reveal these letters for jest and play".[43] The idea that the letters have some hidden meaning is supported by all our *mufassirūn* [exegetes] and by a few verses in the Qur'ān such as *sūrat Āl-'Imrān* 3:7, "We believe in it; all of it (clear and unclear verses) is from our Lord".[44] The following is Abdullah Yusuf Ali's translation of the verse:

> Those who believe (in the Qur'ān), and those who follow the Jewish (scriptures), and the Christians and the Sabians, and who believe in Allah and the Last Day, and work righteousness, shall have their reward with their Lord on them shall be no fear, nor shall they grieve.[45]

---

41   Ibn Kathīr, *Tafsir Al-Qur'ān Al-Azim*, Vol. 1:101.
42   The term polytheist is used here to describe all non-monotheists living in Mecca at the time.
43   Ibn Kathīr, *Tafsir Al-Qur'ān Al-Azim*, Vol. 1:1–2.
44   Abū Ja'far Muhammad B. Jarīr Al-Tabarī, *The Commentary on the Qur'ān* [Jāmi al-Bayān 'an ta'wīl āy al-Qur'ān], ed. L. J. Cooper (Oxford: Oxford University Press; Hakim Investment Holdings (M. E.) Limited, 1987), Vol. 1:83–5, 88–9. Al-Tabari offers ten possible reasons for the significance of the letters, before offering his own opine that their meaning remains a mystery.
45   The Presidency of the Islamic Researches and IFTA, *The Holy Qur'ān*, 27.

The Occasion of Revelation

According to tradition, the *asbāb an-nuzūl* [occasion of the revelation] of the verse follows the first conversation that took place between Muhammad and Salman al-Farisi. The story is vividly recounted in a *hadīth* narrated by two renowned *tabi'un*, Al-Suddi and Mujahid ibn Jabr.[46] Here, Salman al-Farisi, born a Zoroastrian, describes his journey from Jundishur, in former Persia, to meeting the prophet Muhammad. He explains that one day he and his friend, the son of the King of Jundishur, were out hunting in the desert when they met a Christian monk praying alone. The monk read to them from the Gospel and explained the meaning of the verse. As a result of the encounter both men had what can only be described as a deep religious experience and each man "submitted to God". Soon after their return to Jundishur, Salman left his former life to join the monk and his community near the town of Mosul. While with the monks he was told of the pending arrival of a man who would be called a prophet. One of the signs by which to recognize this prophet is that he would not accept charity, but may accept gifts. Later, while travelling, Salman fell into the hands of robbers who sold him into slavery. He is later bought by a woman from the tribe of Kalb who lives near the village of Yathrib (Medina). She employs Salman to tend her sheep along with another one of her servants. One day Salman hears of a man in Mecca claiming to be a prophet. Salman leaves the sheep with the other servant and sets off for Mecca to see if the stories he has heard are true. When Salman meets Muhammad he watches him for a long time before approaching him. He offers Muhammad food, and Muhammad asks him, what is this? Salman says it is charity, and so Muhammad promptly refuses. After a while Salman approaches Muhammad again with meat and bread, and again Muhammad asks, "what is this?" This time Salman says, "it is a gift". Muhammad accepts the gift and the two men sit and eat the food together. While Salman describes the monks that had told him to expect the arrival of a prophet, Muhammad declares these men are *ahl al-nar*

---

46 Ibn Jabr Mujahid, *Tafsir Mujahid Ibn Jabr*, ed. Dr Muhammad Abdul-Salam Abu Al-Neel, 1st edn (Medina Nasr, Cairo, Egypt: Dar Al Fiqr, Modern Islamic Ideology, 102h), 204.

[people destined for the fire]. Salman is naturally quite disturbed by this remark and proceeds to defend the virtues of his former colleagues, whom he says, "prayed and fasted and believed in you and attested to the fact that you would be sent as a prophet".[47] It is then that the verse is revealed.[48]

Belief, and Those Who Believe

Turning to the opening phrase of the verse, *those who believe*, the commentary of Mujahid explains there is a seismic shift in the nature of belief after the arrival of Muhammad and the revelation of the Qur'ān. Prior to Muhammad people were required to follow the dictates of their religion as well as their prophets and would be judged accordingly. However, following the arrival of Muhammad, Mujahid considers belief in the prophethood and the Qur'ān now essential for true believers.[49] Al-Tabari examines the meaning of "belief" first in general terms, then moves to the particular. He describes in a general sense that "belief" may include what one professes coupled with how one lives one's life.[50] Moving to the phrase's particular import is the decisive challenge to the People of the Book to believe in the authentic mission of Muhammad as prophet: "those who attest the veracity of the Messenger of God and the truth that he brought them from God. Their faith in this is their attesting its veracity".[51] This highly conditional interpretation of the word *imān* [believe] is a minimum requirement for anyone now expecting to be considered a believer. The designation of believer is highly contentious from an interfaith perspective, especially

---

47 McAuliffe, *Qur'ānic Christians*, 108.
48 Al-Tabarī, *Tafsīr Al-Tabarī*, Vol. 1:360–4. Martin Lings, *Muhammad, His Life Based on the Earliest Sources* (India: Allen & Unwin, 1983), 105–8. McAuliffe, *Qur'ānic Christians*, 105–6.
49 Mujahid, *Mujahid, Dr. M. Abdul-Salam, Kuwait University*, 204, fn. 2.
50 Al-Tabarī, *Tafsīr Al-Tabarī*, Vol. 1:94–5. According to the available editions of the Tafsir of Mujahid there is very little commentary from Mujahid. Most of what is known of his commentary is found in the commentary of other *mufassirūn*.
51 Ibid., Vol. 1:356.

when examining attitudes and directives regarding the identity of the opposite, those who are labelled unbelievers, *kāfir*.[52]

Ibn Kathir begins his approach to the problem of belief and disbelief by allowing one verse in the Qur'ān to explain another. He examines the context of the verse in question by examining the preceding verse. This verse (2):61 discusses the people who will receive the most punishment on the Day of Resurrection. The verse states, "The People who will receive the most torment on the day of Resurrection are: a man who was killed by a prophet or who killed a prophet, an unjust ruler and one who mutilates [the dead]". These are the people who have defied God's commands and who "transgress set limits by committing prohibited acts". Therefore, *sūrat al-baqarah* (2):62 explains the opposite; those believers (*mu'min*) who need not fear. Ibn Kathir interprets the verse as indicating that those who lived in earlier times, that is, before the prophet Muhammad, and who followed previous prophets and messengers and were righteous shall receive their *ajruhum* [reward]. These people need not fear what will happen in the future or grieve for what has been lost in the past.[53]

Similarly, Rida sees the reconciliatory thrust of *sūrat al-baqarah* (2):62 in contrast to the condemnatory character of the preceding verse.[54] His explanation of the verse does not concentrate on any particular person or group, but rather, he chooses to universalize the message to encompass the weakness found in all people in general who willingly ignore the guidance of God and the limits that He sets.[55] Verse 62 offers hope for salvation to all people who turn to God and obey Him and his messengers. For Rida the thrust of the verse is such that correct belief and correct action are intrinsically linked. In an effort to further elaborate the point Rida cites the words of his teacher Muhammad Abduh:

---

52   Interestingly, modern scholars also examine the meaning of khafir in Chapter 4 of this dissertation.
53   Ibn Kathīr, *Tafsir Al-Qur'ān Al-Azim*, Vol. 1:247.
54   Rida, *Tafsir Al-Manar*, Vol. 1 & 2:277.
55   Ibid.

... belief in relation to actions will be pure from whispers of infatuations and hallucinations. As a result, a believer rises with his faith to such heights where he would begin to experience the glory of the Lord. So, when he raises his eyes to the highest plane, he lowers them out of awe and falls to the ground in servitude to Allah in fear and awe. And if he looks at what is in his hands, upon which Allah has bestowed upon him, he feels honoured by Allah while finding strength in what he does with whatever is under his control. He does not transgress the limits and does not stand without moving towards the purpose assigned to him until he reaches it. So he remains to be a servant of Allah, a chief of everything after Him.[56]

In strictest terms, *those who believe* refer to those who say they accept and follow the prophet Muhammad. However, true belief is not as simple as that. One's life must reflect one's stated beliefs. Rida stresses that the faith acceptable to God nurtures and educates the individual, and motivates them to do what is good with their life. Belief in religion is a requisite, and one is required to believe unequivocally in Allah and the message of the prophets, so that those who fail to accept the meaning of the verse in its entirety are those who would be chastised in *sūrat al-baqarah* (2):8: "And there are those people who say: we have believed in Allah and the Final Day, and they are not believers". Accordingly, the verse states, it is not their lack of correct belief in Allah and the Final Day, or Muhammad, that causes their ultimate demise, but the lack of self-control, their unwillingness to allow God to transform their lives, to the extent that their stated belief is of little merit to them.[57]

Jews, Christians and Sabians

Examining the phrase *those who are Jews* ... Al-Tabari begins the identification of the members of *ahl al-kitāb*. This is the first community to receive direct revelation from God in the form of the *Torah*. The name for Jews, *hādu* is analysed as coming from the verb *hada* meaning "they repented".[58]

---

56 Ibid. Trans. Abdul Haseeb, ed. Richard Kimball.
57 Ibid., Vol. 1 & 2:278.
58 Al-Tabarī, *Tafsīr Al-Tabarī*, Vol. 1:356–7. Idem, Vol. 1:31.

Following the rational supported by Ibn Jurayj, the Jews are called *yahūd* because they said, "We have turned to you in repentance".[59] Ibn Kathir while agreeing with Al-Tabari over the meaning of the word *yahūd* prefers to explain the origins of the Jews from a slightly more historical perspective. He contends the Jews are followers of the Prophet *Musa* (Moses). They are a people who refer to the *Torah* for judgement and that they are called *yahūd*, which means that they sought repentance from God for their sins and were kind to one another. Another possibility offered for the origin of the name is that it comes from their ancestor *Yahūda* (Judah) a son of the Prophet Yaqub (Jacob).[60]

As for the phrase *and those who are Christians* Al-Tabari begins with an etymological analysis of the word used for Christians in the Qur'ān, *nasārā*. He further explains that *nasārā* is the plural of *nasrāni*, and that there is also the rare feminine form of the word, *nasrāna* and a rare plural form *ansār*.[61] The connection with the word *ansār* [helpers] is interesting. Accordingly, one of the reasons *nasārā* is used to denote Christians is because the Christians would *nusra* [help] one another.[62] This theory is supported by *sūrat as-saff* (61):14, where Jesus asks his followers, "Who will be my *ansāri* [helpers] to the work of Allah?" and they reply, "We are Allah's *ansāru* [helpers]!" Another explanation of the term *nasārā* more recognizable to western Christians posited by Al-Tabari relates to the land called Nāsirah, or Nazareth. This theory is supported by a *hadīth* transmitted from Ibn Juraij. A variation of this theory that is supported by Ibn Abbas and Qatadah, contends that Christians are called *nasārā* because this is the name of the town that Jesus came from, making him the *nāsirī* and by extension his followers *nāsirīyūn*. Ibn Kathir by and large follows the same

---

59   Ibid., Vol. 1:356. The etymological origins of the word *"yahūd"* Judah, see Gen 29:35, differs from Strong's Concordance, [3063] 1507. Eugene H. Maly. *The Jerome Biblical Commentary*, 2 vols (Englewood Cliffs, NJ: Prentice-Hall, 1968), 30.
60   Ibn Kathīr, *Tafsir Al-Qur'ān Al-Azim*, Vol. 1:249.
61   Al-Tabarī, *Tafsīr Al-Tabarī*, Vol. 1:357.
62   Ibid. Cf. Rodney Stark, *The Rise of Christianity: How the Obscure, Marginal Jesus Movement Became the Dominant Religious Force in the Western World in a Few Centuries*, 2nd edn (San Franscisco, CA: Harper Collins, 1997), 74.

Ahl al-Kitāb: *The Qurʾānic People of the Book*   27

explanation as Al-Tabari for the origins of the name "*nāsirī*".[63] As for Rida, the etymology of names for Jews, or Christians is not terribly important. From a historical perspective, the Jews and Christians referred to in the verse are those groups of people who were known by these names or titles at the time. They are people who followed prophets before Muhammad. Allah described some of them as Jews who adopted Judaism. Similarly, the *nasārā* were supporters of the Messiah, and other people simply became known as Sabians.[64]

Tafsīr Mujahid focuses on the identity of the obscure people known as the Sabians. He describes them as "Those people who are between the Magi and the Jews, and have no religion".[65] He warns that their slaughtered food is not to be eaten nor are their women eligible for marriage to Muslims.[66] In effect he is challenging their inclusion as members of *ahl al-kitāb*, the repercussions of which are still felt today. Al-Tabari begins his analysis of the Sabians with an etymological pursuit of the name. He defines Sabians, or *Sābiʾūn*, as the plural of *sabiʾi;* deriving from the verb *sabaʾa*. An interesting use of the word is given in comparison to the stars at night: "so-and-so came suddenly (*sabaʾa*) upon us at such-and-such a place". *Sabiʾi* [convert], the noun in general form, is the label given to a person who converts to a new religion.[67] Al-Tabari continues to examine many theories purporting to identify the origins and beliefs of the Sabians. He mentions two opinions offered by Mujahid pertaining to the Sabians mentioned above.[68] There is a third opinion narrated by Ibn Juraij who again draws upon the work of Mujahid. This narration refers to a conversation between Mujahid and another *Tabiʾun*, this time, Ata ibn Abi Rabah, where the above two points

---

63   Ibn Kathīr, *Tafsir Al-Qurʾān Al-Azim*, Vol. 1:249. Griffith, *The Church in the Shadow*, 7.
64   Rida, *Tafsir Al-Manar*, Vol. 1 & 2:278. The identity of the Sabians is very complex. Confusion follows these people even today, especially as to whether those who claim to be Sabian should they be afforded protection as People of the Book.
65   ibn Jabr Abu al-Hajjaj al-Makhzumi Mujahid, *Tafsir Mujahid*, ed. Abd al Rhman Tahir al-Surati, trans. Sumia Bel Haj, sponsored by Emir of Qatar, Sheikh Khalif Ibn Hamad Al Thani edn (Islamabad, Pakistan: Islamic Research Center, Islamabad), 77.
66   Mujahid, *Mujahid, Dr. M. Abdul-Salam, Kuwait University*, 204.
67   Al-Tabarī, *Tafsīr Al-Tabarī*, Vol. 1:357.
68   Ibid. "L'exégèse" Vol. 1:31–2.

are discussed and an additional point is made. This third opinion states that the *Sābi'ūn* are like the tribe of Sawad, neither like the Magians, Jews or Christians. The two *tabi'un* both report that Muhammad was called *Sābi'ūn* by the polytheists because he left his religion.[69] Other possible meanings, or identities, of the group, come in the form of a *hadīth* that originates from ibn al-Nu'man Qatadah. This *hadīth* discusses their worship of angels and that they pray facing the direction of Mecca. A *hadīth* narrated by Al-Hasan Al-Basri adds that they prayed five times a day. Muhammad wanted to exempt them from the *jizyah* (poll tax) until he was informed that the *Sābi'ūn* worshipped angels.[70] In a *hadīth* narrated by Ibn Zaid, Muhammad postulates that the *Sābi'ūn* are a people from Mesopotamia, near Mosul. In general terms the *Sābi'ūn* profess, there is no god, but God. However, they do not accept Muhammad as prophet, nor do they have any scripture or other prophets. The final opinion suggested by Al-Tabari comes from a *hadīth* narrated by Al-Suddi and simply confirms "Others said that they were a religious group among the people of the scripture".[71]

Like Al-Tabari, Ibn Kathir finds the Sabians difficult to define. His own opinion is in line with the description based on the thoughts of Mujahid: "The Sabians are between the *Majūs*, [Zoroastrian], the Jews and the Christians. They do not have a specific religion". Nor are they polytheists. They lived according to their *fitrah* [instinctual nature]. For this reason, Ibn Kathir goes on to say, some idolaters used to describe converts to Islam as *sabi'i*, meaning that they have abandoned all other religions on earth.[72] Other opinions considered by Ibn Kathir relate that the Sabians did not possess any particular message, nor did they have their own prophet. He reports that the Sabians were a sect from the *ahl al-kitāb* who read from the *Zabūr* (psalms).[73] Rida's understanding of the Sabians is slightly different. He posits the idea that the Sabians may well have been an offshoot

69 *Tafsīr Al-Tabarī*, Vol. 1:358.
70 Ibid. This is an interesting example where the Muslim community was able to inform and influence the decision of Muhammad in matters of interpretation.
71 Ibid.
72 Ibn Kathīr, *Tafsir Al-Qur'ān Al-Azim*, Vol. 1:250.
73 Ibid.

Ahl al-Kitāb: *The Qurʾānic People of the Book*

of Christianity. He suggests this possibility because of the practices they have held in common with mainstream Christianity; namely that Sabians worshiped on Sundays, practised baptism and confession. He notes as well that they practise a number of innovations in their religious practices that regrettably have little or nothing to do with their original prophetic tradition.[74]

The Requisites of Salvation

The next phrase from the verse under discussion is, *Whosoever believes in God and the Last Day, and works righteousness ...* This phrase is explained by Al-Tabari as defining the basic tenet of belief common to and requisite of those who may be confident that they will be rewarded by God: "*their wage awaits them with their Lord*". Unfortunately, the inclusive air of this phrase is soon tempered by the exclusivist terms of the commentary. Al-Tabari posits the question to himself, where is the completion of God's words, "Surely they that believe, and those who are Jews, and the Christians, and the Sabians?" His answer is slightly rhetorical and introduces a condition; "whoso believes in God and the Last Day, their wage awaits them with their Lord".[75] This condition develops whereby there would appear to be a subset from among the Jews, the Christians and the Sabians who are saved rather than their entire respective communities.

In his developing argument Al-Tabari looks at the grammatical issue arising from the apparent lack of agreement between the variations of the word "believe" found in the first phrase "they that believe" and "whoso believes" The problem arises as to "how can those who believe come to believe?"[76] The word examined in the first instance is *āmana*, found in "they that believe". This word is compared with *āmanū*, employed in the phrase

---

74   Rida, *Tafsir Al-Manar*, Vol. 1 & 2:280. Here he is referring to the inappropriate attention paid to celestial bodies.
75   Al-Tabarī, *Tafsīr Al-Tabarī*, Vol. 1:359.
76   Ibid.

"[Believe] in Muhammad and what he brought".[77] For Ibn Abbas and many others, the grammatical issue suggests there is a definite necessity for the People of the Book to come to believe in Muhammad. In fact Ibn Abbas as well as Ibn Kathir hold that the entire verse with its inclusive language is *mansūkh* [abrogated], by *sūrat Āl-'Imrān* (3):85. This verse states, "whoso desires another religion than Islam, it shall not be accepted of him; in the next world he shall be among the losers". On the other hand Al-Tabari examines the possibility that the verse is *muhkam*, meaning [firmly established] and therefore not abrogated by *sūrat Āl-'Imrān* (3):85.[78] This possibility leads to a subtler distinction, that people who remain faithful to their religion, without any change must come to believe and accept Muhammad as prophet (without becoming his follower). Then "whoever among them comes to believe in Muhammad, in what he brought and in the Last Day, and works righteousness, and does not alter or change so that he dies in his 'faith' the reward for his deeds and his wage awaits him with his Lord, as He has described".[79] The phrase *and no fear shall come upon them, neither shall they sorrow* is interpreted to refer to the judgement of the Last Day. Jews, Christians and Sabians who come to believe in Muhammad will not be concerned with judgement of the Last Day when they see the reward that God has prepared for them.[80]

Al-Tabari, while reflecting on the various opinions offered above, summarizes the opinion of Mujahid, who maintains that after the revelation of the verse, Muhammad added, "Whosoever dies in the religion of Jesus and dies in submission to God before he hears of me is in a good 'position,' but whosoever hears of me today and does not believe in me is doomed".[81] In his closing remarks he concludes, "God has not specified the wage of righteous

---

77 Ibid.
78 Ibid., Vol. 1:364. McAuliffe, *Qur'ānic Christians*, 119. Cf. Khaalad Muhammad Khaalid, *Men around the Messenger* [rajil hwul al rasul], ed. Aelfwine Acelas Mischler, trans. Sheikh Muhammad Mustapha Gemeiah Al Azhar Administration (El-Mansoura: Dar Al-Manarah, 2003), 443–50.
79 Al-Tabarī, *Tafsīr Al-Tabarī*, Vol. 1:359.
80 Ibid., Vol. 1:360.
81 Ibid., Vol. 1:364.

action together with faith for some of His creatures rather than others, and the statement in his words 'whoso believes in God and the Last Day' applies to everyone he mentioned at the beginning of the verse".[82] Al-Tabari's commentary thus establishes a precedent that opens the way for Muslims to accept the faith of the People of the Book as potentially salvific, as long as the role of Muhammad is accepted as authentic.[83] No doubt this conditional acceptance remains a challenge for many Muslims and Christians.[84]

Ibn Kathir maintains a much more exclusivist line of argument. For him the inclusivist language of the verse is conditioned and abrogated to the point where the language offers little consolation to the People of the Book. Ibn Kathir demonstrates his understanding of the requisites of salvation by employing verses from *sūrat Āl-'Imrān* (3):85, mentioned above, as well as *sūrat Yunus* (10):62 and *sūrat fussilat* (41):30, that promise those who say, "our lord is Allah (alone)" have no need to fear death for they shall receive glad tidings of Paradise …[85] In addition he draws support from a *hadīth* attributed to Ibn Abbas that emphasizes the importance of accepting Muhammad as prophet: "Allah does not accept any deed or work from anyone, unless it conforms to the Law of Muhammad, that is, after Allah sent Muhammad. Before that, every person who followed the guidance of his own Prophet was on the correct path, following the correct guidance and was saved".[86] For Ibn Kathir then, to be a true believer after the arrival of Muhammad necessitates belief in Muhammad as prophet. He states his position clearly that Allah sent the prophet to all mankind, as the last and final prophet and messenger. All mankind is required to believe in him, obey him, and refrain from what he prohibited; "those who do this are true believers".[87]

---

82   Ibid., Vol. 1:359, 64.
83   Samir Khalil Samir, "Le Commentaire De Tabari Sur Coran 2/62 Et La Question Du Salut Des Non-Musulmans", *Annali: Istituto Orientale de Napoli* 40, no. 30 (1980): 586. This important point is emphasized by Samir, noting the break with traditional commentary.
84   Rashid Rida examines this idea in greater detail in *sūrat al-māʾidah* (5):48.
85   Ibn Kathīr, *Tafsir Al-Qurʾān Al-Azim*, Vol. 1:248.
86   Ibid., Vol. 1:249.
87   Ibid., Vol. 1:250.

After engaging in lengthy exposition of the *taqlīd*, traditional commentary of the verse Rida seems most willing to engage in *ijtihād*, and offer his own opinion, quoting from *sūrat an-Nisā'* (4):123–4 in support of his argument concerning who is saved:

> Not your desires, nor those of the People of the Book (can prevail): whoever works evil will be requited accordingly. Nor will he find, besides Allah, any protector or helper. If any do deeds of righteousness, be they male or female, and have faith, they will enter Heaven, and not the least injustice will be done to them.[88]

It would appear, according to Rida, that personal responsibility and one's response to God strongly affects whether or not one enters Paradise rather than what he describes as "superficial religiosity". God alone decides who will enter Paradise and who will not. He warns Muslims not to be complacent with outward signs of faith, thinking that because they say they believe in Allah and the Last Day they will enter Paradise.[89] He asserts that God will judge all according to one principle and that The People of the Book will receive the reward Allah has promised them if they have lived their lives according to their divine precepts.[90] In defence of his position Rida examines three general categories of people discussed by Imam Ghazali: The first category offered are people like the American Indians. It is not thought they ever received a pure divine message. Therefore these people are thought to be safe from condemnation. The second category describes those who received, or came across the message of Muhammad, but might have been too stubborn or arrogant to consider its import. These people it is said, will certainly have to account for their disbelief. Then there are those who receive the message in an incomplete or distorted form, they like the American Indians, could not be condemned for not accepting Islam. Another category added by Rida, includes people who have been socially conditioned from an early age to reject Muhammad and Islam. These people would be pardoned because the erroneous information they received influenced their ability to appreciate

---

88   Rida, *Tafsir Al-Manar*, Vol. 1 & 2:278. Translation of An-Nisa (4):123–4 by Abdullah Yusuf Ali.
89   Ibid., Vol. 1 & 2:279–80.
90   Ibid., Vol. 1 & 2:278, af. 7.

the message objectively.⁹¹ In today's world this could cover a large percentage of non-Muslims. In summary of his own position on the verse Rida says, "Correct faith is the one that is the top controller of the heart and the will that further controls the limbs during actions. When the worldly desires challenge this control, then this person tries to beat it in the tussle. 'Indeed, those who fear their Lord, when an impulse touches them from Satan, they remember (Him) and at once they have insight'".⁹²

Commit No Excesses in Your Religion, *Sūrat an-Nisā'* (4):171

Sūrat an-Nisā' (4):171 is a Medinan *sūrah*.⁹³ The verse presents ample opportunities for the discussion of a wide range of important themes contrasting Islam and Christianity. Through analysis of this verse the exegetes examine the nature of Jesus, the concept of Trinity, the relationship between Jesus, his mother, God the Father, and the Holy Spirit. The People of the Book are encouraged to believe in the messages of the previous prophets including belief in the Paraclete, interpreted by Muslims as referring to Muhammad. How these topics are discussed varies within certain limits, as does the willingness of the exegetes to engage with extra-Qur'ānic materials that help illuminate the discussion. Abdullah Yusuf Ali's translation of the verse is as follows:

> O People of the Book! Commit no excesses in your religion: nor say of Allah aught but the truth. Christ Jesus the son of Mary was (no more than) a messenger of Allah, And His Word, which He bestowed on Mary, and a Spirit proceeding from Him: so believe in Allah and His messengers. Say not "three": desist: It will be better for you: For Allah is one God: glory be to Him: (Far exalted is He) above having a son. To Him belong all things in the heavens and on earth. Enough is Allah as a disposer of affairs.⁹⁴

---

91 Ibid., Vol. 1 & 2:280–1.
92 Ibid., Vol. 1 & 2:281. Citing *sūrat al-araf* (7):201.
93 Ibn Kathīr, *Tafsir Al-Qur'ān Al-Azim*, Vol. 2:367.
94 *The Holy Qur'ān*, 271–2.

Tafsīr Mujahid does not discuss *sūrat an-Nisā'* (4):171 directly. It could be that the specific themes referred to in the verse were matters of common knowledge during his lifetime and therefore did not merit discussion. Alternatively, his specific comments, if they ever existed, may have become lost with the passage of time. In any case the preceding verses, 157–160, do offer some indications of his reflections on the subjects discussed. These verses discuss what the Qur'ān describes as the *shubbiha lahum* [apparent crucifixion] of Jesus. They confirm the status of Jesus as Messiah and messenger of God. Mujahid then continues to defend the honour of Mary against allegations made by the Jews concerning the nature of the conception of Jesus. His ending comments say that God promises the People of the Book that "all will come to believe in Jesus before they die".[95]

Al-Tabari begins his commentary by considering the phrase, *O People of the Book! Commit no excess in your religion*. In his commentary, he singles out Christians as being the subject of the verse. In the phrase, *nor say of Allah aught but the truth*, his focus narrows to one of the Christological titles of Jesus as the "Son of God". This he asserts is a false statement. Interpreting the title literally, Al-Tabari bases his argument on the Qur'ānic retort, that God does not produce offspring.[96]

Ibn Kathir begins by stating that Allah forbids the "People of Scriptures" (an alternative translation), from going to extremes in their religion. This serious error is one that he declares Christians are especially prone to and he therefore devotes a great deal of attention to this community and their religious beliefs. In support of his position he employs several *tafsīr* techniques. First, the Qur'ān is used to help interpret the Qur'ān, then he quotes several *hadīth* before making interesting use of the writings of a particular Christian cleric. The excesses that Ibn Kathir challenges include the nature of Jesus, like the previous exegetes, and extend to the credence given by Christians to the disciples of Jesus and Church leaders. He says:

---

95 Mujahid, *Mujahid, Dr. M. Abdul-Salam, Kuwait University*, 296.
96 Al-Tabarī, "L'exégèse" Vol. 1:289. Mujahid does not provide any commentary on this verse.

> The Christians exaggerated over Isa until they elevated him above the grade that Allah gave him. They elevated him from the rank of prophethood to being a god, whom they worshipped just as they worshipped Allah. They exaggerated even more in the case of those who they claim were his followers, claiming that they were inspired, thus following every word they uttered whether true or false, be it guidance or misguidance, truth or lies …[97]

In this regard, the credence Christians place on the words of the followers of Jesus and Jews place on the words of their rabbis, is considered by Ibn Kathir as the motivational force behind *sūrat at-tauba* (9):31, "They took their rabbis and their monks to be their lords besides Allah". In the next phrase, *nor say of Allah except the truth*, he reiterates the basic tenets of *tawhīd* [oneness of God] whereby Allah is "glorified, praised and honoured in His might" without partners. This is in defence of Christian claims, as understood from the verse, of Jesus being His son and "Maryam his wife".[98] Ibn Kathir interprets the faith claims and the reprimanding words of the Qur'ān as truth versus lie, as if the faith claims of Christians could not possibly be the product of sincere misinterpretation of the words of Jesus, as received, or the words of the prophets of the Torah.[99] In response to the alleged inappropriate praise Christians bestow upon Jesus, Muhammad warns his followers of not making the same mistake with him. In a *hadīth* narrated by Imam Ahmad, through Ibn Abbas, 'Umar recalls Muhammad as informing his followers of the appropriate description of his relationship to Allah and warning them not to exaggerate "Do not unduly praise me like the Christians exaggerated over Isa, son of Maryam. Verily, I am a servant, so say, 'Allah's Servant and His Messenger'".[100] A form of counter compensation at least in part, influences the exaggerations of Christians, over reaction to Jewish disbelief in Jesus as Messiah.[101] However he insists that Christian claims concerning Jesus and his message are illogical. He states the true message of Jesus is consistent with Jewish respect for monotheism.

---

97   Ibn Kathīr, *Tafsir Al-Qur'ān Al-Azim*, Vol. 3:55.
98   Ibid., Vol. 3:56.
99   Ibid.
100 Ibid., Vol. 3:55.
101 Rida, *Tafsir Al-Manar*, Vol. 6:67–8.

Accordingly, Jesus taught the Children of Israel to worship one God, to be conscious of God in their lives, and refrain from giving preference to earthly pleasures over the values of God's Kingdom. In addition, Rida explores the belief that Jesus taught his disciples to wait for arrival of "the comforter", the final prophet who will stand over his teachings and set people on the right path.[102] More will be said about this subject below.

Jesus the Messiah

With the phrase, *Christ Jesus, the son of Mary was (no more than) A Messenger of Allah*, Al-Tabari touches upon the Qur'ānic significance of Jesus commonly neglected by Christians. The Qur'ān affirms Jesus as *al-masih*, the Messiah, the Christ, and the "good news".[103] The significance of this statement is of seminal importance. Analysis of the term *al-masih* or the role of the Messiah, through the Qur'ān produces some interesting questions. In the Judeo-Christian tradition there are at least five recognized uses of the Hebrew term *mashiach* [messiah], that range from the ordination of priests starting with Aaron, an honour bestowed on the gentile ruler, Cyrus of Persia, the anointing of kings and prophets, and finally to the eschatological Messiah.[104] There is of course little agreement between Jews and Christians on either the person, or role of the Messiah, and although the Qur'ān agrees with Christians by affirming Jesus as *al-masih* [the messiah] there are significant differences in respective expectations as well.

The use of the definite article in the Qur'ān stresses the uniqueness of Jesus as *al-masih*. In this light the term, *son of Mary*, acts as both a corrective to the Christian title "Son of God" and as a positive affirmation of the unique birth of Jesus and the uniqueness of Mary. The phrase, *is*

---

102   Ibid. Cf. Geoffrey Parrinder, *Jesus in the Qur'an* (Oxford: Oneworld Publications, 2003), 96–100.
103   Al-Tabarī, "L'exégèse" Vol. 1:289.
104   Richard L. Kimball, "An Exploration of the Concept of Messiah through Judaism, Christianity and Islam" (St Andrews: St Mary's College, School of Divinity, University of St Andrews, 2008).

Ahl al-Kitāb: *The Qur'ānic People of the Book* 37

only the messenger of God, contributes to the description of the Messiah as well as to set boundaries for the role of the Qur'ānic Messiah. Various translations either translate the word *rasūl* as "the" messenger of Allah or "a" messenger of Allah.[105] The use of the definitive article is interesting since all three Abrahamic religions agree that there have been many messengers of God. Suffice it to say then, the use of the definitive with *rasūl* contributes to the uniqueness of Jesus as God's messenger and Messiah without detracting from the mission of God's other messengers. Al-Tabari describes the suggestion that the Messiah is the begotten "Son of God", as simply erroneous.[106]

On the other hand, the accusation often heard from some Christian commentators that Islam reject Jesus, or that in Islam, Jesus is just another prophet could not be further from the truth.[107] The differences between the Qur'ānic Jesus and the Jesus of Christianity are much subtler. Christians often neglect the fact that the Qur'ānic rejection of Christian claims of the divinity of Jesus, in no way implies that Jesus is not the Christ. The Qur'ān affirms that Jesus is authentically sent by God to be a blessing to mankind.[108] The title "Messiah" is reserved for Jesus, his birth is unique, comparable only to Adam, the miracles and teachings are all affirmed, and none can consider themselves a Muslim unless they accept Jesus as the

---

105 For comparisons see the English translations of the Qur'ān by Yusuf Ali, and Mohsin Kahn. The use of *tashkīl* in the Qur'ān developed over several generations as the recitation of the Qur'ān progressed from oral tradition to written form. Therefore, there are some slight variations between texts, primarily due to dialectal concerns between authorized texts. Cf. William Montgomery Watt in *The Cambridge History of Islam*.
106 Al-Tabarī, "L'exégèse" Vol. 1:289.
107 In this genre there is a wide spectrum ranging from Pastor Terry Jones, to the many Christian apologetic works that include academic endeavours. Cf. Norman L. Geisler and Abdul Saleeb, *Answering Islam*, 2nd edn (Grand Rapids, MI: Baker Books, 2006), 233.
108 From the very beginning, a common reaction from Christians is to consider its teachings false and reject the prophethood of Muhammad. Cf. Doctrina Jacobi, and John Moschus, *Pratum Spirituale*, citing Sophronius, Patriarch of Jerusalem, and John of Damascus, *Fountain of Knowledge* in Robert Hoyland, *Seeing Islam as Others Saw It: A Survey and Evaluation of Christian, Jewish and Zoroastrian Writings on Early Islam*, vol. 13 (Princeton, NJ: Darwin Press, 1997), 57, 63, 485–9.

Christ.[109] The Qur'ān states the position of the Messiah in relation to an omnipotent God, one who is not in need of auxiliaries and therefore the Qur'ān rejects the idea of begotten, physical sonship, or divinity.

In fact, the phrase the Qur'ān emphatically states Jesus is, *His word, which He bestowed on Mary and a spirit proceeding from Him*. For Al-Tabari Jesus is thus "a spirit" from God, given unto, or bestowed upon Mary from Gabriel.[110] Ibn Kathir's focus is concerned with Jesus as "the word" bestowed upon Maryam, or if he is the product of "a word". He explains "*Jibril* (Gabriel) blew the life of Isa into Maryam by Allah's leave, and Isa came into existence as a result. This incident was in place of the normal conception between man and woman that results in children".[111] According to the logic of the statement, and in terms close to what Al-Tabari writes, Ibn Kathir states that Jesus is called a *rūh* [spirit] and a word created by Allah, because Jesus is the product of the word "Be" that God uttered and sent with Jibril (Gabriel). Jesus is accordingly, a word created by God, "a creation" of God, and not the creating word of God.[112] In support of this argument Ibn Kathir cites from *sūrat al-mā'idah* and a couple of *hadīth* to demonstrate that Jesus is one of God's messengers, a servant of God, favoured (with signs and miracles), and a creation of God's. The nature of Jesus is compared to Adam because he was created by God's command, "Be".[113] In a *hadīth* that comes down through Al-Bukharī (Fath Al-Bari 6:547) Muhammad explains the acceptable bounds of belief concerning the nature of Jesus and religious faith in general:

> If anyone testifies that none has the right to be worshipped but Allah alone Who has no partners, and that Muhammad is His servant and Messenger, and that Isa is Allah's servant and Messenger and His Word which He bestowed on Maryam and a spirit created by Him, and that Paradise is true and Hell is true, then Allah will admit him into Paradise with the deeds which he performed.[114]

---

109 See *sūrat n-nisa* (4):171, *sūrat Āl-'Imrān* (3):48, 59 & *sūrat Maryam* (19):16–34, *sūrat az-zukhruf* (43):59. 63–4.
110 Al-Tabarī, "L'exégèse" Vol. 1:289.
111 Ibn Kathīr, *Tafsir Al-Qur'ān Al-Azim*, Vol. 3:56.
112 Ibid.
113 Ibid., Vol. 3:57–8.
114 Ibid., Vol. 3:58.

Rida's examination of the "word" employed to create Jesus is similar in manner to the other commentators. His particular interest focuses on the use of the word *rūḥ*. He begins his examination of the characteristics of the spirit found in the Qur'ān. He points out that the spirit of God, in the form of the Angel Gabriel, creates, guides and strengthens Jesus, as for example in *sūrat al-baqarah* (2):253; *sūrat al-mā'idah* (5):111; *al-anbiya* (21):91 and *as-sajdah* (32):8–9. There are, however, many uses of the word "spirit" in the Qur'ān. He states that the sending of the "spirit" is not unique to Jesus, as is demonstrated in *sūrat ash-shura* 42:52 and *an-nahl* 16:2: "thus We revealed to you an inspiration (same word used as spirit) by Our command" and "He sends down an 'inspiration' by his command on whoever He pleases".[115]

Rida further demonstrates through the examination of several passages from the New Testament several ways in which God sends his spirit. These examples demonstrate that Jesus does not uniquely receive strengthening by the Spirit. Therefore, receiving the Spirit should not be used as an argument for equating Jesus with God. He examines the nativity story found in the first chapter of Luke describing how the Holy Spirit (the angel Gabriel) not only appears to Mary, but also to Elizabeth, John and Zakaria. Further to the point, the same words are used to describe how the Holy Spirit strengthens Jesus' disciples, even Judas. Therefore, Rida surmises that it does not make sense to say something that is a creation, or strengthened by God through the Holy Spirit, or that is sent by God, could be His equal.[116]

Believe in His Messengers

The next phrase discussed is ... *So believe in Allah and His Messengers*. Al-Tabari and Ibn Kathir consider this phrase simply states where faith should be directed; meaning believe God is one, alone without son, or wife, and believe in His messengers. *Jesus is God's servant and messenger.*[117] Allowing

---

115   Rida, *Tafsir Al-Manar*, Vol. 6:69.
116   Al-Tabarī, "L'exégèse". Rida, *Tafsir Al-Manar*, Vol. 6:70. Matthew 1:18 is also quoted.
117   Al-Tabarī, "L'exégèse". Vol. 1:289. Ibn Kathīr, *Tafsir Al-Qur'ān Al-Azim*, Vol. 3:59.

one verse of the Qur'ān to help interpret another, Ibn Kathir looks specifically at *sūrat al-mā'idah* (5):75 "*al-Masih* (Isa), son of Maryam, was no more than a Messenger; many were the Messengers that passed away before him. His mother Maryam was a woman of truth, they both ate food". This phrase reiterates the above point by identifying Jesus as one in a line of Messengers sent by God. Hence, Jesus is a human being called upon by God to be a messenger like one of the many messengers before him.[118] Rida pays particular attention to the Gospel of John. Here he observes inferences to the Spirit of God that have special significance for both Muslims and Christians. Rida examines the promises made by Jesus to send the comforter, the Spirit of Truth. For instance, John 15:26 reads, "The comforter that I will send you from the Father, the Spirit of Truth, that is with the Father will proceed, he will bear witness to me". In John 16:7, 13–14, Jesus explains the necessity for his leaving and details the continuity of purpose of God by sending the Comforter/Paraclete after Jesus. The possible meanings of this phrase are explored in great detail. He rejects the idea that proceeding from the Father should be interpreted, as Christians do, that the Spirit is a division of God, and therefore evidence of the Trinity. Rather Rida sees this comforter as pointing to the prophet Muhammad who, "because he does not speak on his own, but will utter what he hears, and he will inform you of what is to come. And he will bring honour to me because it is from me that he will take and he will inform you".[119] The word identified as referring to Muhammad in John's Gospel is *menahhemana* in Aramaic, *paráklētos* in Greek. It is commonly translated into English as counsellor, life-giver, comforter, spirit of truth, or advocate. In Arabic, the word is *ahmad*, a variation on the name and meaning of Muhammad.[120] Rida notes that there are discrepancies with various

---

118   The statement regarding food is very interesting and not one discussed by the exegete.
119   Rida, *Tafsir Al-Manar*, Vol. 6:70–1.
120   Ibid., Vol. 6:70. The Arabic Bibles including the Arabic New Testament, Trinitarian Bible Society and the Coptic, Arabic Van Dyke translate the word as *ilmahzi*. George M. Lamsa translates the word as "comforter" in John 16:7, and "Spirit of truth" in 16:13 in his translation of the Aramaic of the Peshitta. *Holy Bible, from the Ancient Eastern Text*, trans. George M. Lamsa (New York: Harper One, 1933), 1075–6. A Hebrew word associated with paraclete is *Manaem*, Samir Khalil Samir challenges the Islamic linking of the Syriac *menahhemana* and Greek *parakletos* (consoler) with

translations, interpretations and synonyms of the meaning of *menahhemana* and Paraclete, but for Muslims the use of the word is a clear indication of the coming of the prophet Muhammad, not only because of the similarities of his name, but also because of the message that he brought to humankind. Perhaps somewhat tongue-in-cheek, Rida, follows the deductive logic of "what comes from God is God", to infer that Christians should then take up belief in a "quadrity", rather than the Trinity. Since as he explains, this comforter, is not the same as the Holy Spirit, but is something new from God.[121]

Trinity & Tawhīd

The next subject examined is the concept of Trinity. Al-Tabari opens his remarks on the phrase, *Say not "three": desist, it will be better for you;* with a synopsis of the inconsistencies he sees, especially with the idea that Jesus could be a god.

> Among Christians, there is the reigning doctrine that Jesus is a god, that he is one of the three gods who are called the Father, the Son and the Holy Spirit. What is astonishing, in addition to their belief that Jesus would be a god, is that they believe that Jesus ate, drank, slept, and that he had been crucified, whereas these characteristics are those of humans. Moreover, they also recognize that he was formed in the belly of his mother Mary.[122]

Al-Tabari's commentary neglects, as do all the exegetes, a central theme in the Christian understanding of the nature of Jesus by ignoring the fact that the humanity of Jesus is an integral component of Christian belief. His synopsis of the doctrine of the Trinity omits the insistence by Christians of *tawhīd*. Criticism of the concept of the Trinity is a central theme of Islam and there are several verses of the Qur'ān where this is expressed.

---

the Greek *periklytos* (praised). Samir Khalil Samir, *111 Questions on Islam, on Islam and the West* [Cento Demande Sull'Islam: Intervista a Samir Khalil Samir], ed. Wafik Nasry, trans. Claudia Castellani (San Francisco, CA: Ignatius Press, 2008), 191.
121 Rida, *Tafsir Al-Manar*, Vol. 6:70–1. A similar line of logic is queried by Kenneth Cragg, *The Arab Christian: A History of the Middle East* (London: Mowbary, 1994), 79, 91.
122 Al-Tabarī, "L'exégèse" Vol. 1:289.

Shirk [the association of any partners with God] is strictly forbidden in Islam.[123] Al-Tabari chides those who use the term saying, "Cease telling the lie, which is in fact association (polytheism), that will be better for you than divine punishment".[124] The Qur'ān and Al-Tabari's assessment, leave no margin of tolerance. The Qur'ān is unequivocal with its distaste for any allusion to associating partners with God. Yet, the use of the term Trinity, whether it is appropriate or not, it is certainly not a lie. There is no intention to deceive. Rather the word chosen is intended to name an experience, a felt sense of the authenticity and connectedness between the Creator, the Messiah, and the Spirit that touches all creation.

Continuing with the theme of *tawhīd* through the phrase, *Allah is a single God*, Al-Tabari says, "The adored God is rather only one God, who has neither offspring nor parent".[125] Coupled with the next phrase, *glory be to him: (far Exalted is He) above having a son*, Al-Tabari repeats the phrase for emphasis, "Far above is He from having a son"![126] He further explains the phrase as exemplifying the omnipotence of God as creator. Contrasting then the place of the Qur'ānic Messiah there is the phrase, "With Him belongs what is in the skies and on Earth".[127] Once again rejecting any notion of the Messiah being co-creator our exegete expounds the greatness of God as the creator, and the place of the Messiah, Jesus as one of his creations, "all that there is in the skies and on the Earth, angels, humans and other creatures belong to Him; how could the Messiah be his son, while he belongs to the whole as one of the creatures of God"?[128] The closing phrase of the verse captures the trajectory of the argument succinctly, "God is enough of a protector!" Al-Tabari's commentary paraphrases the statement adding that God is enough for worshipers as governor, and provider.[129]

---

123   Al-Khudrawi, *Dictionary of Islamic Terms*, 217.
124   Al-Tabarī, "L'exégèse" Vol. 1:289.
125   Ibid.
126   Ibid.
127   Ibid. Here citing from *sūrat t al-jathiya* (45):13.
128   Ibid.
129   Ibid.

Ibn Kathir takes a slightly different view of the Trinity by linking the mother of Jesus with the concept of Trinity. He offers his assessment of the verse, "Do not elevate *Isa* and his mother to be gods with Allah. Allah is far holier than what they attribute to Him".[130] Using the Qur'ān to help explain the meaning of the statement, Ibn Kathir refers to two verses from *sūrat al-mā'idah*. In *sūrat al-mā'idah* (5):73, it says, those who say, "Allah is the third of three" are disbelievers.[131] Further, in (5):116 Allah asks Jesus "O Isa, the son of Mary! Didst thou say unto men, 'Take me and my mother for two gods beside Allah?'" Jesus responds "Glory to thee! Never could I say what I had no right (to say). Had I said such a thing, thou wouldst indeed have known it. Thou knowest what is in my heart, though I know not what is in thine".[132] He explains that it never even crossed the mind of Jesus to ask people to worship him and his mother.[133] In his defence Jesus adds, "Never did I say to them ought except what you (Allah) did command me to say".[134] His association of Mary with the Trinity picks up on a very interesting Qur'ānic theme that may come as some surprise to many Christians. Simply put, there are no Christians that consider Mary part of the Trinity. Yet, in the interest of accuracy, it has to be said that there used to be. Historically, a Christian sect called Collyridians did in fact worship Mary as God.[135]

Ibn Kathir demonstrating his awareness of Christian creedal variations briefly discusses the origins of three major Christian denominations. In pursuit of this aim he paraphrases the Melkite Patriarch of Alexandria, Sa'id bin Batriq's assessment of the Council of Nicea convened during the reign of the Emperor Constantine. Accordingly, Constantine, seeing the Council divided over the formation of doctrine, strategically chose to support the sect with the most supporters over all the other groups. This sect

---

130   Ibn Kathīr, *Tafsir Al-Qur'ān Al-Azim*, Vol. 3:59.
131   Ibid.
132   *The Holy Qur'ān*, 326–7.
133   *Tafsir Al-Qur'ān Al-Azim*, Vol. 3:304–5.
134   Ibid., Vol. 3:305.
135   Spencer J Trimingham, *Christianity among the Arabs in Pre-Islamic Times* (Beirut: Libraire Du Liban, 1990), 68.

thrived, "churches were built and doctrines were taught to young children, who were baptized on this creed".[136] In time dissenting voices broke away from the Western Church, or the Melkite Church, and went on to be called the Jacobites and Nestorians. He says, "These three sects agreed that Isa was divine, but disputed regarding the manner in which Isa's divinity was related to his humanity; were they in unity or did Allah incarnate in Isa! All three of these sects accuse each other of heresy".[137] For this reason Ibn Kathir remarks rather comically, "if ten Christians meet, you would end up with eleven sects"![138]

Rida offers a brief history of the Trinity that he sees as an ancient pagan theme found in many cultures. Stepping beyond the normal bounds of *tafsīr*, Rida traces pre-Christian examples of Trinitarian ideologies through the works of several western historians and anthropologists like Thomas Maurice, George Stanley Faber, Thomas William Doane, John Fiske, and others. Rida examines the beliefs of Hindus, Buddhists, Ancient Egyptians, Romans, Greeks, Zoroastrians even Northern European folklore. His review presents some uncanny similarities between pagan religious beliefs and creedal formulas enshrining Christian Trinitarianism.[139] Noteworthy from the commentary is the narrative that reportedly takes place between a Thulius, a Pharaoh and an Egyptian priest where Thulius asks if there is anyone greater than he. The priest replies, "Yes. There is one greater than everything and that is Allah before everything. Then there is the 'word,' and with them the 'holy spirit.' And all these three are one in nature and they are one in person, and from them is the eternal power".[140] Rida surmises that the revelation of the creative word of God and the spirit of God

---

136   Ibn Kathīr, *Tafsir Al-Qur'ān Al-Azim*, Vol. 3:60.
137   Ibid., Vol. 3:60–1.
138   Ibid., Vol. 3:60.
139   Rida, *Tafsir Al-Manar*, Vol. 6:73–8. Cf. Thomas William Doane, *Bible Myths and Parallels in Other Religions: Being a Comparison of the Old and New Testament Myths and Miracles with Those of Heathen Nations of Antiquity Considering Also Their Origin and Meaning*, ed. J. W. Bouton, 4th edn (New York: The Truth Seeking Company, 1882), 372–5.
140   Rida, *Tafsir Al-Manar*, Vol. 6:74–5. Here Rashid Rida is quoting from Doane, Thomas, William. 1882. *Bible Myths and Their Parallels in Other Religions*, 373.

to be revealed. Therefore, whatever permissible matters you find in it, then consider them permissible. And whatever impermissible matters you find in it, then consider them impermissible".[153] This verse therefore is immensely influential in debates concerning the theme of *mansūkh* [abrogation].

The verse ostensibly demonstrates the trajectory of God's revelation beginning with the *Torah* continuing on to the Bible and culminating with the Qur'ān, that is *muhaymin* [guardian], over God's revelation. Through the ensuing discussion of the trajectory of revelation, the verse indelibly links the People of the Book to the *ummat al-mu'minīn* [Community of the Believers] of Islam. An uncritical reading of the verse suggests a sense of religious *détente*, where the People of the Book and the People of the Qur'ān should let their lives speak for them through their respective tradition; leaving to God, whom we all serve, to sort out our differences. In fact, part of this verse is probably one of the most oft quoted phrases by proponents of interfaith dialogue. Yet, the traditional commentary of the verse clearly demonstrates how far an uncritical reading may stray from the established understanding and by default, epitomizes the necessity for comparative theology. Abdullah Yusuf Ali's translation of the verse follows:

> To thee We sent the Scripture in truth, confirming the scripture that came before it, and guarding it in safety; so judge between them by what Allah hath revealed, and follow not their vain desires, diverging from the Truth that hath come to thee. To each among you have We prescribed a Law and an Open Way. If Allah had so willed, He would have made you a single people, but (His plan is) to test you in what He hath given you: so strive as in a race in all virtues. The goal of you all is to Allah; it is He that will show you the truth of the matters in which ye dispute.[154]

Muhayminan, Guarding in Safety

Mujahid's commentary is brief. He confirms a central theme of the Qur'ān as guardian over the sacred books and providing a divine law revealed to

---

153   *Tafsir Al-Qur'ān Al-Azim*, Vol. 3:71.
154   *The Holy Qur'ān*, 300–1.

Muhammad for all to follow.[155] Similarly Al-Tabari begins his commentary with the phrase *to thee we sent the scripture in truth*. The scripture in question is identified as the Qur'ān and the recipient is Muhammad. He reiterates that the message of the Qur'ān is clear and without doubt. The purpose of the text is writ plain by the phrases *confirming the scriptures that came before it and guarding it in safety*. He conveys that the Qur'ān confirms the truth of the scriptures that preceded it, guarding what has truthfully been revealed, while challenging and correcting what is false.[156] He supports his opinion by quoting the teaching of Ibn Abbas that Jewish and Christian scholars have altered the true message of the People of the Book. Therefore "the Qur'ān is the guardian of the Torah and the Gospel, judge between them by what God has revealed".[157] This means that what has come before the Qur'ān is subject to the Qur'ān and Muhammad is repeatedly warned to judge by the revelation given to him and not to be distracted by "their vain desires".[158]

Ibn Kathir's explanation of the verse in question is clustered together with the preceding verses 40–47. These state that God has dominion over all the earth. He punishes and forgives whom he wills. God consoles and warns Muhammad that there are those who would prefer to follow any lie than to follow the truth. These people reject not only what is given to Muhammad, but also what was revealed in the past to them in the form of the Torah, "the plain command of God".[159] The law of retribution is found in verse (5):45. However, it may come as a surprise that the verse endorses the teachings of Jesus concerning forgiveness, "But if any one remits the retaliation by way of charity, it shall be for him an expiation".[160] Continuing in the same trajectory, verse (5):46 attests that God sent Jesus,

---

155 Mujahid, *Mujahid, Dr. M. Abdul-Salam, Kuwait University*, 310.
156 Al-Tabarī, "L'exégèse" Vol. 1:316.
157 Ibid.
158 Ibid.
159 *The Holy Qur'ān*, 298. *Sūrat al-mā'idah* (5):44. Cf. Ibn Kathīr, *Tafsir Al-Qur'ān Al-Azim*, Vol. 3:185.
160 *Tafsir Al-Qur'ān Al-Azim*, Vol. 3:192. *The Holy Qur'ān*, 198. Cf. fn. 754 and 754. In a *Sunnah* that comes down through Ubadah bin As-Samit and recorded by Imam Ahmad (Ahmad 5:13) Muhammad says, "Any man who suffers a wound on his body

the son of Mary, and gave him the Gospel. The Qur'ān says of the Gospel, "therein was guidance and light and confirmation of the Torah that had come before it, a guidance and an admonition for those who have *taqwā* [consciousness of God]". Verse (5):47 further states "Let the People of the Injil judge by what Allah hath revealed therein", repeating a similar proviso given to the followers of the Torah, "And whosoever does not judge by what Allah has revealed, such are the rebellious". Ibn Kathir contends that the verses imply that if they were to accept the teachings of the Torah and the Gospel then they would have to accept all teachings that are in these books, including the predictions that point to the coming of Muhammad and the commands to believe in him.[161]

With the above context of the verse in mind *sūrat al-mā'idah* (5):48 becomes clearer. Ibn Kathir interprets the first phrase *to thee We sent the Scripture in truth, confirming the scripture that came before it, and guarding it in safety*, to mean that the Qur'ān confirms the Torah and the Gospel that were sent before it and guards these teachings.[162] Ibn Kathir explains that the previous scripture foretells of the coming of the Qur'ān through God's servant and Messenger Muhammad. Those who understood the scriptures were strengthened in faith and kept Allah's commands, as confirmed by *sūrat al-isrā'* (17):107.[163] Ibn Kathir further expands the meaning of verse (5):48 to confirm the pre-eminence of the Qur'ān *vis-à-vis* all other Scriptures. One word, *muhayminan*, is extensively examined and presented as affirming the position of the Qur'ān. There are slight varying interpretations of the word. Ibn Kathir, who draws upon the commentary of Al-Tabari for support, discusses these variations at some length. Ibn Kathir records that Ibn Abbas, based on the narrations of Sufyan Ath Thawri, Abu Ishāq and At-Tamimi, considered the word *muhayminan* to mean, "entrusted over"

---

and forfeits his right to retaliation as a way of charity, then Allah will pardon him that which is similar to what he forfeited".
161 *Tafsir Al-Qur'ān Al-Azim*, Vol. 3:194. Some verses that are thought to allude to the coming of Muhammad are found in Deuteronomy 18:15; 18:18, John 16:7–8; Acts 3:17–24.
162 Ibid., Vol. 3:195–6.
163 Ibid., Vol. 3:196.

(Al-Tabari 10:378). While Ali bin Abi Talhah believed Ibn Abbas taught the word means "The trustworthy", implying that the Qur'ān is trustworthy over all preceding Divine Books. This opinion is also held by several reliable sources including Mujahid, Qatadah, Al-Suddi, and Ibn Zayd (Al-Tabari 10:379; 10:377–80). Ibn Jarir, similarly, taught that the use of the word *muhayminan* implies "The Qur'ān is trustworthy over the Books that preceded it. Therefore, whatever in these previous Books conforms to the Qur'ān is true, and whatever disagrees with the Qur'ān is false".[164]

Rida's understanding of the verse is the closest to a literal interpretation. Central to his understanding is his appreciation for cultural diversity and interpretation of the legal prohibitions and commands. This enlightened view endorses a plurality of interpretations of *Shari'ah*, as methods of guidance for society while strongly endorsing the established universal truths of religion, the oneness of God, the need to submit to his will, the necessity to have one's life reflect one's values and to believe in the Last Day. These he argues are the basis of religion common to all the prophets and held in common with the People of the Book.[165] Similarly to the other *mufassirūn* Rida states that the Qur'ān confirms the teachings of the past prophets that have been lost, or misconstrued, over the years. For this reason, God revealed the Qur'ān to Muhammad, acknowledging the Qur'ān as the trustworthy guardian of revelation that is to be preferred to the Torah and Injil. The meaning of the word *muhayminan* is explored by comparing the definition of the word championed by Ibn Abbas, and other noted scholars whose collective opinion oscillates between "the guardian" as in trustworthy, witness, or shielding.[166]

Abrogation of the Verses

The point being made by Rida is that the Qur'ān represents perfection in religion and that the People of the Book have lost much of their authentic

---

164 Ibid., Vol. 3:197.
165 Rida, *Tafsir Al-Manar*, Vol. 5 & 6:339.
166 Ibid., Vol. 5 & 6:340.

message, rendering their opinions completely untrustworthy.[167] A *hadīth* preserved by Jabir and narrated by Ahmad Al-Bazaar vividly expresses Muhammad's opinion of the unreliability of the Torah.[168] The companion Omar copied a book of the Torah into Arabic and came to read it to Muhammad. As he started reading the prophet's face changed, so that one of the *ansār* [helpers], interrupted Omar and Muhammad said, "Do not ask the People of the Book anything, they are a nation who have gone astray. And you can (have a choice), deny the truth or accept falsehood. By Allah, if Moses was amongst you, he would not have a choice except to follow me".[169] This implies therefore that the veracity of the Torah and apparently the Gospel, have been so badly compromised that even to take advice from the People of the Book in matters of faith leaves a person likely to deny something that is true or to accept a false teaching. According to the traditional commentary, the only testimony from the Torah and Gospel that can be trusted is that which affirms the Qur'ān.[170]

The next phrase discussed is, *So, judge between them by what Allah has revealed*. Ibn Kathir interprets this phrase based on the commentary of Al-Tabari to be a counsel to Muhammad to rule by the revelation of the Qur'ān.[171] Rida shares this assessment without reference to earlier commentary.[172] Interestingly, Ibn Kathir reports on the authority of the companion Ibn Abi Hatim, that Ibn Abbas said, that Muhammad initially had the choice to either judge affairs by the Qur'ān or to let non-Muslims decide their own affairs according to their own traditions. However, these arrangements were abrogated with the further revelation, *and follow not their vain desires, diverging away from the truth that has come to you*.[173]

---

167 Ibid.
168 Ibid., Vol. 5 & 6:341.
169 Ibid.
170 It is worth noting that this statement is the basis of one of the rules of *tafsīr*, whereby the Torah and *Injil* are only consulted to support what is in the Qur'ān, rather than as evidence in their own right.
171 Ibn Kathīr, *Tafsir Al-Qur'ān Al-Azim*, Vol. 3:197–8.
172 Rida, *Tafsir Al-Manar*, Vol. 5 & 6:341.
173 Ibn Kathīr, *Tafsir Al-Qur'ān Al-Azim*, Vol. 3:195–8. Rida, *Tafsir Al-Manar*, Vol. 5 & 6:341.

Many Roads Lead to God

Having asserted the supremacy of the Qur'ān over the Torah and Injil the next phrase under discussion re-affirms the authenticity of the revelation given to the People of the Book and that given to Muslims, *To each among you have We prescribed a Law and an Open Way"*. Al-Tabari's commentary differentiates between religion and law. He says that the religion before Allah does not change, but the message from the prophets differed in detail, for each community, "A clear path to follow".[174] The following phrase acknowledges God's intent for diversity amongst peoples, *if Allah so willed; He would have made you a single people. But His plan is to test you in what He has given you*, meaning that all communities will be judged according to their actions and belief in order to establish those who are obedient from those who are rebellious.[175] Ibn Kathir believes that each community was given a clear path to God. People should strive to do God's will, "following His Laws that abrogated the laws that came before it. And believing in His Book, the Qur'ān, which is the Final Book that He revealed".[176] Surprisingly, Ibn Kathir notes that Ad-Dahhak considered the phrase, *So strive as in a race in good deeds* to be directed only to Muslims, and not a challenge to all people.[177]

Rida develops this phrase much further. He accepts that there has been a progression of revelation culminating in the Qur'ān, each abrogating the tenets of the former. However, he then examines the philosophy behind revelation and law. He states that the purpose of revelation and laws are to purify and improve the lives of those who follow them and that *Shari'ah* differs with changing contexts "based upon the conditions of the community and the readiness of the people". He further explains *dīn*, religion. Rida identifies the main precepts of religion common to all the messengers. These are the oneness of God, the need to submit one's will to God, and performing righteous deeds. He then introduces the term *ihsān*, a beautiful word meaning, the

---

174 Al-Tabarī, "L'exégèse" Vol. 1:316–7.
175 Ibid.
176 Ibn Kathīr, *Tafsir Al-Qur'ān Al-Azim*, Vol. 3:199.
177 Ibid., Vol. 3:200.

constant striving for perfection, minimizing pain and conflict.¹⁷⁸ As part of his examination of the phrase, Rida looks at the *tafsīr* of Qatadah. Qatadah describes the Torah, the Injil and the Qur'ān as *Sharī'ah;* they respectively are ways or traditions, *sunnah*. God will judge between those who obey Him from those who do not. The *Sharī'ah* are practical laws that differ from one tradition to the other, they may be interpreted through a judicial system. Religion on the other hand, is not changeable. This idea of the religion not changing is supported by *sūrat ash-Shūra* (42):13, "He has ordained for you of religion what He enjoined upon Noah and that which We have revealed to you, [O Muhammad] and what we enjoined upon Abraham and Moses and Jesus, to establish the religion and not be divided".¹⁷⁹ Having given the impression that *Sharī'ah* is somewhat relative, Rida further comments on the phrase by re-stating that the Laws found in the Qur'ān are for all people and for all times, because they have been given to the last prophet. The laws that came before had a time and a place of relevance, but are no longer practical. He uses as an example the rigidity of the Torah in worship and the impracticality of the Christian call to bow before every ruler, no matter how corrupt, and every enemy. Rather, Islamic laws are necessary for the stability of society and for the development of humanity making *ijtihād*, here translated as "reason", obligatory.¹⁸⁰ He compares the differences in methods as being those appropriate to a people's maturity and material capabilities. God will test each according to what they have been given, meaning their religion, legal codes and methods. And he emphatically states that the purpose of religion is to motivate all people, not just Muslims, as seen with the commentary of Ibn Kathir, to initiate righteousness and strive towards achieving this goal.

The last phrase is, *the return of you all is to Allah; then He that will inform you about that in which you used to differ*. For Al-Tabari the phrase describes the Day of Judgement when we will all stand before God and be judged according to our actions. On this day God will divide the righteous from those who have been mistaken.¹⁸¹ Similarly for Ibn Kathir the phrase

---

178 Rida, *Tafsir Al-Manar*, Vol. 5 & 6:342. Cf. Al-Khudrawi, *Dictionary of Islamic Terms*, 96.
179 Rida, *Tafsir Al-Manar*, Vol. 5 & 6:342.
180 Ibid., Vol. 5 & 6:347.
181 Al-Tabarī, "L'exégèse" Vol. 1:317.

is a reminder to all people that our final destination is to God. God will set the record straight concerning issues that are disputed. He will reward the sincere and punish the disbelieving for their rebelliousness. For Rida the same sentiments apply. However, there is a much more universal concentration on striving to do the beautiful and making laws that help in this regard, rather than making laws that are the cause of enmity.[182]

The Curse of Taqlīd

If one were to stop here then the theme from the first half of the verse would appear to imply that Islam is the pure religion, but that Judaism and Christianity, for all their faults, are still valid roads to God and salvation. Jews and Christians were given "a way" that they may choose to follow according to God's precepts and to compete with other communities, to see who could do better. However, the succeeding verses amplify the critical connotations found in verse 48 concerning dialogue with Christians and Jews. The commentary shows that Islam is the true way and that Christians and Jews have compromised the authentic message that they have received.

A brief glimpse at the commentary from the scholars reveals an apparently insurmountable obstacle, a wholly unedifying caricature of the Qur'ānic construct of the People of the Book. For Al-Tabari the message of the above verses is quite clear. Christians and Jews are the enemies of believers.[183] The abridged edition of his *tafsīr* lacks any historical context that could somehow mitigate the severity of the proclamation. Ibn Kathir and Rida shed some light on the context. They pick up on the theme that there are Jews who wish to "turn" Muhammad and the nascent community away from the revelation of the Qur'ān and its teachings. In an interesting *hadīth* transmitted by Ibn Abbas, and recorded by Muhammad bin Ishāq, Ibn Kathir describes the occasion of the revelation of *sūrat al-mā'idah* (5):49. Here four members of the Jewish community in Medina, Ka'b bin Asad, Ibn Saluba, Abdullah bin Surya and Shas bin Qays, conspired together to attempt to misguide

---

182   Rida, *Tafsir Al-Manar*, Vol. 5 & 6:347.
183   Al-Tabarī, "L'exégèse" Vol. 1:317–8.

Muhammad concerning "his" religion. They went to Muhammad and said, "O Muhammad! You know that we are the scholars, noblemen and chiefs of the Jews. If we follow you, the Jews will follow suit and will not contradict us. But there is enmity between us and some of our people, so we will refer to you for judgment in this matter, and you should rule in our favour against them and we will believe in you".[184] Muhammad did not accept their request, and in turn he received the revelation, *And so judge between them by what Allah has revealed and follow not their vain desires, but beware of them lest they turn you far away from some of that which Allah has sent down to you ... sūrat al-mā'idah* (5):49. Ibn Kathir, Al-Tabari and Ibn Abi Hatim maintain that the revelation concerning the above *hadīth* concludes with *sūrat al-mā'idah* (5):50, *Do they then seek the judgment of (the days of) ignorance (jāhiliyya)? And who is better in judgment than Allah for a people who have firm faith?*[185]

Ibn Kathir explains the meaning of the verse as God criticizing those who choose to ignore His guidance, preferring their own ignorant misguidance and lustful contrivances.[186] This explanation is important for several reasons. In simple terms the word "*jāhiliyya*" means ignorance. It is translated by Ibn Kathir in verse (5):50, to represent a period of time before the Prophethood of Muhammad, "Do they then seek the judgment of (the days of) ignorance?" Describing the time before Muhammad as the time of ignorance insinuates that those who followed the teachings given by God, namely the Torah and Gospel in previous times were also following their own opinions and desires so to speak. Yet, the Qur'ān uses the word "*jāhiliyya*" to refer to the perennial problem of people who choose to ignore God's revelation or choose to abide by some parts of Divine Law while ignoring others. Ibn Kathir seems quite willing to accept Al-Tabari's assessment of non-Muslims: "Whoever does this, he is a disbeliever who deserves to be fought against, until he reverts to Allah's and His Messenger's decisions, so that no law, minor or major, is referred to except by His Law".[187]

---

184 Ibn Kathīr, *Tafsir Al-Qur'ān Al-Azim*, Vol. 3:201. Rida, *Tafsir Al-Manar*, Vol. 5 & 6:347. Here the Jewish leaders are described as rabbis.
185 Ibn Kathīr, *Tafsir Al-Qur'ān Al-Azim*, Vol. 3:202.
186 Ibid. Mujahid, *Mujahid, Dr. M. Abdul-Salam, Kuwait University*, 310.
187 Ibn Kathīr, *Tafsir Al-Qur'ān Al-Azim*, Vol. 3:202. Over time the concept of *jāhiliyya* evolves from implying, "ignorance" to referring to the "period of ignorance".

Looking just a little further ahead to verse 51, it says, "O ye who believe! Take not the Jews and the Christians for your friends and protectors". It would appear therefore that Muslims are prohibited from taking Jews and Christians, as friends. The *tafsīr* of Al-Tabari and ibn Kathir certainly tend to lean in this direction, seeing Jews and Christians as potential enemies of the true community of believers.[188] However, the *tafsīr* of Rida examines the context specifying to whom the prohibition applies and when. In this regard he examines various *hadīth*, some that suggest a blanket prohibition, as well as the evidence that suggests that the prophet Muhammad did not practise such a prohibition himself, nor did he intend such a universal interpretation. Muhammad made many treaties with Christian and Jewish tribes. Some were honoured and some were broken. For example, the Bani Awf were a Jewish tribe from Medina that enjoyed amicable relations with Muhammad, as did the Bani al-Haritha, Sa'dah, Jasm, Aws and Tha'laba.[189] Therefore the *sunnah* of Muhammad shows a distinction between the enemies of Islam and those with whom friendships are accepted and encouraged.

In fact, Muhammad classed non-believers in three categories. There were those as mentioned above, who had benign relations with the Muslims and did not obstruct the mission of the prophet or his community in any way. Then there were those who fought openly against Muhammad, and lastly there were those who tried to remain neutral in order to see how events would unfold. Rida reports, some of these tribes secretly wanted Muhammad and Islam to succeed while others wished he would fail.[190] Accordingly the verse has both a general and a specific context to explain the harshness of the words. Muhammad made peace with the three other Jewish tribes of Medina, the Bani Qaynuqa, Bani an-Nadr and the Bani Quraydah.[191] Each in turn reneged on their

---

188 Al-Tabarī, "L'exégèse" Vol. 1:218. Ibn Kathīr, *Tafsir Al-Qur'ān Al-Azim*, Vol. 3:203–6.
189 Rida, *Tafsir Al-Manar*, Vol. 5 & 6:350. Cf. Bernard Lewis, *The Jews of Islam* (Princeton NJ: Princeton University Press, 1984); ibid., 10–11, 96.
190 Rida, *Tafsir Al-Manar*, Vol. 5 & 6:350.
191 Cf. Ali Muhammad As-Sallaabee, *The Noble Life of the Prophet, Peace Be Upon Him*, trans. Faisal Shafeeq, 3 vols (Riyadh: Dar-us-Salam, 2005), 1366–8.

agreement and fought aggressively against him. At this time there were individual Muslims who had personal agreements with these tribes.[192] These Muslims needed to choose to whom they would remain loyal, to the Jews in this instance, or to Muhammad. For instance, Abdullah bin Ubay bin Salool had a treaty with the Bani Qaynuqa tribe, which he chose over loyalty to Muhammad. Ubadah ibn As-Samit, from the Bani Awf bin al-Khazraj tribe, also had an agreement with the Bani Qayuqa, but he renounced all his former allegiances and said, "My loyalty is on the side of Allah, His messenger and the believers. And I move towards Allah and His messenger from the oath I had with these *kuffars* and from supporting them".[193] Those who refused to declare wholeheartedly for Muhammad and kept their contacts up with Jewish and Christian friends, to the potential detriment of the Muslim community, were called the hypocrites. They tended to keep their options open so they too were included in the context of the verse. In Rida's opinion the prohibition against contact has to do with aiding and abetting anyone who was fighting against the prophet and the Muslim community and has nothing to do with religion *per se*.[194] In fact Rida refers to *sūrat al-mumtahanah* (23):7–9, to demonstrate the opposite:

> Perhaps God will put, between you and those to whom you have been enemies among them, affection. And God is competent, and God is Forgiving and Merciful. God does not forbid you from those who do not fight you because of religion and do not expel you from your homes-from being righteous toward them and acting justly toward them. Indeed, God loves those who act justly. God only forbids you from those who fight you because of religion and expel you from your homes and aid in your expulsion [forbids] that you make allies of them. And whoever makes allies of them, then it is those who are the wrong doers.[195]

---

192 Rida, *Tafsir Al-Manar*, Vol. 5 & 6:350–1.
193 Ibid. Vol. 5. & 6. 351. Al-Tabarī, "L'exégèse" Vol. 1:318. Here the intention is to expose Abdallah ibn Saloul and the other "hypocrites".
194 Rida, *Tafsir Al-Manar*, Vol. 5 & 6:352.
195 Ibid., Vol. 5 & 6:353–4. This teaching is in contrast with the teachings of Zamakhshari, al-Baydawi and others who would go as far as to say that a Muslim should not even see the fires of Christians and Jews used for cooking.

Nearest in Love to the Believers Wilt Thou Find, *Sūrat al-māʾidah* (5):82–3

This final cluster of verses under discussion, *sūrat al-māʾidah* (5):82–3 explore the varying Qurʾānic stereotypical responses to Islam to be expected by both Christians and Jews.[196] On the one hand these verses appear to offer the potential for a spiritual rapprochement between Christians and Muslims and on the other hand there is the seeming irreconcilable animosity to be expected from Jews. The commentary stereotypically reinforces images of the Qurʾānic construct of Christians in general by examining specific nuanced themes. Included in this cluster of themes are the pre-Qurʾānic Muslims, and the differences between those who continue in their submission to God to accept Muhammad as prophet and those who do not. However, as straightforward as the verses appear, there are subtle differences between the exegetes leading to differences between an uncritical understanding and one based on close textual analysis. Abdullah Yusuf Ali's translation of the verses is as follows:

> Strongest among men in enmity to the believers wilt thou find the Jews and pagans; and nearest among them in love to the believers wilt thou find those who say, "We are Christians" Because amongst these are men who have renounced the world, and they are not arrogant. (82) And when they listen to the revelation received by the messenger thou will see their eyes overflowing with tears, for they recognise the truth: They pray: "Our Lord! We believe, write us down among the witnesses". (83)[197]

Destined for Enmity

Mujahid reserves his comments for the identification of the Christians concerned stemming from the occasion of the revelation of the verse and for monasticism. Both these themes will be dealt with more thoroughly

---

196 Here, Jews and Christians are the People of the Book.
197 *The Holy Qurʾān*, 313.

below. The opening phrase *Strongest among men in enmity to the Believers wilt thou find the Jews and Pagans* offers quite a disparaging assessment of the potential for relations between Muslims and Jews. The phrase is explained by Al-Tabari as generalizing the arrogance and stubborn nature of the Jews as well as idol worshippers.[198] Ibn Kathir offers little attempt to soften the impact of the literal reading. He affirms that the phrase describes the Jews because their disbelief "is that of rebellion, defiance, opposing truth, belittling of other people, and degrading the scholars".[199] He goes on to call God's continued curse upon them until the Day of Resurrection for killing many of their prophets, for inciting the polytheists to hatred of Muhammad, and for allegedly trying to poison Muhammad.[200] Rida largely agrees with this assessment. However, he qualifies his remarks by insisting that the experience of the community of believers is a generalization from the context of the period of revelation and not necessarily true for individual cases or for all times. In fact, he notes that theologically Muslims and Jews are very similar, but the worldly interests of the Jews motivated them to rebel against Muhammad. In support of his argument he cites historical examples where Jewish reaction to Islam was quite positive, for instance, following the conquest of Syria, the Holy Land and in Andalusia.[201] However, having valiantly demonstrated how the reaction of the Jews within the Hijaz should be contextualized, he proceeds to qualify his comments by citing that in those countries the advent of Islam served their interest, as they felt oppressed by the Christian regimes. He further states, "Indeed, they did not really change their habits and did not leave what was their character of plotting, and that is they do not do anything except for a benefit".[202]

198 Al-Tabarī, "L'exégèse" Vol. 1:331.
199 Ibn Kathīr, *Tafsir Al-Qur'ān Al-Azim*, Vol. 3:246.
200 Ibid.
201 Rida, *Tafsir Al-Manar*, Vol. 7 & 8:6–7.
202 Ibid., Vol. 7 & 8:7.

Christians as Believers

In contrast, the appraisal of Christians is far more optimistic, *and nearest among them in love to the Believers wilt thou find those who say: "We are Christians:" because amongst these are men devoted to learning and men who have renounced the world qissīsīn* [priests] *and ruhban* [monks], *and they are not arrogant.* An uncritical understanding of the verse may lead one to universalize this glowing assessment of the relationship between Muslims and Christians. However, this high honour is conditional and represents an excellent example of the *theoretical construct* referred to by McAuliffe.²⁰³ The conditions of praise are apparent when the possible occasion of the revelation is examined.

Mujahid relates that the verse refers to the delegation from Abyssinia who came with Ja'far and his companions after they sought refuge from persecution from the pagans of Mecca.²⁰⁴ Al-Tabari, based on a *hadīth* from Ibn Abbas, describes this possible occasion in greater detail:

> This divine matter was revealed about the Christians from Abyssinia, who had been dispatched to Medina by their king the Najāshī. When the Qur'ān was recited to the envoys, their eyes filled with tears, they recognized truth and believed. That is indicated in the continuation of the revelation: and that they are without arrogance. When they hear what has been revealed to the envoy, you see their eyes water, so much they recognize truth there, at the point of saying: "Our Master, we believe. Include us among the witnesses". (5):83.²⁰⁵

Here is a clear example of Qur'ānic praise for Christians who convert to Islam. Members of the Christian delegation were able to recognize the truth when they heard it, because they were not arrogant and as a result they were open to the truth that they recognized and converted to Islam. For Al-Tabari and Ibn Kathir the conversion of the delegation from Abyssinia to Islam represent only one of the possible occasions to which the verse

---

203   McAuliffe, *Qur'ānic Christians*, 288.
204   Mujahid, *Tafsir Mujahid*, 202. McAuliffe, *Qur'ānic Christians*, 285–92.
205   Al-Tabarī, "L'exégèse" Vol. 1:331. Translation by this author. Ibn Kathīr, *Tafsir Al-Qur'ān Al-Azim*, Vol. 3:245.

could refer. For instance, Al-Tabari in a *hadīth* transmitted by Ibn al-Nu'man Qatadah considers that the verse could have been any group of Christians. He says "They were followers of the religion of Isa [Jesus], son of Maryam, who when they saw Muslims and heard the Qur'ān, they became Muslims without hesitation".[206] Ata bin Abi Rabah, a student of Ibn Abbas, identifies the group in question as the Abyssinians who embraced Islam after Muslims migrated there and lived amongst them. Al-Tabari keeps the identity of the people concerned vague and says that it could be applied to anyone who fits the description, whether they are from Abyssinia or not.[207] The reaction of these Christians is therefore held up as the normative example of good Christians. In his own opinion, Ibn Kathir relates that the phrase, *and you will find the nearest in love to the believers those who say: "We are Christians"* to refer in very general terms to those, "who follow the religion of the Messiah and the teachings of the Injil", offering perhaps his personal admiration for the teachings of the Gospel. In support of this opinion he quotes from *sūrat al-hadīd* (57):27 "And We ordained in the hearts of those who followed him (Jesus), compassion, mercy, and monasticism" without mentioning that the end of the phrase describes monasticism as something Christians invented themselves.[208] Further Ibn Kathir says that in the religion of the Messiah fighting is prohibited, while citing a verse similar to Matthew Chapter 5, "He who strikes you on the right cheek, then turn the left cheek for him".[209] Ibn Kathir says that Christians generally are more tolerant of Islam and Muslims, "because of the mercy and kindness that their hearts acquired through part of the Messiah's religion".[210] Rida's commentary seeks to identify those to whom the phrase might include. First, he believes it is addressed to Muhammad. The second audience in

---

206 *Tafsir Al-Qur'ān Al-Azim*, Vol. 3:245. Quoting Al-Tabari 10:501. Cf. 246–8.
207 Ibid. McAuliffe, *Qur'ānic Christians*, 205–6.
208 Ibn Kathīr, *Tafsir Al-Qur'ān Al-Azim*, Vol. 3:246. Mujahid stresses that monasticism was not something ordained by God, rather God has given us the means to enjoy life in a proper way, through Islam, Mujahid, *Mujahid, Dr. M. Abdul-Salam, Kuwait University*, 313–4.
209 Ibn Kathīr, *Tafsir Al-Qur'ān Al-Azim*, Vol. 3:246.
210 Ibid.

most general terms would be everyone. "The people" represent multiple possibilities; they are the Jews, polytheists and the Christians of Abyssinia, at the time of revelation. Moving to a more general meaning of the phrase, he opines that the meaning extends to every nation and to all generations.[211]

Invitations to Islam

Further to the point, Rida examines the particular response to letters of invitations to Islam sent by Muhammad to some kings and leaders surrounding the Hijaz. He summarizes the response from Christians as favourable, irrespective of whether they accepted Islam, or not. In particular he examines the cases of Heraclius, the Christian emperor; Cyrus, the Coptic Patriarch of Alexandria; Jaifar bin al-Jalandi, the king of Oman, and his brother Abd. The reception of these leaders to the invitation was courteous and attentive. Eventually Jaifar bin al-Jalandi and his brother both convert to Islam. According to Rida, Heraclius and Cyrus did not convert, but neither did they reject Muhammad and his message. With these examples Rida re-introduces some common themes concerning the continuity of true religion found in Islam and the prophethood of Muhammad as foretold by the previous prophets. What keeps otherwise faithful people from accepting Islam, he maintains, has more to do with worldly concerns rather than disbelief. Their reasons for remaining Christian are in keeping with the possible acceptable reasons given in his examination of the *sūrat al-mā'idah* (5):48. These reasons vary from loss of power, not properly understanding the message of Islam and a "false" sense of loyalty to the *taqlīd* of their own religion. Cyrus for instance upon receiving Hatib bin Abi Balta'ah, the messenger from the prophet replies, "we have a religion that we will not abandon except for something better".[212] In response Hatib explains that the message from Muhammad is the perfection of the religion of the Messiah: "The good news that Moses gave about Jesus is like the good news that Jesus gave regarding Muhammad. And our invitation to

---

211   Rida, *Tafsir Al-Manar*, Vol. 7 & 8:4.
212   Ibid., Vol. 7 & 8:4–5.

you is to the Qurʾān, just as you invite the people of the Torah to the Injīl. Every prophet has a nation that he was sent to, and it is your duty to obey him. We do not ask you to refrain from the religion of the Messiah, but we ask you to follow it".[213] Cyrus responds, "I have looked into the affairs of this Prophet, and I have found that he does not command that which is disliked, and does not prevent that which is desirable. I also did not find him to be a misguided magician, or a lying soothsayer. And I have found out that he carries the signs of prophethood when he made hidden apparent, and telling that which people whisper".[214] As a sign of friendship Cyrus gave Muhammad many gifts including two slave girls. Mariah, a Christian, became his wife and bore his son, Ibrahim.[215]

Learned and Sincere

For Al-Tabari the phrase, *because amongst these are men devoted to learning and men who have renounced the world and they are not arrogant*, implies that from among the Christians there are priests, and those who practise monastic life. These Christians are humble and recognize the truth.[216] He posits two interesting theories regarding the identity of the priests and monks in question. The first is based on a *hadīth* that comes from Ibn Abbas that proposes that they are Jesus' disciples. This theory describes them as *al-islam* [submitting to God]. Jesus thus called them to *daʾahum ila al-islam* [follow him in submitting to God]. The second theory, based on *hadīth* that come from Abu Salih al-Misri and Saʾid b. Jubayr, places the identity of the priests and monks within the context of the verse, with the delegation from Abyssinia.[217] These scholars, who he describes as *ahl dinin* [people of a religion], are credited for instilling into their communities the values of the teachings of Jesus

213 Ibid.
214 Ibid., Vol. 7 & 8:5.
215 Lings, *Muhammad*, 277, 86, 315.
216 Al-Tabarī, "L'exégèse" Vol. 1:331.
217 McAuliffe, *Qurʾānic Christians*, 218.

and thus making Christians more receptive to Islam.[218] For Ibn Kathir, priests and monks exemplify that among the Christians are men who are humble, seek knowledge, truth and fairness.[219] This phrase is taken in conjunction with verse 5:83 *And when they listen to the revelation received by the Messenger, thou wilt see their eyes overflowing with tears, for they recognise the truth.* For Al-Tabari the phrase implies that when the delegation heard the Qur'ān recited they recognized that it is God's truth, and their eyes could be seen to fill with tears.[220] For Ibn Kathir the phrase refers to "the good news that they have about the advent of Muhammad". In light of the truth they have found the Christians respond as the verse concludes, "*they pray: 'Our Lord! We believe; write us down among the witnesses'*". In support of this opinion Ibn Kathir discusses two very important verses that explain and affirm the positive disposition of Christians towards Islam, *sūrat Āl-ʿImrān* (3):199, which he translates as, "And there are, certainly, among the People of the Scripture, those who believe in Allah and in which has been revealed to you, and in that which has been revealed to them, humble themselves before Allah". This verse alludes to the Qur'ānic theme of the continued sequential nature of revelation and the fidelity of the Christians who continue in faith to enter Islam. The other verse is *sūrat al-qasas* (28):52–5, which brings into play the concept of Christians as pre-Qur'ānic Muslims; Abdul Yusuf Ali translates the verses:

> Those to whom We sent the Book before this, they do believe in this (Revelation); (52) and when it is recited to them, they say, "We believe therein, for it is the Truth from our Lord: Indeed we have been Muslims (Bowing to Allah's Will) from before this. (53) Twice they were given their reward, for that they have persevered, that they avert evil with good, and that they spend (in charity) out of what We have given them. (54) And when they hear vain talk, they turn away there from and say: "To us our deeds, and to you yours; Peace be to you: we seek not the ignorant".[221]

---

218   Ibid., 218–9.
219   Ibn Kathīr, *Tafsir Al-Qurʾān Al-Azim*, Vol. 3:247.
220   Al-Tabarī, "L'exégèse" Vol. 1:331–2.
221   The Presidency of the Islamic Researches and IFTA, *The Holy Qurʾān*, 1135–6.

Ahl al-Kitāb: *The Qur'ānic People of the Book*

It is often forgotten that the Arabic language pre-dates Islam by more than 1,500 years.[222] Therefore the terms used to describe a person who submits their will to God, that is, a *"Muslim"* or is called to follow God, *"da'ahum ila al-islam"* could have been used in the period of *jāhiliyya*, to name a person of faith. The use of the phrase is quite complimentary and should not be forgotten as a phrase that potentially includes a faithful Christian even if only in rare usage. In fact, this author has heard this verse and similar phrases quoted by Palestinian Christians to their Muslim brothers and sisters, usually followed by, "You have your Islam and I have mine".[223] In the following chapters the use of Islamicized Arabic terms will be examined in greater detail. In any case Christians who do satisfy the above description and enter Islam are praised in the Qur'ān for their perseverance and fidelity.

Rida agrees with the other exegetes extending the praise for respect for the truth to priests, monks and to Christians in general.[224] He observes that there are good and bad people in both religions. The character of the Jews is contrasted to the Christians with a quick examination of the historical factors affecting their disposition; that the problem with the Jews originates with their enslavement in Egypt and the command of God to keep separate from the pagans once the Jews entered the Holy Land. At first this separation from other peoples was necessary. He argues that if the Jews had mingled with pagans their monotheistic religion would have been overcome by the pagan practices. However, what started out as a means of training a nation, eventually led to a nationalization of *tawhīd*. This practice eventually produced some undesirable attributes like arrogance, superficial religiosity, and excesses in materialism and rituals, things that Jesus came to reform. Following in the sequence of divine revelation, God sent Muhammad as the Paraclete, "the spirit of truth" who would guide humanity in all that is good for the body and the soul. The people of faith, including priests and monks, who accepted and propagated the teachings of Jesus, whether they were from Jewish backgrounds or not, were closer in affection and belief to Islam, even with their concept of Trinity. They were

---

222 Trimingham, *Christianity among the Arabs*, 8–10.
223 Cf. *Surat al-Kafirun* (109).
224 Rida, *Tafsir Al-Manar*, Vol. 7 & 8:7–11.

therefore, more predisposed because of the teachings of Christ to accept the truth of Islam when it was presented to them.[225] Rejecting the notion that the concept of the Trinity, as a form of polytheism, might in some way negatively affect the relationship between Muslims and Christians; Rida remarks that the concept of Trinity is a very complicated concept introduced into Christianity "when it was not even understood and comprehended" and ironically, probably facilitated people's conversion to Islam.[226]

The general common theme of the character of believers is traced through history in order to demonstrate its continued veracity and to acknowledge missed opportunities. Rida briefly examines some of the reason for the historical aggression between Christians and Muslims. Reflecting on the crusades, the rise of the Ottoman Empire, and extending into modern times he sees the aggression as a product of worldly ambitions, misconceptions and racism for which both sides have been guilty. Turning to Muslims, Rida condemns the Muslims of his time for their weakness in the practice of following the Qur'ān and for tolerating corrupt governments and politicians. He further condemns the backwardness of their educational systems and social developments that have made a mockery of Islam in contrast to western Christian countries that have modernized. If it were not for these factors he argues, whereby Muslim countries would be as developed as western countries, economically, socially and politically; the friendliness between Christians and Muslims would be even greater, as would conversion to Islam. He ends his assessment of the causes of strife aptly with a curse on the *provocateurs* that might cause any strife between Muslims and Christians, "May the curse of Allah be upon those who provoke animosity and hatred among the servants of Allah in utter self-interest or to please their masters".[227]

Rida contends that Christians who are not arrogant, or not filled with haughtiness, when they hear the message of the Qur'ān and contemplate its meaning, they are more likely to recognize it as Gods truth and accept Islam. They may respond, as did the delegation from Abyssinia, *"Our Lord!*

---

225   Ibid., Vol. 7 & 8:7–8.
226   Ibid., Vol. 7 & 8:7–11. McAuliffe, *Qur'ānic Christians*, 231.
227   Rida, *Tafsir Al-Manar*, Vol. 7 & 8:10.

We believe; write us down among the witnesses". Being witness in this case infers membership of the community of Muhammad, having previously followed the teachings of Jesus. This includes Jesus' teachings concerning the Paraclete. Rida then narrates from Ibn Abbas, that the witnesses are those referred to in *sūrat al-baqarah* (2):143, "And thus we have made you a medium (just) nation that you may be bearers of witness to the people and the prophet may be a bearer of witness to you".[228]

Conclusions

This chapter employs the hermeneutical method of traditional commentary, *tafsīr*, to examine the commentary of four Islamic scholars concerning a selection of verses from the Qur'ān that discuss Christians and Christianity. A close textual analysis of the commentary portrays the following theoretical construct. *Sūrat al-baqarah* (2):62 defines the communities of the People of the Book. The commentary discusses the issue of correct belief. At stake is whether or not *whosoever believes* could encompass those who do not accept Muhammad as prophet. For Mujahid and Ibn Kathir, Christians who do not follow from belief in Jesus to belief in Muhammad are no longer true believers; they will be doomed in the next life. Al-Tabari considers correct belief implies belief in Muhammad, but maintains that the promises of the phrase, *and no fear shall come to them, neither shall they sorrow*, for *whosoever believes in God and the Last Day and works righteousness*, remains established, *muhkam*. This suggests the possibility of salvation for all who believe in God and who live their lives according to their beliefs and thus need not fear the Last Day. Rida, also considers the value of deeds, letting one's life speak, are far more important than membership of a particular religion, or superficial religiosity. Therefore, although both Al-Tabari and Rida acknowledge the importance of accepting the

---

228 Ibid., Vol. 7 & 8:11–12.

prophethood of Muhammad, they do not exclude those who remain in their faith from God's salvation.

The idea of following the evolution of belief through successive revelations from all the prophets to Muhammad is central to the theoretical construct outlined by McAuliffe. There is strong evidence to maintain that even from the classical period of exegesis, and arguably from the formative period as well, there is an element of inclusive salvation reserved for Christians as well as for others. What remains pivotal however, is the need for those who do not follow Muhammad, to refrain from being antagonistic to his message and community. This is not unlike the necessity for those who do not accept Jesus to refrain from rejecting the one who sent him, as in Luke 9:50 or Mark 3:28–9. What is clear from the debate is the need to understand the area of abrogation and context. The context of the revelation of a verse is where the verse is soundly understood. To generalize, or universalize, on the specific meaning of a verse is an act of interpretation that can be challenged by alternative interpretations. The context of *sūrat al-baqarah* (2):62 concerned the Salman al-Farisi and his former Christian colleagues. His example of steadfastness to following the sequence of revelation forms part of the normative example of Qur'ānic Christians. The necessity of accepting Muhammad as an authentic prophet of God appears not unreasonable if indeed Muhammad was the man he claimed to be. Yet not every person is afforded the honour of the company of a prophet in order to ascertain his character and authenticity. Nevertheless, it behoves Christians then to consider what it is they reject about Muhammad while remaining within their own *taqlīd*.

The commentary for *sūrat an-Nisā'* (4):171 criticizes Christian excesses in religion. Here the main issue concerns *tawhīd*, the oneness of God. Christians are accused of elevating Jesus and his mother to be gods, rather than servants of God. The verse does not mention any particular denomination or community specifically. Therefore, the criticism acts as a corrective to the theoretical construct of Christians in general. The appellation of "Son of God" is discussed at length and is roundly denounced as *shirk*, association of partners with God. The nature of the Qur'ānic Jesus as Messiah is presented and discussed. He is a creation of God, through the word of God, and strengthened through God's Spirit. This is not viewed in itself as an exclusive event, since the Spirit of God is active in the world and strengthens others. Examples of God sending His Spirit to others are examined through verses of the Qur'ān and Gospel. Here again the *menahhemana*/Paraclete is mentioned as another form of God's creation that God sent to strengthen people's faith. Ibn Kathir reflects that Jesus taught strict *tawhīd* in keeping with Judaic tradition. He cites *sūrat al-mā'idah* (5):166 for support. In this verse Jesus squarely denies instructing anyone to worship him or his mother. Ibn Kathir mentions with great respect that Jesus taught people to worship God alone, to be conscious of God in all aspects of their life, *taqwā*, and to renounce the pleasures of this world. The blame for the error in Christian dogma falls squarely on the followers of Jesus, the monks and priests, who Ibn Kathir says Christians follow as lords. Ironically, in another context it is the priests and monks from Abyssinia that are singled out for praise for their recognition of Muhammad as a prophet. Rida in his commentary embarks upon a study of the concept of Trinity found in ancient cultures. The gist of his argument is that the sin of *shirk* is something societies are prone to adopt and often feed upon each other's mythologies, anthropomorphizing the concept of father, son and spirit to be a divine triune entity. Therefore, as he sees it, Christians have only slipped into the oft-repeated folly of distorting the truth of their revelation by associating partners with God. Moreover, Rida curiously mentions the possibility that this exaggeration may be the result of over compensating for the refusal of most Jews to accept Jesus and/or the result of translating the Semitic concept of Messiah to a predominantly gentile world.

Sūrat al-mā'idah (5):48 appears at first glance to acknowledge that the People of the Book received divine revelation as part of a sequence of revelation. Each community is to persist in faith and practice, consciousness of God, to see who can better serve God. However, the commentary presents quite a different picture. Here the key to the opening phrase is the term *muhayminan*, meaning to guard over. The Qur'ān is presented as guardian over all previous revelations, keeping what is true in safety from alteration. The choice is God's guidance or the return to the days of *jāhiliyya*. Therefore not all the texts are equal, the Qur'ān is superior to the Torah and Gospel because the divine truth given to these communities has been lost or distorted. The occasion of revelation instructs Muhammad to remain steadfast to the revelation that has been given to him in judgement with certain Jews of Medina rather than seek to use his office in a dispute with their own people. For his services they would offer their conversion. Further the commentary differentiates between the way to God, meaning the different prescriptions of life for each community, or *Sharī'ah*, which may differ slightly from one culture to another, and true religion, which does not change from one prophet to the next. In short, true religion is simple, belief in one God, the need to submit one's life to God, and to ever strive to let one's life reflect one's belief with righteous deeds, thus ever striving for perfection in faith and practice, *ihsān*. This is the same religion that was enjoined upon all the prophets. The final phrase from the verse reflects the omnipotence of God; in the end, God will judge all our differences.

Sūrat al-mā'idah 5:82–3 gets to the heart of the image of the theoretical construct of praiseworthy Christians. Here in strongest terms Christians are described as the nearest to Muslims. The reasons have to do with the values of Jesus' message that predispose Christians to humility and mercy. This verse praises priests and monks. These are the Christians who from a scholarly perspective are able to recognize the truth of the Qur'ān, referring to the teachings of Jesus that relate to the *menahhemana*/Paraclete. The most plausible specific example of such Christians is that of the delegation from Abyssinia, although in general terms the verse could apply to all Christians who respond in kind. Christians who convert to Islam, or as Hatib bin Abi Balta'ah would say, continue to follow in the religion of Jesus by accepting Muhammad as the *menahhemana* are praised and promised a double reward for their steadfast perseverance in faith. Pre-Qur'ānic Christians are praised for following Jesus and described as pre-Qur'ānic Muslims for responding to Jesus' call to Islam. Those who do not convert to Islam in the time of Muhammad are understandably not praised, but neither are they condemned.

PART II

Challenging the Constructs:
Expanding *Tafsīr* of the Qur'ānic People of the Book

Part II attempts to shed light on two important theoretical constructs emerging from the examination of the People of the Book through the hermeneutic *tafsīr*. The first concerns the social and historical environment of the context of the Qur'ān and its importance as a factor influencing *tafsīr*, while the second concerns the Christian response to theological representations of Christian doctrines. Through this inquiry, it is hoped that both Muslims and Christians will be encouraged to appreciate what the Qur'ān and Gospel have to say regarding the oneness of God, and God's relationship with his word. Through this examination it is hoped certain challenges and opportunities for more fruitful dialogue and cooperation will emerge.

CHAPTER 2

Beyond *Al-jāhiliyya*: The Social and Historical Context of the People of the Book in Pre-Islamic Arabia

> Utruku al-habasha mā tarakūkum.
> [Until the Abyssinians attack you, do not attack them.]
> — MUHAMMAD

Introduction

In Islamic culture the name given to the period of time on the Arab peninsula prior to the arrival of Islam is *al-jāhiliyya*.[1] Tradition has it that this was a barbaric period in matters of social conduct and faith.[2] This period is frequently contrasted with the seminal shift in the relationship between man and God, with the inlibration of his word in the form of the Qur'ān and the prophethood of Muhammad. Some might argue that here humanity once again faced the choice between *islām*, submission to God's guidance, and negotiating matters of faith and conduct based on the misguided norms of flawed beliefs. Yet, as the Qur'ān mentions, and as discussed in the previous chapter, God has always offered his guidance to his creation, beginning with Adam and spoken through all the prophets, even on the Arab peninsula. Those who followed God's guidance could be found in the

---

1   Muhammad bin 'Abdil-Wahhaab, *An Explanation of Aspects of the Days of Ignorance*, trans. Isma'eel Alarcon (New York: Sanatech, 2005), 15.
2   Ibid., 13–22. Cf. Tarif Khalidi, *Arabic Historical Thought in the Classic Period* (Cambridge: Cambridge University Press, 1996), 1, 7, & 11.

communities of the People of the Book and in the lives of individuals who through the exercise of reason and conscience also lived righteous lives. So, what qualifies as *al-jāhiliyya*? What is the difference between submission to God's will before and after the arrival of Islam?

More specifically, is Qur'ānic criticism of the People of the Book based solely on faith and creed, which varied significantly between various communities extant on the peninsula, or is there an element of particularity at work, that determines whether a community might be predisposed, or not, to congenial coexistence with Muhammad and Islam?[3] Due to the importance of these questions it is unfortunate that there is a dearth of primary source material remaining from pre-Islamic Arab communities. An examination of the period identifies two main Arab/Islamic sources of information. One interesting genre of information comes from the poetry left behind by nomadic Arabs. This is referred to as *al-jāhiliyya poetry*.[4] Then there is the vast repository of Islamic literary material found in the *sīra*, *hadīth* and *tafsīr* collections that are based on verses of the Qur'ān mentioning *al-jāhiliyya*.[5] These sources, although quite suitable for homiletic purposes, fall short of answering key social and anthropological questions about the people and time in a broader sense that might contribute to a greater understanding of the varied relationship between Muhammad's nascent community and the communities they encountered. Fortunately, the image we have of the period is enhanced by information supplied by other external societies, Abyssinian; through legend as with the *Kebra Nagast*; through the extra-canonical Jewish *Rabbanan d'Aggadta* stories, as well as some material from the social sciences. Since the period is critically important for Muslims, Christians and Jews in gaining an understanding of the context of the Qur'ān, the period of *al-jāhiliyya* necessitates closer analysis.

The communities extant at this time are important to the future development of Islamic culture, as they set precedents for interaction for the generations that follow, even to the present day. The principal communities

---

3   Darren M. Slade, "Arabia Haeresium Ferax (Arabia Bearer of Heresies)", *American Theological Inquiry (online)* 7, no. 1 January 2015 (2014): 43–53.
4   Khalidi, *Arabic Historical Thought in the Classic Period*, 6.
5   Ibid., 1–39.

concerned are the Christians and Jews extant on the Arab peninsula during the time of revelation, in particular the Jews of the Hijaz, Medina and to a lesser extent Himyar as well as Christians from Abyssinia and Najrān.

Before examining this period, it is worth considering what the term *al-jāhiliyya* means and how it is employed. *Jahl* is the root of the word *jāhiliyya*. In Islamic theology the term *jahl* represents a lack of knowledge or rejection of God's guidance.[6] Derivatives of the term appear numerously in the Qur'ān translated into English as *ignorant, ignorantly, ignorance, ignore* and even as *foolish*.[7] The term *al-jāhiliyya* appears only four times in the Qur'ān. In each instance the use of the term suggests a slightly nuanced meaning that is explained by the context of the verse. In *sūrat Āl-'Imrān* (3):154 the context that suggests the term implies a wavering faith or doubt in God and his prophet. In *sūrat al-mā'idah* (5):50 the phrase refers to more self-serving use of interpreting Jewish traditions in favour of one group of Jews over another. In *sūrat al-ahzab* (33):33 the term refers to immodest displays of wealth by women and instructs the wives of Muhammad to conduct themselves modestly and dutifully in their faith. The last use of the term in the Qur'ān is in *sūrat al-fath* (48):26, here the believers are given the gift of *sakinah*, calmness, in face of a heated discourse with nonbelievers and those who preferred the ways of the days of ignorance.[8] One noteworthy historical use of the term worth mentioning involves Abu l'Hakam, who ignominiously gained the title Abu Jahl, *the father of ignorance*, for his vociferous opposition to Muhammad and for his persecution of defenceless Muslims.[9]

The use of the term *al-jāhiliyya* in the Qur'ān suggests that the initial audience is familiar with pre-Islamic culture. Consequently, people are

---

6 Dr Rohi Baalbaki, "Al-Mawrid", in *A Modern Arabic-English Dictionary* (Beirut: Dar El-Ilm Lilmalayin, 2007), 409 & 37. Possible antonyms for *jahl* are *islām*, submission to God, *ilm* knowledge, or *hilm*, moral reasonableness, or self-control.
7 M H Shakir, "Concordance of the Qur'ān: Extracted from the M. H. Shakir Translation of the Qur'ān", in *Concordance of the Qur'ān: Extracted from the M. H. Shakir Translation of the Qur'ān* (New York: Tahrike Tarsile Qur'an, Inc., 2005), 586–7.
8 Reuven Firestone, *Journeys in Holy Lands: The Evolution of the Abraham-Ishmael Legends in Islamic Exegesis* (Albany: University of New York Press, 1990), 5, n21.
9 Lings, *Muhammad*, 58.

offered the choice of living by God's guidance, the way of *islām* and thus becoming a person who submits to God, a *Muslimūn*. However, the universal import of the term makes defining the boundaries of *al-jāhiliyya*, either in time or place, an elusive task, due to the many nuanced meanings and applications of the term. For instance, since pagan Arabs are named does this imply monotheist Arabs are possibly exempt from accusations of rejecting God's guidance? Alternatively, is living in the light of *islām* conditional to a perennial personal choice? As mentioned in Chapter 1, Islamic scholars use the term in the generic sense to name the time and spiritual condition of the Arabs prior to the arrival of the prophet as well as in its specific Qur'ānic context in *tafsīr* literature. The exegesis of Al-Tabari and Rashid Rida suggest that there is a possibility of living a righteous life, living *islām*, but failing for matters of conscience, albeit prejudiced from an Islamic perspective, to accept the religion of Islam and requisite belief in the prophethood of Muhammad. In modern times some Islamic schools and social movements equate the gross failings in society, both in Western, as well as in Islamic countries analogous to a return to *al-jāhiliyya*.[10] Muhammad bin 'Abdil-Wahhaab, for example, is as critical of Islamic leaders as he is with non-Muslims. Sayyid Qutb, for his part, prefers to focus on the image of complete separation between Muslim Society and all other influences in order to achieve a more utopian Islamic Society.[11]

The problem with the association of *al-jāhiliyya* of the pre-Islamic period with modern society, or any other period of time, is that very few people (if any) truly understand pre-Islamic Arabian culture well enough to make a fair comparison. Therefore, this author contends that the concept of *al-jāhiliyya* runs the risk of misinterpretation by theologians, or by social-political movements, who might oversimplify the concept and

---

10   "The Worldview of Sunni Arab Fundamentalists: Attitudes Towards Modern Science and Technology", in *Fundamentalisms and Society: Reclaiming the Sciences, the Family, and Education*, ed. R. Scott Appleby and Martin E. Marty, The Fundamentalism Project (Chicago: University of Chicago Press, 1997), 91.
11   Here the works of Muhammad bin 'Abdil-Wahhaab and Sayyid Qutb come to mind. See 'Abdil-Wahhaab, *Days of Ignorance*, 13, 285, 303–4. Cf. Sayyid Qutb, *Milestone*, Sime (USA 2005), 6–11.

undervalue the state of spiritual growth on the Arab peninsula prior to Muhammad. Therefore, just as the theoretical construct of the People of the Book obscures paths to interfaith dialogue, so too, the resulting theoretical construct of *al-jāhiliyya* risks obscuring the subtle nuances that are possibly found in the context of the revelation of verses.[12] Lack of clear understanding of *al-jāhiliyya* threatens the relationship between Muslims and People of the Book. For how can a contribution to dialogue be valued when one of the contributors is considered to wilfully reject God's guidance as is the case with the pedagogical works of Sayyid Qutb and 'Abdil-Wahhaab?

From these quite varied views, what can be said about the boundaries between belief and disbelief of those who do not convert to the religion of Islam, yet practise *islām*? The former case might be true for those Christians, or Jews, who met Muhammad, accepted that he was an authentic servant of God, but remained within their tradition, as well as those who may never have met Muhammad or been aware of his teachings. Further to the point, in discourse with this genre of pre-Islamic society a more soul-searching dialogue surely took place. Questions like these underscore the importance of understanding how the term *al-jāhiliyya* may have been applied at the time of the revelation of the Qur'ān, in order to understand the merits of the correct use of the term today.

It is hoped that a better understanding of the pre-Islamic period will demonstrate that Islamic criticisms of the People of the Book is more dependent on the specific context of the revelation than is generally accepted. The implications are that the Islamic criticisms of Christianity are less reliable beyond the context of revelation. This is especially true after the death of Muhammad, as the followers of Muhammad struggle to interpret and apply his teachings in new and changing contexts of time and place. Further to the point, unless the specific context is adequately

---

12   The idea here is that of the *sociology of consciousness*, how well do future generations truly understand the authentic mission, or intention of Muhammad, verses an inevitable element of interpretation in light of one's own context. For instance, 'Abdil-Wahhaab's use of *ahl al-jāhiliyya* infers a universal rejection of divine revelation for both non-believers and the People of the Book at the time of Muhammad and as an ever-present danger to Muslims.

understood, it is not possible to employ the methodological discourse of *tafsīr* properly, leaving the interpretation of the Qur'ān with its timeless import, obscure to future dialogue.

The Children of Abraham in Arabia

In an attempt to understand the particular Abrahamic culture of Arabia it is worth stepping back to try and comprehend how monotheism may first have arrived there. To begin, when most western people think about the Jews of antiquity they are likely to imagine the Jews of the Old Testament, a people perfectly content to live in Eretz Yisrael, the very land that God promised to Abraham and to Moses. Similarly, a westerner may have paid scant attention to the fate of Ishmael and his descendants, nor to the promises made to Abraham and Hagar on Ishmael's behalf. What of the fate of the other children of Abraham's wife Hagar, not to mention the children of his concubines? The descendants of all these people slip conveniently away from the common image of Abraham. Then there are the "other" peoples of the region, the Amorites, Canaanites, Hittites, Girgashites, Horites and Amalkites who often fought the Children of Israel and were subject to the *ban* in reprisal.[13] Perhaps a brief examination of Biblical sources and the corpus of material left behind by the *Rabbanan d'Aggadta* may provide clues as to how, in a theological if not a historical sense, the religion of Abraham came to Arabia and what social perspective this may have inspired.

---

13   The *ban* is the Hebrew term used for offering the sacrifice of one's enemies as tribute to God. Here one is required to slaughter men women, children livestock and crops. The direction is given by Moses to annihilate the Amalekites for their sin of attacking the Children of Israel while they were weak and wandering the desert. Cf. Hagai Mazuz, "Massacre in Medina" *Segula: The Jewish Journal Through History*, no. 3 (2010). See also Jack Cohen, *The Reunion of Isaac and Ishmael* (New York: Mosaic Press, 1987), 30.

Beyond Al-jāhiliyya

All Nations Will Be Blessed

From the outset, the fates of the lives of the children of Abraham seem intertwined. In Genesis the future patriarch of the Arabs, Ishmael, is born to Abraham and Hagar.[14] When he reaches the age of thirteen he is circumcised on the same day as Abraham, as a sign of the everlasting covenant between Abraham and God, along with all the other males from Abraham's household.[15] Abraham and Hagar are assured that God will bless Ishmael, despite the blessings bestowed upon Sarah's son Isaac. Indeed, after Ishmael and his mother are sent away to wander in the desert of Paran, the angel of the Lord repeats God's promise that Ishmael will be the father of a great nation.[16]

The Bible does not mention any further contact between Abraham, Hagar and Ishmael. Picking up the trail requires an examination of Jewish *Rabbanan d'Aggadta* material as well as Islamic sources.[17] These sources

14   Hagar is the gift of Pharaoh to Sarah. Muhammed Ibn Ismael Al-Bukharī, *The Translation of the Meaning of Sahih Al-Bukharī* trans. Dr Muhammad Muhsin Khan (Riyadh: Darussalam, 1997), Vol. 4, Book 60, ¶3348, ¶59. Cf. Louis Ginzberg, *The Legends of the Jews*, trans. Henrietta Szold, 6th edn (Philidelphia, PA: The Jewish Publication Society Of America, 1909), 223, fn. 74, 37. Here, drawing upon the Targum Yerushalmi, Hagar is discussed not only as a gift from Pharaoh, but also his own daughter. "The Legends of the Jews", in *The Legends of the Jews*, ed. Boaz Cohen (London: John Hopkins University Press, 1998), 7:199. Here Hagar is identified as Keturah, the woman Abraham marries after the death of Sarah. *Jewish Legends*, 1:298. In the *Pseudo-Jonathan* Hagar/Keturah is both the daughter of Pharaoh and granddaughter of Babylonian king Nimrod. Florentino Garcia Martinez, Hagar in Targum Pseudo-Jonathan (Brill, 2011). 263–74.
15   *The Holy Bible: English Standard Version* (Wheaton, IL: Good News Publishers, 2001). Genesis 16.
16   Ibid. Genesis 21. D S. Margoliouth, *The Relations between Arabs and Israelites Prior to the Rise of Islam*, The Schweich Lectures 1921 (London: Oxford University Press, 1924), 12.
17   The *Rabbanan d'Aggadta* are stories or legends employed by the Rabbinic Jews of the Diaspora for homiletic purposes. Torah and copious servings of the moral imagination blend to fill in the blanks between the outlines provided by the canonical texts and the needs of the teacher. This is especially true with the Jewish versions of the relationship between Ishmael and Isaac as well as the pre-maternal relationship

discuss stories concerning visits to Ishmael, their bond, as well as the future reconciliation between Isaac and Ishmael. One romantic story recounts the reunion of Abraham and Hagar. Accordingly, following the death of Sarah, Isaac recognized the grief of his father and set off to find Hagar, his father's other love. By now Hagar is recognized by Abraham and his family for her righteousness. Hagar never relinquished her fidelity to Abraham in spite of their separation, nor her faith to his God. She joyfully accepts Isaac's invitation and returns with him. Reunited, Hagar, is given a new name, Keturah, meaning incense, referring to the manner in which her *teshuvah* [repentance], was accepted for her pride over Sarah.[18] Reunited, Keturah bore Abraham six more sons as well as a daughter.[19]

Another very important legend relates to the building of the Ka'bah in Mecca referred to in *sūrat al-baqarah* (2):125 & 127.[20] Muslim scholars identify this temple as the temple mentioned in Psalms 84.[21] Here again

---

between Sarah and Hagar. See Ginzberg, *Jewish Legends*, 237–44. Concerning Hagar and Sarah and the birth of Ishmael, Cf. 263–6 where Ishmael is sent away and 266–9 where Abraham visits Ishmael. Cf. Cohen, *Reunion*, 167–9.

18 Rabbi Binyamin Efrati, *"Sh'ma B'ni" a Treasury of Stories and Lessons from the Weekly Parashah* [Otzar HaTorah LaYeled], ed. C. D. Sklar, trans. Rabbi Yaakov Yosef Iskowitz, 2005 edn (Jerusalem: Feldheim Publishers, 2005), 25–6. Here citing (Parash 25:1). Cf. <http://jwa.org/encyclopedia/article/keturah-midrash-and-aggadah> accessed 2 May 2016.

19 Ginzberg, *Jewish Legends*, 290–3, 98. Cf. Genesis 25 for a discussion of Keturah as the wife of Abraham.

20 See *sūrat al-baqarah* (2):127, *sūrat Āl-'Imrān* (3):96–7 & *sūrat al-hajj* (22):26. Al-Bukhārī, *The Translation of the Meaning of Sahih Al-Bukhari* Vol. 4, Book 60, ¶3364 & 65, 355–9. Abraham I. Katsh, *Judaism in Islām* (New York: New York University Press & Bloch Publishing Company, 1954), xxv, 101–3. Vera B Moreen, "Ish[H]Ma'iliyat: A Judeo-Persian Account of the Building of the Ka'ba", in *Judaism And Islam Boundaries, Communication And Interaction: Essays in Honor of William M. Brinner*, eds John L. Hayes, Benjamin H. Hary, Fred Astren (Leiden: Brill, 2000), 185–99.

21 This presumption is the source of great debate. Part of the problem stems from possible alternative locations for the place name "Baka Valley" as suggested by 2 Samuel 5:23 & 24, 1 Chronicles 14:14 &15 which places Baka near the valley of Rephaim, closer to Jerusalem.

we see the example of the bond between Ishmael and Abraham where the faith of Abraham is passed on to his beloved son and for the generations that follow. The importance of this legend is that it provides a common place for pilgrimage for the descendants of Ishmael as well as later generations of Jews. If mention of the site in Psalms is authentic then Mecca was indeed a place well known to Jewish travellers with a solid link to their own tradition.[22] There is a story recounted by Ibn Ishāq that goes back to the pre-Islamic period. This story mentions how the Jews used to worship at the Ka'bah. As the story goes, the King of Yemen, Tibān As'ad Abū Karīb, a proselyte to Judaism, intended to destroy the temple, because he learned that the people there were engaged in idol worship. Two rabbis from Yathrib, who explained the origins of the temple, dissuaded him. These two rabbis were the sons of Isrā'il b. ishāq b. Ibrāhīm otherwise known as, the friend of al-Rahmān. They travelled with Abū Karīb to Yemen and helped bring Judaism to his Himyarite Kingdom.[23] More will be said of this incident below.

Continuing in Genesis 25, Abraham nearing death, sends the children of Hagar/Keturah, and their children away to the east country with gifts.[24] Some of the tribes and towns of Arabia bear their names.[25] When Abraham dies his sons Ishmael and Isaac bury him with his wife Sarah in the field purchased from the Ephron in the cave of Machpelah in present day Hebron.[26] The names of the descendants of Ishmael are peppered throughout the Old Testament. In Genesis 37 the Ishmaelites purchase Joseph from his brothers and sell him into slavery in Egypt. Later, after generations of servitude, Moses marries a daughter of Jethro, the priest of

---

22   Lings, *Muhammad*, 4.
23   Ibn Ishāq, *The Life of Muhammad, a Translation of Ibn Ishāq's Sirat Rasul Allah* [Sirat Rasul allah], trans. Alfred Guillaume, 22nd edn (Karachi: Ameena Saiyid, Oxford University Press, 2009; repr. 1967), 7–10.
24   Ginzberg, *Jewish Legends*, 298–9.
25   Peoples such as the Nebaioth and Kedar (from whom Muhammad traces his ancestry), towns such as Dedan, Teyma were Jewish towns in pre-Islamic Arabia.
26   This tomb serves as both a Mosque and Synagogue, for a time the Greek Orthodox Church also used the building.

Midian.²⁷ The tribe of Midian is descendent of Abraham and Keturah.²⁸ Moses first confides in his father-in-Law the calling he received from God. Jethro reacts by celebrating the event with a sacrifice in honour of God's might. In Exodus 18 Jethro advises Moses to establish a council to help him judge the affairs of the people.²⁹ In Isaiah a few of the other children of Abraham are mentioned including the prophet Kedar, 42:9–13. Muslims believe that this prophet refers to Muhammad, just as the descendants of Ishmael mentioned in Genesis 25:12–18 are considered the ancestors of the Prophet.

Pre-Islamic Poetry as a Backdrop to Pre-Islamic Culture

Coexisting on the Arabian Peninsula were two distinct ways of life that were, by and large, mutually beneficial.³⁰ These were the ways of the *badawah* [Bedouin], and of the sedentary life of the *hadarah* [town or village]. These two distinct way of life allowed for the development of two coexisting social paradigms. On the one hand there is the cyclical life of the Bedouins based on *dahr* [an ephemeral sense of time as a natural phenomenon].³¹ Here the future held little promise other than a repetition of the past. Time

---

27 Another name for Jethro is Shu'ayb. Jethro is regarded as a pre-Islamic Muslim. Cf. Moshe Gil, "The Origin of the Jews of Yathrib", in *The Arabs and Arabia on the Eve of Islam*, ed. F. E. Peters, The Formation of the Classical Islamic World (Aldershot, Hampshire: Ashgate Publishing Limited, 1999).
28 Chronicles 1:29–33.
29 Brown, Fitzyer, and Murphy, *The Jerome Biblical Commentary*. Ibid., 49–50, 55–6.
30 Lings, *Muhammad*, 23–5. As part of the culture, families from large towns would often pay to have their babies reared by Bedouin tribes until the child was well into its childhood. For instance, Halīmah, from the tribe of Bani ibn Bakr reared Muhammad for eight years.
31 Mohammed A Bamyeh, *The Social Origins of Islam: Mind, Economy, Discourse* (Minneapolis: University of Minnesota Press, 1999). 67; Khalidi, *Arabic Historical Thought in the Classic Period*, 3.

Beyond Al-jāhiliyya

lay ahead, always over the horizon, just as the next halting site. Neither did the Bedouins have any great need for a god to account to, or an afterlife to worry about. All of the individual's needs were contained and shared within the fate of the tribe. In this environment an outcast was doomed.[32] The rich pre-Islamic Arab culture of the Bedouin survives in the poetry. On the other hand, the sedentary life of the *hadarah* with the creation of surplus value from crops and trade possibly encouraged the *hadarah* to develop more formal social structures.[33]

The *Muʾallaqāt*, or the Seven Classic Pre-Islamic Odes, represents the lore and values of their day.[34] In each *qashīda* [poem], the poet tells one side of a narrative in an entertaining way. Often the poem is the only record of the events discussed. It is worth remembering that the poetry is not a historical record, but rather as the participants, both poet and collector, choose to recall events. What survives was collected during the reign of Muʾawiya, the second Caliph of the Umayyad Dynasty (680 CE).[35] There are a few literary approaches to studying the poetry. These are listed and discussed in the article by Jonathan A. C. Brown.[36] This study accepts the practicalities of the Source and Tradition Critical Approach.[37] For reasons

32   Bamyeh, *The Social Origins of Islam*, 67, 96. Trimingham, *Christianity among the Arabs*, 309. Trimingham considers Bedouin fidelity to any god or religion no more than a form of insurance policy.
33   Bamyeh, *The Social Origins of Islam*. 30, Economic stability allowed for greater political and social development in towns that was lacking in the Bedouin life. Cf. Ibn Khaldûn, *The Muqaddimah: An Introduction to History* [The Muqaddimah], trans. Franz Rosenthal, vol. 1 (Princeton, NJ: Princeton University Press, 2005; repr., 1969), 91–3. Trimingham, *Christianity among the Arabs*, 310.
34   Bamyeh, *The Social Origins of Islam*, 89. Cf. M. J. Kister, "The Seven Odes", in *Studies in Jāhiliyya and Early Islam*, ed. M. J. Kister, Variorum Collected Studies Series; C S 123 (London: Variorum, 1980), 35–6.
35   Cf "Studies in Jāhiliyya", 34.
36   Jonathan A. C. Brown, "The Problem of Literary and Historical Sources", *Arab Studies Quarterly* 25, no. 3 (2003).
37   When possible collaborating historical, anthropological or sociological evidence will be added to accounts, veering towards the Critical Alternative Approach adopted by Suzanne Pinckney Stetkevych, *The Mute Immortals Speak* (Ithaca, NY: Cornell University Press, 1993).

of brevity and by way of example this study confines itself to A. J. Arberry's collection of 'Amru Ibn Kalthum, Imr al-Qais' and Zuhair Abu Salmā.

'Amru Ibn Kalthum

The life and poetry of 'Amru Ibn Kalthum, from the Christian tribe of Banū Taghlib, epitomizes the precarious lifestyle of the pre-Islamic times.[38] Perhaps most surprising is the claim by Arberry that the sentiments expressed in the following tale would not be out of place in modern times.[39] Here there is a description of the life of a man born to be the leader of his community. Depicted in his *qashīda* is a portrayal of the beauty and horror of Bedouin life. There are colourful portrayals of hedonism, loyalty to family and tribe, but also infanticide, intertribal warfare with obligations for mutual defence and honour killings.

The story of 'Amru Ibn Kalthum begins with the realization that he might never have been born if his mother did not have a lucky escape from the practice of female infanticide. It is reported that her father, Muhalhil Ibn Rabī'a decided to dispose of the new born child as soon as he heard his wife gave birth to a girl.[40] Fortunately, the child's mother, Hind, begged a servant to hide the baby. That night Muhalhil dreamt he heard a voice that chanted:

> How many a youth of promise,
> How many a goodly chieftain,
> What armoury of glory lurks in Muhalhil's daughter's womb![41]

Startled by the dream Muhalhil immediately rose and sought his infant daughter's whereabouts. At first his wife Hind pretended that the child

---

38 Trimingham, *Christianity among the Arabs*, 174.
39 A. J. Arberry, *The Seven Odes: The First Chapter in Arabic Literature* (London: George Allen & Unwin, 1957), 201.
40 Ibid., 188.; The practice of infanticide is a prime example of one of the significant changes ushered into Arabic culture by Islam. See *sūrat at-takwir* (81):1–14.
41 Ibid.; Khaldûn, *The Muqaddimah*, 1.

Beyond Al-jāhiliyya

had been killed as he intended. It was only when Hind sensed his remorse and realized that her husband wished the child no harm that she told him the truth. He then commanded the child be nurtured on the finest foods. The child was given the name Lailā and she grew to be a princess. Years later Lailā wed Kulthūm Ibn Malīk. When Lailā in turn was pregnant her husband dreamed he heard a voice say:

> What a son shall be yours, Lailā!
> Impetuous as a roaring lion,
> Sprung of Jusham's fertile loins
> No lie is this that I am telling.⁴²

When Lailā's son 'Amru Ibn Kulthūm was one year old, Lailā also dreamt that she heard a voice exclaim his virtues.

> Mother of 'Amr, I promise you
> A glorious son of noble stock,
> Braver than a maned lion,
> Strong to smite and strenuous,
> People's leader at fifteen.⁴³

So it was, 'Amru Ibn Kulthūm seemed destined for a great life. His poetry preserves the culture of his people as well as his own achievements. It is reported that he lived to an exceedingly great age of 150. He lived long enough to observe the rise of Islam and to embrace it.⁴⁴ As leader of the Banū Taghlib he led his people against the Banū Bakr ibn Wā'il over the latter's refusal to allow the Banū Taghlib access to water.⁴⁵ Water rights were denied seemingly due to past grievances between the tribes. As a result, seventy men died of thirst. In retaliation, the Banū Taghlib prepared for war, while the Banū Bakr prepared to receive them. Before the first battle cry, as the tribes stood face-to-face in the heavy silence there was time

---

42 Arberry, *The Seven Odes*, 189.
43 Ibid.
44 Ibid., 190–2. Fr Louis (Rizqallâh) Cheikhô places his death around the year 600 CE.
45 Trimingham, *Christianity among the Arabs*, 173. This Battle may have taken place around 480 CE.

to reflect on the fact that their last feud lasted some forty years and cost many lives.[46] Perhaps the gravity of the situation sobered their lust for *ijāra*, mutual protection, unfortunately history does not say. Legend tells us that the leaders of the Banū Taghlib and the Banū Bakr opted for mediation. They chose the neighbouring King ʿAmr Ibn Hind of al-Hira.[47]

Restoration of the peace was chillingly simple. King ʿAmr Ibn Hind required that the Banū Bakr provide seventy men from noble stock as escrow for the lives of the seventy men from the Banū Taghlib. One person from each tribe would plead the merits of their tribe's case. If ʿAmr Ibn Hind judged the Banū Taghlib to be in the right then the men would be handed over to pay with their lives. If the king found in favour of the Banū Bakr the men would be set free.[48] Thus agreed, the battle of the odes began. ʿAmru Ibn Kalthum naturally agreed to represent the defence of the Banū Taghlib. The Banū Bakr's King al-Harīth begrudgingly agreed to speak on behalf of his tribe.

Al-Harīth was a leper and detested the fact that he was required to stand behind seven veils to address King ʿAmr Ibn Hind and that his footprints would later be sprinkled with water as soon as he left the company of ʿAmr Ibn Hind.[49] Yet, none of his subjects could deliver the defence that he composed to his satisfaction.

All accounts credit al-Harīth with a remarkable performance. As al-Harīth delivered his defence the separating veils were set aside one by one and the footprints of al-Harīth were allowed to remain. In fact, ʿAmr Ibn Hind was so moved that the king allowed al-Harīth's to take food from his own bowl. Then King ʿAmr Ibn Hind instructed that anyone reciting al-Harīth's ode in the future must first perform ablutions out of respect. As a sign of good faith King ʿAmr Ibn Hind gave al-Harīth the forelocks of the seventy men.

---

46 Arberry, *The Seven Odes*, 187, 89. Al-Muhalhil led the Banū Taghlib at this time. The war concerned a murder and reprisal of tribal members. A feature of retribution concerned the value of some apropos the value of others.
47 Ibid., 67–8. Arberry reports that ʿAmr Ibn Hind was the son of Hind, a Christian princess.
48 Ibid., 193.
49 This author is not sure whether the ritual served as protection against leprosy or to conform to some protocol before a king.

Beyond Al-jāhiliyya

That said, it was now the turn of 'Amru Ibn Kulthūm to make his case on behalf of his tribe. In the ode the young leader arrogantly reminded the king of the Banū Taghlib's exploits and warned against judging *his* community too harshly.[50] In fact the ode merely cautioned King 'Amr Ibn Hind not to make his people their enemy with a rash decision, hardly the tact required to win friends let alone influence a king.[51] Here is an extract:

> ... With what purpose in view, 'Amr Ibn Hind,
> Should we be underlings to your chosen princelet?
> Threaten us, then, and menace us; but gently!
> When, pray, were we your mother's domestics?
> ... When any boys of our's reaches his weaning
> the tyrants fall down before him prostrating.
> We have filled the land till it's too straight for us,
> And we are filling the sea's black with our vessels.
> So let no man act foolishly against us,
> Or we will exceed the folly of the foolhardiest.[52]

The sequence of events that followed is unclear. Arberry reports that there are two explanations regarding the inspiration of the poem and the fate of King 'Amr Ibn Hind.[53] One issue is universally accepted. That is 'Amru Ibn Kulthūm beheaded King 'Amr Ibn Hind following an incident in which King 'Amr Ibn Hind's mother, Queen Hind, insisted that 'Amr Ibn Kulthūm's mother Lailā serve her, by passing some food at a banquet. In one version, 'Amru Ibn Kulthūm mother was dining in a separate room with 'Amr Ibn Hind's mother when she yelled for help. Fearing the worst 'Amru Ibn Kulthūm reacted by grasping King 'Amr Ibn Hind's own sword and dispatched his head, then broke into ode over the corpse.[54]

---

50   Bamyeh, *The Social Origins of Islam*, 182.
51   Arberry, *The Seven Odes*, 204–9.
52   Ibid. 204–9.
53   Ibid., 185–7.
54   An alternative version places the banquet sometime after the battle of the odes, on an occasion when King 'Amr Ibn Hind conspired to orchestrate a situation where Lailā would unwittingly perform some act of subservience for Queen Hind.

Imr al-Qais'

Hunduj Ibn Hujr Ibn al-Hārith, was the son of King Imr al-Qais from the Christian Kinda tribe. He is more commonly known as Imr al-Qais', the Wandering King.[55] His choice of occupations, not to mention the risqué nature of his poetry, did not sit well with his family. They banished him from the tribe, making him a *sa'lūk* [outcast].[56] By all accounts he led a very exciting life. He is noted for his sexual conquests and bohemian lifestyle, which one would find difficult to match, especially one imagines, in Arabia after the dawn of Islam.[57] His life epitomizes the pre-Islamic virtue of belonging to a tribe, and in his case, the contrast, a life of an outcast. The style of his poetry is very traditional in comparison to 'Amru Ibn Kulthūm. He begins his poem by calling his companions to halt at a location that spurns a memory of times past and of course, for Imr al-Qais', the memory of a lover, Unaiza. Her memory sends him off into verse.

> Halt, friends both! Let us weep, recalling a love and a lodging
> By the rim of the twisted sands between Ed-Dakhool and Haumal,
> Toodih and El-Mikrat, whose trace is not yet effaced
> for all the spinning of the south winds and the northern blasts;
> there, all about its yards, and away in the dry hallows
> you may see the dung of antelopes spattered like peppercorns,
> Upon the morn of separation, the day they loaded to part,
> by the tribe's acacias it was like I was splitting a colocynth;
> there my companions halted their beasts awhile over me
> saying, "Don't perish of sorrow; restrain yourself decently!"
>
> Yet the true and only cure of my grief is tears outpoured:
> What is there left to lean on where the trace is obliterated?
> ... Oh yes, many a fine day I've dallied with the white ladies
> and especially I call to mind a day at Dāra Juljul,

---

55 Richard Bell, *The Origin of Islam in Its Christian Environment; the Gunning Lectures, Edinburgh University, 1925*, ed. Jon Ralph Willis, 2nd edn, vol. 10, Islam and the Muslim World (Edinburgh & London: Frank Cass And Company Limited by arrangement with Macmillan and Co. Ltd, 1925; repr., 1968), 43.
56 Bamyeh, *The Social Origins of Islam*, 187, 93–5.
57 Arberry, *The Seven Odes*, 35.

and the day I slaughtered for the virgins my riding-beast
(and oh, how marvellous was the dividing of its loaded saddle),
and the virgins went tossing its hacked flesh about
and the frilly fat like fringes of twisted silk.
Yes, and the day I entered the litter where Unaiza was
And she cried, "Out on you! Will you make me walk on my feet?"
She was saying, while the canopy swayed with the pair of us,
"There now, you've hocked my camel, Imr al-Qais'.
Down with you!"
But I said, "Ride on, and slacken the beast's reins,
And oh, don't drive me away from your refreshing fruit …

… Many the pregnant woman like you, aye, and the nursing mother
I've night-visited, and made her forget her amuleted one-year-old;
Whenever he whimpered behind her, she turned to him
With half her body, her other half unshifted under me".[58]

The story of Imr al-Qais' begins in the fifth century when the Kinda tribe, under the tutelage of the king of Yemen, attempted to establish a new social order, based on a monarchy, to compensate for the increasing prominence of *ghazw* [raids], between tribes. This was during the reign of his grandfather who once ruled al-Hira, expelling al-Mundhir III from the Lakhmid kingdom. Al-Mundhir III was the client of the Sassanian King Qubādh.[59] As the story goes, his grandfather was soon driven out by Anūshīrwan and massacred by the succeeding al-Mundhir along with 50 members of his family. Consequently, the affairs of the Banū Asad passed to Imr's father. This tribe killed him in his sleep setting off a long chain of retribution killings that would cost many lives including Imr al-Qais himself and the son of the Jewish poet, Samau'āl, whose fidelity to Imr al-Qais is the origins of the phrase, *as faithful as Samau'āl*.[60]

Here is a brief sketch of the ordeal. When the Imr al-Qais learned of the circumstances of his father's death he was playing backgammon with a friend. For a time he continued to play, insisting that he did not want to

---

58 Ibid., 61–6.
59 Trimingham, *Christianity among the Arabs*, 169.
60 Arberry, *The Seven Odes*, 39. Samau'āl's extension of fidelity to Imr al-Qais cost him the life of his son.

spoil his companion's turn. Then he said, "He left me to rot when I was a boy, and now I am a man he's loaded me with his blood".[61] Legend has it that he continued to drink and revel for seven days, then vowed not to eat flesh, nor drink wine again, nor anoint himself, neither touch a woman, until he had avenged his father. He swore to "kill one hundred of the Banū Asad and shear the forelocks of another hundred".[62]

For a time Imr al-Qais pursued his vow with a vengeance, until his companions judged he achieved the measure of his vow.[63] Once the *asab al-tha'r* [revenge duty] had been exceeded his companions left him. The return of a kingdom did not merit the continuance of the campaign, not even from amongst his family. Thus, Imr al-Qais sought the help of the Byzantines to restore the monarchical experiment.[64] By this time his enemies regrouped. Bolstered by support of King al-Mundhir from the Lakhmid Kingdom, they set out to track down the now isolated Imr al-Qais. He fled from one tribe to another until he reached Samau'āl ben Ādiyā, a Jewish Arab living in Taima.[65]

From the safety of Samau'āl's castle, Imr al-Qais planned his counter attack. With a letter of reference from Samau'āl to al-Hārith, the leader of the Ghassan and Byzantium phylarch of Syria and enemy of al-Mundhir, Imr al-Qais set forth to enlist the aid of the Emperor Justinian. Events progressed as planned. Imr al-Qais succeeded in convincing al-Hārith and Emperor Justinian that his campaign was in their mutual interests. What happened next is not clear. Imr al-Qais may have been promised an army; another theory is that he was appointed Governor of Palestine, but something caused the emperor to have second thoughts. One explanation suggests Imr al-Qais may have captured more than the heart of the emperor's daughter, and true to form, celebrated the deed in verse. We will never know. Justinian, without giving anything away, sent Imr al-Qais a gold embroidered mantle along with a letter wishing him well and requested to be kept informed of his progress. However, no one would have expected the robe

---

61   Ibid., 36.
62   Ibid., 36, 37.
63   Bamyeh, *The Social Origins of Islam*. 51. Arberry, *The Seven Odes*, 37.
64   Bamyeh, *The Social Origins of Islam*. 52. Arberry, *The Seven Odes*, 37.
65   *The Seven Odes*, 38.

to be laced with poison. As soon as Imr al-Qais put on the robe he broke out in sores that covered his whole body and caused an agonizing death.⁶⁶

Zuhair Ibn Abu Salmā

Zuhair Ibn Abu Salmā is the final poet to be examined in this chapter. Arberry refers to Zuhair as the Moralist. According to Mumayiz, he was born around 520 CE in al-Hajer, south of modern day Riyadh.⁶⁷ His father died when he was a boy. His love of poetry was nurtured by his stepfather 'Aws b. Hajar (d. 620). Caliph 'Umar b. al-Khattab referred to Zuhair as "the poet of poets" and said that he never praised anyone without merit.⁶⁸ Many of the phrases he coined live on in Arab culture as proverbs, some form part of school curricula.⁶⁹ For example, "After a crass life, the old could not with wisdom glow, but youth, after a crass phase, may to wisdom grow".⁷⁰ Arberry notes that Zuhair struggled with his verse preferring to write using ordinary everyday language, rather than burden his audiences with convoluted oration.⁷¹ Unlike other *al-jāhiliyya* poets he abstained from the excesses of life, preferring to draw the attention of his audience to thoughts of conducting one's life in pursuit of wisdom in preparation for the final Day of Judgement before God.⁷² In fact, one of the outstanding features of Zuhair's poetry concerns not the praise of his own feats, or moral conduct, but rather his praise for these qualities in others.⁷³

---

66   Ibid., 38–9. Ibrahim Mumayiz, "Imru' Al-Qays and Byzantium", *Journal of Arabic Literature* XXXVI, no. 2 (2005): 151. Alternatively, Mumayiz believes Imr al-Qais simply contracted Bubonic plague.
67   *Society, Religion and Poetry in Pre-Islamic Arabia*, eds Ahmed Allaithy & Abied Alsulaiman, trans. Arabic Translators International (Antwerp-Apeldoorn: Garant, 2010), 155.
68   Ibid.
69   Ibid.
70   Ibid., 164.
71   Arberry, *The Seven Odes*, 98.
72   Ibid., 98–9.
73   Ibid., 90. Mumayiz, *Society, Religion and Poetry*, 155.

The religion of Zuhair is a bit of a mystery. It is not certain whether he converted to Islam or not.[74] Lewis Cheikho believes he may have been a Christian, although Carl Brockelmann contends that he remained a pagan. The verse below denotes clear evidence that Zuhair's personal religious views were far advanced from traditional pagan lore.

> Do not conceal from Allah whatever is in your breast
> Hoping it may be hidden; Allah knows whatever is concealed
> And either it's postponed, and put in a book, and stored away
> For the Day of Reckoning, or it's hastened, and banished betimes.[75]

The context of the *mu'allaqa* of Zuhair takes place in the aftermath of a friendly horse race between the chieftain of the 'Abs, 'Qays ibn Zuhayr and the chieftain of the Dhubyān, Hudhayfa b. Badr for a prize of 100 camels. In the middle of a thrilling race some men from the Dhubyān drove the horse belonging to 'Qays ibn Zuhayr off course, allowing the mare belonging to Hudhayfa b. Badr to win. Naturally enough the 'Abs declared victory, but the Dhubyán refused to pay even a single camel. From here events progressed from bad to worse as 'Qays slew a brother of Hudhayfa, setting in train a war that would last "40" years.[76]

The legend of the events that led to the peace is a highly entertaining story that shows that behind every great man is a great woman, even in *al-jāhiliyya* times.[77] The catalyst to the peace is a vain discussion between the soon to be peacemakers, Al-Hārith son of 'Auf ibn Abū Hāritha and his cousin Khārija ibn Sinān. One day al-Hārith asked his cousin, "What do you think, is there anyone in the world who would refuse me if I asked his daughter's hand in marriage?" To which Khārija replied, "Yes, 'Aus ibn Hāritha ibn La'm of the tribe of Taiy".[78] So, as if in a boyish dare, the two

---

74 Arberry, *The Seven Odes*, 98–9. Citing R. A. Nicholson; Mumayiz, *Society, Religion and Poetry*, 155–6. Both Arberry and Mumayiz relate that the paths of Muhammad and Zuhair did cross.
75 Arberry, *The Seven Odes*, 98.
76 Ibid. "40" may well have been a colloquial expression for a long time. 90–1.
77 Mumayiz, *Society, Religion and Poetry*, 155.
78 Arberry, *The Seven Odes*, 91–2.

rode off on their camels in the direction of 'Aus ibn Hāritha ibn La'm to settle their wager. When they met 'Aus ibn al-Hāritha, they greeted him in the customary fashion exchanging pleasantries. Eventually, 'Aus inquired as to the occasion of the visit. Al-Hārith replied risibly, "I've come to look for a wife". Al-Hārith's manner offended the proud father. 'Aus told al-Hārith, "You've called at the wrong address", then turned and walked away.[79]

When 'Aus's wife learned the nature and identity of the visitors she became very annoyed and demanded 'Aus go back out and persuade al-Hārith to return. She exclaimed, "Well, don't you want to marry off your daughters?" And "if you won't marry any of them to the Lord of the Arabs, who will you marry them to?" 'Aus, his honour now at stake, complained, but his wife would hear none of it. She told 'Aus exactly what to say and sent him off to coax al-Hārith back.[80] When 'Aus caught up with al-Hārith he explained that the question of marriage to one of his daughters caught him off guard and that if he returned he would get what he came for.[81]

At that 'Aus informed each of his three daughters individually of the nature of al-Hārith's visit; one by one offers of marriage were made. The first daughter declined the invitation citing that she wasn't very pretty. She confessed to an awkward character and that since al-Hārith was not kin, he might eventually get bored and divorce her. The second daughter considered the offer, but declined, citing that she was a bit of a fool with no accomplishments. She was afraid that after a while al-Hārith might also divorce her, leaving her in an awful mess. To each daughter 'Aus gave his blessing then asked for the youngest daughter Buhaisa.

Buhaisa considered the offer, not knowing what her sisters had said, only that they refused. She then reasoned, "Well, I'm the pretty one. I'm accomplished, I've a lofty character and a most distinguished father", with a smile. "If he divorces me, God will never be good to him again".[82] 'Aus blessed Buhaisa and give al-Hārith the good news. Buhaisa's mother prepared the bridal trousseau and Buhaisa was prepared for the wedding.

79   Ibid., 92.
80   Ibid., 92–3.
81   Ibid., 93.
82   Ibid., 94.

A tent was pitched close to Buhaisa's home and Aus invited al-Hārith to make his abode there. In due course Buhaisa entered as his new bride. However, just as al-Hārith advanced to consummate the marriage Buhaisa cried, "stop that! What, here in front of my father and brothers? That's utterly impossible".

So, there was little option but for al-Hārith and his cousin and Buhaisa to bid farewell and set off for the lands of al-Hārith. On route al-Hārith signalled for Khārija ibn Sinān to continue on as he and his pretty, accomplished bride veered off the beaten track to make camp.[83]

Yet, the pair soon caught up with the cousin who looked rather questioningly at al-Hārith and asked, "Finished?" To which al-Hārith replied, "No, by God. She said to me, 'what, would you treat me like a slave girl out of the market, or a woman taken in battle? No, first you must kill the camels and slaughter the sheep and invite all the Arabs, and do all that should be done for the likes of me'". The cousin smiled approvingly and said to al-Hārith, "Ah, I see she's a girl of spirit and good sense, I've high hopes she'll be a wife who'll bear you fine sons, *inshallah* [God willing]".[84]

The trio returned to al-Hārith's country and a great feast was prepared. Al-Hārith entered the boudoir, but soon re-emerged. "Finished?" inquired the cousin. "No" cried al-Hārith. "What happened this time?" inquired the cousin. Al-Hārith pleaded, "I went to her, desiring her mightily. You see, we have made ready the flocks. Then Buhaisa said, 'I was told you are a man of honour. I don't see much sign of it in you.' How is that?" Al-Hārith pleaded. Buhaisa replied, "Why, how is it you find time to go about marrying women, while the Arabs are busy killing each other?" To which al-Hārith responded zealously, "Then what do you want me to do?" Buhaisa said, "Go out and make peace between those people, then return to your family, and you shan't miss anything this time".[85]

"Ay" said the cousin, "I see she's a girl of spirit and good sense. She's spoken well".[86] With that al-Hārith and his trusted cousin, Khārija ibn Sinān, set off to face the warring factions. After a great effort, many trials

---

83   Ibid., 95.
84   Ibid. *Inshallah* is a beautiful word with many applications.
85   Ibid.
86   Ibid.

Beyond Al-jāhiliyya

and tribulations, a peace was brokered. Al-Hārith and Khārija ibn Sinān collected the blood-dues of 3,000 camels; and in spite of one serious infringement, the peace set. Al-Hārith returned to Buhaisa. True to her word, Buhaisa bore him several sons and daughters and Al-Hārith's name and deeds live on.[87] Below is a sample of Zuhair's *mu'allaqa* immortalizing the search for peace and reconciliation:

> I swore by the house which men circumambulated, men of Quraysh and Jurhum who built it.
> In truth, worthy you will be praised for what you've assailed, in ease and in hardship, steadfast you've well prevailed.
> You stopped the Abs-Dhubyán war which both could have doomed, and all those slain whom "Mansham" had perfumed.
> You said: A possible lasting peace we all could see, with money, and good deeds, from war we could be free.
> By so doing you have done yourselves so much good. From the sin of serving blood ties, well away you stood.
> In all the glories of "Ma'aad" greatest you have seemed, for he who wins in glory's treasure, great will he be deemed.
> Through such pedigree camels, wounds are fully healed. For use as stars by those who no crime did yield.
> Those who the blood money assesses for the war dead, have not bloodletting cupful of blood had shed.
> For another tribe's use, one tribe these foals have paid, though not a cup of blood had they payment made.
> To the allies, from me, this one message conveys, to Dhubyán: will you faithful to the sworn peace stay?
> Do not hide from God what is in your breast concealed. For whatever is concealed, to God his will revealed.
> What you conceal, the charge against you God will defer, till Judgment Day, or, you'll now his vengeance incur.
> War is what you've known of it, and tasted it well, not what idle, baseless chatter of it would tell.
> Should you wage war, what's the loathsome and vile is what you'd wage. Kindle it, and out of control
> it'll wildly rage ...[88]

---

87   Ibid.
88   Mumayiz, *Society, Religion and Poetry*, 159–60.

The pre-Islamic poetry examined provides a glimpse into the context in which the mission of Muhammad operated. The challenges that the culture of the day presented are immense. Examples of infanticide, honour killings, raids, sexual promiscuity and drunkenness are all addressed. In contrast, at each stage there are tales of inspiration, where individuals emerge as heroes, who challenge the prevailing ignorance. These are found in the grandparents of 'Amru ibn Kalthum who refrain from murdering a daughter at birth, who in time becomes the mother of one of *al-jāhiliyya's* greatest poets. Then there is the fidelity of Samau'āl and the heavy price he paid for keeping his word. Still the poetry of Zuhair provides the greatest example of selfless heroism in the exemplary actions of Al-Hārith and Khārija ibn Sinān, inspired by his wife Buhaisa. In this particular *mu'allaqa* the madness of war, revenge duty and the opposite, the expiation of blood debt, are praised through the actions of those not directly involved in the war. In this environment, the idea that Muhammad succeeded in his own lifetime to provide a solid foundation from which Islam would venture forth to the ends of the earth, is a testimony to the faith he inspired.

The Jews of the Hijaz

There are many plausible theories that attempt to explain the origins of Judaism on the Arabian Peninsula. Attempting to provide a definitive answer to the question is probably not possible since it is far more likely that there is an element of truth behind several theories. The safest explanation is to accept that some form of limited migration to Arabia by Jews began in Biblical times, that is, in the time of the prophets and continued for centuries as an alternative to migration within Byzantine or Persian Empires.[89] One theory posits that

---

89   Gil, "Jews of Yathrib", 206–12. Jacob Lassner, *Jews, Christians, and the Abode of Islam: Modern Scholarship, Medieval Realities* (Chicago & London: University of Chicago Press, 2012), 131. Cf. Ben Abrahamson and Joseph Katz, "The Persian Conquest of Jerusalem in 614ce Compared with Islamic Conquest of 638ce: Its Messianic Nature

Beyond Al-jāhiliyya

Saul sent a contingent of soldiers, on God's order, to slaughter the Amalekites. After conducting a ruthless campaign against the people and property of the Amalekites the soldiers fail to kill the king's son. For this act of mercy they were forbidden to re-enter the Promised Land. Now exiled, these soldiers simply returned to the land that they had lain waste and remained in loose contact with their kin in Judea and Samaria.[90] Another theory posits that thousands of Jews fled to Arabia after the fall of the First Temple.[91] In fact the Talmud speaks of some 80,000 rabbis fleeing to join other Jews in the Hijaz.[92] Similarly there may have been scores of refugees seeking shelter in Arabia after the fall of Jerusalem in 70 CE, following other messianic mis-adventures starting with the Bar Kokhba revolt 132–6 CE, or as a consequence of the Mar Zutra revolt in Mahoza, Persia, 502 CE. Other plausible reasons may include the failed Jewish uprising in Yemen led by Yūsuf Dhū Nuwās's in 518 CE, or as late as the collapse of Persian/Jewish control of Jerusalem in 614 CE, with Exilarch Nehemiah ben Hushiel as governor.[93] Interestingly, both Jewish and Islamic sources acknowledge the presence of Jews from southeastern Palestine throughout the Hijaz from the earliest times and as the original inhabitants of Yathrib.[94] Therefore Jews of Arabia may well have considered themselves both native to the land and to a lesser degree, *resident aliens*, since the major narratives explaining their origins contain an element of tragedy.

---

      and the Role of the Jewish Exilarch", *Alsadiqin: the Committee for Historical Research in Islam and Judaism Copyright* (1954): 13.

90   Mazuz, "Massacre in Medina ". Cf. note 12 above. Cf. Exodus 17:8–16; Deuteronomy 25; 1Samual 15.

91   Lassner, *Jews, Christians, and the Abode of Islam*, 132.

92   Gil, "Jews of Yathrib", 206, Cf. n15.

93   Matthew V. Novenson, "Why Does R. Akiba Acclaim Bar Kokhba as Messiah?", *Journal of the Study of Judaism*, no. 40 (2009): 559–60, 64; Roi Porat; Hanan Eshel; Amos Frumkin, "Finds from the Bar Kokhba Revolt, from Two Caves at En Gedi", *Palestine Exploration Quarterly* 139, no. 1 (2007): 48–9. Isaiah M. Gafni, *Land, Center and Diaspora: Jewish Constructs in Late Antiquity*, eds Lester L. Grabbe, James H. Charlesworth, vol. 21, Journal for the Study of the Pseudepigrapha (Sheffield: Sheffield Academic Press Suppliment Series, 1997), 64–72. Interestingly there is no mention of a contingent of men from Medina joining the Persian/Jewish campaign to take Jerusalem from the Romans.

94   Gil, "Jews of Yathrib", 203–4.

Yet, as plausible as these explanations may seem, there are many scholars who contend that these Jews were anything but real Jews. This opinion does not reject the idea that at least some of those that identified themselves as Jews were birthright Jews, but rather suggests that because the culture was thoroughly integrated with the rest of the Arab culture that many of those claiming to be Jewish may simply have been proselytes.[95] Nua for instance, makes the case that almost all of the "Jews" mentioned in the *sīra* have Arab names, but looked to the Jews of Himyar for spiritual guidance.[96] D. S. Margoliouth considered the Jews of Hijaz as emerging from the growing monotheist, or *rahmānist*, religious identity rather than from ethnic stock.[97] Offering an alternative analysis, Torrey and Hirshberg propose the opinion that the majority of the tribes professed the Jewish faith as legitimate.[98] Similarly Arab Muslim sources accept the *bona fides* of the self-definition of those claiming to be Jews without equivocation.

Economy, Education & Developed Community

The Jews of the Hijaz were quite an advanced community in many regards. Bamyeh argues that their identification with the Torah, as God's chosen people, would have given them a unique worldview largely absent from their neighbours.[99] Jewish communities largely inhabited most of the agricultural land of the Hijra. These towns and villages include those found along the caravan trails leading north, including Yathrib (Medina), Uhud, Khaibar, al-Hijr, Tayma, Tabuk, up to Ma'an and the southern regions of Palestine.[100] Although many

---

95   Ibid., 209.
96   Ibid., 209. François Nau, *Les Arabes Chrétiens De Mésopotamie Et De Syrie Du Viie Au VIIIe Siècle* vol. 1, Cahiers De La Société Asiatique (Paris: Imprimerie Nationale, 1933), 113–4.
97   Margoliouth, *Relations*, 69–71.
98   Gil, "Jews of Yathrib", 209, fn. 19. Cf. Charles Cutler Torrey, *The Jewish Foundation of Islam*, The Hilda Stich Stroock Lectures (New York: Bloch Publishing Co., 1933), 8–27.
99   Bamyeh, *The Social Origins of Islam*, 26, 30, 62–3, 67.
100 David Nicolle, *Historical Atlas of the Islamic World* (London: Mercury Books, 2004), 22–32.

of these towns held annual market-fairs it is not known if they had their own set festivals for pilgrims, as did Sana'a, Mecca, Ukaz or Duma.[101] Nevertheless they had the ability to diversify their means of livelihood between trade, agriculture, crafts or even *ghazw* [plunder], if deemed necessary.[102]

The Jews of the Hijaz were among the first to use irrigation and therefore had an advantage over other communities reliant on seasonal rains.[103] Dates were one of the major food crops. Their ability to create a surplus through agriculture and trading endeavours assisted the advancement of their communities. This gave them a great advantage over their Bedouin neighbours who relied primarily on herding.[104] For this reason they attracted migrant labour that often chose to remain within the region. This agricultural surplus aided their transition from purely agriculture economy to a mixed economy offering services and trade.

Since the second century Jews have been obliged to educate their sons.[105] There is evidence that some form of formal education system existed in Medina during *al-jāhiliyya*. For instance, Caliph Uthman was criticized for choosing Zaid Ibn Thābit, one of Muhammad's secretaries, as the scribe of the Qur'ān, because, as Abdullah b. Mas'ūd said, "I was reading the Qur'ān while Zaid was still a boy with two sidelocks of hair playing amongst the Jewish children in the literacy (Torah) school".[106] Ironically, Mas'ūd may have attended the same school, as did seven of the twelve tribal leaders that took part in the Great Aqaba.[107] Some of the Jewish converts

---

101 Bamyeh, *The Social Origins of Islam*, 11–12.
102 Ibid., 17, 30.
103 Ibid., 19, 153. These fortified agricultural communities were often Jewish communities.
104 Werner Caskel, "The Bedouinization of Arabia", in *The Arabs and Arabia on the Eve of Islam*, ed. F. E. Peters, The Formation of the Classical Islamic World (Aldershot, Hampshire: Ashgate Publishing Limited, 1999), 34.
105 Maristella Botticini and Zvi Eckstein, "From Farmers to Merchants, Conversions and Diaspora: Human Capital and Jewish History", *Journal of the European Economic Association* 5, no. 5 (2007): 16.
106 The education system in pre-Islamic Medina is an area well worth further research, Cf. Michael Lecker, "Zayd B Thābit: 'A Jew with Two Sidelocks' Judaism and Literacy in Pre-Islamic Medina (Yathrib)", *Journal of Near Eastern Studies* 56, No. 4 (1997).
107 Ibid., 271.

to Islam such as Abdullah ibn Salaam were highly regarded as scholars by the Jews of Medina, at least until they converted to Islam.[108]
Interestingly, none of the aforementioned opinions express any merit in the possible evangelical nature or "universal mission" that the Jews of the Diaspora may have felt for their neighbours.[109] Lecker, for instance, suggests that the Banū Māsika teachers in the Torah School would have encouraged the Arab children to convert to Judaism.[110] If anything the challenge to the purity of the Jewishness of the Jews of the Hijaz could be viewed positively, as evidence of the willingness of Arabs in pre-Islamic times to convert to the Jewish faith. Gil, citing the work of Suhaylī, draws attention to the fact that Arab women used to vow to bring their children up *tahawwadathu* [Jewish], if they survived.[111] Further, citing Samhūdī, Gil posits that several other Bedouin tribes in Medina, including the B. Harīth b. Ka'b of the Ghassān and Judhām also accepted Judaism.[112] In a sense then, questions surrounding the purity of the Jews of Hijaz is evidence that to a large degree the birthright Jews in the region are at least in part, victims of their own success in spreading the message of monotheism, making alliances through marriages, as well as challenging the underlying polytheist culture around them.[113] Perhaps because of the mystique of their origins the pre-Islamic Jews of the Hijaz are one of the most fascinating and influential communities to feature in the life of Muhammad, the Qur'ān and the

---

108 As-Sallaabee, *The Prophet*, 2:819–20. Lecker, "Zayd B Thābit: 'A Jew with Two Sidelocks' Judaism and Literacy in Pre-Islamic Medina (Yathrib)", 262, 69. Evidence supports the idea that there may well have been other literate Jewish converts including Ka'b al-Ahbār, Hudhayfa b. al-Yamān and possibly Mu'adh b. Jagbal.
109 Gil, "Jews of Yathrib". Yakov M. Rabkin, *A Threat from Within: A Century of Jewish Opposition to Zionism* [Au nom de la Torah, Une histoire de l'opposition juive au sionisme], ed. Brenda Conroy, trans. Fred A. Reed (Black Point, Nova Scotia: Fernwood, 2006), 128–9.
110 Lecker, "Zayd B Thābit: 'A Jew with Two Sidelocks' Judaism and Literacy in Pre-Islamic Medina (Yathrib)", 259.
111 Gil, "Jews of Yathrib", 210.
112 Ibid.
113 Lecker, "Zayd B Thābit: 'A Jew with Two Sidelocks' Judaism and Literacy in Pre-Islamic Medina (Yathrib)", 271.

formation of Islam. Like the Jews of Himyar, the Jews of the Hijaz were fiercely independent.[114] They appear to have avoided becoming a client of either the Byzantine or Persian Empires.[115] Thus the evidence seems to support the image of the Jews of the Hijaz as a people highly developed and respected by their peers.

Demographic Change and Expectations of a Messiah

With the arrival of the Aws and Khazraj from the Himyar in the fifth century the non-Jewish inhabitants of Medina increased their influence over the city. The demographic change increased tensions in the region leading to poor relations between individuals and tribes.[116] For this reason the Jews of Median taunted the Aws and Khazraj with the threat that they would soon regain control of Medina. It is noted that the Jews threatened their neighbours saying, "A prophet is now about to be sent. We will follow him and we will slay you as 'Ād and Iram were slain".[117] This boast reveals a lot about the outlook of the Jews of Medina and the Hijaz. At the time this statement was made the Babylonian Talmud was nearing completion. In the Talmud there are clear invocations to focus on study and against adding to the defeat of Bar Kokhba. In fact, the thrust of Rabbinic Judaism was opposed to waiting for a prophet. Instead the emphasis was on following the Torah.[118] Yet these Jews threatened their adversaries with the intervention of a prophet. So, what kind of prophet would seventh-century Jews of the Diaspora be waiting for? If they followed the Talmud, that is to say they were Rabbinic Jews, they would have been conscious of living

---

114 Nicolle, *Historical Atlas*, 30–1.
115 Gil, "Jews of Yathrib", 205, n7. The text suggests that the Jews of Medina might have collected a poll tax on behalf of the Persians.
116 Lings, *Muhammad*, 108. Lassner, *Jews, Christians, and the Abode of Islam*, 132–5.
117 Lings, *Muhammad*, 105. Citing Heinrich Ferdinand Wüstenfeld translation of Ibn Ishāq's biography of Muhammad, 287. Ishāq, *Sirat Rasulallah* 93.
118 B. M. Bokser, "Messianism, the Exodus Pattern, and Early Rabbinic Judaism", in *The Messiah: Developments in Earliest Judaism and Christianity*, ed. James H. Charlesworth (Minneapolis, MN: Fortress Press, 1992), 239–58.

in post-prophetic times. Is it possible they were waiting for more than a prophet? Perhaps they expected the, שילה, *Shiloh* [the one to whom it belongs] as in, "until the *Messiah* to whom the kingdom belongs comes".[119]

The concept of waiting for God to send His prophet and the opposite, of Jews appointing, or following a prophet/messiah are discussed in the Babylonian Talmud.[120] In general terms, liberation from exile is God's gift and Jews should not try to force the hand of God. Rabbinical Jews interpret the *galut* [dispersion], as fitting into God's universal plan of salvation, to be followed in due course, by God's beckoning. Through their redemption, will follow the *Aliyá* [gathering of the Nation] and return to the Promised Land. In order to preserve the remnants of Judaism following the destruction of the second Temple, rabbinic sages devised three oaths to counter any future pre-emptive military campaign to retake the Holy Land.[121] The consequence of falsely stirring the passions of expectations of this entity is a curse of damnation, whereby the guilty are forever ostracized from their community.[122] Perhaps because of the failure of previous rebellions against the Romans and the disastrous consequences this held

---

119 Michael B. Shepherd, "Targums, the New Testament, and Biblical Theology of the Messiah", *Journal of the Evangelical Theological Society* 51/1, no. March 2008 (2008): 54. Cf. David Mendel Harduf, *Rabbinic Exegesis of Biblical Names and Narratives (in the Talmud and Midrash)*, 2nd edn (Willowdale: Beit Ra'if Publishing, 2002), 46.

120 An excellent thorough brief discussion of the subject is found in Jacob Immanuel Schochet, *Mashiach: The Principles of Mashich and the Messianic Era in Jewish Law and Tradition* (New York: S. I. E. , 1991), 13–57. "Babylonian Talmud: Kethuboth", in *Hebrew-English Edition Of The Babylonian Talmud*, ed. B. A. Rabbi Dr I. Epstein, PhD, D. Lit. (London: Soncino Press, 1971), 111a.

121 Cf. Reuven Firestone, "Holy War in Modern Judaism? 'Mitzvah War' and the Problem of the 'Three Vows'", *Journal of the American Academy of Religion* Vol. 74, No. 4 (2006): 964–71.

122 Cf. Gafni, *Land, Center and Diaspora*, 21, 35. Rabin discusses further the origins and development of the *Messianic Caution* from the earliest Rabbinic sources, 71–81. Firestone, "Holy War in Modern Judaism? 'Mitzvah War' and the Problem of the 'Three Vows'". The penalty for not waiting for God is described as, the flesh of the Jews to be consumed like that of gazelles or hinds of the field, 961. Cf. "Babylonian Talmud", 111a.

Beyond Al-jāhiliyya

for Judaism in general, it is probable that the Jews of the region, if they held any heightened expectation of a prophet, would be somewhat ostracized by other Jewish communities, especially those in Baghdad, a major centre of Judaism in the Rabbinic times of the Diaspora.[123] Yet, prior to Muhammad's migration to Medina the expressed interest of members of the Aws and Khazrajites in allying themselves with Muhammad, at the first Aqaba, was in order to ensure that if Muhammad was indeed the prophet that the Jews anticipated, that they would be on the right side of any ensuing conflict. This is especially true if the acceptance of Muhammad meant that the adherents saw themselves as submitting to God rather than to a rival tribe.[124]

Now, it is one thing to threaten your neighbours with the imminent arrival of the *Shiloh*, the Messiah, or some ruler of divine origin, and quite another for this entity to live an eleven camel-day ride to the south. The implications of the arrival of the promised deliverer are momentous to say the least. The responsibility of the leaders of Medina to endorse, or not, the claims of a non-Jewish king, a Messiah who will "rule over all the children of humanity", should not be underestimated.[125] The endorsement of another false *Shiloh* would surely be a disaster for all Jews living in the region.

It is impossible to say to what degree this idea of the imminent arrival of a prophet influenced the reception of Muhammad. The fact that the Jews lived with a heightened expectation is further evidenced by the existence and presentation of a letter to Muhammad by Abu Ayyūb (Khalid b. Zayd), an *ansār* [helper], from the Khazraj in whose house Muhammad stayed when he first arrived in Medina.[126] This letter belonged to the Tubba, the king of the descendants of the Qahtān, also known as the Saba', a people discussed in

---

123 Rabkin, *A Threat from Within*, 6, 15, 195.
124 Bamyeh, *The Social Origins of Islam*, 152–4.
125 Shepherd, "Targums", 54.
126 Gil, "Jews of Yathrib", 211. Citing Samhūdī, I. 189. He may have been a distant relative of the prophet Vol. 1. 632; Lecker, "Zayd B Thābit: 'A Jew with Two Sidelocks' Judaism and Literacy in Pre-Islamic Medina (Yathrib)", 270.

sūrat saba' (34):15–19 *and sūrat l-dukhān* (44):37.[127] Ibn Isḥāq's biography of Muhammad gives some indication as to the contents of the letter. Here the two rabbis that accompanied Tibān As'ad Abū Karīb to Yemen persuaded the Tubba' not to destroy Yathrib after a man from Yathrib killed his son. In their explanation, they describe a future prophet (named Ahmad) coming from the tribe of Quraysh who will come to settle in Yathrib as a *Muhājir* [refugee], and whose reign will last till the end of time.[128]

For this reason, perhaps Ibn Ubayy, the king in waiting, was willing to step aside to give Muhammad a chance to prove himself.[129] One could only imagine the mixed emotions experienced by Ibn Ubayy. Not only may he have felt the disappointment of not becoming the leader of Medina, which must have been heartbreaking on a personal level, but as a leader of his community he may well have felt a sense of responsibility to discern the acceptance, or rejection, of a prophet. He needed to weigh Muhammad's growing popularity against his willingness to embark on what appeared to be foolhardy military campaigns against Medina's former allies and to cast aside traditional allegiances based on blood bonds in favour of the *ummat al-mu'minīn*, community of believers. One can imagine that Ibn Ubayy was searching for affirmation, or not, that Muhammad was indeed the prophet his fellow Jews were expecting. He was becoming increasingly anxious that the Jews of the Hijaz and Medina were in danger of falling once again for a false prophet, whose defeat would shatter the stability of the Jewish community in Arabia; just as the sixth-century defeat of Yūsuf Dhū Nuwās's failed to curtail the spread of Christianity to the south and

127 Ibn Kathir tells us that the Tubba refers to an ancient people, possible descendants of Noah's son Shem. They once tried to attack Medina over the death of the king's son. However, they eventually came to mutually satisfactory terms to the extent that the Tubba adopted Judaism and brought it to Yemen. Ibn Kathīr, *Tafsir Al-Qur'ān Al-Azim*, 8:74–80 & 686–9.
128 Ishāq, *Sirat Rasulallah* 7. Harry Munt, "Writing the History of an Arabian Holy City: Ibn Zabāla and the First Local History of Medina" *Arabica*, no. 59 (2012): 22. Citing al-Samudī *Wafā'* III, 378–9.
129 Lassner, *Jews, Christians, and the Abode of Islam*, 139. Bamyeh, *The Social Origins of Islam*, 200–1. Lings, *Muhammad*, 108, 29. Here Ibn Ubayy is mentioned as a leader of the Khazraj.

the fall of Exilarch Nehemiah ben Hushiel brought an end to Jewish/Persian control of Jerusalem just three years before.[130]

Muhammad's Relationship with the Jews of Medina Pre-Hajj

The Jews of Medina are considered distant kin to Muhammad with links on his Great Grandparent's side.[131] They are amongst Muhammad's earliest allies, affording Muhammad safe haven when his own community turned against him and his followers in Mecca.[132] From the biographical material of the life of Muhammad it is very clear that the Jewish reception of Muhammad, as a leader and as possible prophet is generally cautious. Setting the advantage of hindsight aside, and beginning with the perception that the Jews of Medina were prone to the expectation of a prophet/messiah, it is not much of a surprise that the Jews of the Medina begin their interrogation of the credentials of Muhammad as a would-be prophet, from a messianic perspective.[133] In fact given the likely origins of the Jews of Medina and the Hijaz it is not surprising that they might greet

---

130   There will be greater discussion of the Dhū Nuwās's below. Cf. *The Book of the Himyarites; Fragments of a Hitherto Unknown Syriac Work*, ed. Axel Moberg, trans. Axel Moberg, vol. VII, Skrifter Utgivna Av Kungl. Humanistiska Vetenskapssamfundet I Lund (Leipzig: Lund, C. W. K. Gleerup, 1924), xxv–xxxv. Gafni, *Land, Center and Diaspora*, 21, 64–72.

131   Lings, *Muhammad*. Salmà (bint 'Amr) from the tribe of Khazraj marries Hashīm the great-grandfather of Muhammad, also mother Aminah's half-sister (Salmà bint Qays) lived in Medina 8, 27, 231. Cf. Michael Lecker, "A Note on Early Marriage Links between Qurashis and Jewish Women", in *Jews and Arabs in Pre-and Early Islamic Arabia*, ed. Michael Lecker (Aldershot, Hampshire: Ashgate Publishing Limited, 1998), 18, 24, 27–28. Pre-Hajj converts from the Medinan tribes of the Aws and Khazraj pledge at Aqabah to submit to Muhammad and to protect him. As-Sallaabee, *The Prophet*, 1:582–6 & 631.

132   Here the author accepts that there is no evidence that the Jewish leaders made a decision to afford Muhammad and his followers safe-haven. Their "wait and see" attitude may have been influenced by a desire to improve relations between the warring tribes of Medina. Lings, *Muhammad*, 108.

133   Ibid., 16. Cf. As-Sallaabee, *The Prophet*, 2:803–4.

Muhammad with both open arms and a degree of trepidation. Certainly the arrival of the rumoured prophet would create intense interest. Perhaps some had heard of the accolades bestowed on the young man by the monk Bahīrā or Nestor.[134]

Entry into Medina and the Treaty

One can only imagine the excitement that Muhammad's initial entry brought to the people of Medina. Anticipation of a prophet that most had only heard about surely ushered a sense of *détente* whereby the senseless feuding would no longer dominate daily life.[135] How many would remember the approach of the envoys from the Quraysh, enquiring as to what to make of this man that declared himself prophet and his response to the three questions posed by the rabbis?[136] An image of this festiveness is characterized by the fact that a non-supporter is acknowledged as the first to sight the approach of Muhammad's entourage from the top of his castle and shouted the news of Muhammad's approach to Qubā, at the outskirts of Medina.[137] He called to those waiting, "Sons of Qaylah, he is come, he is come!"[138] Then there is the hearty confusion as the people mistakenly greet the elder Abu Bakr as the prophet, only realizing their mistake when Abu Bakr shaded Muhammad from the sun.[139] In Medina

---

134   Lings, *Muhammad*, 29–30, 34.
135   Ibid., 82, 108.
136   Ibid., 77. These questions are: The legend of the Sleepers of Ephesus. It is quite an odd story for rabbis to present since it is considered a legend of Christian origin. The second question, concerned tidings of a far traveller. And the third, concerned the Spirit of God. Cf. Sidney H Griffith, "Christian Lore and the Arabic Qur'ān: The 'Companions of the Cave' in Surat Al-Kahf and in Syriac Christian Tradition", in *The Qur'ān in Its Historical Context*, ed. Gabriel Said Reynolds (Abingdon, Oxon: Routledge, 2008).
137   As-Sallaabee, *The Prophet*, 2:668–9. Ishāq, *Sirat Rasulallah* 227.
138   Lings, *Muhammad*, 121. As-Sallaabee, *The Prophet*, 2:668–9. A slightly different wording is uttered in this rendition, "O group of Arabs, here comes your grandfather ...".
139   *The Prophet*, 2:669–9.

Beyond Al-jāhiliyya

Muhammad playfully allowed his camel Qaswā decide where he would stay. Qaswā wondered to a courtyard in the district of the Bani Malik branch of the Najjār that belonged to two brothers, Sahl and Suhayl. While accommodation was prepared Muhammad stayed with Abu Ayyūb Khalid, the man who possessed the letter from the Tubba.[140]

Not long after Muhammad arrived he set about to unite the different communities in Medina into a community of believers. This new community was not only to be comprised of the *ansār* and *muhājirah* [emigrants], but Jews as well. Muhammad's effort to unite Medina came in the form of a Treaty.[141] In short the treaty forms more of a social contract of mutual defence and security without seeking conversion.[142] The Treaty began by defining the residents of Medina that believed in one God as *Al-Ummah*, the nation, creating a new social entity.[143] This is a very important detail since one characteristic of *al-jāhiliyya* is that blood ties and tribal loyalties defined the political and social interaction.[144] *Ansār* and *muhājirah* were thus united as a brotherhood by belief in Muhammad as prophet and in following *Sharī'ah*. An important fact, however, is that the Treaty did not insist that Jews accept Muhammad as a prophet, although the treaty referred to him as such. The Jews could follow their own laws and practices.[145] In fact an important aspect of the Treaty states, "The Jews of the Banū Auf are a nation with the believers".[146] Muslims and Jews enjoyed equal status as citizens and all were free to worship as their conscience prescribed. If a person was wronged then it was incumbent on Jews and Muslims to come to their assistance. In cases of peace

---

140 Lings, *Muhammad*, 123, 24. The Adī branch of the Bani Najjār is reported to be distant kin to Muhammad. They are part of the Khazjarite clan.
141 Ishāq, *Sirat Rasulallah* 231–3. Cf. Lassner, *Jews, Christians, and the Abode of Islam*, 137–8.
142 Tariq Ramadan, *The Messenger, the Meanings of the Life of Muhammad* (London: Penguin, 2007), 88–90.
143 As-Sallaabee, *The Prophet*, 2:788–92.
144 Ibid., 2:788–9.
145 Lings, *Muhammad*, 125. Cf. As-Sallaabee, *The Prophet*, 2:790–1.
146 *The Prophet*, 2:791–2. Here As-Sallaabee is citing the work of Dr Diyaa Al-'Umaree, *As-Seerah An-Nabawiyyah As-Saheehah*.

or war between tribes, neither party would make a separate treaty that threatened the peace of Medina.[147] All of the signed parties accepted the final arbitrator in matters of dispute between inter-communal rivalries rested with God and Muhammad.[148]

The treaty provided a means by which aggrieved parties could forgo revenge without losing face, since the signatures were in effect submitting to Allah and his prophet. In theory the Treaty also made provisions for the People of the Book to maintain their existing beliefs.[149] To a greater degree the Treaty successfully united the Aws and Khazraj. Surprisingly, Jewish support for the Treaty was tendentious at best. On occasion they would, however, avail of Muhammad's services as an arbitrator. A very positive example reinforces the ability of an offended party to remit retaliation as a charity and this act of forgiveness would count as expiation for any sin that a person may have committed.[150] This is thought by Ibn Kathir to be the occasion of revelation for *sūrat al-mā'idah* (5):45 examined in Chapter 1.

Alternatively, a less sincere example comes from *sūrat al-mā'idah* (5):49. Here four members of the Jewish community in Medina, Ka'b ibn Asad, Ibn Saluba, Abdullah bin Surya and Shas bin Qays, conspired together to misguide Muhammad concerning "his" religion. They went to Muhammad and said, "O Muhammad! You know that we are the scholars, noblemen and chiefs of the Jews. If we follow you, the Jews will follow suit and will not contradict us. But there is enmity between us and some of our people, so we will refer to you for judgment in this matter, and you should rule in our favour against them and we will believe in you".[151] Muhammad's response to this particular request for arbitration is captured in the exegesis of *sūrat al-mā'idah* (5):50 that specifically mentions *al-jāhiliyya*. The context of the request demonstrates that the

---

147   Lings, *Muhammad*, 125.
148   As-Sallaabee, *The Prophet*, 2:792–3. Cf. Qur'ān 4:104.
149   Ibid., 2:792.
150   Ibid., 2:795. The case involved blood money in feuds between two Jewish tribes, the Banū Nader and the Banū Qurayzah.
151   See above Chapter 1.

rejection of Muhammad as prophet and leader of Medina had little to do with sincere matters of faith and more to do with traditional allegiances and worldly gain. The verse asks, "Do they seek then the judgment of the Days of Ignorance? And who is better in judgment than Allah for a people who have firm faith?"[152]

From Treaty to Enmity

It is unfortunate that interaction with the Jews of Medina became increasingly contentious. Historians and the biographers of Muhammad agree that relations between Muhammad's *Al-Ummah* deteriorated rapidly and with devastating effect. The fate of the Banū Khazraj, the Banū Nadir and the Banū Qaynuqa: death, conversion, or submission, echo through the ages.[153] Within a few short years all Jews would come to be described as hypocrites and those most likely to have enmity for the believers, as in *sūrat al-mā'idah* (5):82 examined in Chapter 1. Yet, history is also replete with examples of co-operation and compassion. From a Jewish perspective, as well as peace, the arrival of Muhammad changed the social, political and religious landscape of Medina in an unanticipated way. The new facts on the ground exposed weaknesses within the worldview/ontological view of the Jews of Medina to challenges that would prove to be their undoing. An underlying factor being their understanding of "chosen".[154] As Ling points out, they could not accept that God would send a non-Jew as a prophet.[155] Whereas the Jews were masters of the art of survival under the traditional order, they lacked faith in the new untested way.[156]

---

152 Ibn Kathīr, *Tafsir Al-Qur'ān Al-Azim*, 3:202.
153 Lewis, *The Jews of Islam*, 10. Cf. Kister The Massacre of the Banū Qurayza, M. J. Kister, *Society and Religion from Jāhiliyya to Islam*, Collect Studies Series; Cs327 (Aldershot, Hampshire: Variorum, Gower Publishing Group, 1990).
154 Cf. Rashid Rida in the previous chapter.
155 Lings, *Muhammad*, 16, 126–7. Another question the defeat of Exilarch Nehemiah ben Hushiel raises is whether, or not, help from a non-Jew was ever interpreted as not waiting for God and forcing God's hand.
156 Ibid., 127.

Before Muhammad arrived the Jews of Medina looked to God to destroy their enemies, not to provide the conditions of coexistence.[157] It would seem that the promise of universal salvation through Abraham, found in the Torah, and the command to spread the faith of Abraham, found in the Talmud, did not and could not possibly include the Arabs of the Hijaz. On the other hand, Muhammad's willingness to take on all opposition in Arabia and the high cost of his early military campaigns failed to convince the sceptics of his prophethood, especially those expecting God's messenger to be a little less fallible.

Looking at the evidence of opposition to Muhammad in light of the three oaths and in conjunction with recent devastating defeats of Jewish campaigns that tried to pre-empt the hand of God; it is a great pity that more empathy is not afforded to Judaism in general, and these historical Jews in particular, by modern exegetes. History certainly attests to the fact that the Jews of Medina are guilty, if anything, of a gross error of judgement with regard to Muhammad and Islam.[158] Their willingness to cling to the ways of *al-jāhiliyya*, as seen through the eyes of Islam, proved to be their undoing.

Christians of Abyssinia

In *al-jāhiliyya* Christians could be found the length and breadth of Arabia, in towns, amongst the settled communities, as well as within the Bedouin communities. The spread of Christianity on the Arab peninsula is a very interesting subject. Seminal in this field of research is the enterprise of J. Spencer Trimingham in his *Christianity Among the Arabs in Pre-Islamic Times*.[159] Trimingham follows the slow and steady spread of Christianity from the time of the Evangelists to the dawn of Islam, from Syria to Yemen, from Petra to Baghdad. He also examines the spectrum of diversity that thrived in an area beyond the reach of control of Byzantine Church

---

157 Ibid.
158 Lewis, *The Jews of Islam*, 10.
159 Trimingham, *Christianity among the Arabs*.

Beyond Al-jāhiliyya

authorities who sought to enforce the oscillating edicts of the various Church Councils. Consequently, the Qur'ān, rather than responding to heretical notions of the nature of Christ is making its own statements in the milieu of what will develop into mainstream Christian Melkite, West Syriac Jacobites, East Syriac Nestorians as well as mainstream Ethiopian *Tawahedo* creedal formulae.[160]

Through the exegesis of the verses examined in the previous chapter it is possible to present a Qur'ānic image of Christians that is generally quite favourable in comparison with Judaism. The Qur'ān accepts that Christians follow divine revelation in the form of the Gospel through the ministry of Jesus, the Messiah. It is, however, a matter of dispute within Islam just how much of Jesus' authentic teachings remain intact and where, or how, changes came about. Equally, however, it believes that enough of the authentic message of Jesus to lead sincere Christians to salvation and even to Islam.

Sūrat al-mā'idah (5):82–3 examines the potential for Christians to be considered nearest to Muslims. The *asbāb an-nuzūl* of this verse is thought to relate not to Christians on the Arab peninsula, but rather to Christians from the Kingdom of Abyssinia. These Christians are believed to have travelled with Ja'far and the refugees, as a delegation from the King of Abyssinia to Muhammad in Medina. The text suggests that they are true Christians, because their faith, their submission to God, *islām*, encourages them to move from the teachings of Christ to recognizing Muhammad as the Paraclete, the "comforter", that Jesus promised he would send.[161]

---

160 Sidney H Griffith, *The Bible in Arabic: The Scriptures of the "People of the Book"*, eds William Chester Jordan and Peter Schäfer Michael Cook, Jews, Christians, and Muslims from the Ancient to the Modern World (Princeton, NJ: Princeton University Press, 2013), 26–7. David D. Grafton, "The Identity and Witness of Arab Pre-Islamic Arab Christianity: The Arabic Language and the Bible", *Hervormde Teologiese Studies* 70, no. 1 (2014): 6–7.

161 Mujahid, *Tafsir Mujahid*, 202. Interestingly, the religion in Ethiopia prior to Christianity may well have been Judaism. Cf. Acts 8:26–40; Abebe Zegeye, "The Construction of the Beta Israel Identity", *Social Identities* 10, no. 5 (2004). Here Zegeye contends the Jews of Ethiopia may have originated with the tribe of Dan, or like the Jews of the Hijaz, migrated during the Babylonian captivity.

However, the exegesis moves from the specific to the general, in order to suggest a potentially favourable reception of Muslims by any Christian, not just Abyssinians, unless their attitude towards Muslims and, or, Islam is influenced by ulterior motives. This amicable theological construct is the basis for considering Christians as potential pre-Qur'ānic Muslims.[162] This implies that the faith of Christianity was essentially *islām* before the coming of Muhammad and reified Islam, as a religion in its own right. The potential for harmonious relations is epitomized by the relationship between early Muslims and the Kingdom of Abyssinia to the extent that during the period of conquest Muhammad instructed his army, *utruku al-habasha mā tarakūkum* [Until the Abyssinians attack you, do not attack them], and "As long as they do not bother you and let you live in peace, you too should not bother them [allow them] also to live in peace".[163] In fact, in classical times, Abyssinia was the only country to earn the designation, *dār al-hiyād* [realm of neutrality].[164]

Social Political Considerations

This section seeks to briefly describe the Christians of Abyssinia and to investigate whether the favourable relationship between early Muslims and Abyssinians was based on some social, political or theological commonality or was simply a matter of congenial personalities. Dr Farooq Hassan believes that the Abyssinian model of coexistence is one that has several lessons for today's society. He contends that there were certain characteristics of Abyssinia that first prompted Muhammad to encourage early Muslims to emigrate there in order to escape persecution in Mecca.

---

162   See also *sūrat al-qasas* (28): 52–5.
163   Dr Farooq Hassan, "Re-Examining the Possibility of Peaceful Co-Existence of Muslims and Non-Muslims in the West Based on the Abyssinian Model," *Interdisciplinary Journal of Contemporary Research in Business* 3, no. 11 (2012): 878.
164   F. Peter Ford, "Christian-Muslim Relations in Ethiopia: A Checkered Past, a Challenging Future", *Reformed Review*, no. Spring (2007): 3. Cf. Haggai Erlich, *Ethiopia and the Middle East* (Boulder, CO: Lynne Reinner Publishers, 1994), 15.

Beyond Al-jāhiliyya

These characteristics concern the type of society that existed and the reputation of the *Negus* [king], Ashama ibn Abjar or Najāshī, as he was commonly known.[165] Muhammad advised the Muslims in 615 CE, "Migrate to [Abyssinia] Ethiopia and live there till Allah relieves the hardship you face here as that is a *land of justice* and *truth*. There is a king who loves justice; no one is treated unjustly by him".[166]

Ethiopia, where Abyssinia is located today, can truthfully claim to be one of the world's oldest civilizations.[167] Its trading links to the Mediterranean world can be traced back to pre-historic times. Items exported include ivory, tortoise shells, incense, fragrant gums, precious stones and pearls, spices, exotic animals, elephants, pottery, glass, metals and slaves. In return traders brought cloth, olive oil, wine, iron tools, gold and silver.[168] Later trade via the Red Sea connected Abyssinia beyond the Mediterranean world to Persia, India and the Far East. The development of several ports along the coast such as Adulis and Ptolemaist Theron (near Suakin) as well as inland towns such as Aksum and Koloe facilitated this trade.[169] By the sixth century CE, Abyssinia controlled trade along the Red Sea, allowing for the development of a prosperous society. Alongside trade came the development of maritime skills and agriculture, including the cultivation of coffee.[170]

The ruling Aksum dynasty came originally from southern Arabia. Accordingly, people from southern Arabia migrated across the Red Sea, while

165 There are several scholarly variations of the name of the King of Abyssinia.
166 Hassan, "Abyssinian Model", 871–2. It seems that this meeting point can be interpreted in a negative way as well. Through this interpretation Abyssinians are seen as the powerful nemesis of Islam because once the king converted he needed to keep his new faith secret. See Erlich, *Ethiopia*, 17.
167 Paul B Henze, *Layers of Time: A History of Ethiopia* (New York: Palgrave, 2000), 1–2. Cf. The Rift Valley Chris Johns, *Valley of Life, Africa's Great Rift* (Charlottesville, VA: Thomas-Grant, 1991), 27.
168 Henze, *Layers of Time*, 15–19.
169 Ibid., 16–18.
170 Ibid., ibid., 16–18., 16–18.

maintaining links to southern Arabia.¹⁷¹ This would account for the fact that many of the Abyssinian towns grew along the most practical routes to the sea and the towns show strong southern Arabian influences.¹⁷² When the Aksums left southern Arabia they maintained a nominal interest in the establishment of military outposts. Abyssinia was for centuries an ancient superpower alongside Persia, Byzantium and China.¹⁷³ Abyssinia can rightly claim to be the only African country that was not colonized.¹⁷⁴ In spite of its military ability, Abyssinia did not venture to expand beyond the region of the Horn of Africa.¹⁷⁵ Fortunately too, Abyssinia and its Aksum empire were remote enough not to merit envious attention from the Persians and Byzantines.¹⁷⁶

Biblical Abyssinia & Post-Apostolic Christian Mission

The Bible attributes the origins of monotheism in Abyssinia to Noah's son Cush, and his two grandsons Seba and Sabta (Gen 10:67; Chron. 1:8–10). These sons are thought to have been the original settlers of Ethiopia.¹⁷⁷ Other references mention that Moses married a Cushite woman (Numbers 12:1). Judaism is traced to the love affair between the young Ethiopian Queen Makeda of Sheba and the wise King Solomon (1Kings 10:1–14).¹⁷⁸ Closely connected to this affair is how the Ark of the Covenant, built by Moses

---

171 Trimingham, *Christianity among the Arabs*, 287 & 92. Gradually these ties weakened; by around 340 CE Himyarites formed a separate kingdom with Zafār as its capital.
172 Henze, *Layers of Time*, 16–21.
173 Ibid., 22. Here Henze is citing the Persian prophet Mani.
174 Wendy Murray Zoba, "Guardians of the Lost Ark: Ethiopia's Christians Stake Their Identity on Being Heirs of Solomon and Keepers of His Treasure", *Christianity Today* 43, no. 7 (1999): 60.
175 Henze, *Layers of Time*, 33.
176 Ibid., 30. Here Henze is citing Munro-Hay.
177 Zoba, "Guardians of the Lost Ark: Ethiopia's Christians Stake Their Identity on Being Heirs of Solomon and Keepers of His Treasure", 60.
178 E. A. Wallis Budge, *The Kebra Nagast: The Queen of Sheba and Her Only Son Menyelek* [Kebra Nagast], trans. E. A. Wallis Budge (London: Forgotten Books, 2007; repr., 2007), 132–5.

(Exodus 25:10), is claimed to rest in the Church of Saint Mary of Zion, Aksum.[179] The Christian era begins with Philip's encounter with the Ethiopian eunuch in Gaza (Acts 8:26–40). In addition, the disciples Matthew, Nathanael and Thomas are purported to have preached in Abyssinia.[180]

Prior to the adoption of Christianity as its main religion, the religious make up of Abyssinia was a mix of Judaism, Christianity, Sabeanism and other African religions.[181] The origins of Christianity in Abyssinia may well have begun as early as the first century.[182] However, more is known about the development of the Church from the fourth century onwards. According to Ethiopian tradition, the story begins with two Syrian boys, Aedisius and Frumentius, who were shipwrecked and sold into slavery.[183] The Emperor Ella Aminda employed them in his royal court. Over time, through hard work and dedication, the young men were granted their freedom and earned the emperor's and the queen's respect and admiration. Indeed, the queen was so impressed with their character that when her husband died she asked Aedisius and Frumentius to stay on to help educate her son Ezanas.[184] During this time the two encouraged Christian traders to build churches to help spread the good news of the Gospel.[185]

---

179 Ibid., 176. Zoba, "Guardians of the Lost Ark: Ethiopia's Christians Stake Their Identity on Being Heirs of Solomon and Keepers of His Treasure", 60–1.
180 "Guardians of the Lost Ark: Ethiopia's Christians Stake Their Identity on Being Heirs of Solomon and Keepers of His Treasure", 60.
181 The pre-Christian history of Ethiopia is a field of study is far beyond the scope of this chapter. Suffice it to say that if Acts of the Apostles is accurate then sometime in the first century CE Christian teachings first impacted on the Empire. See further Zegeye, "Beta Israel Identity". Trimingham makes reference to a Sabaean King Shāmir Yuhar'ish ruling Axum as well as southwest Arabia Trimingham, *Christianity among the Arabs*, 288.
182 John Binns, "Theological Education in the Ethiopian Orthodox Church", *The Journal of Adult Theological Education* 2, no. 2 (2005): 103. Cf. Harold G. Marcus, *A History of Ethiopia* (Berkeley: University of California Press, 1994), 5–7.
183 Steven Kaplan, "Dominance and Diversity: Kingship, Ethnicity, and Christianity in Orthodox Ethiopia", *Church History and Religious Culture* 89, no. 1–3 (2009): 293.
184 Bell, *The Origin of Islam*, 10, 80.
185 Marcus, *A History of Ethiopia*, 7. Cf. Kaplan, "Dominance and Diversity", 293–4. Gay L Byron, "Manuscripts, Meanings, and (Re)Membering: Ethiopian Women in Early Christianity", *Journal of Religious Thought* 59/60, no. 1 (2006): 93.

In 303 CE Frumentius travelled to Alexandria in Egypt to request that the Patriarch Athanasius assign a bishop to Abyssinia. To his amazement Athanasius appointed Frumentius.[186] This began a centuries long relationship between the Egyptian Orthodox Church and the Ethiopian Orthodox Church, whereby the Egyptian Orthodox Church appointed the bishops of the Ethiopian Orthodox Church.[187] Athanasius, one of the great Church Fathers, was very active in Church politics and frequently suffered the consequences of his convictions. Once declared "the Column of Orthodoxy", Athanasius suffered numerous stints in exile for his opposition to Arianism.[188] He was a strong advocate of the Nicene formulation, which stood against Arianism.[189] Frumentius stayed in Egypt for two years preparing for his role as bishop. On his return he converted Ezanas and his family.[190] The conversion of the royal family was one thing; conversion of the country to Christianity was another. The top down approach took several generations.

Overtime Christianity replaced Judaism and Sabeanism as the country's predominant religion. Those who remained Jewish are referred to as *Beta Israel* [House of Israel], or *Falashas* [exiles, or strangers].[191] History (*c.* 351 CE) records one attempt by the Emperor Constantius, an Arian, to recall Frumentis to Alexandria so that the newly installed Bishop George of Cappadocia could investigate his conduct and beliefs. Frumentius and the Ethiopian Church however remained loyal to Athanasius and his anti-Chalcedonian ideals.[192] By the fifth and sixth centuries Ethiopia was quite

---

186 Marcus, *A History of Ethiopia*, 7. Cf. Ninian Smart, *The Phenomenon of Christianity* (London: Collins, 1979), 260.
187 Kaplan, "Dominance and Diversity", 294.
188 Khalid Anatolios, *Athanasius: The Coherance of His Thought* (New York: Routledge, 1998), 86–7. 86–7; Timothy D. Barnes, *Athanasius and Constantius: Theology and Politics in the Constantinian Empire* (Cambridge, MA: Harvard University Press, 1993), 19–33.
189 *A New Eusebius: Documents Illustrative of the History of the Church to A. D. 37*, 7th edn (London: S. P. C. K., 1957), 270–1, 79.
190 Marcus, *A History of Ethiopia*, 8. Cf. Kaplan, "Dominance and Diversity", 293.
191 Zegeye, "Beta Israel Identity". Citing Kessler, 1982, 4.
192 Marcus, *A History of Ethiopia*, 7–8. Bell, *The Origin of Islam*, 10, 30–1, 35.

a developed country economically and a regional military force.¹⁹³ King Kaleb and his son Gabra Masqal (The Servant of the Cross) consolidated Christian authority in Ethiopia by establishing a new law code, commencing a massive church building program while simultaneously destroying pagan temples and synagogues.¹⁹⁴ Legend has it that it is during this period that the *Kebra Nagast*, the formative epic narrative of Ethiopian History was composed.¹⁹⁵

Some Theological Considerations

Ethiopian Christians name their unique Christology as Tawahedo, meaning union. Here the human nature of Jesus is described as gradually uniting with the divine, forming a single nature.¹⁹⁶ This concept was rejected by the Council of Chalcedon (451 CE) who preferred the description of the nature of Jesus as, "perfect God and man, consubstantial with the Father and consubstantial with Man, one sole being in two natures, without division or separation and without confusion or change".¹⁹⁷ A poetic description of the Ethiopic position might be the participation, or deification, of man through union with the Divine Light. This idea stems through the experience of humanity with the sacrifice of Jesus and through his taking on of human nature, as Athanasius once said, "He became man in order that we might become divine".¹⁹⁸ The Ethiopian Orthodox Tewahedo Church defines their belief in the Trinity as,

---

193 Byron, "Manuscripts", 88.
194 Kaplan, "Dominance and Diversity", 295.
195 The Kebra Nagast describes the Solomon and Sheba "Israelite" origins of Ethiopian Judaism, including procurement of the Arc of the Covenant by their son Menelik. The Arc is thought to rest in Lalibela, Ethiopia. The dating of the text is much debated. It was not written down until the fourteenth century. Cf. Ibid., 296, fn. 10.
196 Ibid., 302. 302; Marcus, *A History of Ethiopia*, 7.
197 *A History of Ethiopia*, 8. Kimball, "An Exploration", 55–6.
198 Gerald Hiestand, "Not 'Just Forgiven:' How Athanasius Overcomes the under-Realised Eschatology of Evangelicalism", *Evangelical Quarterly* 84, no. 1 (2012); Smart, *Christianity*.

> The Father is the begetter and not the begotten. The Son is the begotten and not the begetter. And the Holy Spirit is the one who comes out from the Father, and takes up from the Son; three names, one God, the Father and the Son and the Holy Spirit. Their Kingdom is one and their authority is one, and from the angels and humans they bow down to them once, and we also having believed, bow down to the Father and the Son and the Holy Spirit, forever and ever, Amen.[199]

This creed offers a unique blend of Syriac monotheism and Coptic Orthodox teachings. It is partially derived from events in the fifth century, where following anti-Monophysitism prosecution in the Byzantine Empire, refugees began to arrive from Syria and eastern controlled Byzantine countries.[200] These refugees, known as the Tsadkan [the Righteous Ones] followed an Antioch Greek version of the Old and New Testaments.[201] Amongst the refugees were nine men who became known as the 'Nine Saints.' These 'Nine Saints' are celebrated for translating the Bible into Ge'ez".[202] The unique theological blend of Syriac and Egyptian remained preserved and unquestioned until the Portuguese invasion in the sixteenth century. After the Portuguese expulsion, the Ethiopian Orthodox Church struggled to formulate a unifying systemized articulation of the nature of Jesus. The resulting debates left three competing options; *Tawahedo* [Union], as described above; *Qebat* [fully unified] through the Holy Spirit; and *Sost Ledat*, an [adoptionist] approach.[203]

---

199   Roger W Crowley, *Ethiopian Biblical Interpretation: A Study in Exegetical Tradition and Hermeutics*, vol. 38, University of Cambridge Oriental Piblications (Cambridge: Cambridge University Press, 1988), 284.
200   Trimingham, *Christianity among the Arabs*, 288–9. Cf. Bas ter Haar Romeny, "Athanasius in Syriac", *Church History and Religious Culture* 90, no. 2–3 (2010): 249–50.
201   Barnes, *Athanasius and Constantius*, 19, 120. Marcus, *A History of Ethiopia*, 8–9. Marcus here is a little sceptical of these claims. The language of Ge'ez was first written in Sabaean Arab letters. Ge'ez as a literary language developed in the fourth century for the translation of Christian texts. See further Byron, "Manuscripts", 89, fn. 24.
202   Niall Finneran, "Hermits, Saints, and Snakes: The Archaeology of the Early Ethiopian Monastery in Wider Context", *International Journal of African Historical Studies* 45, no. 2 (2012): 258–9.
203   Kaplan, "Dominance and Diversity", 301.

Asylum, Dialogue & Détente

From the above description of the history and faith of the Ethiopian Orthodox Church one can state that they maintained a strong allegiance to the teachings of Athanasius. They believe in the Trinity, and also that Jesus is the true Messiah, one in substance with the Father through the action of the Divine Spirit, that is, the true begotten son of God. Nothing about the creed of the Abyssinian Church could in the slightest way be misconstrued as anything other than Christian. Yet, it was to this community, ruled by King Ashama ibn Abjar, that Muhammad sent members of his nascent community around 615 & 616 CE so that they might escape persecution from the enemies of Islam in Mecca.[204] As Martin Ling, citing Ibn Ishāq reports, Muhammad instructs those most oppressed, "If ye went to the country of Abyssinia, ye would find there a king under whom none suffereth wrong. It is a land of sincerity in religion. Until such time as God shall make for you a means of relief from what ye now are suffering".[205]

In Abyssinia, Muslims let their lives speak. They were not encouraged to proselytize, but encouraged instead to nurture relations with Christians. Some Muslims chose to remain in Abyssinia even when it was safe to return to Arabia.[206] The *hijra* [migration] to Abyssinia is a monumental meeting in history. Here the prophet of God sent his people not only to another country for protection, but also to a country that devotedly followed another religion, namely Christianity.

The question is, was this instruction prompted by God, or was it merely a well-known fact that the Kingdom of Abyssinia would offer refuge to any person or group suffering persecution?[207] Either way, this is a true example

---

204 Hassan, "Abyssinian Model", 871–2.
205 Lings, *Muhammad*, 80.
206 Hassan, "Abyssinian Model", 874. Henze, *Layers of Time*, 43. An interesting caveat to this relationship is the fact that some emigrants chose to remain in Abyssinia. They settled and are buried in the Negash in eastern Tigray.
207 As-Sallaabee, *The Prophet*, 1:490–1. Here As-Sallaabee examines a few of the issues involved in the choice of Abyssinia, such as the character of the king and the relative social and political autonomy his kingdom enjoyed from influence of the Meccans.

of crisis, faith and response.²⁰⁸ In the history of the world there are occasions when the fate of humanity comes down to simple choices. This is one of them. Muhammad must have deliberated the circumstances and accepted that he could not protect all of his community. He needed help. The King of Abyssinia, for his part, would have to choose to provide a safe haven for refugees, at the request of a stranger purporting to be a prophet, or honour his longstanding friendship with the people of Mecca. The decisions each man made set an exemplary standard for future generations to follow.

Martin Lings reports that the first emigrants numbered no more than eighty. They were well received and free to worship as their conscience dictated.²⁰⁹ The Quraysh responded by sending a team headed by ʿAmr ibn al ʿAs to bribe the king's generals to persuade the king to send the refugees back. It is the measure of the man that King Ashama ibn Abjar first insists the refugees are given a chance to state their case.²¹⁰ The king asked them "What is this religion wherein ye have become separate from your people, though ye have not entered my religion nor that of any other of the folk that surround us?"²¹¹ Jaʿfar ibn Abī Tālib explained to the king,

> O King, we were a people steeped in ignorance, worshipping idols, eating unsacrificed carrion, committing abominations, and the strong would devour the weak. Thus we were until God sent us a Messenger from out of our midst, one whose lineage we knew, and his veracity and his worthiness of trust and his integrity. He called us unto God, that we should testify to His Oneness and worship Him and renounce what we and our fathers had worshipped in the way of stones and idols; and he commanded us to speak truly, to fulfil our promises, to respect the ties of kinship and the rights of our neighbours, and to refrain from crimes and from bloodshed. So we worship God alone, setting naught beside Him, counting as forbidden what He hath forbidden

---

208　Another way of looking at the issue is to consider the choices as a matter of cause and effect, the choices made have long lasting effects. See further ibid., 1:479–84.
209　Lings, *Muhammad*, 82.
210　Ibid. 82. Possible origins for the king's love of justice stem from the fact that he was sold into slavery as a child following his father's murder. Due to lack of a suitable replacement the enslaved king was liberated and returned to the throne. Since then he felt free from the need to show favouritism and chose the purest path in matters of conscience. Cf. Ishāq, *Sirat Rasulallah* 153–4.
211　Lings, *Muhammad*, 83.

Beyond Al-jāhiliyya

and as licit what He hath allowed. For these reasons have our people turned against us, and have persecuted us to make us forsake our religion and revert from the worship of God to the worship of idols. That is why we have come to thy country, having chosen thee above all others; and we have been happy in thy protection, and it is our hope, O King, that here, with thee, we shall not suffer wrong.[212]

Once Ja'far's speech was translated, the king asked if he had any revelation from their prophet and Ja'far recited from *sūrat Maryam* (19):16–21:

And make mention of Mary in the Book, when she withdrew from her people unto a place towards the east, and secluded herself from them; and We sent unto her Our Spirit, and it appeared unto her in the likeness of a perfect man. She said: I take refuge from thee in the Infinitely Good, if any piety thou hast. He said: I am none other than a messenger from thy Lord, that I may bestow on thee a son most pure. She said: how can there be for me a son, when no man hath touched me, nor am I unchaste? He said: Even so shall it be; thy Lord saith: It is easy for Me. That We may make him a sign for mankind and a mercy from Us; and it is a thing ordained.[213]

The king and his bishops were visibly moved by Ja'far's presentation of Islam and by his recitation of the *āya* [verse] from *sūrah Maryam*. To those assembled the king said, "This hath truly come from the same source that which Jesus brought". Then the king turned on Amr and his colleague Abdullah and said, "Ye may go, for by God I will not deliver them unto you; they shall not be betrayed".[214]

Amr and Abdullah accepted they had lost the day. However, they continued to conspire to upset the balance of this newly formed relationship. Amr decided he would tell the king what Muhammad taught concerning Jesus. Abdullah cautioned against this move since he felt that the king would harm the refugees. Abdullah, in spite of everything, still considered the refugees kin, even if they had gone astray. Amr, perhaps aggrieved by his inability to sway the king the day before, felt no such compassion. The next morning Amr went straight to the king and told him that Muhammad

212 Ibid., 83.
213 Ibid., 83.
214 Ibid., 83.

declares Jesus, son of Mary, no more than a slave. This upset the king and he sent for Ja'far and his companions.²¹⁵

According to tradition, the refugees were frightened. They felt they were in serious trouble. Nevertheless, they decided to say exactly what Muhammad taught them. When they were before the king, the king asked what Muhammad had to say about Jesus. Ja'far responded by saying, "We say about which our prophet brought, saying he is a slave of God, and his apostle, and his spirit, and his word, which he cast into Mary the blessed virgin".²¹⁶ The king was again impressed and said, "By God, Jesus, son of Mary, does not exceed what you have said by the length of this stick".²¹⁷ In front of his generals and court, the king again declared that the refugees were free to remain in his country for as long as they wished. The king returned the gifts that he received from Amr and said that he would not betray the refugees for a mountain of gold.²¹⁸

The analogy of Jesus as a slave is very interesting. This author wonders what the point of common reference would have been between the king, who spoke Ge'ez and Ja'far who spoke in Arabic. It may be of interest to note that Muhammad would later describe the slaves of God as,

> My slave ceaseth not to draw near unto Me with devotions of his free will until I love him; and when I love him I am the hearing with which he heareth and the sight with which he seeth and the hand with which he graspeth and the foot with which he walketh ...²¹⁹

Perhaps the thought of Jesus as a slave to God, his servant, and his word, captured the imagination of the king and his bishops, providing a mental

---

215 Ishāq, *Sirat Rasulallah* 152.
216 Ibid., 152.
217 Ibid., 152.
218 Ibid., 153.
219 Lings, *Muhammad*, 330–1. This *hadīth* is discussed as part of the Greater Holy War, the "The war against the soul" where the soul of the fallen man is against itself ... See further Al-Bukharī, *The Translation of the Meaning of Sahih Al-Bukharī* Vol. 1, Book 8, 275–6. *Gebr/gäbr*, in Ge'ez appears to allow a similar meaning and usage. Both the Qur'ānic Description and the *hadīth* remind this author of the verse in John 14:9–14.

Beyond Al-jāhiliyya

image that reinforced their creedal position. Unfortunately, historical accounts lack further dialogue and explanation. In any case the king was comfortable with the verse recited by Ja'far and pledged his support to the refugees. Stories concerning correspondence between Muhammad and the Negus are well celebrated amongst Muslims and Christians. Sometimes the friendship put a strain on their respective communities, who may have been more willing to focus on doctrinal differences.[220] Others try to explain the friendship by erasing differences, as may be the case of those Muslims who contend that the Negus not only accepted Muhammad as prophet, but actually embraced Islam.[221] Whatever the case, several conclusions can be deduced from this initial meeting between Christianity and Islam that can provide a normative example for the present.

Potential fraternal admiration is facilitated by shared values and respect for justice. However, significant doctrinal differences do exist. Issues like Trinity, crucifixion, sonship, Paraclete, forgiveness of sin, and a myriad of religious rituals certainly present issues of contention. Yet in spite of all the possible reasons to differ, it would seem that respect for the sincerity of believers allowed for a healthy portion of tolerance between the two communities. This tolerance and respect provided a backdrop, even in

---

[220] Sergew Hable Sellassie, *Ancient and Medieval Ethiopian History to 1270* (Addis Ababa: United Printers, 1972), History, 185. There were two rebellions against the king while the immigrants resided in Abyssinia. The first was purely political, beyond the River Nile. The other was in the capital and concerned the king's alleged conversion to Islam based on the writings of Al-Tabari.

[221] Sergew Hable Sellasie sees the contention of the king's conversion as a leap of faith. However, Islam had not developed its distinct theology at the time to challenge the beliefs of the king or his bishops. See further ibid., 185–90. Henze, *Layers of Time*, 42–3. In Ishāq, *Sirat Rasulallah* 657. Correspondence between Muhammad and the Negus implies that the king accepts all the tenets of Islam. The king even offers to join Muhammad; However in Lings, *Muhammad*, 318. Muhammad leads the funeral prayers for the king *in absentia* without referring to the king as a Muslim. Muhammad describes him thusly, "This day a righteous man hath died. Therefore arise and pray for your brother Ashamah". Another source contends that the king recited the *shahada* in the company of Ja'far but remained a secret Muslim for fear that his people would riot. 9, Cf. fn. 23, E. Cerulli, "L'Islam Etiopico, in his *L'Islam di leri e di Oggi*, 113–133.

al-jāhiliyya, for the invocation of Muhammad not to attack the Abyssinians unless they attack you and to allow the Christians of Abyssinia to live in peace as long as Abyssinians allow Muslims to live in peace. The fact that not every generation decides to honour such an understanding is not a reflection on Islam or Christianity, but rather on the sincerity of the individuals concerned.[222] The fact remains that even when there are substantial theological differences, as with the case of the King of Abyssinia and the early Muslim community, it is possible to create sincere fraternal relations.[223]

The People of the Book in the Himyar Region of Southern Arabia

In southern Arabia monotheism progressed from Sabeanism to Judaism to Christianity.[224] The story of this transition is as fascinating as the history of faith in Abyssinia or al-Hijaz. The Christians of Najrān, for instance, are discussed in more than eighty verses in the Qur'ān.[225] It is therefore important to understand as much as possible about this community, in order to better understand the nuanced way the Qur'ān and its exegesis deal with this community in comparison with other Christian communities from different social, political and theological contexts.

---

222 Erlich, *Ethiopia*, 9. Following the death of Muhammad there have been various occasions when both sides have attempted to undermine the timelessness of the *hadith* with political and economic motives, fortunately the aggressor paid a higher price.
223 Ibid., 16. Sheikh Nimr al-Darwish is a founding member of the Islamic Movement in Israel with close links to the Popular Front for the Liberation of Palestine.
224 Andrey Korotayev, "Apologia for 'the Sabaean Cultural-Political Area'", *Bulletin of the Oriental and African Studies, University of London* 57, no. 3 (1994); Bell, *The Origin of Islam*, 10, 33. Trimingham, *Christianity among the Arabs*. 293, describes the form of monotheism prevalent as worshipping *rahmanān* (the merciful), around 384 CE, found in (GI 389).
225 Ishāq, *Sirat Rasulallah* 272.

From Sabean to Judaism

According to the composite legends narrated by Ibn Kathir that draw upon renditions of stories collected by Imam al-Ḥāfiẓ, ibn Isḥāq, as well as several others, the people of southern Arabia descend from Sām bin Nūh, otherwise known as Shem, son of Noah. Alternatively, Sahih al-Bukharī reports that the Aslam people, a tribe of the *ansār*, who had settled in Medina from Yemen, before the prophet arrived, descended from the family of Ishmael, because they were archers. Both variations draw upon the legend of the Queen of Sheba as recorded in the Ethiopian legend.[226] The story of the Tibān As'ad Abū Karīb, mentioned above, advances another variation of the introduction, or reintroduction of Judaism to the region. This marks the establishment of the Jewish Himyarite Kingdom replacing the Sabaean hegemony.[227]

Regrettably, a major feature of the propagation of faith in *al-jāhiliyya* included strong inclinations towards superstition and sectarianism.[228] When Abū Karīb's returned to Yemen/Himyar he invited his people to accept Judaism. Understandably, they would not convert until they could test to see if Judaism was better than their own religion. The test involved *mubāhala* [an ordeal by fire].[229] According to Ubaydallah, the two rabbis accompanying Abū Karīb wore their sacred books around their necks and stepped into the fire along with some Yemenites with their sacred books

---

[226] Ibn Kathīr, *Tafsir Al-Qur'ān Al-Azim*, 8:74–6. Genesis 10 relates that the lands inhabited by Shem extend from Mesha to Sephar to the hill country in the east, otherwise known as Himyar or Yemen. Rosalie Rakow & Lynda J. Rose, *Sana'a City of Contrast* (Burke: Tandem Publishers, 1981), 1.

[227] Trimingham, *Christianity among the Arabs*, 296. There were Jews in this region going back to the return of the Queen of Sheba. This theory is also accepted by Lecker, "The Conversion of Himyar to Judaism and the Jewish Banū Hadl of Medina", 635.

[228] Isḥāq, *Sirat Rasulallah* 9. The story of the conversion to Judaism of Tibān As'ad Abū Karīb relates that Jews used to worship at Mecca, as a sanctuary built by Abraham, but later avoided worshipping there, because the rituals of the pagan pilgrims included blood sacrifices.

[229] The ordeal of fire was used to decide guilt and innocence. If a person could withstand more heat than their adversary it was considered truthful.

and idols. The Yemenites could not stand the heat and wished to come out, but their companions urged them to stand their ground. The Yemenites remained, but soon perished. The rabbis emerged from the fire sweating profusely, but unharmed.[230] Thus Judaism became the religion of the land.

Abū Karīb's kingdom did not last beyond the lives of his sons. Due to an act of fratricide the kingdom fell asunder to a truly despotic leader by the name of Lakhnī'a Dhū Shanātir.[231] Lakhnī'a was a sodomite who raped the sons of the Himyarite nobles so that each was publicly humiliated. This way he thought that no one would emerge as a leader to challenge him. However, when Zur'a Dhū Nuwās, the younger son of Abū Karīb, learned that Lakhnī'a's guards were coming to seize him he slipped a knife between his foot and sandal. The guards came and delivered Dhū Nuwās, just as the others. Dhū Nuwās waited till he was alone with Lakhnī'a, then sprung up and attacked Lakhnī'a, cutting off his head. He emerged from the chamber and motioned to the guards to look inside. Greatly relieved at what they saw, they thanked Dhū Nuwās and asked him to be their king. Zur'a Dhū Nuwās took the name Yūsuf, with the title "The King of all the Sabaeans" and reigned over all of Himyar for many years.[232] The religion of the land remained Judaism. In Himyar there was the general perception at the time that Judaism was a religion independent of all foreign influence.[233] However, Christianity and the power struggle beyond the borders of Himyar soon began to take root.

---

230   Ishāq, *Sirat Rasulallah* 10. There is an alternative, less ghastly variation of the story as well.
231   Ibid., Trimingham, *Christianity among the Arabs*, 297. Trimingham contends that the Abyssinians installed this ruler based on a Syriac letter of Simeon of Beth Arsham.
232   Ishāq, *Sirat Rasulallah* 13–14. Korotayev, "Apologia for 'the Sabaean Cultural-Political Area'", 472.
233   Bell, *The Origin of Islam*, 10, 37. Trimingham, *Christianity among the Arabs*, 289, 97–8.

The Beginnings of Christianity

There are several variations as to how Christianity spread throughout Himyar.[234] In one version Ibn Ishāq credits a Syrian ascetic by the name of Faymiyūn. This man travelled around Syria offering his services as a builder in order to earn a living.[235] One day while he and his companion Sālih were walking in the desert they were abducted and sold into slavery. They were sold to two noblemen from Najrān. At the time the people of Najrān worshipped a palm tree.

Gradually, the people of Najrān accepted Faymiyūn as a hardworking, virtuous man, who often prayed alone at night in his room and whose prayers were answered.[236] It was also noticed that while he was alone praying in his room, his room would become bright. Out of curiosity his master inquired as to his religion. Faymiyūn replied that he was a Christian. His master then challenged Faymiyūn to produce a single miracle to prove the veracity of his religion. In return, if Faymiyūn could produce such a miracle, his master pledged that he and the people of Najrān would leave their religious customs and become Christians too. So, Faymiyūn prayed and cursed the palm tree that the people worshipped. As he prayed a strong wind came and uprooted the tree and threw it on the ground and the people of Najrān converted to Christianity.[237]

A more historically traceable account follows the missionary efforts of the Arian Bishop Theophilus in 356 CE.[238] He too was once a slave, who may originally have been a native of the island of Dibu, off the coast of Himyar. Theophilus was sold into slavery and sent to Syria where he became a Christian.[239] As a deacon he requested to be sent back to his own country.

---

234 *Christianity among the Arabs*, 290–1, 94–5. Here Trimingham describes some early missions to southern Arabia.
235 Suleiman A Mourad, "Christians and Christianity in the Sira of Muhammad", in *Christian-Muslim Relations: A Bibliographical History*, ed. David Thomas, et al. (Brill, 2009), 6–61.
236 Ishāq, *Sirat Rasulallah* 14.
237 Mourad, "Christians in the Sīra", 60. Ishāq, *Sirat Rasulallah* 15–16.
238 Bell, *The Origin of Islam*, 10, 34.
239 Ibid., 34–5. Glaser believes his home is close to Anfuda on the Red Sea coast.

Emperor Constantius and his Arian co-religionists handsomely endorsed the mission of Theophilus with gifts for the King of Himyar. In due course the king converted and in his new zeal built three churches from his own resources.[240]

Later Theophilus travelled to Abyssinia, the Axum Empire, in an attempt to undermine the efforts of Frumentius' mission. As discussed above Frumentius and the Christians of Abyssinia closely followed the teachings of Athanasius. Athanasius' teachings were out of step with the Arianism of Constantius and Theophilus. Theophilus considered it his duty to replace the teachings of Frumentius with those acceptable to the emperor. To this end Constantius issued a letter to the Emperor Ezana and his brother Shaizana requesting that they send Frumentius to Egypt to give account of his teachings on the nature of Christ and explain his allegiance to the teachings of Athanasius.[241] It is thought that the motivation behind the mission included the worldly desire to bring Himyar and Abyssinia closer to Byzantium. This mission failed in Abyssinia and had only limited success in Himyar.[242]

The People of the Trench

What follows next in the region is a period of sectarianism that attests to an underlying hatred of Abyssinian rule in Himyar, including Christianity. The steady spread of Christianity brought with it a real or perceived change in the allegiance of the local population away from Dhū Nuwās. The nature of the rivalry between Judaism and Christianity in the south of Arabia is a story that merits further investigation that is beyond the remit of this

---

240 Ibid., 34–5. Sellassie, *Ethiopian History*, 101. These churches are situated in Zafār, Adane and the name of the third is unknown but described as a Persian market town.
241 *Ethiopian History*, 101–2. Emperor Ezana was the emperor of Abyssinia (Aksum), Himyar and Saba.
242 Ibid., 102. Bell, *The Origin of Islam*, 10, 35–6. Frumentius remained in Abyssinia and the Church there remained loyal to Athanasius. Across the Red Sea Christianity remained a mix of Arianism and Ethiopian Orthodoxy. Politically the Church may have been viewed as being marginally closer to Byzantium.

present study.²⁴³ Suffice to say there are hints of ruthless sectarianism against native Jews before the winter of 523 CE, when Dhū Nuwās "The King of all the Sabaeans" attacked the Abyssinian Christian garrison of Zafār.

Dhū Nuwās' target and timing were well chosen. During the winter months it would have been very difficult for Abyssinia to send reinforcements to its outposts in Himyar. Zafār was the largest garrison town. Dhū Nuwās was aware that if his soldiers could take Zafār there would be limited resistance in the rest of Himyar.²⁴⁴ However, Zafār was well fortified. After several days of fighting Dhū Nuwās realized he would have to come up with a better plan. His solution required a promise to allow the soldiers to return safely to Abyssinia. He sent priests to the gates of the town to convince the soldiers of his sincerity. The soldiers took the bait. Three hundred soldiers along with their leader marched out to meet Dhū Nuwās. Dhū Nuwās prepared a feast for them to keep them off guard, but he had already ordered his soldiers to stay beside every Abyssinian soldier and to cut off their heads while they slept. This they did. In the morning 300 heads were presented to Dhū Nuwās and he proceeded to march on Zafār. There he burnt men, women and children in churches as they prayed. He gave instructions to the Jews of Zafār and all of south Arabia that if they tried to hide a Christian they would have their property confiscated and that they too would be burnt alive.²⁴⁵ Following Zafār, Dhū Nuwās proceeded to attack the Christians tribe of Ash'ar then the port of Mokhār, inhabited by the Christian Farasān tribe, a branch of the Taghlib.²⁴⁶ The repercussions of attacking his next target, the Christians of Najrān, are remembered to this day.²⁴⁷

Dhū Nuwās employed similar tactics at Najrān. He first requested support from the garrison of Abyssinian soldiers, claiming he was under attack by pagans. An indication of just how well Dhū Nuwās caught the

---

243 Hans Kung, *Islam: Past Present and Future*, trans. John Bowden, 1st edn (Oxford: Oneworld Publications, 2007), 32–3.
244 Trimingham, *Christianity among the Arabs*, 298. Sellassie, *Ethiopian History*, 128. ibid., cv–cvi.
245 *Ethiopian History*, 128. *The Book of the Himyarites*, VII, cv–cvi.
246 Trimingham, *Christianity among the Arabs*, 298.
247 The Feast Day of the Martyrs of Najrān in the Roman Catholic tradition is 24 October.

Christians by surprise is the fact that the entire garrison marched out in support, leaving the town unprotected. On the way, the army met a Christian who asked where they were going. Then he informed them of the massacre at Zafār. The soldiers returned to Najrān immediately, while Dhū Nuwās plotted another ruse. This time he arrived at the town and declared to the inhabitants that he was now king of all Arabia and if the people accepted him, he would forgive them for closing the gates against him. 150 people from several nationalities living in the town decided to meet him at his camp to agree terms.[248] When they arrived he offered them a simple choice, renounce Christ, become Jewish or die. They refused and were killed on the spot. Dhū Nuwās then took the town, burnt the churches, and tortured and murdered the remaining Christian population.[249]

Among the many descriptions of the torture and perseverance in faith of the Martyrs of Najrān is the testimony of Habsa, daughter of Hayyān, one of those responsible for spreading the Christian faith in Himyar. As the massacre progressed Habsa begged her Jewish neighbour to turn her over to Dhū Nuwās' men. Habsa's neighbour reluctantly succumbed to her request, after she threatened to turn him in for hiding her. Two of Habsa's friends joined her. Habsa beseeched the soldiers to allow them the honour of martyrdom, but the soldiers were reluctant to touch Habsa, a woman of noble reputation, without consulting Dhū Nuwās. So, Habsa along with her two friends were brought face to face with Dhū Nuwās. Habsa said to him "I am the daughter of Hayyān of the family of Hayyān, the teacher, him by whom our Lord sowed Christianity in our land. But Hayyān, my father, once burned your synagogues".[250] Dhū Nuwās intimated to Habsa that she was of the same opinion as her father and if given the chance would burn synagogues as well. To which she replied no, that she would prefer to be a martyr and cursed him

---

248 Trimingham, *Christianity among the Arabs*, 295–6. It would seem Najrān was a very metropolitan Christian centre with different denominations of Christians present as well as indigenous and non-native citizens.
249 Sellassie, *Ethiopian History*, 129. *The Book of the Himyarites*, VII, cv–cvi. Kung, *Islam*, 32. Kung, *Islam*, 32. Kung, *Islam*, 32. Kung, *Islam*, 32. Kung, *Islam*, 32. Kung, *Islam*, 32.
250 *The Book of the Himyarites*, VII, cxxiii.

Beyond Al-jāhiliyya   131

for all his evil deeds. Dhū Nuwās gave Habsa and her companions a chance to convert. Habsa declined preferring martyrdom. Habsa's friends also declined adding, even if we did not speak the words of Habsa we agree with all she said. Dhū Nuwās granted their wish and they met a tortuous end.[251]

Eventually, news of the massacres leaked out to the Christian world; winter ended and the army of Ellā-Asbehā (Caleb in Ethiopic), King of Abyssinia crossed the Red Sea to avenge the murder of his citizens and fellow Christians.[252] Dhū Nuwās' call to arms to all the local leaders, including Mundhir III of Hira, fell on deaf ears.[253] Alone, Dhū Nuwās faced a very large and angry army. The King of Abyssinia crossed the Red Sea with some 230 ships; some provided by Justin I, as well as more than 70,000 soldiers.[254] He landed near Mokha, the main port in south Arabia. Dhū Nuwās managed to stave off the first expedition against him by retreating up into the mountains. Caleb entered Zafār victorious and rebuilt the churches, then appointed Sumuyafa' 'Aswa', a Himyarite by birth, ruler of the region. Caleb met those who apostatized. He spoke to them at length then arranged a service for them and ordered the priests to forgive them and intercede with God on their behalf.[255] However, as soon as Caleb returned to Abyssinia Dhū Nuwās began to attack the garrison. In 525 CE Caleb returned well equipped with 100,000 soldiers in order to pursue Dhū Nuwās by land and sea.[256] This time Dhū Nuwās could not escape, in defiance he rode his horse into the sea, never to be seen again. Caleb left general Abreha in charge of the garrison in Zafār, officially commissioned, in the Holy Trinity Church with Bishop Grigentius.[257]

251 Ibid., cxxiii–cxxvi.
252 Trimingham, *Christianity among the Arabs*, 299; Sellassie, *Ethiopian History*, 131–5. Citing Ryckman, *La persécution des chrétiens himyarites au sixième siècle*. 17 and A. A. Vasiliev, "Justin and Abyssinia": *Byzantinishe Zeitschrift* (1933), 33.
253 *Ethiopian History*, 129–30.
254 Trimingham, *Christianity among the Arabs*. 299. Sellasie dates this first expedition at 523 CE in the fifth year of Justin I's reign. 133.
255 *The Book of the Himyarites*, VII, cxl–cxli.
256 Sellassie, *Ethiopian History*, 135.
257 Ibid., 135, 43. According to the historian Procopius, Abreha might at one time have been a slave. The Greek and Roman Churches consider Caleb a saint. Caleb's feast day is 24 October.

Soon after his return to Abyssinia, Caleb abdicated his reign and embraced the ascetic life.[258] Whatever loyalty Abreha felt towards Caleb did not transfer to the new emperor Sumuyafa Aswa. Aswa sent several expeditions to Himyar to restore order, but each failed. In face of the expedition led by the accomplished general Ariat, Abreha seemed as destined to fail as Dhū Nuwās. Yet, bizarrely, Abreha challenged the general to a duel, claiming that they were both trying to serve the king and that their soldiers should not shed each other's blood. Ariat an accomplished soldier agreed. However, Abreha had no intention of losing. He positioned one of his trusted soldiers, Arangada, in hiding, with instructions to kill Ariat if Ariat got the upper hand. When Abreha began to lose Arangada thrust his spear into Ariat. As a reward Abreha granted Arangada the first night with every new bride in Yemen.[259]

The Reign of Abreha and the Birth of the Prophet

In many ways Abreha's reign over Himyar was beneficial to both Abyssinia and the people of Himyar. Once secure in position he paid tribute to Abyssinia.[260] Abreha moved the capital from Zafār to Sana'a, placing his capital on the main route north through the towns of Al-Ta'if, Mecca and Medina, to Damascus. He conquered the northern tribes and consolidated power both eastward and southward to include Hadramawt. This allowed the Abyssinians to realize their goal of controlling the spice route. Along with Bishop Grigentius, he improved the administration of the region and set out a common code of law. He embarked on an ambitious development plan that saw the reconstruction of the famous dam at Ma'rib. He also built many churches, including the Cathedral of Sana'a in the style of

---

258 Ibid., 137, 43. He stayed in the hermitage of Abba Pentelḗwon and he sent his crown to Jerusalem to hang from the Holy Sepulchre.
259 Ibid., 145–6.
260 Ibid., 145.

Beyond Al-jāhiliyya

Hagia Sophia of Constantinople, using stones from the ruins of the castle of the Queen of Sheba.[261]

Sellasie explains that the Cathedral served two important purposes. One was to help propagate the faith after the reign of Dhū Nuwās. The second was to tap into some of the wealth that made the Quraysh of Mecca rich, namely pilgrims. Ibn Ishāq tells that Abreha wrote to the Emperor of Abyssinia, "I have built a church for you, O King, such as has not been built for any king before you. I shall not rest until I have diverted the Arabs' pilgrimage to it".[262] In order to help spread the Christian faith Bishop Grigentius advised Abreha to take measures against pagans and Jews to encourage them to accept Christianity.[263] Shortly afterwards, and quite conveniently, a man from Mecca defiled the church, thus giving Abreha reason to attack Mecca and destroy the Ka'bah.[264]

Abreha's expedition to Mecca in 570 CE is remembered as *ām al-fīl* [the Year of the Elephant].[265] Both Muslim and non-Muslim sources accept the broad outline of the events of the expedition. On the journey north, forces led by Dhū Nafr al-Himyarī and Nufayl in Khatham attempted to save the

---

261 Ibid., 146–50. The Arab word is *al-qalis* from the Greek *Ecclesia*. According to Albright, the Dam can be dated to 750 BCE. An inscription, 136 lines long, commemorates the building of the great church in Sana'a.
262 Ishāq, *Sirat Rasulallah* 21.
263 Sellassie, *Ethiopian History*, 150. In light of the campaign of Dhū Nuwās against the Christians it is difficult to imagine the encouragement left little choice.
264 Kister, *Society and Religion*, 44, 63 & 65. This church is thought to have been desecrated by Nufayl b. Habīb al-Khath 'amī, citing Al-Tabari, Ta'rikh Cairo 1939 I. 556, as well as al-Zurqānī, Mughultāy. Attacks on rival pilgrimage sites were not uncommon. The sanctuary built by Banū Murra at Buss was destroyed by the Meccans for attempting to compete with the Ka'bah; Sellassie, *Ethiopian History*, 151, 53. Sellasie reports an alternative reason for attacking Mecca concerned the grandson of Abreha, who was attacked and robbed by men from Mecca. Following the incident, they looted the church in Najran; According to L. Caetani a man from the tribe of Banū Fugayn Harīth ben Malik desecrated the church. Trimingham, *Christianity among the Arabs*, 304–5.
265 There is a slight variation of the dates of this expedition based on Sabaean inscriptions examined by Ryckman. This year is remembered as the year Muhammad was born, but historians consider this probably not accurate. Cf. *Christianity among the Arabs*, 304–5. 304–5; Sellassie, *Ethiopian History*, 152–3, fn. 35. Bell, *The Origin of Islam*, 10, 4.

Ka'bah from destruction. Both attempts failed miserably. As Abreha's army approached Mecca his soldiers raided the surrounding region. Some of the villagers lost quite significant quantities of livestock, including Abdul Al-Muttalib, the grandfather of Muhammad, who lost approximately 200 camels. The raids intimidated the Meccans to such a degree that they abandoned the city, stating that only God could defend the Ka'bah.[266] Before the invasion began, 'Abdul Al-Muttalib brazenly approached Abreha demanding his camels back. Abreha comments on the request as odd, inquiring why 'Abdul Al-Muttalib did not plead for his sacred Ka'bah. To which 'Abdul Al-Muttalib replied, "The camels are mine, but the temple belongs to another, who will defend it". Abreha retorted, "He cannot defend it from me". 'Abdul Al-Muttalib said calmly, "That is your affair; only give me back my camels".[267]

The next morning Abreha began his assault, his war elephant (Mahmūd) in the lead. Yet, no matter what they did the elephant would not march towards Mecca. According to Lings, a man named Nufayl, one of the prisoners previously taken in battle, had learned from the elephant's keeper the command to stop and whispered this into the elephant's ear. Dutifully the elephant knelt down and would not take a step towards Mecca even when beaten.[268] Then the sky grew dark, swift-flying birds filled the air, each carrying three small stones between their claws and beak. They pelted the soldiers causing them to retreat in panic. The velocity of the stones pierced through their coats of mail. As the soldiers made their retreat, each man struck by a stone fell dead. The skin of the soldiers began to rot like those stricken with small pox. Some of the soldiers died quickly others died slowly including Abreha.[269]

Following the death of Abreha, his sons Yaksum and Masruk took over. Within a few short years the political power of Abyssinia and Byzantium

---

266 Sellassie, *Ethiopian History*, 151–2. Bell, *The Origin of Islam*, 10, 40–1. Ishāq, *Sirat Rasulallah* 22–3.

267 Kister, *Society and Religion*, 65. Sellassie, *Ethiopian History*, 152. Abreha give Abdul Al-Muttalib back his camels and this encourages a delegation from Mecca to approach Abreha and offering a third of their wealth to him if he spares the Ka'bah, but he refuses the offer.

268 Lings, *Muhammad*, 20–1.

269 Ibid., 21; Ishāq, *Sirat Rasulallah* 26–7. Sellassie, *Ethiopian History*, 152–3.

Beyond Al-jāhiliyya

weakened in the region and Persian control increased. Many of the natives of Himyar, led by Sayf b. Dhū Yazan, preferred the rule of Babylon to that of the Abyssinians. To this end the Persians joined with locals to massacre the remnants of Abyssinians in Himyar.[270] Gradually the Christian faith became increasingly diversified. Bishop Grigentius is thought to have favoured Byzantium, while most people of Himyar remained loyal to the Abyssinian Church. Nestorian Christians inhabited the island of Socotra and the coastal region of Yemen. In Yemen Christianity stagnated primarily due to the perceived rivalries between different factions of Christians.[271] This state of disarray of beliefs, warring and sectarianism provides the backdrop to *al-Jāhiliyya* in south Arabia at the time of the delegation of Najrān.

Christian Deputation from Najrān

Towards the end of Muhammad's life he received many delegations and envoys from communities all over Arabia including several from Himyar.[272] In the tenth year after the Hijra a delegation of Christians from Najrān of the Byzantine Rite arrived.[273] It is noteworthy for several reasons. The

---

270 *Ethiopian History*, 154–8.
271 Trimingham, *Christianity among the Arabs*, 302–3. 302–3. Bell, *The Origin of Islam*, 10, 41–2.
272 Lings, *Muhammad*, 319, 24. According to calculations this is year 9 A. H. or 631 CE. Elsewhere the Romans led by Heraclius, recaptured Jerusalem from Jewish and Persian control, around 626–9 CE. Four Himyar princes wrote to Muhammad informing him of their acceptance of Islam. The princes were informed of their duties as Muslims including their obligations to protect the People of the Book who agreed to pay taxes.
273 Ibid., 326. Trimingham, *Christianity among the Arabs*. 273. Mourad, "Christians in the Sīra", 65. Suggests the date is closer just before 622 CE. According to A. Guillaume's translation of Ibn Ishāq, Christian kings of Byzantine funded churches and paid Bishop Abū Harithā a subsidy. He also reports that there were slight variances in the expression of the Christology of the deputation. These variances may be indicative of the creedal debates of the time. For instances he relates that some would describe Jesus as God, others as Son of God, or that Jesus is part of the Trinity. Ishāq, *Sirat Rasulallah* 271.

deputation comprised some sixty delegates, including fourteen nobles, two leaders, Abd al-Masīh and al-Ayham and the patriarch, Bishop Abū Harithā.[274] In contrast to the deputation from Abyssinia that sought to discern the character of Muhammad, this deputation, came prepared to defend their religion.[275] Nevertheless, when it came time for the delegation to pray Muhammad invited them to use the Masjid al-Nabawi.[276]

One very important aspect of the visit is that the Islamic literature records a brief summary of the arguments the Christians employed in defence of their beliefs. According to Ibn Ishāq's the logic of their belief that Jesus is God and Son of God is based on the miracles he performed. For instance, that Jesus used to raise the dead, heal the sick and could declare the unseen. Among the miracles mentioned are some obscure miracles only found in eastern Christian traditions. These miracles include fashioning clay birds and bringing them to life by breathing into them and that he spoke when just a baby in the cradle. They declared Jesus God's son, because he did not have an earthly father; that he is third of three, because God says, We have done … We have commanded … We have created and We have decreed. Therefore if God was one he would have said, I. Here the Christians are remembered as associating Mary and Jesus with God as part of the Trinity.[277] They responded to Muhammad's call to Islam with the retort, "We were *Muslims* before you were born".[278] This raised the ire of Muhammad who told them, "You cannot be Muslims since you ascribe a son to God, [and] worship the cross".[279]

---

274 Mourad, "Christians in the Sīra", 65. One might expect Bishop Abū Harithā's defence of Christianity to be similar to the arguments of other Byzantine Christians of later generations, that is, Theodore Abū Qurrah.
275 Ibn Kathīr, *Tafsir Al-Qur'ān Al-Azim*, 2:176.
276 Lings, *Muhammad*, 326.
277 Ishāq, *Sirat Rasulallah* 271–2. Bell, *The Origin of Islam*, 10, 9. Referring possibly to terms like *theotokos*. Cf Tarif Khalidi, *The Muslim Jesus: Sayings and Stories in Islamic Literature*, 12 vols, Convergences (Cambridge, MA: Harvard University Press, 2001), 51–218.
278 Mourad, "Christians in the Sīra", 65–6. Cf. Kung, *Islam*, 35. Here Arabic is discussed as a Christian language.
279 Mourad, "Christians in the Sīra", 66. Here citing Ibn Hishām; Ishāq, *Sirat Rasulallah* 272. As-Sallaabee, *The Prophet*, 3:1929–32.

Beyond Al-jāhiliyya

So, began a hearty exchange of positions on faith and doctrine concerning the nature of Jesus as Messiah and Son of God as well as many other tenets. The delegation remained in Medina for a few days. One night during their visit Muhammad reportedly received more than eighty verses for the beginning of *sūrat Āl-'Imrān* as well as three for *sūrat al-qasas* that deal with Christians and their doctrines.[280] These verses could be interpreted as part of the Islamic challenge to the beliefs of *al-jāhiliyya* held by the delegation that the mission of Muhammad intended to correct. The gist of the verses discuss the oneness of God (3):18, the right for only God to be worshipped (3):18, the likeness of Jesus to Adam (3):59, that is, without an earthly father, but rather as commanded by God to "be" (3):47. There is a requisite acceptance of Muhammad as prophet and messenger of God and the need to follow what Muhammad teaches in order to be a believer (3):31. There are verses that chastise Christians for contorting scripture to suit their own wills rather than following clear guidance (3):24.[281] Many of the verses praise Mary as the most virtuous woman (3):42–4. Several verses discuss Jesus as Messiah, affirming his miracles, even his intercession on behalf of some believers (3):49. Yet, the same verses specify unreservedly that the acts Jesus performed were intended as signs for mankind, accomplished only by God's leave (3):45.[282] So too, the Qur'ān makes the point

---

280 Mourad, "Christians in the Sīra", 65–6. *Sūrat al-Qasas* 28:52–5. Cf. Ibn Kathīr, *Tafsir Al-Qur'ān Al-Azim*, 2:107–205.
281 *Tafsir Al-Qur'ān Al-Azim*, 2:111–7. Here there is a concise explanation of the interpretation, *ta'wīl*, of scripture based on verses that are *muhkamāt*, easy to understand, or *mutashābihāt*, difficult to interpret. If verses that are *muhkamāt* are employed to interpret verses that *mutashābihāt* a correct interpretation is possible. However, if the opposite is attempted, it is quite possible to develop an overly esoteric interpretation that may be completely misguided. Only God knows the correct interpretation of the difficult verses (3:7). Verse 3:24 can then be applied directly to Christians and an explanation is given as to how Islam perceives changes developed away from Jesus' original teachings. Cf. 170–1, 176–7.
282 Ibid., 160–1. Jesus' intercession on behalf of "some people" is Ibn Kathir's explanation of the verse, "Held in honour in this world and the Hereafter, and will be one of those near to Allah". Accordingly, this ability to intercede is granted by God. It is not something Jesus has any ability to do without God's leave.

that a true prophet has never called people to pray to them, but rather God is always the focus of worship (3):79.

Famously, the verses reveal the challenge of *mubāhala* to settle the veracity of the message of Muhammad in relation to the beliefs of the deputation (3):60–3. When the delegation received the challenge, they asked for some time to consult.[283] The next day Muhammad arrived with his daughter Fatimah, her husband Ali and their children, Hasan and Hussein. Muhammad spread a large cloak on the ground for the five of them, known as "the People of the Cloak", to stand on. The delegation from Najrān, whose people had previously suffered martyrdom rather than convert to Judaism, responded to Muhammad's challenge by saying, we are not prepared to carry the disagreement so far as *mubāhala*.[284] Now, either they lost their nerve, or the differences between them and Muhammad did not merit putting God to the test. The deputation left on good terms, agreeing a settlement that allowed them the freedom to practise their religion, in exchange for accepting Muhammad as a ruler.[285]

The dramatic challenge of *mubāhala* perhaps overshadows other verses that leave both parties equally committed to their own faith and religion, yet at the same time diffuses any animosity generated by the evident contradictions. The first set of verses outline the duties and limits of the responsibilities of Muhammad towards those who refuse to follow his guidance. These are *sūrat Āl-'Imrān* (3):18–20, where the closing *āya* says, "And say to those who were given the Scriptures (Jews and Christians) and to those who are illiterate (Arab pagans): 'Do you also submit yourselves?' If they do, they are rightly guided; but if they turn away, your duty is only to convey the message".[286] Verse (3):64 opens the way for each generation to discuss the recurrent questions of faith, not as an inherited tradition,

---

283 Lings, *Muhammad*, 326. Ibn Kathīr, *Tafsir Al-Qur'ān Al-Azim*, 2:176–9.
284 Lings, *Muhammad*, 326.
285 Ibid., 326–7. Mourad, "Christians in the Sīra", 66. Abd al-Masīh, one of the delegation leaders said to the bishop that if they wished to remain Christians they should conclude a peace treaty with Muhammad, for they were certain he was certainly a prophet with a genuine message.
286 Ibn Kathīr, *Tafsir Al-Qur'ān Al-Azim*, 2:131.

but experienced. Say: "O people of the Scripture: Come to a common word that is just between us and you, that we worship none but Allah the same, and that we associate no partners with Him, and that none of us shall take others as lords besides Allah".[287] Admittedly a challenging verse for Christians, but one that allows Christians to discuss their submission to God and not just defend a formula of words.

Conclusions

It is hoped that this exercise of reconstructing the image of the communities' extent on the Arab Peninsula and its surrounds during the pre-Islamic period helps provide greater understanding of the *sabab an-nuzūl* and the varying factors that might have influenced their initial meeting with Muhammad and Islam. The Time of Ignorance, *al-jāhiliyya*, is a term Muslims use to describes this period as well as man's condition prior to the arrival of Muhammad and the revelation of the Qur'ān. The term *al-jāhiliyya* describes the way of life, the habits, beliefs and traditions of the people of that time that are out of keeping with God's guidance. However, not everyone from the period was out of keeping with God's guidance. Some were living *islām* if the term is used in its un-reified sense, as submitting to God. The difference between pre-Islamic ignorance and pre-Qur'ānic *islām* are highly nuanced, since submission to God, *islām*, is the same for all times. With the revelation of the Qur'ān, those who follow the true teachings of God are expected to recognize the authority of the teachings of Muhammad and to follow him.

Nevertheless, it is important to note that failure to accept Muhammad does not mean damnation. The Treaty of Medina as well as the agreements with delegations from Najrān and Abyssinia testifies to the fact that allowances for matters of conscience are acceptable, and under such circumstances,

---

287   Ibid., 2:180.

coexistence is preferable. Sincerity, deeds and peaceful intention seem to be key factors governing whether or not those who do not follow Muhammad in *islām* are friend or foe, not adherence to any particular form of creed.

At the dawn of Islam the Jews of Medina gave sanctuary to Muhammad and protection from those who wished to harm him. They failed however, to embrace Muhammad as the chosen prophet with whom they had threatened their neighbours and with whom Islam identifies in their sacred text. In fact, a great deal of the Islamic literature focuses on the inability of the Jews to leave the ways of *al-jāhiliyya* behind. By and large the Jews of Medina and Hijaz worked against Muhammad's attempts to create a new community based on faith in one God, rather than traditional tribal ties. Nevertheless, when the gradual demise of Judaism in the region from Jerusalem to Abyssinia to Yemen is taken into consideration it may be easier to understand their reticence. They certainly paid a very heavy price for their failure to accept Muhammad.

An interesting question concerns why the Jews of the Hijaz, who by all accounts were waiting for a messianic figure, did not migrate to Jerusalem to escape their demise when a Persian army supported by Jewish soldiers captured the city in 614 CE from the Byzantines. In contrast the Jews of the Levant, as People of the Book, adopted an entirely different attitude to Islam following the capture of Jerusalem a few years later. The relationship that ensued demonstrates that enmity between Muslims and Jews need not necessarily prevail. In our modern world, with all its troubles, people have the choice to construct the conditions for peace, whereby citizens of the global *ummah* may respectfully encourage each community to live in harmony.

The Christians of Abyssinia in many ways represent the ideal Qur'ānic Christians. They progressed in faith from one form of monotheism, to the next, from Sabeanism, to Judaism to Christianity and Islam; at least this is how the Islamic sources recount the outcome of the delegation to Medina and the response of King Ashama ibn Abjar. Even those who do not convert to Islam, and this would include the citizens of the Kingdom of Abyssinia, their faithfulness and solidarity to nascent Islam is revered. In fact, their reception of Islam is contrasted with the Jews in the other half of *sūrat al-mā'idah* (5):82 where it says, "And nearest among them in love to the believers wilt thou find those who say, 'We are Christians'".

Beyond Al-jāhiliyya

In addition, there is the *hadīth* from Muhammad, *utruku al-habasha mā tarakūkum* [until the Abyssinians attack you, do not attack them].

Theologically the Abyssinian Christians are devoted Trinitarians following the Tawahedo formula. There is therefore no obvious reason why their reception of the refugees should be any different to any other Christian community. According to Islam, they remained guilty of the sin of *shirk*, by associating partners with God. Yet, as the Islamic literature describes, the king found very little difference between their beliefs and offered friendship. Perhaps, then, the defining factors have more to do with the moral fiber of the king in addition to the social and political factors of the day. Consequently, the paradigm of relations between the first Muslims and the Christians of Abyssinia remains an inspiration and one that today's Christian societies need to cherish and promote.

The ancient Kingdom of Himyar offers another perspective for both Jews and Christians. Here again Judaism replaces the religion of Sabeanism. Within a few generations Christianity threatens the Jewish hegemony. The words of Habsa concerning the deeds of her father reveal volumes, even if the deeds till this day lie hidden. In an article written by Michael Lecker, there is a note that Dhū Nuwās came to Najrān after the Jews there complained that the Christians were trying to dominate them.[288] Could there have been attacks on synagogues, intimidation, or incidents of forced conversion that have gone unrecorded? Could the reign of Lakhnī'a Dhū Shanātir, installed by Abyssinia, explain the ferocity of the attacks against the Christians at this time? These questions might provide avenues for further study. Although the literature does not describe the levels of sectarianism as *jahl*, certainly the extension of tribal warfare to religious persecution qualifies as an aspect of *al-jāhiliyya*.

The story of the delegation from Najrān to Medina marked the first recorded in-depth exchange of views in defence of Christian dogma.[289] This meeting should be considered in light of the previous sectarianism

---

288 Lecker, "The Conversion of Himyar to Judaism and the Jewish Banū Hadl of Medina", 636.
289 Cf. Griffith, *The Bible in Arabic*, 35–6. Griffith makes the compelling argument that Islamic criticism of Christian beliefs is in response to extant Christian views

between Jews and Christians, as well as the provocation in the Year of the Elephant. The *sīra* and *tafsīr* material attest that the delegation, which included Bishop Abū Harithā, was anything but a diplomatic exchange of niceties, or one political entity acknowledging the rise of a new regional leader. This delegation defended the Christian faith in earnest. The views of the Christians from Najrān inspired more than eighty verses of the Qur'ān. The image of the exchange is heated, not reflective. They respond to Muhammad's call to Islam with their own declaration that they were *Muslims* before Muhammad was born. In spite of their differences the delegation departed on amicable terms, agreeing a treaty that allowed them to keep all of their property, run their own affairs and practise their own faith, *shirk* and all.

---

represented by Melkite, Nestorians, Jacobites and Ethiopian confessions spreading through the Arab peninsula at the dawn of Islam.

CHAPTER 3

Resisting the Construct: Post-Conquest Christian Theological Responses to Islam

Lā ilāha 'illa Allāh
[There is no God but God]

Introduction

This chapter examines the post-conquest Arabic-speaking Christian responses to aspects of the theoretical construct of Christianity created by traditional Qur'ānic *tafsīr*.[1] In specific terms the chapter examines how Arabic-speaking Christians responded to accusations of "excesses in your religion" that the traditional commentary draws attention to in *sūrat an-Nisā'* (4):171. These "excesses" include the Incarnation or Sonship of Jesus and the description of God in Trinitarian terms.[2] In order to address this task effectively this chapter briefly outlines the consolidation of Islam on the Arab peninsula following the death of Muhammad and the outward expansion of Islam throughout the conquest period. From here an overview is offered of the types of theological reactions to the conquest as Christians adjust to the new political and social reality as People of the Book.

---

1   The term Levant is used here to describe the region covering: Gaza, Palestine to Sidon, and Syria.
2   Griffith, *The Church in the Shadow*, 93. Cf. "Christian Theology in Islamic Terms", in *Thinking the Divine in Interreligious Encounter*, eds Norbert Hintersteiner and François Bousquet (Amsterdam: Rodopi 2012), 151.

One of the key features of the conquest is that Christians in the region of all denominations gradually adopted Arabic as their *lingua franca*. This presented their religious leaders with a dilemma, since the new language, closely linked to Islam, systematically excluded the meanings desired for expressing theological truths previously expressed in Greek and Syriac. In addition, they faced the challenge to prove that the standard Christian teachings, namely the Incarnation or Sonship of Jesus and descriptions of God in Trinitarian parlance, are found in the Bible and are not the product of Byzantine emperors or Church Councils.[3] This chapter examines three texts by three Chalcedonian scholars who lived between the early ninth to the thirteenth centuries of the Abbasid Dynasty (*c.* 749–1258 CE). These interlocutors are Theodore Abū Qurrah (d. 820 CE), Sulaymān ibn Hasan al-Ghazzī (b. 940 CE) and Paul of Antioch (*c.* 1200 CE). This chapter explores the continuity and diversity of their theological and rational arguments in light of the social and political environment in which they lived.

Setting the Scene: From the Death of Muhammad to Al-Quds

It had been barely two years since the delegation from Najrān visited the prophet Muhammad and prayed in al-Masjid an-Nabawi.[4] On 8 June 632 CE, as Usāma prepared to lead the Muslim army north to Syria, Muhammad at the age of sixty-three, succumbed to an ailment that had plagued him for some time.[5] Following Muhammad's death Abu Bakr is reported to

---

3   *The Church in the Shadow*, 94–5. Cf. "Muslim and Church Councils; the Apology of Theodore Abu Qurrah", in *The Beginnings of Christian Theology in Arabic: Muslim-Christian Encounters in the Early Islamic Period* (Hampshire, Burlington: Ashgate Publishing Limited, 2002), 274.
4   Mourad, "Christians in the Sīra", 65.
5   Lings, *Muhammad*, 343. Cf. As-Sallaabee, *The Prophet*, 3:1606. Vol. 3. 1606. As-Sallaabbee records that Muhammad acquired this illness after tasting poisoned meat in Khaibar.

have said, "O people, whoso hath been wont to worship Muhammad-verily Muhammad is dead; and whoso hath wont to worship God-verily God is living and dieth not". Then Abu Bakr recited from *sūrat Āl-'Imrān*, "Muhammad is nothing but an apostle. Apostles have passed away before him. Can it be that if he were to die or be killed you would turn back on your heels? He who turns back does no harm to God and God will reward the grateful".[6]

Almost immediately the orphaned community faced some very serious challenges that would test their resolve to understand and follow the teachings of Muhammad as well as maintain their newly formed alliance to the *ummat al-mu'minīn*. The challenges were threefold; record the hitherto oral Qur'ān; preserve the *hadīth*; and stave off the dissension to Islamic rule on the Arab Peninsula described as the Wars of Apostasy.[7] Muhammad's dearest friend and companion Abu Bakr valiantly met these challenges, followed by his successors 'Umar ibn Al-Khattāb and 'Uthmān ibn 'Affān (632–56 CE).[8]

The Apocalypse or Days of Redemption

For centuries Christians in the Levant lived under the confident vision *in hoc signo vinces*, "under this sign you will conquer". This Christian battle cry heralded back to the days of Emperor Constantine who encouraged Christians

---

6   Lings, *Muhammad*, 345.
7   Ibid. Here Ling identifies Musaylimah of the Bani Hanīfah, Tulayhah a chief of the Bani Asad, Aswad ibn Ka'b of the Yemen, along with Sajāh, who claimed to be a prophetess. Cf. Leone Caetani, "The Art of War of the Arabs, and the Supposed Religious Fervour of the Arab Conquerors", in *The Expansion of the Early Islamic State*, ed. Fred M Donner, The Formation of the Islamic World (Hants: Ashgate Publishing Limited, 2007), 9. Caetani makes the point that within a very short period of time the very same Arabs who were suppressed by Muhammad's army during the Wars of Apostasy (*Ridda*) joined those fighting for an Islamic empire.
8   Fred M. Donner, *Muhammad and the Believers: At the Origins of Islam* (Cambridge, MA: The Belknap Press of Harvard University Press, 2010), 97–106.

to link political and military success with God's favour.⁹ However, as the Muslim army advanced, the seismic shift in fortunes prompted many to consider the conquest in apocalyptic or eschatological terms.¹⁰ In fact the earliest historical accounts of the conquest originate amongst the non-Chalcedonian communities, who perceived part of the success of the conquest due to the errors of the Chalcedonians and therefore perhaps, justification of their own Christological formulations.¹¹

There are several theories regarding the success of the Arab invaders. Bousquet suggests the reasons for the swift success of the Arabs were multi-faceted and included the poor state of the Byzantine army in contrast with the invaders. Bousquet also considered the promise of the spoils of war a strong motivational factor, thus reducing the image of the invaders to marauding mercenaries.¹² Gil considers religious motivation a key factor of the conquest, as Muslim soldiers may have believed, after the death of the prophet, that they were waging war in the "End of Days" to impose the mastery of the new religion on the world.¹³ Caetani downplays religious zealousness as a driving force behind all but the earliest followers of Muhammad, while suggesting hunger and material poverty as the real catalysts.¹⁴

Bell posits that local interests saw the conquest as potentially beneficial to their own concerns, citing the fact that Jews in the vicinity of Jerusalem acted as guides for the Muslim army in retaliation for sectarian abuse

---

9   John C. Lamoreaux, *Theodore Abū Qurrah*, trans. John C. Lamoreaux, vol. 1 (Provo, UT: Bringham Young University Press, 2005), xviii. Cf. M A Smith, *From Christ to Constantine* (Leicester: Inter-Varsity Press, 1976), 170–1.
10 Cragg, *The Arab Christian: A History of the Middle East*, 52, 56. Cf. Griffith, *The Church in the Shadow*, 24–5. Cf. Hoyland, *Seeing Islam* 13, 26–31, 57, 257–335, 526–31.
11 Walter E. Kaegi, "Initial Byzantine Reactions to the Arab Conquest", in *The Expansion of the Early Islamic State*, ed. Fred M. Donner, The Formation of the Classical Islamic World (Hants: Ashgate Publishing Limited, 2007), 122–3.
12 G. H. Bousquet, "Some Critical and Sociological Remarks on the Arab Conquest and the Theories Proposed on This", ibid., The Formation of the Islamic World, 20.
13 Moshe Gil, *A History of Palestine, 634–1099* [Erets Yisra'el ba-tekufah ha-Muslemit ha-rishonah (638–1099)], trans. Mrs Ethel Broido, vol. 1 (Cambridge: Cambridge University Press, 1993), History, 12–13.
14 Caetani, "The Art of War", 9–10, 11–12.

suffered following Heraclius's recapture of Jerusalem.[15] In fact Gil makes an excellent argument that the Jews of Palestine may have regarded the Muslim conquest as a harbinger of the messianic "Days of Redemption".[16] Sebeos suggests that earlier generations of displaced Jews approached the Muslims for aid and "informed them of their blood relationship through scripture".[17] It is interesting to note that under the Covenant of 'Umar Jews were not initially allowed to live in Jerusalem in order to placate Christian concerns. However, after a period of three years the Jews were allowed not only to return and live in Jerusalem, but one was appointed Governor.[18] This ended a 500-year-old Roman/Byzantine ban that was only briefly interrupted a generation before with the aid of the Persians.[19]

Donner notes that the invading armies employed a simple strategy that relied heavily on winning the hearts and minds of rural communities, before eliciting their support to communicate with urban populations. Consequently, the generous terms offered to the People of the Book that submitted to Muslim rule, including religious freedom, thus ensured that heavy fighting only took place on rare occasion. These terms required communities to pay the *jizyah* tax and not "aid the enemies God".[20] There is certainly more to the story of the conquest than Muhammad's great commission, for what other reasons would inspire even the Christian tribes of the Judhām, Lakhm and Taghlib to join the conquering army?[21] The period of conquest represents a fascinating aspect of Islamic history that will need to be set-aside for present purposes. Whatever the deciding factors may

---

15   Bell, *The Origin of Islam*, 10, 164–5.
16   Gil, *A History of Palestine*, 1, 61–4.
17   Sebeos, *The Armenian History Attributed to Sebeos*, trans. R. W. Thomson, vol. 31 (Liverpool: Liverpool University Press, 1999), Part 1, 94–8.
18   Donner, *Muhammad and the Believers*, 114. Donner translates the Armenian word for *prince* as governor. See further Sebeos, *Armenian History*, 31, Part 1, 103.
19   Hoyland, *Seeing Islam* 13, 127. Donner, *Muhammad and the Believers*, 51, 68–74, 297.
20   *Muhammad and the Believers*, 117, 21–4. Cf. Gil, *A History of Palestine*, 1, 140–2. Cf. Sebeos, *Armenian History*, 31, Part 1, xxvi–xxx, 94–113, 32–54.
21   Trimingham, *Christianity among the Arabs*. 124. Donner, *Muhammad and the Believers*, 114, 24.

have been, there is little disputing that the invading Islamic army rapidly conquered the Levant and with lasting repercussions.

People of the Book, Dhimmitude or Détente

Once the military campaigns concluded, Christians and Jews of all denominations, as People of the Book, benefitted by a certain *dhimmī* [protected] status that guaranteed protection. As a result, quite possibly for demographic reasons, Christians who for decades outnumbered the Muslim population in vast areas of the Middle East were relatively free to govern themselves and practise their own religion in exchange for social and political submission.[22] In a sense, the conquest of Islam throughout the Levant provided an accord between the People of the Book and the ruling Muslim community not dissimilar to the Treaty of Medina, or the accord between Muslims and the Christians of Najrān.[23] It is now accepted that the spread of Islam did not require the forced conversion of Christians, or Jews, nor were Christians exiled from their lands.[24] Interestingly, Donner surmises that part of the reason for this accord may be that acceptance of Muhammad as prophet was not a dominating expression of the conquest.

22   Cragg, *The Arab Christian: A History of the Middle East*, 56–7. Cf. Laura Veccia Vaglieri, "The Patriarchal and Umayyad Caliphates", in *The Cambridge History of Islam*, eds P. M. Holt, Ann K S Lambton, and Bernard Lewis, The Central Islamic Lands from Pre-Islamic Times to the First World War (Cambridge: Cambridge University Press, 1995), 64–5. Cf. Lewis, *The Jews of Islam*, 42–3.
23   Ali Muhammad As-Sallaabee, *The Biography of Abu Bakr as-Siddeeq* [Sira Abu Bakr As-Sideeq], trans. Faisal Shafeeq (Riyadh: Darussalam, 2007), 690–4. M. A. Muhibbu-Din, "Ahl Al-Kitab and Religious Minorities in the Islamic State: Historical Context and Contemporary Challenges", *Journal of Muslim Minority Affairs* 20, no. 1 (2000): 116, 22. Cf. Gil, *A History of Palestine*, 1, 114.
24   Joshua Starr, *The Jews in the Byzantine Empire 641–1204*, ed. Nikos A Bees, Texte Und Forschungen Zur Byzantinisch-Neugriechischen Philologie (Hants: Gregg International Publishers Limited, 1969), 1–11, 83–5. Richard W. Bulliet, *Conversion to Islam in the Medieval Period* (Cambridge, MA: Harvard University Press, 1979), 1, 3, 41, 106–7. Bousquet, "Some Critical and Sociological Remarks", 15–16.

As evidence Donner examines the coinage from the period that inscribes the first half of the *shahādah* [testimony of faith], without mention of Muhammad.[25] In contrast to *tafsīr* literature, this idea finds support from the testimony of escaped prisoners of war who claimed their captors believed Muhammad was calling Arabs, as children of Abraham, back to monotheism.[26] Undoubtedly however, for ruling Christians, the conquest was an outright disaster. They lost power and control of society and were set on an equal footing with adversaries whom they once ruled.

As one might expect, co-operation between the newly subject people and their overlords varied from one community to the next.[27] For instance, there is archaeological evidence to suggest that Christians and Muslim occasionally shared sacred space.[28] For the People of the Book in general and specifically for minority Jewish and Christian communities, who had been previously suppressed by their co-religionist, the Islamic conquest brought a modicum of stability and relief.[29] In fact this new parity benefitted greater ecumenical scholarship whereby non-Chalcedonian Christian communities were free to make contributions to the development of Arabic Christian literature.[30] It is very important to keep in mind that the degree of toleration exhibited by Muslims rulers stands in marked contrast to the sectarian strife that preceded it during the conquest of Jerusalem by the Persians in around 614 CE and the subsequent reconquest by Heraclius in around 629 CE, or indeed the circumstances surrounding the pre-Islamic massacres in Najrān and Himyar discussed earlier.[31] This is not to say, however, that the

---

25 Donner, *Muhammad and the Believers*, 71–2, 111–5.
26 Hoyland, *Seeing Islam* 13, 128–9.
27 Gil, *A History of Palestine*, 1, 140.
28 Donner, *Muhammad and the Believers*, 115. Bell, *The Origin of Islam*, 10, 170.
29 Hoyland, *Seeing Islam* 13, 181–2. Cf. Griffith, *The Church in the Shadow*, 11, 12, 27. Cf. Will Durant, *The Age of Faith*, 11 vols, vol. 4, The Story of Civilization (New York: MJF Books, 1950), 218–9.
30 Gutas, *Greek Thought*, 15. Cf. Thomas W. Ricks, *Early Arabic Christian Contributions to Trinitarian Theology: The Development of the Doctrine of the Trinity in an Isamic Milieu*, 1st edn, Emerging Scholars (Minneapolis, MN: Fortress Press, 2013), 4–5.
31 Gafni, *Land, Center and Diaspora*, 21, 64–72. Cf. Lewis, *The Jews of Islam*, 3, 8. Cf. Katz, "The Persian Conquest of Jerusalem", 13–20. CF. Maher Y. Abu-Munshar,

People of the Book did not on occasion face severe persecution. In simple terms, they did. The work of Hoyland, Friedman, Yousef Courbage and Philippe Fargues, for example, testify that on occasion and generally as part of other extenuating social and political and economic circumstances, Christians and Jews did face severe persecution at the hands of those from whom they were promised protection.[32] Conversely, it must be noted that under Islamic rule many People of the Book, due to their protected status, retained and rose to high rank in their professions as doctors, politicians, merchants and scribes.[33] Nevertheless, Christians faced an ever-increasing challenge to maintain their own faith communities in the face of social and theological challenges that were responsible for the slow but constant diminution of Christianity in the Holy Land.[34]

Early Arab-Speaking Christian Response to Islam

For some time, the written and spoken languages of Christians of the Levant following the period of conquest remained the traditional languages of Greek, Armenian, Syriac and Coptic. These languages represent the liturgical languages of what would become the Coptic, Chalcedonian, Nestorian, and Jacobite Christian denominations. The Arabization and Islamicizing of the culture accompanied with the adoption of Arabic as the everyday language took generations.[35]

Islamic Jerusalem and Its Christians: A History of Tolerance and Tensions (London: I. B. Tauris, 2013), 87–97.

32 Griffith, *The Church in the Shadow*, 148–9. Cf. fn. 60–4.
33 Ibid., 17–18. Cf. Hoyland, *Seeing Islam* 13, 339. Cf. Lawrence Conrad, "Ibn Butlān in Bilad Al-Shām: The Career of a Travelling Christian Physician", in *Syrian Christians Unser Islam: The First Thousand Years*, ed. David Thomas (Leiden: Brill, 2001), 131–58.
34 Cragg, *The Arab Christian: A History of the Middle East*, 58. Cf. Bulliet, *Conversion to Islam*, 41, 107. Cf. Griffith, *The Church in the Shadow*, 147–9.
35 Cf. *The Church in the Shadow*, 23–74. Cf. Hoyland, *Seeing Islam* 13, 67, 92, 480.

Beginning as early as the first Abbasid century (*c.* 750 CE), Christian scholars in Palestine and elsewhere began to write in Arabic.[36] The first tracts were translations of catechist type literature designed for everyday worship. Over time a second genre of more apologetic literature developed whose dual purpose was not only to defend the particular creedal formula of one denomination against other Christian formulae, but also to provide reassuring arguments to Christians tempted to convert to Islam.[37] These tracts were composed with an air of confidence with full knowledge that Muslims may learn of such works. Sometimes the works suggested that any right-thinking Muslim would understand the reasonableness of their arguments and convert to Christianity, if it were not for fear of losing their position in society.[38] Perhaps coincidentally, these types of responses echo the sentiments Christians are said to have expressed when rejecting Muhammad's invitations to Islam.

Early Arabic-speaking Christians drew upon an array of tools in order to recommend the soundness of their doctrines. These tools include rational arguments based on Greek philosophy, clever analogies and scriptural defences from the Old and New Testaments as well as from the Qur'ān and from Islamic idiom.[39] These scriptural defences provided several functions in support of the Christian understanding of the oneness of God, by responding to accusations of "excesses" in religion often by challenging or inverting Muslims arguments against Christian doctrines.[40]

---

36 Sidney H Griffith, "The Monks of Palestine and the Growth of Christian Literature in Arabic", *The Muslim World* 78, no. 1 (1988): 2.
37 Ibid., 4–6. "First Christian Arabic Theologians", 63.
38 "The Monks of Palestine", 4. Cf. *The Church in the Shadow*, 38. Cf. L L. D. William Muir K. C. S. I., *The Apology of Al Kindy: Written at the Court of Al Māmūn, (A. H. 215, A. D. 830) in Defence of Christianity against Islam* (Charleston: Bibliolife, 2014; repr., Bibliolife LLC), 2, 4–8, 11, 20–2, 58–9.
39 Griffith, "First Christian Arabic Theologians", 81. Cf. "Christian Theology in Islamic Terms", 153.
40 Ricks, *Early Arabic Christian Contributions*, 171.

On the Triune Nature of God

An excellent example of scriptural apology is offered by one of the earliest Arab Christian works, *On the Triune Nature of God*.[41] Here the anonymous author expresses a defence of the concept of Trinity, the Messiah in the history of salvation, the doctrine of the Incarnation, and the Great Commission, in terms that are both striking in their simplicity and ingenious in their theology.[42] The text is replete with expressions of tenets of the Christian faith that are in sympathy with Islam including the ongoing debate amongst the Muslim *Mutakallimūn* over the Divine attributes.[43] For example the anonymous author writes, "To thee (shall we) return; Thou art almighty, to Thee be the praise, O God, Creator of the heavens and the earth, and all that is therein by thy Word and Spirit".[44] The author employs Islamic idiom to define the basic similarity and difference between Christian and Muslims as; "we do not distinguish God from his Word and His Spirit".[45] This of course echoes *sūrat an-Nisāʾ* (4):171, where the Qurʾān describes Jesus as the Messiah, an apostle of God, His Word and a Spirit proceeding from Him.[46] A further example illustrates the author's focus on the grammar of the Qurʾān to illustrate the

---

41 Anonymous, *An Arabic Version of the Acts of the Apostles and the Seven Catholic Epistles*, ed. Margaret Dunlop Gibson, trans. Gibson, 1st edn, vol. VII, Studia Sinaitica (Piscataway, NJ: Gorgias Press, 2003). Cf. Mark N. Swanson, "An Apology for the Christian Faith", in *The Orthodox Church in the Arab World, 700–1700: An Anthology of Sources*, eds Samuel Noble & Alexander Treiger, The Orthodox Christian Series (DeKalb: Northern Illinois Press, 2014), 40–59.

42 "The Apology", 41–3. Note the use of the well-known pairing of Islamic names for God as a triad, "You are the Merciful-in-Deed, the All-merciful, the Merciful-in-Self.

43 Richard M. Frank, "Attribute, Attribution, and Being: Three Islamic Views", in *Classical Islamic Theology: The Ashʿarites*, ed. Dimitri Gutas (Aldershot, Hampshire: Ashgate, 2008), Chapter V, 258–78. Cf. Griffith, "Christian Theology in Islamic Terms". 153–5.

44 Anonymous, *An Arabic Version*, VII, 2. Cf. *sūrat al-māʾidah* (5):18, 48, 105. Other translations or paraphrase of the phrase اليك المصير reveal other verses. The other phrases leading up to "*by thy Word and Spirit*" also have Qurʾānic parallels.

45 Ibid., 3. Frank, "Attribute, Attribution", 261. In contrast the Muslim scholar Abū l'Hudhayl Jubbāʾī separated the act of the creation from the thing, *shāy*, being created.

46 *The Holy Qurʾān*, 271–2.

use of the first person plural, rather than the singular, when God creates man, "*We* created man in misery and *We* have opened the gates of Heaven with water pouring down, and have said, And now are ye come unto *Us* alone, as *We* created you at first".[47] Drawing direct parallels with what is identified as excesses in the Qur'ān the author reminds Muslims, "Ye have said that ye believe in God and His Word and the Holy Ghost, so do not reproach us, O men! That we believe in God and His Word and His Spirit: and we worship God in His Word and His Spirit, one God and one Lord and one creator".[48] The author surmises "that this is our faith and our testimony".[49]

Further, *On the Triune Nature of God* draws upon several themes that later interlocutors will employ. The text makes use of interesting analogies of Jesus as begotten in the manner of the sun begetting rays, the mind words, or fire heat. In each case the author notes that one could not exist before the thing begotten, nor is the use of the term begotten by Christians anything like begotten in a worldly sense.[50] The author humbly acknowledges that Christians do not understand exactly how this is, as the ways of God are beyond human comprehension.[51] Perhaps a key strength of the text is the fact that a little humility goes a long way. Moreover, the text draws upon miracle stories found in scripture, Christian lore, as well as the Qur'ān, such as creating birds from clay. There is also the example of Jesus sending his disciples the gift of the *Paraclete*, here meaning the Holy Spirit, something the author says only God can do.[52] An interesting enculturation of the author's apology concerns the use of the word "beloved" in place of the word "begotten" when describing the baptism of Jesus. The author has the Father bear witness from Heaven, "This is my *beloved son*, in whom I am well pleased".[53] These arguments attempt by way of testimony and use

---

47 Anonymous, *An Arabic Version*, VII, 5. Here the author is citing *sūrat al-balad* (90): 4, *sūrat al-qamar* (54): 11, and *sūrat al-an'ām* (6):94.
48 Ibid., 6. Sidney H Griffith, "The Melkites and the Muslims: The Qur'ān, Christology, and Arab Orthodoxy", *Al-Qantara* XXXIII 2, no. July-September (2012): 430.
49 Anonymous, *An Arabic Version*, VII, 6.
50 Ibid., 5.
51 Ibid., 5.
52 Ibid., 12, 13. From (*sūrat al-mā'idah* (5):110), 34 fn. 132b-133b.
53 Ibid., 6.

of Christian and Islamic idiom to build a bridge between Islamic and Christian understanding of faith in one God.

Graeco-Arabic Translation Movement

Today some tend to underestimate the influence of Greek science and philosophy on cultures outside the Byzantium Empire during the early medieval period. However, Greek studies wielded remarkable influence stretching from Spain to India.[54] One of the most influential facets of Greek influence is seen in the popularity of the Greek translation movement, which in point of fact began long before the Islamic conquest.[55] From the dawn of Christianity, Greek philosophy had a pervasive influence on Christian theology. In addition Christian missionaries with Greek philosophical underpinnings aided the dissemination of Greek scholarship wherever Christianity spread. Christians, especially from what was emerging as the Nestorian formulation of Christianity, were at the forefront of the early translation movement in Baghdad.[56] Yet, the diffusion of Greek culture, the process of Hellenization that took place across Persia and into Asia, was not dependent on any particular religious, or ethnic grouping, but took place over several centuries and was driven by many factors.[57]

With the Islamic conquest and with the adoption of Arabic as the main language by Christians, a social phenomenon took place across lands controlled by the Abbasid Dynasty that is on par with the Italian Renaissance, or the scientific enlightenment that occurred during the sixteenth and seventeenth centuries.[58] This is the Graeco-Arabic translation movement that centred in Baghdad and blossomed under caliph al-Mansur and his son

---

54 David C. Lindberg, *The Beginnings of Western Science: The European Scientific Tradition in Philosophical, Religious, and Institutional Context, Prehistory to A. D. 1450*, 2nd edn (Chicago: University of Chicago Press, 2007), 163, 66.
55 Ibid., 163–4.
56 Ibid., 165. Cf. Ricks, *Early Arabic Christian Contributions*, 6.
57 Lindberg, *The Beginnings of Western Science*, 165. Cf. Gutas, *Greek Thought*, 7.
58 *Greek Thought*, 8.

al-Mahdi. They commissioned the translation of Aristotle's Topics (On the Art of Argumentation).⁵⁹ In turn, the translation of Greek works into Arabic helped Muslims formulate a defence of their beliefs using similar language and concepts.⁶⁰ For more than two centuries the Graeco-Arabic translation movement captured and held the attention of people from all levels of society, from caliphs and engineers, to theologians, across all religious lines and linguistic demarcations.⁶¹ The reasons for its popularity defy general explanations such as altruistic motives of Syriac-speaking Christians or the open-mindeness of a few rulers who saw themselves as the intellectual descendants of the ancient Greeks and Persians.⁶² The need to transform the new Islamic empire from tribal rule to centralized State rule should not be underestimated.⁶³ The increasing requirements to manage the empire required greater sophistication than the followers of Muhammad could ever have envisioned. Perhaps it is fair to say that each facet of the emerging empire saw within the Greek classics their own reasons for sustained interest, including proselytizing.⁶⁴ By the end of the tenth century scholars from the extant spectrum of society translated almost all of the Greek books including works on mathematics, geometry, medicine, astrology, botany, wisdom sayings and all the works of Aristotle available in the Near East.⁶⁵

Bayt al-Hikma, House of Wisdom

One of the early seminal figures in the Graeco-Arabic translation movement is the Nestorian Christian physician Hunayn Ibn Ishāq (d. 873 CE).⁶⁶ Hunayn Ibn Ishāq administered a school of translation in the famous Baghdad library *bayt al-hikma* [*The House of Wisdom*], with his son, Ishāq ibn Hunayn and

---

59   Lindberg, *The Beginnings of Western Science*, 168–71.
60   Ricks, *Early Arabic Christian Contributions*, 9–10.
61   Gutas, *Greek Thought*, 3–5.
62   Ibid. Ricks, *Early Arabic Christian Contributions*, 9–10. Lindberg, *The Beginnings of Western Science*, 170.
63   *The Beginnings of Western Science*, 168.
64   Ibid., 170–1.
65   Gutas, *Greek Thought*, 1.
66   Ibid., 2, 14, 109, 24, 33–6. Griffith, *The Church in the Shadow*, 119.

nephew, Hubaysh. Together they adopted a method of translation that differed from other translators. They did not translate word for word, *ad verbum*, but rather sought to ascertain the meaning of the text, offer a translation *ad sensum*.[67] No doubt this method made the consumption of the translated material more accessible to the reader. Another really interesting figure from this early period is Abū Yusūf Ya'qūb b. Ishāq al-Kindī (d. 873).[68] He is described as the first Arabic Muslim philosopher.[69] It is thought al-Kindī was born in Basra, but moved at an early age to Baghdad where he received his education. He was a contemporary of Hunayn Ibn Ishāq and is thought to be a direct descendant of Imr al-Qais, the poet discussed in Chapter 2, and al-Ash'ath b. Qays, a king of the Kinda tribe, and a companion of Muhammad.[70] In addition to the many works translated by Al-Kindī there are over 300 of his own writings recorded by the tenth-century book merchant Ibn al-Nadīm in *Al fihrist*, chief amongst these is *On First Philosophy*.[71]

Ilm al-kalām, Theological Discourse

One exciting consequence of the translation movement is the opportunity afforded Muslim and Christian scholars to draw upon Neoplatonic or Aristotelian logic as a common vehicle for *kalām* [discourse].[72] This *kalām* facilitated the systematic defence of aspects of Christian faith like

67   Ibid., 141–150. Cf. Lindberg, *The Beginnings of Western Science*, 171–2.
68   Griffith, "First Christian Arabic Theologians", 81.
69   Peter Adamson, *Al-Kindī*, ed. Brian Davies, vol. 8, Great Medieval Thinkers (New York: Oxford University Press, 2007), 3. Cf. Griffith, "Christian Theology in Islamic Terms", 165–6. Cf. Adamson, *Al-Kindī*, 8, 52. This Muslim Al-Kindī should not to be confused with the Nestorian Al Kindy (Al-Kindī) discussed above by William Muir who also participated in the translation movement.
70   *Al-Kindī*, 8, 4, 5. Cf. Tony Abboud, *Al-Kindi: The Father of Arab Philosophy*, ed. Munir A. Shaikh, Great Muslim Philosphers and Scientists of the Middle Ages (New York: Rosen, 2006), 12–30.
71   Adamson, *Al-Kindī*, 8, 7, 9.
72   Griffith, "First Christian Arabic Theologians", I 67, 75; III 161. Cf. "Christian Theology in Islamic Terms", 151, 55. "Faith and Reason in Christian Kalām: Theodore Abū Qurrah on Discerning the True Religion", in *Christian Arabic Apologetics During the Abbasad Period (750–1258)*, eds Samir Khalil Samir and Jørgen S. Nielsen (Leiden: Brill, 1994), 1–6.

the concept of the Trinity and Incarnation just as Muslims from both the Mu'tazilite and Ash'arite traditions developed the tools necessary to grapple with important Islamic themes including the conundrum of absolute *tawhīd* in light of the multitude of *sifāt Allah* [divine attributes].[73] Yet describing Neoplatonic logic or reasoning as a common language requires qualification. It is true Muslims and Christians both found Greek logic a valuable tool to augment the expression of their respective faiths. Nevertheless, it is critically important to understand that Muslims and Christians both employed logic to different ends.[74] In fact for Muslims one of the pitfalls of using Greek philosophical terms in their theological discourse was the threat of being accused of defining their religion in similar terms as Christians. This problem is highlighted in the writings of as-Sahrastānī against his co-religionists' discussion of the divine attributes.[75] Similarly the Neoplatonic body of thought associated with Jahm ibn Safwān (d.746) drew the wrath of both Mu'tazilite and the school of Islamic law associated with Ahmad ibn Hanbal, because it was perceived that he was willing to engage in independent reasoning, *ijtihād*, with Christians using common philosophical conceptions in contrast with basic Islamic principles.[76] This problem underscores this present author's thesis. For all the theological apologetics, for all the *kalām*, very little can be classed as an attempt to embark upon a mutual exploration of our experience of God.[77] This represents both a challenge and an opportunity.

It would seem that one of the root obstacles to understanding one another is be found in the different ways Muslims and Christians derive authoritative knowledge of God. Traditionally for Muslims true knowledge of God

---

73 *The Church in the Shadow*, 17–19. Ricks, *Early Arabic Christian Contributions*, 1, 11. Cf. Richard M. Frank, *Beings and Their Attributes* (Albany: State University of New York Press, 1978), 8–28.
74 Griffith, *The Church in the Shadow*, 19. Taneli Kukkonen, "Al-Ghazālī on the Signification of Names" *Vivarium* 48 (2010): 55, 58, 62, 74.
75 Griffith, "First Christian Arabic Theologians", 80–1, fn. 79.
76 Ibid., 81–2. Cf. Gibrīl Fouād Haddād, *The Four Imams and Their Schools* (London: Muslim Academic Trust, 2007), 363–5.
77 Griffith, "Christian Theology in Islamic Terms", 155. Griffith notes the degree of mutual influence is debatable.

comes from reading and understanding the Qurʾān.[78] That is through *tafsīr*. Christians, on the other hand, believe they can derive authoritative knowledge of God by use of their own reasoning faculties.[79] Another way of looking at the difference is to consider that Christians are by tradition quite content to think of theology as faith seeking answers, but for Muslims *ʿilm al-kalām* [theological discourse], should lead one to faith, since all the primary doctrines of Islam are held to be rationally demonstrable.[80] Therefore the discourse between Muslims and Christians at this time should be seen very much as a product of the ongoing renaissance of learning and mutual exploration through the science of Greek philosophy in light of their competing faith claims. Rather than suggest definitive solutions, *kalām* literature gives *ishārāt* [points] to meanings requiring an understanding of the cultural milieu of the interlocutors who themselves struggled to cross multi-dimensional bridges between faith, experience, tradition, intent and understanding.[81] It would appear that even the best intended efforts to communicate differing beliefs between faiths faced a certain disconnect between the limits of empathy and the barriers constructed by social conditioning, or theoretical constructs, despite sharing a common language and terminology. This is due to the fact that the application of such terms, tends to reflect the differing perspective of both communities. Therefore, a point of convergence is nearly impossible since the participants intend primarily to restate their faith claims without examining what truth the other's faith may impart to them.[82] Dall'Oglio describes this seemingly insurmountable problem (see Chapter 5) as the dialogue of the deaf. Fortunately, in spite of the difficulties of achieving a common understanding, Griffith captures the attractiveness of using Aristotelian logic when Abū Qurrah cites the words of an adversary who says, "Persuade me not from your Isaiah or Matthew, for whom I have not the slightest regard, but from compelling acknowledged, common conceptions".[83]

78 "First Christian Arabic Theologians", 81.
79 Ibid., 78, 80–1. Frank, "Attribute, Attribution", 275.
80 "Kalām", 18–19, 36–7.
81 "Hearing and Saying", 6.
82 Griffith, *The Church in the Shadow*, 18–19.
83 Ibid., 94.

A major theological characteristic of the Christian works going back to the writings of John of Damascus is that they consciously integrated a notable degree of Islamic idiom with reasoning, especially through the use of terms found in the divine attributes, *sifāt Allah*, as expressed in the *al-asmā' al-husnā* [*Beautiful Names*]. These terms were frequently used to demonstrate that the divine attributes of *essence* and *action* may be reduced to three irreducible substantial attributes: *mawjūd* [existing], *hayy* [living], and *nātiq* [speaking].[84] In turn, Christians identify these substantial attributes as the *thalātha aqānīm* [three hypostases], of the Trinity. Furthermore, through discussion of the divine attributes and the application of the rules of Arabic grammar Christian scholars attempted to demonstrate to Muslims the reasonableness of their belief in God's oneness, in light of His multiple attributes.[85]

Three Arabic-Speaking Christian Scholars

The three early Arabic-speaking scholars examined below were chosen from a possible selection of more than a dozen scholars from the Abbasid period whose writings are still extant. They were prolific writers and leaders of their respective Chalcedonian communities whose writings portray scriptural and rational defences of their faith. This research examines Chalcedonian or Melkite Christian scholars, since their creedal formula is similar to western Christianity and might therefore be more readily understood.

Although not devoid of sectarian tensions, the works of Theodore Abū Qurrah provide interesting insights into the time when *ahl al-kitāb* as *ahl adh-dhimma* could consider the new Islamic centres of Damascus and Baghdad

---

84 Ibid., 95–6. Frank, *Beings*, 8–38. Cf. Norman L Geisler, Saleeb, Abdul, *Answering Islam: The Cresent in Light of the Cross*, 2nd edn (Grand Rapids, MI: Baker Books, 2006), 23–8.
85 Ricks, *Early Arabic Christian Contributions*, 11; Griffith, "Christian Theology in Islamic Terms", 160, 62–5.

as their intellectual centres.⁸⁶ The work of Sulaymān ibn Hasan al-Ghazzī however, reveals a sensitive use of Islamic idiom mixed with rational argument at a time of persecution. In contrast, Paul of Antioch's *Letter to a Muslim Friend* demonstrates a less tempered manipulation of the Qur'ān coupled with rational and Biblical argument. It is hoped that the three Christian interlocutors, through their apologetic texts, can add to the debate in defence of the concepts of the Trinity and Incarnation. In addition, it is hoped their work will help inform and inspire Christians and Muslims today in our increasingly integrated societies, to look afresh at the potential for an inclusive appreciation of the sincerity and faith of our fellow believers.

Theodore Abū Qurrah

Theodore Abū Qurrah is the earliest Arabic-speaking Christian *mutakallim* [a person who engaged in dialogue] who is known by name.⁸⁷ The details of his personal life are scarce and generally dependent on his critics.⁸⁸ It is believed that the Mu'tazilite 'Isā ibn Sabīr al-Murdār (d. 840) wrote a refutation of Abū Qurrah, *Against Abū Qurrah, the Christian*. This work is presently lost, but perhaps may be found one day.⁸⁹ The Mu'tazilite 'Abd al-Jabbār al-Hamadhānī refers to the writings of Abū Qurrah when discussing the faith of the Melkites.⁹⁰ The Jacobite Patriarch of Antioch, Michael I, disparagingly considered Abū Qurrah a "sophist", a person who engaged in dialectical debate with his adversaries using reasoned argument to establish the truth of a subject.⁹¹ John C. Lamoreaux provides an extended detail of accusations made by Michael I that suggest Abū Qurrah may have been

---

86 "The Monks of Palestine", 3–4.
87 Ibid., 21.
88 Ricks, *Early Arabic Christian Contributions*, 55.
89 Griffith, *The Church in the Shadow*, 63. Cf. "First Christian Arabic Theologians", 64.
90 Lamoreaux, *Abū Qurrah*, 1, xvii.
91 Griffith, "The Monks of Palestine", 23.

removed from his bishopric for propagating unsound doctrine. Michael I's account however, remains the only source of these accusations and may not therefore be considered entirely unbiased.[92]

The evidence suggests that Abū Qurrah was born in Edessa and was Bishop of Harrān between 792 and 812 CE.[93] It is known that he wrote many works in both Syriac and Arabic, some of which were translated into Greek by the monks of Palestine.[94] He seems to have enjoyed a strong connection with the monks of Palestine, especially with the well-known Judean monastery at Mar Sabas, but he is not thought to have lived there.[95] He travelled the length and breadth of the Levant and Mesopotamia where his writings were of service to the Arabic-speaking Chalcedonian community in opposition to the beliefs of both Muslims and other Christian communities.[96]

In fact, Abū Qurrah's opinions on the authority of the true Church and on seeking true religion merit examination here. In his essay referred to as, *On the Law, the Gospel, and Orthodoxy*, Abū Qurrah defends the authority of the Christian Bible as the word of the Holy Spirit and the authority of the properly convened six Church Councils that affirm the full divinity and humanity of Jesus the Messiah against Christological objections from Nestorians and Jacobites.[97] Of primary importance to Abū Qurrah's apologetic arguments is the authority of the Bible.[98] The authority of the Bible he argues stems from the evidence of the miracles performed by the apostles and disciples in Jesus' name, while the Church Councils derives its authority from the Bible.[99] This defence is primarily aimed at the challenge of Jacobite monothelitism to

---

92 Lamoreaux, *Abū Qurrah*, 1, xv.
93 Griffith, "The Monks of Palestine", 22. Cf. John C. Lamoreaux, "Theodore Abu Qurra", in *The Orthodox Church in the Arab World, 700–1700: An Anthology of Sources*, eds Samuel Noble & Alexander Treiger (DeKalb: Northern Illinois Press, 2014), 60–1.
94 Griffith, "The Monks of Palestine", 23. Cf. Adel Theodore Khoury, *Les Théologiens Byzantins Et L'islam* (Paris1969), 83–105.
95 Griffith, *The Church in the Shadow*, 60. Lamoreaux, *Abū Qurrah*, 1, xiii.
96 Griffith, "The Monks of Palestine", 22–3. Lamoreaux, *Abū Qurrah*, 1, xv–xviii.
97 Griffith, "Muslim and Church Councils", 280–2, 74, 95.
98 This charge of corruption of scripture is levied against the People of the Book through the *tafsīr* of *sūrat al-māʾidah* (5):48.
99 Griffith, "Muslim and Church Councils", 292.

the nature of Jesus. Abū Qurrah sought to prove to Muslims and his fellow Christians that the Chalcedonian Church correctly represented the teachings of Christ.[100] This argument attempts to address the Muslim claim that the Church corrupted and distorted the religion of Jesus.[101]

Despite the exclusivist thrust of his arguments, Abū Qurrah's relations with Muslims must have been amicable. Griffith reports that he made a translation of the pseudo-Aristotle's *De virtutibus animae* for Dhū al-Yamīnayn Tāhir b. al-Husayn, the governor of Mesopotamia between 813 and 820. This translation may have been undertaken while Abū Qurrah studied philosophy near Harrān. Ibn an-Nadīm (d. *c*. 995) records that Abū Qurrah was for a time the bishop of Harrān and that he debated with the Nestorians there.[102] The last historical reference to Abū Qurrah was in the year 829. This is when Abū Qurrah met caliph al-Ma'mūn. During their meeting Abū Qurrah took part in a debate with a group of Muslims in the caliph's presence, apparently while the caliph was preparing to battle the Byzantines.[103]

Abū Qurrah's Defence of the Trinity and Incarnation, On the Trinity

In *On the Trinity* Abū Qurrah provides a defence of the Trinity and Incarnation by employing a variety of arguments. Through the use of scripture, Islamic idiom, philosophy, grammatical considerations and analogy he demonstrates that it is appropriate not only to speak of God in Trinitarian form, but also in terms of begetting and begotten.[104] He begins the discourse by outlining an analogy of what he sees as the possible responses "to faith

---

100 Ibid.
101 Ibid., 282. This opinion is later expressed by 'Abd al-Jabbār al Hamdhānī (d 1025) in his polemic work *Tahbīt dalā'il an-nubūwah* (*The Establishment of the Proofs of the Prophet*).
102 *The Church in the Shadow*, 61. Lamoreaux, *Abū Qurrah*, I, xvii.
103 Griffith, *The Church in the Shadow*, 63. Lamoreaux, *Abū Qurrah*, I, xvii.
104 Ricks, *Early Arabic Christian Contributions*, 88–92, 171–2.

Resisting the Construct 163

in what is from God" that are beyond the intellectual comprehension of people. He claims, when it comes to faith in discerning what is from God there are in general three types of responses. There are those who reject faith because they are too arrogant to accept what their intellect cannot comprehend. There are others who submit their minds humbly to a message from God, yet do not seek intellectual justification for their faith. Then finally there are those who tentatively submit to a message in faith, but do not rest until their minds determine that a message is truly from God.[105]

Focusing on the people who are arrogant and do not accept what their minds cannot comprehend in relation to God, Abū Qurrah makes some interesting analogies. He points out that these same people rely on faith every day without realizing it. For instance, they rely on doctors to prescribe medicine for them when they are ill. People must place faith in the doctor that what is given to them is not in fact a poison.[106] In the same way when people board a boat they must trust that the pilot is capable of controlling the boat. Then there are judges who must listen to the testimony of witnesses in relation to an allegation. They must place faith in the veracity of the testimony and come to a conclusion as to the guilt or innocence of an accused. At some stage a judge, after making all possible enquiries must make a decision based on the best of their ability in light of imperfect knowledge. They must act *in faith*, even though their decision will have consequences for all concerned. Therefore, it is part of life that people place their faith in people and things of whom and which they have limited knowledge and understanding. Abū Qurrah further analyses the motivation of people that reject faith. He concludes, "That they abandoned belief in God's message for fear that it will sully their desires".[107]

On the other hand, Abū Qurrah adds, "The right-directed intellect submits itself to Christianity alone and confesses it alone, nor does it doubt that it was accepted for any other reason than divine wonders, the

---

105 Lamoreaux, *Abū Qurrah*, 1, 175.
106 Ibid., 175–6.
107 Ibid., 176–8. Cf. Griffith, "First Christian Arabic Theologians", 173–4.

performers of which deserve to be believed and followed".[108] Abū Qurrah states that Christianity would be deficient if the Gospel did not complete the Torah, because Christianity is the fulfilment of the Law of Moses and the intervening books. He then reminds the reader that the wise are required to trust in the scriptures, even if they cannot understand all of what the scriptures say.[109]

From Abū Qurrah's introduction it would seem difficult not to choose Christianity. Not to do so would imply that a person is open to the influence of worldly inducements when choosing which religion to follow. Accordingly, the reader is not required to understand precisely how the concept of Trinity works, but rather to accept what they must on faith. Those who cannot do so are reminded that they should not disturb the children of the Church who might also struggle with such issues. He reminds them of the time when Moses was instructed to prepare the People of Israel to hear the voice of the Lord from Mount Sinai (Exodus 19:13). At this time the people were warned on pain of death that they would be stoned if they tried to approach the mountain. Hence those whose faith remains weak after hearing the persuasive arguments should not weaken the faith of others. The persuasive arguments that Abū Qurrah presents entail the use of scripture and rational argument. In a direct way Abū Qurrah links the authority to requisite total submission to the edicts of Church Councils as would be demanded of Moses.[110]

Abū Qurrah's Scriptural Defence

Abū Qurrah utilizes more than twenty scriptural references from the Torah and New Testament, commending the authority of pre-Islamic scripture, in a way that he hopes will resonate with Muslims.[111] He argues that if one

---

108 Lamoreaux, *Abū Qurrah*, 1. Cf. References to proofs of the veracity of Christianity, that is, *Theologus Autodidactus, Against the Jews, that Christianity is from God, On the Characteristics of True Religion*, 1–57.
109 Ibid., 178.
110 Ibid., 179. Cf. Exodus 19:13 and the authority of Moses in relation to edicts.
111 Ricks, *Early Arabic Christian Contributions*, 57, 63–3.

believes in and examines the Gospel, the Law of Moses and the "intervening books of the prophets" one will find mention of the Father as God, the Son as God and the Holy Spirit as God.[112] Therefore the goal of Abū Qurrah's interpretation of Biblical texts is to strengthen the faith of people, so that they can accept in faith that the Biblical references speak of God grammatically as multiple persons, as fully God.[113] Abū Qurrah's defence of God as multiple persons sees God as lord, angel, word, light, power and spirit, as begetter and as begotten.

His scriptural defence begins with Psalms 110. Here David says, "The Lord said to my Lord, 'sit at my right hand, till I place your enemies under your feet'". Thus presenting a visual image of the absolute authority of God as sitting on a throne.[114] Abū Qurrah explains that the one speaking and the one spoken to are both called Lord and that David did not count them as two lords.[115] Continuing he draws further reference to the verse, "I begot you from the womb, before the light".[116] Therefore God begets God, still one God, one eternal begotten and begetter.[117] From Psalms 45:6–7 Abū Qurrah cites, "Your throne, O God is forever and ever. Your royal sceptre is a sceptre of equity; you love righteousness and hate wickedness. Therefore, God your God, has anointed you with oil of gladness above your fellows". The implications suggest that God anointed another. This anointed God is Christ. He became incarnate and was anointed by God. This image draws upon verses 4:25–6; 10:38 of Acts where Jesus is discussed as God's anointed one. In Hosea 1:6–7 God speaks through the prophet and says

---

112 Lamoreaux, *Abū Qurrah*, 1, 178, 79. Ricks, *Early Arabic Christian Contributions*, 62–3.
113 Lamoreaux, *Abū Qurrah*, 1, 179.
114 Ricks, *Early Arabic Christian Contributions*, 60. This image helps build the argument of God as multi person. Abū Qurrah does not make the link later made by Paul of Antioch of hints of anthropomorphism.
115 Lamoreaux, *Abū Qurrah*, 1, 179. This author accepts the given translation of the verses cited. John C. Lamoreaux notes in his introduction that Abū Qurrah often paraphrases Biblical citations, Cf. xxxv and fn. 116.
116 Ibid., 180.
117 Ibid. This challenges *sūrat al-Ikhlas* (112): 2–3 where God is described as neither begetting nor begotten.

that he will save Judea "by the Lord their God shall I save them". Here the one who saves is Lord and God and the one that speaks is also God.[118]

Abū Qurrah examines ten verses from Genesis to demonstrate numerous references to God as multiple persons, while still insisting that there is only one God worthy of worship. In verse 9:6 God says to Noah, "In the image of God I created man". Accordingly, the one who created man is God and the one in whose image man was created is God, but they are not counted as two gods. A similar example is provided with verse 1:27. In verse 16:7, and 10, verses sure to attract the attention of Muslim ears, Hagar the handmaiden of Sarah fled into the desert, "The angel of the Lord found her by a spring in the desert. And the angel of the Lord said to her, 'I shall so greatly multiply your seed that it will not be counted for the multitude'". Subsequently in verse 16:13 "Hagar called the Lord who spoke with her 'the God who is seen'". The one who appeared to Hagar is the angel of the Lord, who is God, as is the one whose angel this is, is God, but they are not counted as two.[119] As is the case in verse 22:11–12 where Abraham is prevented from sacrificing Isaac by the angel of the Lord, as the angel says, "now I know that you fear God, seeing that for me you did not spare your beloved son".[120]

In Genesis verses 31:3, 11, 13 God identifies himself to Jacob as "The *angel* of God". God later refers to himself as "the God who appeared to you at Bethel"; "Thus the angel is God and the one whose angel this is, is God".[121] In verse 35:1 God instructs Jacob, "Arise, go to Bethel, and dwell there; and make an altar to the God who appeared to you when you fled from your brother". Therefore the one who spoke to Jacob is God and the one who appeared to him when he fled his elder brother Esau is also God, but they are not counted as two Gods.[122] Further in verse 48:15–16 Jacob blessed his son Joseph and his other sons saying, "The God whom my fathers Abraham and Isaac served, the God who has fed me from my

---

118   Ibid.
119   Ibid., 181.
120   Ibid.
121   Ibid., 180. Ricks identifies comparisons with "angel of the Lord" to a sort of pre-Incarnate Son. Ricks, *Early Arabic Christian Contributions*, 63.
122   Lamoreaux, *Abū Qurrah*, 1, 181–2.

Resisting the Construct

youth to this day, the *angel* who has delivered me from all tribulations, bless these lads; and in them let my name be exalted, and the name of my fathers Abraham and Isaac; and let them grow into an innumerable multitude on the earth". Consequently, Abū Qurrah assesses that the God whom his fathers Abraham and Isaac served and the God who fed him from his youth is the angel who delivered him from all tribulations. They are not counted as two. "The angel is God, even as Jacob said and the one whose angel this is, is God, but they are not counted as two Gods".[123] In verse 19:24, "The Lord rained from the hands of the Lord fire and sulphur on Sodom". The implications are similar to the previous examples cited: the Lord rained from the hands of the Lord … two references to Lord, but one God.[124]

Exodus 3:2–6 makes the same point, "the angel of the Lord" appeared to Moses in a burning bush. Later in the verse God called to Moses and said, "Moses, do not come near; put off your shoes from your feet, for the place in which you are standing is holy ground". God then identifies himself as, "I am the God of your fathers, the God of Abraham, the God of Isaac, the God of Jacob". Hence, the angel of the Lord is God, who is at the same time the God of Abraham, Isaac and Jacob. "The angel is God and the one whose angel this is, is God".[125] In verse 33:18–19 there is quite a clear indication that the one who is God calls upon God. Moses asks God to show him His glory. God replies to Moses, "I shall pass before you with my glory and I shall call upon the name of the Lord in your presence". As Abū Qurrah says, "Do you not see that God called upon the name of the Lord? Thus God is God and the Lord whose name God called upon is God, but they are not counted as two gods".[126]

In the concluding Biblical references, Abū Qurrah elicits images of God as Word, the Christ and Spirit thus placing his above argument now within an Islamic context.[127] From John 1:1–2 he quotes, "In the beginning was the Word, and the Word was with God and the Word was God. He was in the beginning with God". Abū Qurrah makes the obvious conclusion

---

123   Ibid., 181.
124   Ibid., 180.
125   Ibid., 180–1.
126   Ibid., 182.
127   Ricks, *Early Arabic Christian Contributions*, 62–3.

that the Word is God and with God, but they are again not counted as two gods. Through Paul in Romans 9:5 there is a reference to Jesus as the Christ, as God, "From them according to the flesh, Christ appeared, he who is God over all, who has praises and blessings forever". Thus, Christ is worthy of praise as God and the one Christ praises is God, but not two gods.[128] The last reference employed by Abū Qurrah to reinforce his argument that God can be spoken of in multiple persons as the one God comes from Matthew 28:19. Here he stresses that Christ commissioned his disciples, "Go teach all nations and baptise them in the name of the Father and of the Son and of the Holy Spirit". As Abū Qurrah says, "Human beings would not have been renewed through baptism in theirs and the Father's name if both of them were not as the Father is".[129] Abū Qurrah summarizes his arguments by drawing attention to the fact that whoever directs their faith rightly and governs it with reason must believe in the testimony of the scriptures. He further states that the wise know that scripture comes from God. Consequently, the Father is God, the Son is God and the Spirit is God. These are never spoken of as more than the one God.[130]

Abū Qurrah's Rational Defence

Abū Qurrah's rational defence of the Trinity draws together the Islamic grammatical discourse and Greek Aristotelian logic for its terms of reference. In so doing Abū Qurrah, along with other Christian apologists, demonstrates that the translation movement developed a new common mode of discussion of theological concerns.[131] An important element of his argument requires the understanding of the difference between what are referred to as the "nature" of something and the "person". For instance, Abū Qurrah uses the analogy of names that refer to nature such as "man", "horse" and "ox".[132]

---

128 Lamoreaux, *Abū Qurrah*, 1, 182.
129 Ibid.
130 Ibid.
131 Ricks, *Early Arabic Christian Contributions*, 69.
132 Lamoreaux, *Abū Qurrah*, 1, 183. Ricks, *Early Arabic Christian Contributions*, 67.

All men share the same basic qualities as every other man therefore we can refer to their nature as the nature of "man". All horses share the same basic qualities as every other horse therefore we can refer to their nature as that of a "horse" and all oxen share the same basic qualities as every other ox therefore we can refer to their nature as the nature of "ox". Likewise, the names of persons like "Peter", "Paul" and "John" refer to different men, the individual person, but not to different "man", the nature. Accordingly, it is wrong to speak of three different men, all of whom share the same nature, but different names, because they are different persons. As Abū Qurrah explains, "If you want to count many persons with one nature, you must not predicate number of the name that refers to the nature".[133]

The above analogies appear clear to follow. Issues arise when the logic is applied to God since the Islamicized culture of the audience was quite aware of the Qur'ānic invocation not to associate three with God, or countenance that God would take a "son". In addition, as noted above, Muslims would not accept rational argument as being sufficiently authoritative. One could imagine a mixed crowd of Christians and Muslims nodding their heads in agreement until the same logic applied to animals and men was applied to God. Applying the logic Abū Qurrah posits, "In a similar way, the Father, Son and Holy Spirit are three persons with one nature (that being God). If you count them, you must not predicate number of the name 'God,' which is the name of their nature. If you do, you cause their single nature, to which the name 'God' refers, to be different natures and fall into manifest error".[134] He then uses a brilliant analogy whereby he says, "The Father is God, but God is not the Father; the Son is God, But God is not the Son; the Spirit is God, but God is not the Spirit".[135] This sort of reasoning, although logically sound, is admittedly a little difficult to follow.[136] It is correct to count three persons, but wrong to count three

---

133   Lamoreaux, *Abū Qurrah*, 1, 183.
134   Ibid.
135   Ibid., 183, Cf. 71.
136   I used a similar example on the Postgraduate Day, 12 December 2013, ISE, TCD. Several of the Christian students refused to accept the definition. A few insisted that it is correct to say, "Jesus is God and God is Jesus".

natures, because the nature of God is one. Continuing with the analogy of the crowd, the Muslim heads stop nodding.

Similarly, Abū Qurrah's reasoning includes the definition of "person" as a logical name. He defines the logical name as not belonging to any particular person and therefore can be predicated by number. Whereas it is wrong to predicate number to their common name, their nature. Through this line of reasoning Abū Qurrah explains that it is also wrong to apply number to "particular non-logical names", otherwise there could be further confusion. Wherein number will make each of the numbered entities to be all of them. The example he gives is "Peter, James and John are three, you make each one to be the three of them. Similarly if you say, 'In heaven, the Father, Son, and Holy Spirit are three,' you make each one to be the three of them'".[137] Therefore number should be applied to the logical name only, which is predicated to each of them (the person), but the common name remains singular.

When speaking of God there are limits to analogies to man. It is possible to speak of "man" in different places, taking different forms, having different will and state. However, in relation to God this is not the case. Abū Qurrah reasons that the Father, Son and Holy Spirit share all things in common. It is not conceivable that either would occupy a place where one of the others was not present, or possesses a will contrary to the others. This is the nature of God. The analogy used by Abū Qurrah is of three lamps lighting a dark house. "The light of each is dispersed in the whole house, and the eye cannot distinguish the light of one from the light of the others or the light of all from the light of one. So also, the Father, Son, and Holy Spirit are one God, even though each is fully God".[138] Other analogies are used to make the same point that the union of the Father, Son and Holy Spirit is pure. There should never be a number predicating the nature of God, "that there is no difference among them that effects the hypostasis of one of them, other than that each is different from the other".[139]

In addition to supplying rational reasoning in defence of the Trinity Abū Qurrah also provides readymade responses for ways Christians can counter

---

137 Lamoreaux, *Abū Qurrah*, 1, 184.
138 Ibid., 184–5.
139 Ibid., 185.

criticism of their beliefs by "certain foolish people", while not identifying these people as doubting Christians, Muslims, or Jews.[140] In relation to questions that try to undermine the concept of the union between the Father, Son, and Holy Spirit Abū Qurrah anticipates the question, "Was it three or one that created the world?" To which Abū Qurrah outlines the grammatical pitfalls of answering the question by saying one or three. Typically, with these sorts of questions Abū Qurrah tries to invert a grammatical challenge in favour of the Christian position.[141] He begins by saying that the question itself indicates a sense of unwillingness on behalf of the individual posing the question to accept both Biblical and rational argument. Their motive he implies seeks only to trick the Christian into doubt over the validity of their faith at the cost of the soul of the one posing the question. He says, "Their minds' logic impels them to their souls' destruction".[142] The response he suggests is, "It is one that created the world, and to say this does not prevent each of the other hypostasis from being the creator". Further, Abū Qurrah offers an analogy that relies on grammar to help defend the concept of Trinity. "You say, 'The tongue of the prophet Moses spoke the truth' and are right to do so. You say, 'The prophet Moses spoke the truth,' and are right to do so. You cannot say 'the prophet Moses and his tongue spoke the truth,' for Moses spoke the truth with his tongue".[143] He further suggests as an analogy, "You say, 'The sun gives light to human beings,' and are right to do so. You say, 'The rays of the sun give light to human beings,' and are right to do so. You do not say, 'The sun and its rays give light to human beings,' for the sun gives light through its rays".[144] Abū Qurrah offers several more analogies that employ the rules of Arabic grammar to similar effect before coming to a more direct application of the defence.

As for the Father, the Son and Holy Spirit, it is possible to say, "The Father created the world", and "the Son created the world". Whereas, it is wrong to say, "The Father and the Son created the world", since Christians

---

140   Ibid.
141   Ricks, *Early Arabic Christian Contributions*, 69. Arabic grammar requires agreement between the subject and verb.
142   Lamoreaux, *Abū Qurrah*, 1, 185.
143   Ibid.
144   Ibid., 185–6.

maintain that the Father created the world through his Son (the Word).[145] The point being that it is wrong to associate two nouns with the singular form of a verb. Abū Qurrah supports this statement by slipping into Biblical references; Hebrews 1:2 and John 1:1–3. He further qualifies the uniqueness of the relationship between the Father and the son as, "We do not think that the tongue and the mind or the rays and the sun or the craftsman's hand and the craftsman, or the eye and the brain are more closely united than the Father and the Son-and this, because of the refinement of the divine essence, which is unimaginably more refined than the most refined creatures".[146] In this sense, then, none of the analogies truly represent the unity between the Father and the Son, since the divine nature is not subject to composition as bodies are, nor matter and form. Even though the Father and the Son are different hypostasis, the divine nature is too refined to detect a difference.

Associating Jesus with other divine attributes Abū Qurrah cites St Paul and St John. St Paul in Hebrews 1:20–3 described Jesus as "Son" thus; "In these last days God has spoken to us by his Son, through whom he created the world. He is the light of the Father's glory and the form of his essence".[147] Abū Qurrah reminds the reader that St Paul refers to Jesus in 1 Corinthians 1:24 as, "Christ is the wisdom of God and his power".[148] This Abū Qurrah says is analogous to heat and fire, because heat is the power of fire. In a similar fashion St John refers to Jesus as "Word" in John 1:1, "In the beginning was the Word and the Word was with God, and the Word was God".[149] Through these examples Abū Qurrah says that St Paul and St John wish to demonstrate that as with annexed nouns, the noun annexed and the noun to which annexation is made are not said to do something together, but both are said to do something by themselves apart from the other. This Abū Qurrah phrases slightly different later on, when he surmises that "the Father and the Son are not said to create, even if each is said to create by itself … For this reason each of them (St. Paul and St. John) called the Son 'God' … they taught that he is

---

145 Ibid., 186. Ricks, *Early Arabic Christian Contributions*, 89–90.
146 Lamoreaux, *Abū Qurrah*, 1, 186.
147 Ibid., 187. Ricks, *Early Arabic Christian Contributions*, 91–2.
148 Lamoreaux, *Abū Qurrah*, 1, 187.
149 Ibid.

a full hypostasis and denied that the divine nature was subject to composition, or that change was to be found with regard to each of its hypostasis".[150]

Abū Qurrah applies the same reasoning to the Spirit as annexed to the Father, and that in the same manner that the Spirit can be spoken of as a complete hypostasis like the Father and the Son. Ricks points out that the comparisons between the attributes describing Son and the Spirit are rather vague.[151] The Holy Church thus says that the Father created and that each of the others created, but does not say that they created together. On the one hand, in that the Church teaches that the Son is fully God and that the Spirit is fully God, even though they are annexed to the Father in this manner, she hypostatically counts Son and the Spirit with the Father and speaks of the Father, Son and Holy Spirit; and thus by counting the Son and the Spirit hypostasis with the Father, she has gone beyond the limit of these annexed entities, none of which are hypostatically counted with that to which they are annexed. On the other hand, in the ways mentioned earlier, even as the sun and its rays and its light are one sun, and so on she says that the Father, Son, and Holy Spirit created (singular) the world but does not say they created it. Similarly, she says, "Father, Son, and Holy Spirit have mercy (singular) on me" but does not say, "Have mercy (plural) on me".[152]

Abū Qurrah further employs Biblical quotations to reinforce the point that both the Son and the Holy Spirit are fully God, and not in any way "in" God, in a manner that the examples above might be considered "in" the thing that they are annexed.[153] For those wishing to defend the concept of the Trinity Abū Qurrah provides advice on another line of questioning that he believes attempts to trick Christians into denying the logic of the Trinity, or at least misrepresent it. Here, Abū Qurrah supposes that the Christian is asked, "Tell me. Do you deny every God other than the Father? Do you deny every God other than the Son? Do you deny every God other than the Holy Spirit? Abū Qurrah then explains the pitfalls of answering the question in various ways, labelling the line of question itself crass, before

---

150   Ibid., 187, fn. 86.
151   Ricks, *Early Arabic Christian Contributions*, 91.
152   Lamoreaux, *Abū Qurrah*, 1, 188.
153   Ibid. Cf. Genesis 1:26; 11:7; John 14:23; Isaiah 48:16 & Proverbs 8:22.

providing a theologically sound response. He maintains that the correct way to respond to this line of questioning is to say, "I deny every God other than Christ".[154] The reason why this is the correct response is explained in terms of the difference between the nature of God and the hypostasis of Christ. For the nature of Christ is God, but the hypostasis of Christ as God does not exclude the Father and the Spirit from having the nature of God. Since the divine nature of the Son, Father and Spirit are one and the same. In an effort to drum home this point Abū Qurrah uses further analogies including whether it is correct to say that there is just one "Gospel" or if there are in fact many Gospels through which the Holy Spirit speaks. Then there is the analogy of an image of a person in a mirror, whether or not one of the reflections represents the person, or does all three. This analogy is followed by the countenance of a person drawn on paper and whether or not this image is a true representation of a person's countenance and if so what of the others. To each the difference is whether or not the question speaks of the nature or essence of a thing and not its hypostasis.[155]

Up until now it could be argued that the text provides support for the veracity of the Trinity in face of Jewish criticisms. From here on in, Abū Qurrah goes on the offensive. His new line of argument draws upon the phraseology found in *sūrat an-Nisā'* (4):171, where Jesus is crowned with the appellations of God's Word and Spirit. Although Islam is not mentioned by name the Qur'ānic parallels are too obvious to ignore. In this defence Abū Qurrah sets out the rationality of his argument by establishing that it is agreed that the divine nature is not subject to composition. Next, that it is accepted that the divine hypostases are not subject to change or cannot be amended to. Therefore he asks those who deny the Son and Spirit are divine hypostases for fear of believing in three gods,

> Does God have a Word? If you say that he does not, you have both made him mute and made human beings better than him. There is no escape: you must say that God has a Word. We then ask: with regard to the word of God, is he part of God? If you say that he is part of God, you ascribe parts to God and introduce composition into his nature, which

---

154 Ibid., 189.
155 Ibid., 70, 189–90.

cannot be; nor can you say that God's word is in God as form is in matter or anything else similar to that, for all this is excluded from God, as we have already said. You are thus compelled to make the Word a full hypostasis and to say that he is fully God ...[156]

Abū Qurrah maintains that the same logic can be applied to Spirit. Thus God and his Word and his Spirit are one. It logically follows that the Son and the Spirit are to the Father as a word of a person and the spirit of a person are thought of in terms of one person. This is especially true with the divine because the divine is not thought of in terms of composition. To reinforce the idea that God can be spoken metaphorically in terms of physical attributes without affecting God's unity Abū Qurrah cites Psalms 98:1 where he describes the Son as the right hand and the arm of God and both saved human beings.[157] Likewise in Luke 11:20 and Matthew 12:28, Jesus cast out demons with the finger of God, meaning the Holy Spirit. These examples relate the Son and Spirit to God, indivisibly and without composition understood as fully God. The above defence demonstrates an awareness of a Muslim as well as a Christian audience. His use of grammar, scripture, Aristotelian logic and analogy, work hand in hand to make a convincing and readable argument for the Trinity and the Incarnation.

Sulaymān ibn Hasan al-Ghazzī

The next scholar examined is the former Bishop of Gaza, Sulaymān ibn Hasan al-Ghazzī.[158] Sulaymān was a prolific writer of theological tracts and is considered the first post-conquest Christian to write a *dīwān*, a book of poetry,

---

156 Ibid., 190.
157 Ibid., 191. The use of "Son" here is a prime example of Abū Qurrah's artistic use of Biblical text.
158 Paolo La Spisa, *I Trattati Teologici Di Sulaymān Ibn Hasan Al-Ghazzī, Tomus 53*, vol. 649, Tomus 53, Corpus Scriptorum Christianorum Orientalium (Louvain: In Aedibus Peeters, 2013), v–vii. Cf. Samuel Noble, "Sulaymān Al-Ghazzī " in

in this case spiritual poetry, in Arabic.[159] In fact what is known concerning his life has been extracted from his poetry.[160] Harald Suermann, citing the work of Néophytos Edelby, posits that Sulaymān was born in Gaza in the middle of the tenth century. His father, Hasan, was a Melkite Christian, despite the Muslim name. Nothing is known of his mother except that she left Sulaymān's father.[161] As a very young man Sulaymān entered monastic life, but he did not stay long.[162] After leaving he married and worked as a civil servant in the Fatimid Caliphate where he amassed a small fortune.[163] Surprisingly, most of his works have yet to be studied or translated into a European language.[164]

The era in which Sulaymān lived was for a very long period of time a matter of some debate. Paul Sbath believed Sulaymān lived in the sixteenth century, while I. Maluf and L. Cheikho considered the fourteenth century more likely.[165] Mgr J. Nasrallah, after examining dozens of manu-

---

Christian-Muslim Relations: A Bibliographical History, eds David Thomas and Alex Mallet (Leiden: Brill, 2010), 617–22.

159   Spisa, *Sulaymān Ibn Hasan Al-Ghazzī T53*, 649, Tomus 53. *Dīwān* poetry is a collection of poetry usually of a spiritual nature. Cf. Samuel Noble, "Sulayman Al-Ghazzi", in *The Orthodox Church in the Arab World, 700–1700: An Anthology of Sources*, eds Samuel Noble & Alexander Treiger, The Orthodox Christian Series (DeKalb: Northern Illinois Press, 2014), 160–70.

160   Néophytos Edelby, *Sulaimān Al-Gazzī: Xe-Xie Siècles*, eds Mgr Néophytos Edelby and P. Kh. Samir S. J., Patrimoine Arabe Chrétien (Rome: Pontificio Istituto Orientale, 1984), xxi.

161   Ibid., xxii, xxv–xxviii. Harald Suermann, "Sulaymān Al-Gazzī, Évêque Melchite De Gaza (XIe Siècle): Sur Les Maronites", *Parole de l'Orient* 21 (1996): 190.

162   "Sulaymān: Sur Les Maronites", 190. Johannes Den Heijer and Paolo La Spisa, "La Migration Du Savoir Entre Les Communautés; Le Cas De La Littérature Arabe Chrétienne", *Res Antiquae* 7 (2010): 67. Noble, "Sulayman", 169. Sulaymān would later regret the constraints of family life, especially following the death of his son.

163   Edelby, *Sulaimān Al-Gazzī*, xxiii.

164   Cf. Paolo La Spisa, *I Trattati Teologici Di Sulaymān Ibn Hasan Al-Ghazzī, Tomus 52*, trans. Paolo La Spisa, vol. 648, Tomus 52, Corpus Scriptorum Christianorum Orientalium (Louvain: In Aedibus Peeters, 2013).

165   Ignace Dick, "Samonas De Gaza Ou Sulaïmān Al-Gazzi: Évêque Melchite De Gaza Xie Siècle", *Proche Orient Chrétien* no. 29 (1980): 175. Cf. Élie Khalifé, "Notice Sur

scripts found empirical evidence in the form of a small tract attributed to Sulaymān around 1056 CE entitled, *Discussion by the blessed Samonas, Archbishop of Gaza, with Ahmed the Muslim, demonstrating that the bread and the wine, consecrated by the priest are the body and blood of our saviour Jesus Christ.* Nasrallah deduced that it was highly unlikely that there was a Greek-speaking archbishop by the name *"Samonas"*, engaged in an in-depth dialogue with a Muslim. Therefore, Nasrallah reasons that this hitherto unknown Greek *"Samonas"* must have been none other than Sulaymān. The confusion Nasrallah surmises is down to the difference in the spelling of the name, thought to be the result of a simple clerical error.[166]

Sulaymān lived during the reign of the controversial Fatimid Caliph, Abū 'Alī Mansūr Tāriq al-Hākim. His supporters referred to him as Al-Hākim bi-Amr Allah, "the ruler by God's Command", to his critics he was the "Mad Caliph". It is noteworthy that Al-Hākim initiated a phase of ferocious persecution against the People of the Book, quite uncharacteristic of the time, in spite of the fact that his own mother was a Christian.[167] During this period of persecution many churches were confiscated and turned into mosques and many Christians were forced to converted to Islam.[168] On a personal level Sulaymān's wealth was confiscated. He lost his job, his wife, son and grandson.[169] His poetry encouraged Christians to "bear their cross" to submit to the humiliating conditions of the day rather than emigrate. These conditions included restrictions against public

---

Un Manuscript Du Poète Arabe Chrétien Sulaimān Ibn Hasan Al Gazzi " *Parole de l'Orient* 2 (1966): 161–2.

166 Dick, "Samonas Ou Sulaïmān", 176–8. Apparently an error by a copyist who mistook *Samonas* for Sulaymān left many scholars in doubt as to the identity of Archbishop *Samonas* and the correct era of Sulaymān. Cf. Jugie A. Martin, "Une Nouvele Invention À Mettre Au Compte De Constantin Palaeocappa: Samonas De Gaza Et Son Dialogue Sur L'eucharistie", *Miscellanea Giovanni Mercati* III (1946): 343. Cf. Spisa, *Sulaymān Ibn Hasan Al-Ghazzī T52*, 648, Tomus 52, viii.

167 Edelby, *Sulaimān Al-Gazzī*, xviii, xix.

168 Ibid., xx, xxiv. Nissim Dana, *The Druze in the Middle East: Their Faith, Leadership, Identity and Status* (Brighton: Sussex Academic Press, 2003), 41.

169 Suermann, "Sulaymān: Sur Les Maronites", 190. Edelby, *Sulaimān Al-Gazzī*, xxiv.

worship, destruction of religious buildings, prohibition against wine production and also instituting regulations that publicly differentiated, *libs al-aghiyār*, People of the Book from Muslims. These regulations included an obligation for Christians to wear a wooden cross around their necks.[170] Ignace Dick, citing the work of Nasrallah, adds that Sulaymān's poetry reveals his personal desire for martyrdom.[171] However, his desire was not realized, though he defiantly put himself in harm's way. At an advanced age, having lost all, Sulaymān re-entered religious life and became Bishop of Gaza.[172] This present research examines Sulaymān's tract entitled, *The Faith of the Orthodox Christian Community* in order to gain some insights into his defence of Christianity.[173]

Sulaymān's Defence of the Trinity and Incarnation
Faith of the Orthodox Christian

Sulaymān's opening defence of the Trinity in *Faith of the Orthodox Christian* bears more than a striking resemblance to Islamic idiom, rather than to Biblical verse. He responds to accusations of excesses made against Christians by stating, "God is one", an affirmation of the Islamic principle of *tawḥīd*. Also, that God does not have any partners, a repudiation of the accusation made against Christians of *shirk*. Sulaymān further

---

170 *Sulaimān Al-Gazzī*, xix, xxiv. Dana, *The Druze*, 41–43.
171 Dick, "Samonas Ou Sulaïmān", 177.
172 Khalifé, "Notice Sur Un Manuscript Du Poète Arabe Chrétien Sulaimān Ibn Hasan Al Gazzi " 162, Cf. folio 64, 08, 33.
173 I am deeply grateful to Fr Sidney H. Griffith S. J. for his care and tutorage at Catholic University during the summer of 2013, without which I would not have been able to translate this text. The Arabic is from Spisa, *Sulaymān Ibn Hasan Al-Ghazzī T52*, 648, Tomus 52, Cf, manuscripts examined XI–XV and Spisa's compilation. 31–40, T3 17–24. Sulaymān's use of the term *Orthodox* is an indication of the Melkite Church's perception of correct Christological formulation rather than the modern usage of the term.

describes God using several attributes of the substance of God that orthodox Christians hold to be true and that are in perfectly harmony with the *al-asmā al-husnā*.¹⁷⁴

One garners from the discourse that Sulaymān intends to build a bridge between the attributes of God as seen from a Christian perspective with the attributes of God described in Islam. The use of these bridge building phrases act to assure the reader that there is much common ground between what Christianity and Islam have to say about God, before making a rational defence of the more polemical characteristics of the Christian faith. Therefore, it is possible to make a couple of assumptions about the text. The audience to whom Sulaymān addressed his text included Muslims and Christians familiar with Islamic idiom, or perhaps the type of "wavering" Christians discussed above by Abū Qurrah. The use of Islamic idiom here, therefore, is as much an evangelic tool as it is a bridge-building device, employed to demonstrate the soundness of the Christian faith in line with debates within Islamic circles regarding God and His attributes.¹⁷⁵

Sulaymān's Scriptural Defence

Sulaymān's use of the Gospel and the Qur'ān is economic. He does not quote a verse directly from either to support the concept of the Trinity or the Incarnation of the Messiah in a manner that is similar to Abū Qurrah.¹⁷⁶ Sulaymān's apology relies almost entirely on rational argument, which is examined below. However, his subtle use of scripture makes a poignant case for expanding the readers' horizon of perceiving faith from a Christian perspective, as well as questioning the value of claiming orthodoxy without orthopraxis. Sulaymān describes God and His actions in a manner that borrows directly from Islamic idiom before adding the Christian experience

---

174 Noble, "Sulayman", 162. The Beautiful Names are a list of superlative names that describe God. The list is not definitive, however, a list of 99 names is generally agreed. Cf. Griffith, "Christian Theology in Islamic Terms", 157.
175 Frank, "Attribute, Attribution", 258–78.
176 Dick, "Samonas Ou Sulaïmān", 175. Edelby, *Sulaimān Al-Gazzī*, xxi.

of God in Trinitarian form. He says, "We believe God is one. No partners through eternity, and no match in lordship ... God creates ... He raises the dead ... He forgives sins ... He is the goal of all believers ... a single object of worship ... no god before Him and no god after Him ... until the destruction of time", before adding, "we believe God is the one who has these attributes, one single substance that entails three hypostases".[177]

Sulaymān describes the Gospel as something that is not easily understood.[178] He says "poor folks" only have knowledge because of what is in the Book, according to the interpretation given by the holy apostles. However, the word of the apostles, the message of the apostles was not accepted until signs of their works were visible.[179] When the apostles came to spread the message of the Messiah (as part of the Great Commission) they did not beleaguer people with "obscurities of speech", but rather placed a blessing on the water and immersed the people, in the name of the Father, Son and Holy Spirit.[180] So that the pure water would purify their bodies and the blessings purified their souls and minds, for their longing for faith after infidelity and tyranny.[181] Thus those longing for faith would become pure and not doubt the truth of the Trinity for all who accepted the Messiah.[182]

The verse used to justify true understanding of God comes from the Epistle of James 2:26, "Because knowledge without works is like the spirit without the soul".[183] The context of the quotation refutes the idea that those who say, "God is one" are necessarily virtuous. "As for the healthy spirit, it knows there is no validity except through works of the flesh".[184] It

---

177 Spisa, *Sulaymān Ibn Hasan Al-Ghazzī T52*, 648, Tomus 52, 32–34. Orthodox here implies Melkite expression of faith. Cf. Noble, "Sulayman", 163–67. *"Not All Baptized with Water Are Christians"*.
178 Spisa, *Sulaymān Ibn Hasan Al-Ghazzī T52*, 648, Tomus 52, 39–40.
179 Ibid., 39. In other Christian documents of this nature "works", generally referred to miracles as a sign, or proof of their message, for which Christians claimed Muhammad lacked as far back as the delegation from Najrān.
180 Ibid., 40.
181 Ibid., 39–40.
182 Ibid.
183 Ibid., 38.
184 Ibid.

seems to this present author that Sulaymān is speaking in the context of his contemporary experiences, aware of the harshness of life for Christians under the caliphate of al-Hākim, and bearing witness that claiming to have "exalted" knowledge with regard to an understanding of God is without merit, unless this understanding is visible in the conduct of one's life. The absence of good works Sulaymān says, "is like a spirit without a body", or better yet, "The healthy spirit is only known by works of the flesh".[185] The signs of a healthy spirit, he informs the reader, are humility, love and asceticism in the things of this world and not with concern for religion.[186] It would appear by this statement that Sulaymān is accusing certain people, perhaps religious and political leaders, of purporting to have a superior understanding of the oneness of God while lacking the virtues of a spiritual life, because of their repression of Christians. Sulaymān asserts that a life full of humility, love and asceticism is therefore a requisite to gaining an ability to understand the higher levels of spiritual matters.[187]

Weaving together a rational argument for faith with the Great Commission, Sulaymān discusses the difference between concepts that are heavy (tangible) and subtle (intangible). Certain things he says are difficult to comprehend, especially things that are not visible. "It is difficult for mankind to know something created in his own body, heavy or subtle. It is necessary for him, if he is weak for that, to recognise his inability to know the creator of the world. Praise be His power".[188] Since mankind does not even understand the working of his mind, soul and of his body, he argues, how can anyone possibly claim to know God. The idea that mankind could know the creator is absurd.[189] He says, even the wisest only

185 Ibid. This statement echoes James 2:26, "faith without works is dead".
186 One of the rumours surrounding the disappearance of al-Hākim suggests he later became a Christian and lived his life as a hermit. Cf. Johannes Den Heijer, "Apologetic Elements in Coptic-Arabic Historiography: The Life of Afrahām Ibn Zur'ah, 62nd Patriarch of Alexandria", in *Christian Arabic Apologetics During the Abbasad Period (750–1258)*, eds Samir Khalil Samir and Jørgen S. Nielsen (Christian Arabic Apologetics During the Abbasad Period (750–1258): Brill, 1994), 201, fn. 44.
187 Spisa, *Sulaymān Ibn Hasan Al-Ghazzī T52*, 648, Tomus 52, 38–9.
188 Ibid., 39.
189 Ibid.

possess a fraction of His knowledge and only then because God discloses certain things. Sulaymān further employs the analogy of the sun with its heat and light as it is for the soul and mind and speech, like Abū Qurrah and the author of *On the Triune Nature of God* above, to underscore the point that God is one, but with three hypostases. This understanding of God as Trinity, he says, came to the apostles through the Gospel, alluding to the Great Commission, to baptize the believers in the name of the Father, the Son and the Holy Spirit, a single God, a single object of worship.[190]

Sulaymān's Rational Defence

Sulaymān relies heavily on Aristotelian logic to reinforce his apologetic for the beliefs of orthodox Christians. He tailors his use of Islamic idiom to complement his very important argument that the Divine attributes that are recognized by Muslims can also defend the orthodox Christian view of the Trinity. Sulaymān describes God by His many attributes as one *essence*, one *substance* that *exists* and is *alive* and capable of *speaking*, echoing *sūrat an-Nisā'* (4):171.[191] Therefore it is fitting to describe God as one single substance that entails three hypostases.[192] How Sulaymān supports this statement concerning the uniqueness of the substance or essence of God is quite interesting. He describes God *via negativa*, that His essence is not a physical body, nor is it a composite.[193] God cannot be touched, nor divided, nor is God subject to change.

God is, on the positive side, a substance unlike any other substance, *jawhar*, which occupies space and can be given properties like colour, hot or cold.[194] The essence of God is *qadīm* [primordial], without beginning and staying without end. God is the *khāliq* [creator], or *muhdth* [originator], of all things from nothing, as He willed, *bi-klimitat* [Making creation

---

[190] Ibid., 40.
[191] Ibid., 32–4.
[192] Ibid., 34.
[193] Ibid., 31.
[194] Ibid.

from His Word].¹⁹⁵ God is living and does not die, a single object of *ma'būd* [worship], no other god or lord before or after Him, to him belong *as-subha* [all praises], in heaven and earth.¹⁹⁶ Sulaymān describes God as one single substance that entails three hypostases.¹⁹⁷ He builds his argument by saying God's essence is a *qa'ima binafsi-ha* [substance that exists on its own accord], and is not found in something else, based on *qnômâ*, a term borrowed from Syriac.¹⁹⁸ He rationally asserts that this substance of God must be either living or not living. Since it would be absurd to think that the creator of all would not be living, Sulaymān posits that God must be existentially living or life itself.¹⁹⁹ This statement relies on Arabic grammar to maintain an Islamic friendly conception of God's absolute oneness.²⁰⁰ Another attribute of this existential, alive, being, is that it is not free from speaking, or not speaking. However, Sulaymān points out that he is not referring to the speech of created beings that speak using lips and tongue, but rather the speaking that exists inherently in Him.²⁰¹ From it proceeds all knowledge and wisdom.²⁰² Since it is impossible for the creator of speech to be speechless, Sulaymān says that this speaking is due to the unique self-existing essence that is alive and speaking. The issue then comes down to how to name the self-dependent being appropriately, or as he says, "when as the meaning of names are taken as required by language we will not find this self-dependent being another appropriate name".²⁰³

195 Ibid., 32.
196 Ibid., 31–4.
197 Ibid., 34.
198 "*qah-emah binafis-ha*" is related to the Syriac term *qnômâ* pl. *qnômê*, a perfect thing, not in need of anything else for its substance. It is found in the Syriac edition of John 5:26. Griffith, "Christian Theology in Islamic Terms", 163–4. Griffith states that this term when translated into Arabic carried negative connotations of trism which Christian scholars tried to avoid.
199 Spisa, *Sulaymān Ibn Hasan Al-Ghazzī T52, 648*, Tomus 52, 34–5.
200 Griffith, "Christian Theology in Islamic Terms", 157–61.
201 Spisa, *Sulaymān Ibn Hasan Al-Ghazzī T52, 648*, Tomus 52, 35.
202 Ibid.
203 Ibid.

Sulaymān names the unique essence of the self-existing creator Father, His speech, Son, and His life, Holy Spirit. This he defends by saying that the self-existing being is not an accident, neither is the act of speaking, nor living, meaning, in an Aristotelian sense, of not being changeable or affected by properties or qualities like other substances, Therefore these attributes are part of the one unique substance and not capable of being separated from the unique substance.[204] An excellent summary of his reasoning is provided below:

> The truth of what we say is there is clear evidence that he is one essence, substance, specified by three hypostases, Fatherhood, Sonship and Spirit, each and every one of them possesses what the other has in terms of divinity. Without separation, or subordination, except in terms of the rank of the name. So, we then believe that there belongs to the Father everything belonging to the Son and the Holy Spirit in divinity. Except that He (the Father) should not be named born and generated. And thus it is for the Father, as for the Son and the Spirit in divinity. Except that He should not be named a parent (Father) one issuing forth. Likewise as for the Holy Spirit as the Father and the Son in divinity, except that he is named generator or the one issuing forth. And the meaning of our saying three hypostasis is by way of explanation of the three referents, and is not three parts, and not three powers, and not three substances, and not a third of an accident, but three properties by means by which the oneness of the eternal creator are known. Praise be his name and exalted be the mention of him. Existing in His essence and His Word and Spirit. One in substance not like created substances that occupy space, because the essence of the Father and the Son and the Spirit is a single essence.[205]

Sulaymān defends the use of the concept of the Trinity in spite of the fact that the concept is admittedly quite a difficult concept to comprehend. He states that the oneness of God is confirmed by applying number to terms and "therefore the terms lead a sum to their power to the ears".[206] This author understands this phrase implies that the understanding of the three hypostases, Father, Son and Holy Ghost leads to an understanding of the

---

204 Ibid., 35–6.
205 Ibid., 36–7.
206 Ibid., 37–8. Sulaymān is referring to the Trinity and possibly in relation to a Pythagorean understanding of the number 3, that is, the sum of 1, the first odd number and 2, the first even number. Therefore "3" is the summation of all numbers. Cf. Mark N. Swanson, *Early Christian-Muslim Theological Conversation among Arabic-Speaking Intellectuals*, 12.

oneness of the essence of God. The hearing of this leads to an understanding by the heart, which in turn is gradually understood by the mind, a concept very familiar to Muslims as hearing the recitation of the Qurʾān eventually leads to understanding. Sulaymān acknowledges that comprehending the concept requires faith and even then, not everyone can grasp it. This is of course reminiscent of Abū Qurrah's view that reason only goes so far before faith must take us the rest of the way. Sulaymān reminds the reader that it is impossible for mankind to comprehend even our own bodies, so how then can we expect to know the Creator, since there is nothing visible in the concept of Trinity to aid in its comprehension.[207] Sulaymān seems to be implying that, since even the wisdom of the wisest only achieves a modicum of understanding of what God reveals, a little humility and trust are required on the part of those who doubt.[208]

Similar to Abū Qurrah, Sulaymān says people would understand that just as the sun must have heat and light, the same is true for the soul, mind and speech. The essence of the soul is one, as is the Trinity, "a single God and a single substance, a single force and a single object of worship".[209] Sulaymān ends his article by requesting in the name of Jesus the Messiah for the intercession of "the Lady of Light" to strengthen the faith of the believers.[210]

Paul of Antioch

The third Christian interlocutor examined in this chapter is Paul of Antioch, Bishop of Sidon. Paul lived around the mid-twelfth to mid-thirteenth century.[211] Similar to the other scholars, very little detail is known about

---

207 Ibid., 39. Meaning intestines and the inner functions of the body.
208 Ibid.
209 Ibid., 40.
210 Ibid.
211 David Thomas, "Paul of Antioch's Letter to a Muslim Friend and the Letter from Cyprus", in *Syrian Christians under Islam: The First Thousan Years*, ed. David Thomas

Paul's life. The assumed period of his life is based on the dating of MS Sinai Arabic 448 and 531, which place the earliest copy of the *Letter to a Muslim Friend* to around the death of Elias of Nisibis (d. 1041) who is mentioned in his writings and 1232.[212] It is believed that he was once a monk, possibly from the Monastery of Siméon the Younger.[213] It is believed that he hailed from Antioch as his name suggests.[214] He is credited with the authorship of several texts including the *Letter to a Muslim Friend* and the *Letter from Cyprus*.[215] The former is directly attributed to Paul. The latter is an extension of the former, amended anonymously in Cyprus at the beginning of the fourteenth century.[216] Collectively his works discuss important matters of faith including the Trinity, Incarnation, the miracles of Christ, the authenticity of the scriptures, free will, predestination as well as the oneness of God.

Paul lived in interesting times. If the period assumed above is correct then Paul lived while the western monarchs were still committed to Pope Urban II's vision of liberating the Holy Land.[217] Paul possibly wrote between the Third Crusade involving Richard the Lionheart and Salāh ad-Dīn Yūsuf ibn Ayyūb, and the fratricidal Fourth Crusade that

---

(Leiden: Brill, 2001), 203–4; Sidney H Griffith, "Paul of Antioch", in *The Orthodox Church in the Arab World, 700–1700: An Anthology of Sources*, eds Samuel Noble & Alexander Treiger (DeKalb: Northern Illinois Press, 2014), 217.

212   Thomas, "Paul of Antioch", 203–4. S. K. Samir contends the *Letter* that was written between 1041 (death of Elias of Nisibis, mentioned in the Letter) and 1232, based on MS Sinai Arabic 531. Paul Khoury, *Paul D'antioche: Évêque Melkite De Sidon (Xiie S.)*, trans. Paul Khoury, vol. XXIV (Beyrouth: Imprimerie Catholique, 1964), 10.

213   *Paul D'antioche*, XXIV, 17.

214   Thomas, "Paul of Antioch", 203.

215   Griffith, "Paul", 216.

216   Thomas, "Paul of Antioch", 213–4. Cf. "Idealism and Intransigence: A Christian-Muslim Encounter in Early Mumluk Times", *Mamlūk Studies Review* 13, no. 2 (2009): 85.

217   Malcom C Barber, "The Challenge of State Building in the Twelfth Century: The Crusader States in Palestine and Syria", in *The Stenton Lecture 2008*, ed. Dr Rebecca Rist (Reading: University of Reading, 2009), 4. Cf. Ralph-Johannes Lilie, *Byzantium and the Crusader States 1096–1204* [Byzanz und die Kreuzfahrerstaaten], ed. Wilhelm Fink Verlag, trans. J. C. Morris and Jean E. Ridings, Poikila Byzantina (Oxford: Clarendon Press, 1993; repr., 1988), 1, 246–58.

Resisting the Construct 187

divided the Latin Christian Church from the Byzantine Eastern Church in Constantinople.[218] This occurred during a period of détente following the Treaty of Ramla in 1192, which ended the third crusade.[219] The Treaty allowed Muslims to control Jerusalem while Christians controlled the coast from Joppa to Tyre.[220] A caveat of the treaty guaranteed the free passage of Christian pilgrims and Muslims merchants.[221] If Paul, in fact, wrote the *Letter to a Muslim Friend* (henceforth, the *Letter*) at this time, then he wrote while Antioch and Sidon were part of the Principality of Antioch and the Province of Tripoli respectively.[222] During this period Christians in the Levant might have felt confident to respond frankly to the theological challenges of Islam.[223]

It is generally accepted that the *Risāla* [*the Letter*] is not an original work of Paul of Antioch and since the *Risāla* basically makes the same arguments as the *Letter*, this study will focus exclusively on the *Letter to a Muslim Friend*. The style of writing is interesting compared to the other two documents under consideration. The *Letter* recounts a dialogue between Paul and his Muslim friend concerning the former's travels to Byzantine territories, including Rome and Constantinople, Moldova and the Frankish provinces.[224] Through the dialogue Paul is able to express his understanding of the mission of Muhammad, the Qur'ān and Islam while defending

---

218 David Nicolle, *The Fourth Crusade 1202–04: The Betrayal of Byzantium*, 1st edn (Oxford: Osprey Publishing, 2011), History, 5, 78–88. Cf. Jonathan Phillips, "The Fourth Crusade and the Sack of Constantinople", *History Today* 5, no. 54 (2004): 21–28.

219 James Reston, *Warrior's of God: Richard the Lionheart and Saladin in the Third Crusade* (London: Faber & Faber Ltd, 2001), 298–99. Durant, *Faith*, 4, 601. Abu-Munshar, *Islamic Jerusalem*, 181.

220 Amin Maalouf, *The Crusades through Arab Eyes* [Les croisades vues par les Arabes], trans. Amin Maalouf (London: Al Saqi Books, 1984), 214–5. Thomas Asbridge, "Talking to the Enemy: The Role and Purpose of Negotiations between Saladin and Richard the Lionheart During the Third Crusade", *Journal of Medieval History* 39, no. 3 (2013): 291–2.

221 Reston, *Warrior's of God*, 298–9.

222 Barber, "Crusader States", 1–20.

223 It seems unlikely that Paul would have adopted such a confident tone in his *Letter* if the Church on which he relied were imploding behind him.

224 Khoury, *Paul D'antioche*, XXIV, 169, Arabic 59–60.

aspects of the Christian faith. Whether or not the trip and conversations ever actually took place is an interesting question. Khoury considers that it is plausible that Paul made the trip. As a bishop Paul would have motive and opportunity to attend the 3rd Latin Council held in Vienna in 1179 CE.[225] Could Paul have met western Christians interested in Islam and who would have read the Qur'ān and were familiar with its teachings? According to Khoury there were western Christians beginning to take an interest in Islam around the middle of the twelfth century. In fact, Robert de Ketene completed a translation of the Qur'ān into Latin in 1143 CE. Thomas considers it highly unlikely however, since the Europeans at that time would not have been able to introduce the subtle changes into the text of the Qur'ān that the *Letter* demonstrates.[226] Perhaps the literary personae in Paul's *Letter* are a composite of characters. The dialogue could therefore be a mix of truth and artistic license, useful to convey what Paul would like to say about Islam to his Muslim friend, while leaving Paul free from negative repercussions of any blame for insults deliberate or unintentional.[227]

Paul's extensive use of the Qur'ān in defence of Christian beliefs is ultimately self-serving. Paul selectively draws upon the Qur'ān in support of the Christian faith in ways that Muslims find highly controversial.[228] From a Muslim perspective Paul's use of the Qur'ān would truly qualify for *ijtihād* [independent reasoning] or *bid'ah sayyi'a* [heretical innovation] in matters of religion, since he ignores *tafsīr*.[229] The tone of his *Letter* not

---

225 Ibid., 13.
226 Thomas, "Paul of Antioch", 206–7. Khoury, *Paul D'antioche*, XXIV, 13–4.
227 Griffith, "Paul", 218.
228 Thomas, "Paul of Antioch", 207, 09. Cf. Mark Beaumont, *Christology in Dialogue with Muslims: A Critical Analysis of Christian Presentations of Christ for Muslims from the Ninth and Twentieth Centuries*, eds Kwame Bediako, et al., Regnum Studies in Mission (Eugene: Wipf and Stock Publishers, 2011), 114.
229 Samir Khalil Samir, "The Prophet Muhammad as Seen by Timothy I and Some Other Arab Christian Authors", in *Syrian Christians under Islam: The First Thousand Years*, ed. David Thomas (Leiden: Brill, 2001), 91–106. Respect for traditional *tafsīr* was the common practice of Arab Christian scholars.

only cast Christians in a negative light, but also inspired several polemic texts that influenced generations.²³⁰

Paul of Antioch's Defence of the Trinity and Incarnation, Letter to a Muslim Friend

As the title suggests Paul of Antioch's defence of Christianity is in the form of a letter. He purports to respond to his Muslim friend's queries concerning the views of some noble and learned people that he met on a recent trip to Europe with regard to their opinion of Muhammad and the Qur'ān. Throughout the *Letter* Paul cleverly outlines a defence of Christian beliefs that employs fewer Biblical references in comparison to Abū Qurrah, but extensively quotes from the Qur'ān in a highly cavalier fashion. Therefore it is possible to say that Paul attempts to Christianize the Qur'ān in order to demonstrate its compatibility with Christian doctrines, including the Trinity and Incarnation. Paul's *Letter* is often criticized for intentionally quoting the Qur'ān out of context and for his disregard for traditional *tafsīr* of the texts he invokes which, understandably, Muslims find offensive.²³¹ As a result of his *ijtihād* and perhaps even *bid'ah* Paul's strong arguments in support of Christian use of the terms Father, Son and Holy Spirit and his refutation of allegations of associating partners with God, or accusations of anthropomorphism, find little sympathy.²³² At times Paul hints at an experiential truth that perhaps, with a less confrontational delivery,

---

230 Griffith, "Paul", 217.
231 Three Muslim scholars responded to Paul's letters that remain influential to this day. Shihāb al-Dīn Ahmad b. Idrīs al-Qarāfī (1228–1285) responded to the Letter, while Taqī al-Dīn Ahmad Ibn Taymiyyah and Muhammad Ibn Abī Tālib al-Ansārī responded to the *Risāla*. Cf. Thomas, "Paul of Antioch", 204; "Idealism and Intransigence", 85–103.
232 Khoury, *Paul D'antioche*, XXIV, 177, 83, ¶30, ¶50. Cf. Arabic 70, 78.

might have opened up more fruitful dialogue.²³³ Paul begins and ends his defence by calling for a blessing of perception onto those who desire the right direction. In ways, the opening is slightly reminiscent of the many verses similar to *sūrat Ghāfir* 40:7–8, or *sūrat al-fātiha*, the opening chapter of the Qur'ān that praises God and asks for His guidance for those seeking the right path.

Through his European interlocutors Paul addresses the issue of Christian regard for Muhammad and the Qur'ān. The interlocutors describe how they heard of Muhammad and subsequently obtained a copy of his book, that is, the Qur'ān. This they felt compelled to do since they heard the book often says, "whosoever searches for a religion other than Islam it will not be accepted of him, and in the next life he will be amongst the losers".²³⁴ However, their anxieties soon pass as they read that the Qur'ān states that Muhammad was sent to be a warner to his own people, who had not received one before. Due to the fact that the Qur'ān is written in Arabic and that they have received the Torah and the Gospel in their own tongue, these Christians felt the Qur'ān was not sent to them. A few points can be drawn from this statement. First Paul acknowledges Muhammad as sent by God. The statement also reveals Paul's lack of awareness that Muhammad was in contact with native Arabic-speaking Christians in the Hijaz. In addition, Paul ignores the fact that Arabic was the native tongue for many Christians by this time. Furthermore, the Europeans point out that in the Qur'ān, Muhammad was sent to a people in manifest error, understanding that these people were kin to him, and that through his mission they might follow the right path.²³⁵ Thus the verse, "If anyone seeks a religion other than Islam it will not be accepted of them …" applies to those to whom it arrived in their language and not to others. "Others", they argue, are not obliged to follow Muhammad, nor Islam.²³⁶

In line with traditional *tafsīr* Paul, through the European interlocutors, points out that the Qur'ān has very high esteem for Mary and Jesus.

---

233 Ibid. Paragraph 44. 181. Arabic 85.
234 Ibid., 170. Citing *sūrat Āl-'Imrān* (3):85. Arabic 60.
235 Ibid., 170, ¶6. Arabic 60–1. Griffith, "Paul", 220–1.
236 Khoury, *Paul D'antioche*, XXIV, 170–1. Arabic 60–1. Thomas, "Paul of Antioch", 206–7.

Resisting the Construct 191

However he then cites *sūrat al-ḥadīd* (57):25, but alters the text slightly in order to imply that the mission of the Apostles, as well as the Gospel, is commended over and above Muhammad, to be a warning to Christians not to abandon their faith.[237] In the process he flatly refutes the charge of excesses that Christians have altered the text of the Gospel.[238] In support of his argument Paul brazenly interprets the mysterious *muqaṭṭaʿāt* letters, *alif, lām, mīm*, appearing at the beginning of *sūrat al-baqarah* as an anagram for *al-Masīḥ*.[239] Therefore, in Paul's view where the verse says, *dhālika al-kitāb* [that is the Book], in which there is no doubt, guidance for the pious", the verse, he argues, is referring to the Gospel, not the Qurʾān. If the verse had intended the Qurʾān, Paul further argues, it would have said *hādhā*, [this] Book.[240]

Interestingly, Paul proceeds in a reconciliatory note by citing verses from the Qurʾān that support amicable relations as with *sūrat al-ʿankabūt* (29):46 where it says, "Do not dispute with the People of the Book, unless it is in the better way, except those of them who have been unjust. And say, 'we believe what has been revealed to us and what has been revealed to you. Our God and your God is one, and it is to Him we submit'".[241] Here Paul argues that Christians are not required to follow Muhammad, that they are acknowledged in the verse as believing in the same God, implying that their *Islām* is acceptable to God as is. Otherwise the verse would command Christians to "submit". In addition, he adds that Christians are the closest of the People of the Book to Muslims.[242] Similarly Paul interprets *sūrat al-baqarah* 2:62 to endorse Christianity in an *ipso facto* manner.[243] This interpretation goes far beyond the traditional *tafsīr* examined in Chapter 1.[244]

---

237 Khoury, *Paul D'antioche*, XXIV, 171–6, ¶10–16, ¶23, ¶24. Cf. Arabic 62–4, 67–8. Thomas, "Paul of Antioch", 209. Griffith, "Paul", 222.
238 "Paul", 223.
239 Al-Tabarī, *Tafsīr Al-Tabarī*, 83–89.
240 Khoury, *Paul D'antioche*, XXIV, 173, ¶16. Arabic 65. Griffith, "Paul", 223.
241 Khoury, *Paul D'antioche*, XXIV, 174–6, ¶18–24. Arabic 66–8. Griffith, "Paul", 223.
242 Khoury, *Paul D'antioche*, XXIV, ¶19. Citing Psalms 105. Griffith, "Paul", 224.
243 Khoury, *Paul D'antioche*, XXIV, 175 ¶22. Arabic 67.
244 Griffith, "Paul", 225.

Paul's Scriptural Defence

Paul's cites less than a dozen Biblical verses. Most are different from the verses cited by Abū Qurrah. His use of scripture is different as well. For example, paragraph 19 of the *Letter* makes references to Psalms 106. Here the text is used to distinguish Christians from those Paul claims are the unjust, namely the Jews. In the subsequent verses the Jews are denigrated *en masse*, as people who are guilty of sacrificing their children and engaging in idol worship. In contrast, in paragraph 20, Paul quotes from *sūrat al-mā'idah* (5):82 where Christians are identified specifically as those closest to those who believe and who are praised for the honesty of their actions and the goodness of their intentions.[245] Considering the historical context of the *Letter* these are quite profound analogies. In addition, whereas Abū Qurrah uses scripture to demonstrate that the divine acts under different names, Paul states that God names His divinity Father, Son and Holy Ghost.[246]

Paul's Biblical defence of the Trinity begins about halfway through the text in paragraph 30.[247] In Deuteronomy 32:6 Paul demonstrates that God, speaking through Moses, addresses the sons of Israel, "Is it not the Father who has made you, who created you, acquired you?" In Genesis 1:2, Moses describes how "The Spirit of God hovered over the water". In Psalms 51 through the words of the prophet David, God is described as "Spirit". David says, "Your Spirit does not leave me". In Psalms 33 David also says, "By the Word of God the heavens strengthened and by the Spirit of his mouth all their powers". Paul quotes Job describing the Spirit of God as his "creator" and his "instructor".[248] Through the mouth of the prophet Isaiah in verse 40:7–8 God says, "The astragalus withers and the grass dries, but the Word of God remains forever".[249] Similarly to the views of Abū Qurrah and Sulaymān before him, Paul justifies the hypostases of the Trinity with the

---

245 Khoury, *Paul D'antioche*, XXIV, 174. Arabic 66.
246 Ibid., 177, ¶77. Arabic 70. Griffith, "Paul", 226.
247 Khoury, *Paul D'antioche*, XXIV, 177. Arabic 78–9.
248 Job 33.
249 Khoury, *Paul D'antioche*, XXIV, 177. Arabic 75, translation by this author. Astragalus is a versatile plant found in the Middle East.

words of the Messiah dispatching his disciples on the Great Commission, "Go to all nations, baptise in the name of the Father, the Son and the Holy Spirit, teach them and guard all that I have prescribed for you".[250]

In support of the above Biblical citations Paul seamlessly weaves in verses from the Qur'ān to recall how in Islam God also works through his *Word*. In *sūrat Ghāfir* (40):68, God demonstrates that when He wishes to do anything God merely says "be" and it is. God speaks to Moses with clear Words in *sūrat an-Nisā'* (4):164. In *sūrat al-mā'idah* (5):110 God strengthens Jesus with His Spirit. In *sūrat at-tahrīm* (66):12 God breathed His Spirit into Mary and preserved her virginity. In addition, Paul makes the comparison to the Islamic understanding that Muslims call their Book, God's living word, living and rational, hinting at the inlibration of the Qur'ān. In effect, for all intents and purposes, Paul, like Abū Qurrah above, accepts the credibility of the Qur'ān at least as far as it suits his argument.[251]

From here Paul makes his defence of the concept of the Incarnation of Jesus. In paragraph 33 he says that the Messiah is the Son of God, begotten before the centuries, pre-existing and through him all things came into being. By this Paul says that Christians indicate that there was never a time when the Messiah was not the spoken Word and the Father never ceased to be the Father, speaking. Thus, when the Father sent His Word, the Messiah, the Word did not separate from Him. An analogy Paul uses to describe this relationship is the familiar sunlight and the disk of the sun. Another is the Word of a man from the one who hears, without separating the intellect from the generator.[252] This Messiah is the perfect man, *begotten* by the Holy Spirit and the Virgin Mary, without corruption, without carnal copulation. Paul in paragraph 34 differentiates between Jesus' eternal divine and begotten human nature. This is evident since the divine nature cannot be affected by accidents, in the Aristotelian way, just as God spoke to Moses through the burning bush without the bush being consumed by the flames.[253] Paul further refutes any accusations that Christians are speaking of a carnal sonship by

---

250   Ibid.
251   Ibid., 178, ¶30. Arabic 70–1. Griffith, "Paul", 227.
252   Khoury, *Paul D'antioche*, XXIV, 178. Arabic 71–2. Griffith, "Paul", 227–8.
253   Khoury, *Paul D'antioche*, XXIV, 179. Arabic 72. Griffith, "Paul", 228.

citing *sūrat al-anʿām* (6):101.²⁵⁴ Here it says, "Wonderful originator of the heavens and the earth: How can He have a son when He hath no consort ...?" Yet through *sūrat al-balad* (90):1–3 Paul suggests that the Qurʾān also speaks of the begetter and the begot as referring to the God and his Son, "I swear by the creator and this his begotten". This interpretation of the verse, however, is a gross innovation of traditional *tafsīr*.²⁵⁵

Perhaps a more appropriate defence is presented in *sūrat ash-Shūra* (42):51. In this verse Paul makes the comparison between God speaking through Jesus and God speaking to Moses through the burning bush. The verse reads, "It is not fitting for a man that God should address him accept by revelation or behind a veil".²⁵⁶ Paul says that God appeared to man his most noble creation in this manner, through Jesus. In support of the concept of the Messiah being of two natures Paul cites *sūrat an-Nisāʾ* (4):171 where Jesus is described as a messenger of God, His Word cast into Mary by Him, and a Spirit issuing from Him. Yet, the traditional *tafsīr* from Chapter 1 would only accept this as a sign of the authenticity of Jesus as Messiah, not as proof of his sonship. Another verse Paul cites concerning the nature of the Jesus is *sūrat Maryam* (19):34, "This is the Word of truth, about which they vainly dispute".

Returning to Biblical verse in paragraph 41 Paul reviews the verses cited earlier in paragraph 30. In paragraphs 42 and 43 Paul draws upon analogies such as the tailor sewing a dress and the hand of the tailor sewing a dress; the carpenter and the carpenter's hand making a chair; fire its light and heat; the sun, its rays and warmth, to demonstrate that Christians insist that God and His Word and his Spirit are one sole God.²⁵⁷ These analogies lead to what this present author considers a less guarded and perhaps more personal reflection. Paul posits in paragraph 44 that, "this is how we see God, Holy be His names". He says further that Christians do not deserve blame for what they believe, nor should they give up what they have received for something else; especially since they can find support for their beliefs in the Book brought

---

254 "Paul", 228.
255 Khoury, *Paul D'antioche*, XXIV, 179. Arabic 72. Griffith, "Paul", 228. Ibn Kathīr, *Tafsir Al-Qurʾān Al-Azim*, Vol. 10, 483.
256 Khoury, *Paul D'antioche*, XXIV, 179–80, ¶36. Arabic 72–3. Griffith, "Paul", 228.
257 Khoury, *Paul D'antioche*, XXIV, 181. Arabic 75.

Resisting the Construct 195

by its messenger.²⁵⁸ If this is a sincere statement then Paul is getting to the heart of the matter. Christians don't hold onto a difficult concept like the Trinity just because it comes down through tradition. It is because Christians experience God through the three hypostases.²⁵⁹

Interestingly, Paul immediately moves from a dialogue inspiring statement to some of his more polemic thoughts. He anticipates Muslim reaction to his highly Christianized interpretations of the Qur'ān, or lack of respect for *tafsīr*, by positing the question, that if Christians accept part of the Qur'ān then should they not accept all of it? He answers his own question in paragraph 45 with an analogy of a debt for 100 dinars. If a debt is recorded in a book, but the debt is eventually paid, the creditor cannot reproduce the book and demand payment a second time just because it is written in the book. Paul is insinuating that the payment of the debt abrogates the initial entry into the debt book. For this reason Paul argues his interpretation of the Qur'ān is also valid.²⁶⁰ In paragraph 46 he threatens to cite verse for verse with Muslims from their own Book in defence of Christian beliefs. In paragraph 47 Paul declares that the Qur'ān gives Christians the strongest arguments. Since He says the Qur'ān has "placed Christians over the infidels, until the Day of Resurrection" and because Christians follow Jesus they are "the closest in friendship to those who believe". In addition, Paul recalls that in the Qur'ān it says, "God has placed in our hearts humility and piety". Paul further states that the Qur'ān praises the Gospel, our writings, monasteries and churches and that Christians are recognized for their good deeds. For these reasons and the fact that, "No one has advantage over us", Paul declares the Qur'ān supports Christian beliefs.²⁶¹ He then boldly asserts that not only does the Qur'ān support

---

258 Ibid. Arabic 75.
259 This author is thinking in terms of the juxtaposition between how things are named within a community through a common process of social conditioning and how outsiders interpret these same terms.
260 Khoury, *Paul D'antioche*, XXIV, 181–2. Arabic 76.
261 Ibid., 182. Arabic 76–7. Perhaps the statement, "No one has advantage over us" helps locate the text historically to when Latin and Byzantine Christians were united and held lands they would lose in the Fourth Crusade and later times.

Christian beliefs, but it warns Christians not to abandon what they have received. In paragraph 48 Paul paraphrases *sūrat al-māʾidah* (5):112–115 where the disciples of Jesus seek a sign from God that Jesus is truly God's messenger. God sends down a "communion table" as a sign for the first and the last of them. They accept faith and are given a stark warning of a torment that "no other people have endured", if they abandon what they have received.[262]

Paul's Rational Defence

Paul's rational defence of the Trinity and the Incarnation is a central element of the *Letter*. His argument is similar to his predecessors especially, Sulaymān al-Ghazzī above. In conjunction with his use of reason Paul combines Biblical and Qurʾānic support for his argument. In the process Paul takes great liberties with traditional *tafsīr*, frequently turning Islamic criticism of Christian excesses into support. In his opening statement Paul describes God as Father, Son and Holy Spirit, "whose substance is confessed to be one, and whose hypostases are posited to be three".[263] In so doing he immediately describes God as a thing or substance knowing this is not acceptable to Muslims.[264]

In paragraph 25 Paul presents Muslim disapproval as a misunderstanding of what Christians actually mean by the terms used to describe God. "I say: They disapprove of us in our saying Father, Son and Holy Spirit. 'They say (the European interlocutors): If they (the Muslims) knew that we intended by these words to make more explicit the assertion that God most high is a *living rational thing*, they would not disapprove of this'".[265] He says that by this (God most high is a living rational thing) Christians infer that something else created the things that exist, that they could not create themselves. This *shay* [thing], is not like other things, because

---

262 Ibid. Arabic 77.
263 Ibid., 169. Arabic 59. Griffith, "Paul", 219.
264 Khoury, *Paul D'antioche*, XXIV, 185, ¶55. Arabic 81. Griffith, "Paul", 226.
265 Khoury, *Paul D'antioche*, XXIV, 176. Arabic 69.

it is the creator of all things. Accordingly, it follows that the creator of all must be a *being* in order to deny God nothingness. Paul continues to reason that there are two types of things, living and non-living. God the creator of all things must be living, the more noble of the two, in order to deny God mortality. Living things are further divided between rational and non-rational beings. We say God is the more noble; therefore God is *hayy nāṭiq* [living-rational], in order to deny God is ignorant, *jahl*.[266] The three names represent the one unique God who does not cease to be a living-speaking thing. For Christians, the essence is the Father, the Son is the spoken Word (rational), and the life is the Holy Spirit. In support of this argument he draws upon *sūrat al-baqarah* (2):255 where it says "God, no other God than He, living, *al-qayūm* [self-existing]".[267] The importance here for Paul is the use of the word *al-qayūm*, that is found in the verse and would suggest that there are occasions when it is appropriate in Islam to discuss God as a thing or self-existing substance.

As seen above these statements and the names of the hypostases of God are supported by Biblical verse in paragraph 30 and Qur'ānic verse in paragraphs 31 and where the Qur'ān is described as the Word of God, *living speaking*. Paul states that these are essential attributes and each is different. Yet God is one, not apportioned or divided. Paul further states that at the beginning of the Qur'ān three attributes are mentioned at the exclusion of others where it says, "In the name of God, the compassionate, the merciful".[268] Paul therefore justifies the Christian use Father, Son and Holy Spirit as three attributes at the exclusion of others, because none of the other attributes of consequence are *living rational*. The others attributes depend on these attributes. As for example in *sūrat al-isrā'* 17:110, where it says, "Call upon God, and call upon the Compassionate One; whatever you call Him, His are the most beautiful names".[269]

Paragraphs 33 and 34 discuss the concept of the Incarnation of the Messiah with his human and divine natures. Paul argues that the divine

---

266 Ibid., 176–7. Arabic 69. Griffith, "Paul", 226.
267 Khoury, *Paul D'antioche*, XXIV, 177, ¶29. Arabic 69.
268 Ibid., 178. Arabic 71. Griffith, "Paul", 227.
269 Khoury, *Paul D'antioche*, XXIV, 178. Arabic 71. Griffith, "Paul", 227, fn. 83.

nature of the Messiah, like Sulaymān above, is not affected by accidents. Through paragraph 33–36 Paul explains what Christians mean when they say the Messiah is the begotten Son of God. By this Paul says, without the Christ, the spoken Word of God, nothing came into being. That the Messiah never ceased to be Son, that is the spoken Word and the Father never ceased to be Father, that is speaking. Paul uses two analogies to describe this relationship. The first compares the relationship of the Father and the Son to that of the sun and its rays. The second compares the word of a man that when spoken does not separate from the intellect of the man, the generator.[270]

In reference to the Incarnation Paul says that Christ became the perfect man through the Virgin Mary and the Holy Spirit. Thus the Word became flesh. The Messiah is begotten in his human nature, but not his divine, since it is not possible for the divine to be affected by *'arad* [accident]. Consequently, the virginity of Mary remained intact. Paul refutes the accusation levied against Christians that they believe Jesus is begotten in a carnal manner. Paul supports this philosophical argument with reference to the story of the burning bush found in Exodus 3:2–3 and *sūrat al-anʿām* (6):101 where it denies God a consort.[271] Similarly, the divine nature appears in Jesus not due to carnal physical union, but as something *subtle* appearing in a solid form as with *sūrat ash-Shūra* (42):51, "It is not fitting for a man that God should address him accept by revelation, or behind a veil".[272] Further to his argument Paul cites from *sūrat al-balad* (90):1–3 where he alters the verse to say, "swearing" by the begetter and the begotten.[273]

Paul argues that God operates through this dual nature. That through the Messiah the divine achieves the impossible and demonstrates his humility through his humanity.[274] This is how Christians can say, in face of Islamic

---

270 Khoury, *Paul D'antioche*, XXIV, 179. Arabic 72. This is similar to the description found in the *Triune Nature of God* mentioned above.
271 Ibid. Arabic 72. Griffith, "Paul", 228.
272 Khoury, *Paul D'antioche*, XXIV, 179–80. Arabic 72–3. Griffith, "Paul", 227–8.
273 Khoury, *Paul D'antioche*, XXIV, 179. Arabic 72. Griffith, "Paul", 228. Once again Paul ignores *tafsīr*.
274 Khoury, *Paul D'antioche*, XXIV, 180. Arabic 73. Griffith, "Paul", 228.

claims of excesses, that Jesus suffered crucifixion, in his human nature, but His divine nature did not die. Paul very interestingly supports his argument by referring to *sūrat an-Nisā'* (4):157 where it states, "He was not killed nor crucified, but it appeared to them as such".[275] Paul therefore claims that the Qur'ān supports what Christians say about the Messiah. The Messiah is God's spoken word. God is further described as a thing that is not affected by accident. Paul defends the dual nature of the Messiah, unique in his person, by citing further in paragraph 40 from *sūrat an-Nisā'* (4):171 where its states that Jesus is both the Word of God and a Spirit issuing from Him as well as from *sūrat Maryam* (19):34 where Jesus is referred to as "the Word of truth which they vainly dispute".[276] By analogy Paul uses the example of a blacksmith heating a piece of iron. The heat turns the iron into fire, which retains its nature to provide heat and light while allowing the iron to be affected by the heat.[277]

In paragraphs 49–54 Paul discusses the difference between literal meaning of the words Christians and Muslims use to describe God and the intended meaning. The use of the hypostases for the one unique God, Muslims say, leaves Christians open to accusations that Christians flatly deny, such as a belief in three Gods, or carnal begetting.[278] Therefore the use of logic creates a scenario whereby Christians appear to believe there are three Gods, or three parties and that one is called a son, that is, that God acts anthropomorphically. In paragraphs 50–54 Paul compares verses of the Qur'ān that describe God *tajsīm* [in anthropomorphic terms] as having eyes, and limbs and travelling via clouds in order to demonstrate that Muslims also need to step away from the apparent meaning of terms. Here Paul refutes accusations of excesses that suggest Christians believe in any form of association of partners between three Gods, or paternity, marriage, begetting, because these are accusations Christians curse outright.[279] In paragraph 54 Paul makes references that are partially based on *sūrat*

---

275 Khoury, *Paul D'antioche*, XXIV, 180. Arabic 73. Griffith, "Paul", 228.
276 Khoury, *Paul D'antioche*, XXIV, 180. Arabic 74. Griffith, "Paul", 229.
277 Khoury, *Paul D'antioche*, XXIV, 180. Arabic 73–4. Griffith, "Paul", 228–9.
278 Khoury, *Paul D'antioche*, XXIV, 182–87. Arabic 77. Griffith, "Paul", 230.
279 Khoury, *Paul D'antioche*, XXIV, 184–7 ¶53. Arabic 79. Griffith, "Paul", 231–2.

al-baqarah (2):255 that suggest Muslims believe God has two eyes, hands, a face, a leg, a side and sits on a throne. If read literally these physical features imply Islam supports anthropomorphism. Paul therefore posits that Muslims should not criticize Christians for discussing God in terms of the Trinity, where the literal reading would imply association and assimilation, since, on occasion, Muslims also discuss God in terms not intended literally and deny outright literal interpretations.[280] This remark taken together with the statement made in paragraph 25 that, if Muslims understood what Christians are really saying about God they would not disapprove, suggests further that the Qur'ān supports Christianity.[281]

In paragraph 55 Paul acknowledges that many Muslims are well versed in Greek philosophy and logic. More importantly he acknowledges that, for Muslims, there are limits to the degree to which they will rely on logic to discuss and define the nature of God.[282] For Muslims even naming God a *substance*, a basic premise of the Christian argument, is a step too far, noting the criticism received in earlier centuries. Therefore, even though Christians and Muslims both engaged in dialogue using Greek philosophical reasoning it would appear by Paul's statement that Christians needed to augment their arguments to reflect this obstacle. The misuse of the Qur'ān and *tafsīr* as a means of approval was hardly the correct approach. In paragraphs 56–58 Paul outlines a summary of the argument used to describe the three hypostases of the Trinity making the further distinction that God is *jawhar* [a *subtle substance*], not affected by accidents. He names subtle-substances as the soul, the mind, light, as they are not affected by accidents nor do they occupy space. God is the most noble, a self-subsistent, thus not in need of another for existence. Paul acknowledges, however, that Muslims do not accept that it is appropriate to call God a subtle substance.

In Paul's closing argument (paragraphs 59–64) he discusses the difference between the law of Justice given to Moses to guide the children of Israel and the Law of Grace given by the most magnificent provider, through His spoken Word. The Law of Grace is so perfect that it could come

---

280   Khoury, *Paul D'antioche*, XXIV, 184–5. Arabic 79–80. Griffith, "Paul", 232.
281   Khoury, *Paul D'antioche*, XXIV, 176. Arabic 68.
282   Ibid., 185. Arabic 80. Griffith, "Paul", 232.

from nowhere else. Paul contends that it is necessary that God himself by giving His Word must assume the essence of His most noble of creations to manifest his power and magnificence. He chose to do so by becoming man, through the Virgin Mary. Paul concludes that after this perfection there is nothing more to establish. He argues that everything that preceded this perfection points to its coming and everything after it, even if it is excellent, it must be lower, or will borrow from it.[283] Paul further states that what is borrowed (rather than inspired) is of a type of excellence that no one has need.[284] The implications being that the message of Muhammad is inferior to the message of Jesus and that Christians are thus not required to follow the teachings of Muhammad.

Conclusions

In an attempt to understand the early Arabic-speaking Christian response to Qur'ānic accusations of "excesses in your religion", this chapter offers a brief summary of the rise of Islam from the death of Muhammad to the conquest of the Levant. An observation of the conquest is that it occurred on far more nuanced terms than one might popularly perceive. An interesting characteristic of the Church at this time is the fact that Christianity across the region was anything but unified. Besides socio-cultural differences, communities with distinct creedal formulations were emerging and exhibiting increasing hostility towards each other. Hence some Christians initially interpreted the armies of Islam as an apocalyptic event, while others from minority creedal formulas suggest their position improved under Islamic rule. Likewise, some Jews viewed the conquest as the harbinger of Messianic times. In spite of differences in perception, as *People*

---

283 Samir, "The Prophet Muhammad", 104–5.
284 Khoury, *Paul D'antioche*, XXIV, 187. Arabic 82. Griffith, "Paul", 233–4. Samir, "The Prophet Muhammad", 105. Paul insinuates that Muhammad's teachings are from someone else and not from God.

of the Book, Christians and Jews of all creedal formulations benefited from the new political reality that ensured their safety as *dhimmī*. Historically this represents a great departure from previous conquests throughout the region where Christians and Jews, Byzantines and Persians each extracted revenge for previous atrocities. Nevertheless, peace and security had a price and the price included political and social submission.

Over time the Christians of the Levant settled into their new social and political reality. Eventually their native tongues gave way to Arabic. The first Christian Arabic texts were written in the form of liturgical or catechistic material used to serve their pastoral needs. Gradually a second genre of Arabic writings followed that would defend central tenets of the Christian faith against accusations of "excesses in your religion" posed by traditional Islamic exegesis. Many early Arabic Christian works were written to bolster the faith of Christians at a time when scores were converting to Islam. These writings often suggested that Muslims would readily convert to Christianity if it were not for loss of position in society and their desire for worldly pleasures. Other works, like *On the Triune Nature of God*, were quite prepared for the Muslim reader and respectfully drew upon Islamic idiom to defend the reasonableness of Christianity.

The Greek Arabic translation movement epitomized an incredible period of co-operation between the People of the Book and Islam. For more than two centuries Christian, Jewish and Muslim scholars worked side-by-side translating almost all scientific and philosophical works into Arabic. Through lessons learned from Greek philosophical reasoning, Muslims from both the Mu'tazilite and Ashrite traditions developed the tools to help rationalize the absolute oneness of God, *tawhīd*, in light of the multitude of divine attributes, as expressed in the *Beautiful Names*. Christians saw an opportunity with Muslim interests in Greek philosophy, as well as the debates going on within Islam itself, to respond to accusations of "excesses in your religion" using similar terms as their Muslim interlocutors. The Christian Arabic literature from this period argued that the divine attributes of *essence* and *action* could be reduced to three irreducible substantial attributes of *existing*, *living*, and *speaking*. Christians identified these three substantial attributes as the three hypostases of the Trinity.

However, in spite of the fact that Greek philosophical reasoning provided a common means of conducting theological discourse, Muslims and Christians never truly accepted the credibility of reasoning to the same degree. Whereas Christians were quite comfortable with the thought of discovering authoritative knowledge of God through reasoning, or "faith seeking answers", the same could not be said for their Muslim interlocutors who valued the application of Greek philosophical reasoning only so far as it was able to substantiate values espoused in the Qur'ān and Islamic teaching. Muslim scholars were unwilling to break with Islamic exegesis and risk accusations of innovation or heresy, by adopting the tactics of Christians. Nevertheless, the use of Greek philosophical reasoning provided common concepts for discourse whereby Muslims and Christians could better understand the faith of the other.

This chapter examined texts by three authors who lived in different historical times and circumstances. Although it is impossible to say exactly how these varying circumstances affected their respective defences, it is highly unlikely that the social and political environment did not play some role. Theologically, the defences of Abū Qurrah, Sulaymān al-Ghazzī and Paul of Antioch share many similarities, but also nuanced differences. Abū Qurrah argues that the Torah and all the prophets foretell of the coming of Christ. Sulaymān al-Ghazzī, perhaps with a touch of sarcasm, maintains that the words of the disciples were accepted only after seeing clear signs and works of faith. Paul of Antioch insists that it is only because of Jesus that Christians respect Moses and the Torah, let alone Muhammad and Islam. Each of the scholars employs various means including analogy, grammatical analysis, scripture and reason to defend the Trinity and the Incarnation. In the documents examined here, only Paul refers to the nature of God as a *subtle substance* in order to assure Muslims that the type of substance that Christians have in mind when referring to God is unique and not susceptible to change. Overall, each scholar skilfully advances his respective defence of Christian teaching. Yet, in spite of the common language of Arabic, in spite of the common manner of discourse of *ilm al-kalām*, no matter how lucid the arguments for the veracity of the Sonship, Incarnation and Trinity, the Christian scholars could not counter the fact that the Qurʾān expressly forbids speaking of God in terms of Trinity/ three, or Incarnation or as a substance.

Familiarity with and use of the Qurʾān by these early Arabic-speaking Christians in support of Christian faith and beliefs is inspirational. It demonstrates their lack of inhibition with regard to attempting to understand the Qurʾān and that at the very least it demonstrates that Christianity can be expressed in a culture dominated by Islam. The experience of God through His *Word* and *Spirit* compels Christians to retain the concept of the Trinity and the expression of Jesus as the Incarnation. It is important to keep in mind, as demonstrated by Paul of Antioch, that what the Qurʾān declares to be heresy, to a greater extent than is appreciated, Christians also accept as heresy. This is in spite of the fact that some Christians terms present challenges to Muslims. Each scholar offers the occasional glimpse into what can be described as an understanding of God, through an experience of God that follows faith. Abū Qurrah says as much when he warns that people should not let their intellect stand in the way of what is proven by "the mind's use of analogy", expressed with a certainty approaching that of experiential testimony".[285] For Sulaymān it is in the word and deeds of the disciples who brought the Gospel and baptized the people. Expressing faith in terms of the Trinity and Incarnation came gradually to Christianity following exposure to the Word and with faith. For Paul of Antioch the deciding factor pivots around his fervent belief in Grace as God's perfect gift that could only be delivered by God himself, through the veil of the Messiah. From these scholars it seems clear that there is a need for greater inter-scriptural reasoning on key verses of the Qurʾān and Bible that are problematic. Verses like *sūrat an-Nisāʾ* (4):171 and Matthew 28:19 appear to hold the key to creating mutual understandings, whereby Christians and Muslims can respect the faith claims of the other as somehow including their own.

Interestingly, the historical Christian communities from the nomadic Arabian tribes, Abyssinia, or Yemen who provided the context for the revelation of the verses from the Qurʾān that accuse Christians of "excesses",

---

285 Lamoreaux, *Abū Qurrah*, I, 191–2.

Resisting the Construct

are not an important part of the defence of Christianity during the post-conquest period. This is in spite of the fact that Christians from the post-conquest period were apt to defend the orthodoxy of their own communities in relation to the other emerging Christological formulas.[286] Therefore, at this juncture either Christians of the Levant were basically unaware of the various types of Christians inhabiting Arabia and its environs during the period of nascent Islam (to the degree that it could not be discussed meaningfully), or alternatively they were unwilling to differentiate between their respective positions. On the other hand, perhaps Muslims were reticent to discuss the differences in Christological formulas with Christians for fear of saying anything more than what is stated in the Qur'ān or *tafsīr*? Therefore, it is safe to say that by and large both Christians and Muslims during the post-conquest period are culpable of maintaining a deliberate intellectual disconnect between understanding an important aspect of the occasions of revelation in preference to the theoretical construct produced by the traditional commentary.

---

286 Griffith, *The Church in the Shadow*, 62.

PART III

Contemporary Refiguring of the People of the Book

Thus far this book has explored Christianity as the theoretical construct of the People of the Book through the lens of the Qur'ānic commentary tradition, in the social historical context and through the early Arabic Christian response. The focus now moves to modern discourse in order to ascertain the contemporary challenges and opportunities for interfaith dialogue and understanding of religious pluralism.

The texts from the Muslim and Christian scholars examined here oscillate between fidelity to their respective traditions and immense respect for the tradition of the religious other. Together they highlight a trajectory of thought, an edging closer to the metaphoric swim across the sea of uncertainty described by Jack Renard.[1]

---

1   John Renard, *Islam and Christianity: Theological Themes in Comparative Perspective* (Berkeley: University of California Press, 2011), 223–32.

CHAPTER 4

Contemporary Islamic Use of the Term "People of the Book"

Introduction

This chapter focuses on a number of key texts by modern Islamic scholars. The texts emerge from a plethora of possible sources offering guidance and advice for Muslims living in the modern world. Those selected offer a broad cross-section of material. Each scholar echoes both a call to tradition and a call to engage with a rapidly changing world where the boundaries between faith, secularism and culture are increasingly blurred.

The first texts examined are by the highly regarded scholar Yusuf Al-Qaradawi. He is an Egyptian born scholar and political activist closely associated with the ideology of the Muslim Brotherhood. At the time of writing Al-Qaradawi serves on the boards of a number of international Islamic organizations including the European Council for Fatwa Research based in Dublin, Ireland.[1] The texts examined are *Non Muslims in the Islamic Society* and *Al-Halāl Wal Harām Fil Islam* [*The Lawful And The Prohibited In Islam*].[2] These texts demonstrate an awareness of the critical inquiry concerning the term People of the Book, including aspects of

1   Islamic Cultural Centre Ireland, "Fatwas of European Council for Fatwa and Research", ed. Said Fares Al-Falah Foundation (Cairo: Islamic Inc., 2002), vii.
2   Yusuf Al-Qaradawi, *Non Muslims in the Islamic Society* [غير المسلمين في المجتمع الإسلامي], trans. Khalil Muhammad Hamad Sayed Mahboob Ali Shah (Indianapolis: American Trust Publications, 1985). And *The Lawful and the Prohibited in Islam ((Al- Al-Halāl Wal Harām Fil Islam)* [Al-Halal Al-haram Fil-Islam], ed. Ahmad Zaki Hammad, trans. M. Moinuddin Siddiqui Kamal El-Helbawy, Syed Shuky, 2nd edn (London: Shorouk International Limited, 1985).

social historical studies pursued in the previous chapters, in addition to the complexities of modern pluralistic society.

Confirming a Traditional Islamic View of the People of the Book

Al-Qaradawi defines and outlines the rights and duties of non-Muslim residents of Muslim countries in *Non Muslims in the Islamic Society* (1985). In the preface he says that the purpose of the book is to set the record straight in light of what he sees as an attack by hostile opinions from the West against Islam. He states further that, "the old war against Islam has however, not ceased; only its form has changed".[3] In the introduction to *The Lawful And The Prohibited In Islam* Al-Qaradawi explains that the purpose of the text is to provide educational material for Muslims living in Europe and America and to attract non-Muslims to Islam. He perceives that many Muslims living in the West have distorted views of Islam, confusing what is forbidden with that which is allowed.[4]

The Social Contract

In *Non Muslims and The Lawful And The Prohibited* the People of the Book are defined as a group among non-Muslims whose religions are based on divine revelation, even if this revelation is somehow distorted.[5] In *Non Muslims* the phrase *non-Muslim* frequently replaces the traditional use of the term "People of the Book". For example, while citing *sūrat al-ʿankabūt* (29):46, Al-Qaradawi states, "The words of Qur'an indicate the correct manner of discussion with non-Muslims".[6] This verse unambiguously refers to the People of the Book.

---

3   *Non Muslims*, ii. Henceforth referred to as *Non-Muslims*.
4   *The Lawful and the Prohibited*, 1–7.
5   *Non Muslims*, 1. In *The Lawful and the Prohibited*, 19, 59, 336. In this text the term *People of the Book* refers more strictly to Christians and Jews.
6   *Non Muslims*, 29. *The Lawful and the Prohibited*, 37.

An examination of *Non Muslims* reveals that the description of members defined as the People of the Book, their rights and obligations, follow the time-tested *tafsīr* examined in Chapter 1. Al-Qaradawi emphasizes that Islamic society calls for peace, justice and the highest degree of tolerance for "peoples of other faiths" as long as they do not disturb, or prevent Muslims from practising their faith, as in *sūrat al-mumtahanah* (60):8–9.[7] The life of Muhammad sets a normative example for the *ummah* of the closeness with which Muslims and non-Muslims can coexist. Muhammad always maintained friendly contact with the People of the Book. He met their delegations, allowed Christians to pray in his mosque, consoled their sick, mourned for their dead and conducted business with them.[8] In fact Al-Qaradawi points out that whether Muslims form the majority of society, or not, they are encouraged to foster good relations with the People of the Book.[9]

Protected Citizens

People of the Book when citizens, or residents, in an Islamic society are given a special status as protected people along with other non-Muslim citizens. The designation of *ahl adh-dhimma* or *dhimmī* is one that denotes due regard for the divine origins of the respective revelation and requires that the Muslims offer protection for people and property, including churches, as long as they pay the *jizyah* tax.[10] Al-Qaradawi cites a *hadīth* that says, "Anyone who kills a *dhimmī* will not smell of the fragrance of the Garden."[11] Alternatively, Al-Qaradawi employs other *hadīths* where Muhammad warns, "He who hurts a *dhimmī* hurts me, and he who hurts me annoys Allah", or "Whoever hurts a *dhimmī*, I am his adversary, and I shall be an adversary to him on the Day of Resurrection", or similarly, "On the Day of Judgment I shall dispute with anyone who oppresses a person

---

7 *Non Muslims*, 28.
8 Ibid., 28–31.
9 Ibid., 44–6. *The Lawful and the Prohibited*, 59–61, 183.
10 *Non Muslims*, 2, 7. There are noted violations of the ideal.
11 *The Lawful and the Prohibited*, 336.

from among the People of the Covenant, *ahl adh-dhimma*, or infringes on his right, or puts a responsibility on him which is beyond his strength, or takes something from him against his will".[12]

Interestingly, even items that Muslims are forbidden to possess themselves are not to be denied to protected people including wine and pigs. There are however, some constraints on the businesses of the *dhimmī*, like *ribā* [charging interest], as well as restrictions on outwardly defying Islamic practice like drinking in public or eating pork.[13] The *jizyah* tax is generally in lieu of military service, it is not a punitive tax.[14] Al-Qaradawi goes to great lengths to stress that the level of tax is generally equal to what Muslims pay in *zakāt* [almsgiving that each Muslim pays].[15] This protected arrangement is guaranteed by God, His messenger, and by Islamic communities.[16] This is the ideal, accepted with *ijmā'* [broad consensus], among all schools of Islamic jurisprudence. When this ideal is challenged it is due to external factors, both social and political, as seen above in the time the "Mad Caliph", or with [Daesh], the self-styled Islamic State.[17]

Religious Freedom

Religious diversity in Islam is an ethical reality uniquely ordained.[18] Al-Qaradawi offers numerous verses from the Qur'ān that help bridge the seeming contradictions of faiths in order to allow amity and tolerance such as *sūrat Hūd* (11):118 "If thy Lord had so willed, He could have made

12 Ibid., 338.
13 Ibid., 264.
14 *Non Muslims*, 19, 24, 38, 39. Christians may have their own courts. Muslims who have refused military service have paid the *jizyah* and Christians willing to fight on the side of their Islamic government have been exempt. 'Umar ibn al-Khattab called the tax levied against the Christian Bani Taghlib, *sadaqah* alms.
15 Ibid., 38.
16 Ibid., 20–3.
17 Qasim Rashid, "A Muslim's Ramadan Message to Isis: You Don't Speak for Islam", in *Huff Post* (Huffington Post, 2014).
18 Al-Qaradawi, *Non Muslims*, 53.

mankind one People: but they will not cease to differ". Alternatively, there is *surat ash-Shūra* (42):15 where it says, "I believe in whatever book Allah has sent down; I am commanded to judge justly between you. Allah is our Lord and your Lord! For us (is responsibility for) our deeds, and for you your deeds. There is no contention between us and you. Allah will bring us together, and to him is our goal".[19]

Al-Qaradawi insists that Islam has always extended religious freedom to its non-Muslim citizens, apparently referring to the People of the Book who have paid the *jizyah*. No one is compelled to convert to Islam, citing *surat al-baqarah* (2):256: "Let there be no compulsion in religion".[20] There are several historical treaties that reinforce the ideal that Islam does not demand that the People of the Book leave their religion. The examples given include the treaty between Muhammad and the Christians of Najrān as well as the covenant between 'Umar ibn al-Khattāb and the residents of Jerusalem at the time of conquest. In defence of his position Al-Qaradawi cites Ibn Kathir who explains that the truth of Islam is "self-evident" and does not require the use of force to gain converts.[21] This present author contends that this freedom of conscience needs to be considered against the backdrop of relations between religious groups examined in pre-Islamic times, as discussed in Chapter 2 and in the post-conquest period, as examined in Chapter 3. Muslim rule in the post-conquest period proscribed intra-Christian sectarianism.[22] Al-Qaradawi states however, that there has never been an incident where non-Muslims were forced to convert to Islam.[23]

Accordingly, Al-Qaradawi explains that, "Islam simply wants non-Muslims to consider the feelings of Muslims and respect the sanctity of their religion".[24] It should go without saying that non-Muslims should refrain from publicly insulting Islam, the prophet, or the Qur'ān.[25] Ironically

---

19 Ibid., 31–2.
20 Ibid., 9. Cf. *Sūrah Yunus* (10): 99.
21 Ibid.
22 Ibid., 49–52.
23 Ibid., 10. There are, however, many documented exceptions.
24 Ibid., 10.
25 Ibid., 25.

Al-Qaradawi goes on to express that Christians should refrain from outward displays of religion, including displays of crosses, or the construction of churches in Islamic areas where there had never been churches previously. The logic behind these prohibitions is to maintain public order. Nevertheless, Al-Qaradawi notes that historically prohibitions against religious displays were seldom ever enforced. In fact he observes that there are several famous churches and monasteries in Egypt built during the first century of Islamic rule. Al-Qaradawi remarks this point is not overlooked by the nineteenth-century social scientist Gustave Le Bon, citing the great historian William Robertson who commented that, "Muslims are the only people who possess both a zeal for their own faith as well as a spirit of tolerance toward the followers of other religions".[26]

If it is fair to say that the religious freedom of the People of the Book is safeguarded in Islamic society, as the will of God, an ideal practised by Muhammad, his companions and the Rightly Guided Caliphs, then one must be honest and acknowledge that, in reality, things can be quite different. Otherwise the demographic haemorrhage of Christians fleeing from Islamic lands at the time of writing would not be as marked as it is.[27] Al-Qaradawi acknowledges that often the success of non-Muslims in Muslim societies can cause rancour amongst certain elements of the Muslim population.[28] It would also appear that Al-Qaradawi is not well disposed to allowing non-Muslims to reach senior posts in Islamic society.[29] In spite of his misgivings, according to the Qur'ān, injustice against non-Muslims is forbidden in the same way as injustice against Muslims is forbidden. Instances of discord may be appealed through Islamic *Sharī'ah* courts, whereby even a political or religious leader's conduct can be scrutinized.

---

26 Ibid., 11. Here Al-Qaradawi, citing ancient works, *Arab Civilization* (trans. 'Adil Za'aytar) p128.
27 Cf.: <http://imemc.org/article/59618/> accessed 17 April 2016. Conor Gaffey Janine Di Giovanni, Lara Adoumie, Stav Ziv, "The New Exodus: After Years of Slow and Steady Decline Christians Are Being Driven from the Middle East by Isis", *Newsweek Global* 164, no. 13 (2015): 24–33. Neither article refers to the People of the Book.
28 Al-Qaradawi, *Non Muslims*, 13.
29 Ibid., 14.

Al-Qaradawi gives a historical example involving a case where a Christian was offered the right to strike the head of the Caliph for his son's abuse of power.[30] In general, Al-Qaradawi surmises, periods of oppression are followed by a return of balanced leadership and compensation for iniquities.[31]

Reading through the two documents one finds a sense that Al-Qaradawi is well aware of differences between Christian denominations, though this is not his primary concern. His interest remains largely with the socio-historical context, without exploring diverse creedal differences. The area of divorce provides a notable exception and an opportunity to engage in some inter-scriptural reasoning while also allowing him to display his knowledge of differences between some Christian denominations. In the area of divorce Al-Qaradawi examines the teachings of Jesus from a Jewish context and as interpreted by Catholics and Protestants. He posits that the teachings of Jesus were intended to counter Jewish excesses in the area of divorce. Al-Qaradawi cites Matthew 5:31–32, Mark 10:11–12 and a commentary by the Institute of Coptic Catholic Research that states that Jesus prohibited divorce except for reasons of infidelity and taught that remarrying a divorced person is paramount to committing adultery.[32] He notes that some Protestant denominations, like Catholics, do not allow for divorce, while others permit divorce where there are prolonged irresolvable differences.[33] Al-Qaradawi argues that one of the consequences of such stringent requisites for divorce in the West is that Christians resort to civil legislation, where divorce is granted for quite trivial reasons. Consequently, he argues that the application of the teachings of Jesus to demand that couples with irreconcilable differences remain married must have been a temporary injunction. Al-Qaradawi argues that Islam achieves a balance, even though "Among the lawful things, divorce is

---

30   Ibid., 14–5, 23–4.
31   Ibid., 16. A famous case in point is the Church of St John, Damascus. Where one caliph forced the local Christians to relinquish their church in order to provide more land for the expansion of the Umayyad Mosque. The local Christians bided their time for a more sympathetic caliph who reviewed their case and offered substantial compensation.
32   *The Lawful and the Prohibited*, 208–9.
33   Ibid., 209–10.

the most hated by Allah".[34] He goes as far to say that the teachings of Jesus, in this instance, are therefore abrogated by the teachings of Islam. In Islam, the ability for both men and women to divorce and remarry are granted along with compassionate guidelines as to how couples should conduct themselves before, during and after a divorce.[35]

Modern Western Islamic Use of the Term *People of the Book*

This section examines a number of influential texts by a generation of scholars who have lived a number of years in the West. These texts are: *Christian-Muslim Dialogue In The Twentieth Century* (1997) by Ataullah Siddiqui, a British scholar of Indian origins; *Western Muslims and the Future of Islam* (2004) by Tariq Ramadan, a Swiss scholar of Egyptian origins; *Qur'an, Liberation & Pluralism; An Islamic Perspective of Interreligious Solidarity Against Oppression* (1997), *Muslims Engaging The Other And The Humanum* (2000) and *On Being A Muslim: Find a Religious Path in the World Today* (2002) by Farid Esack, a South African scholar and political activist.[36] These texts tactfully draw upon critical inquiry of the People of the Book. Yet, in contrast to Al-Qaradawi, each are proponents of Muslims living in the West seeking their own contextual solutions to living in pluralist society rather than seeking direction from Eastern Muslims who may not understand Western society. The texts examined deal primarily, but

---

34 Ibid., 307. Abu Daoud records this *hadīth*.
35 Ibid., 211–20.
36 Ataullah Siddiqui, *Christian-Muslim Dialogue in the Twentieth Century*, 1st edn (London: MacMillan Press Ltd, 1997). Cf. Tariq Ramadan, *Western Muslims and the Future of Islam* (New York: Oxford University Press, 2004). Cf. Farid Esack, *Qur'an, Liberation & Pluralism; an Islamic Perspective of Interreligious Solidarity against Oppression*, 2002 edn (Oxford: Oneworld, 1997). "Muslims Engaging the Other and the Humanum", *Emory International Law Review* 14, no. 2 (2000). Cf. *On Being a Muslim: Finding a Religious Path in the World Today* (Oxford: Oneworld, 2002).

not exclusively, with the scenario of Muslims engaging with non-Muslim societies. In the context of modernity and instantaneous communication, events taking place in one part of the world have inevitable repercussions in other parts of the world.

Social Contract, New Contexts Reshaping Coexistence

In *Christian-Muslim Dialogue In The Twentieth Century*, Siddiqui identifies the People of the Book in keeping with the critical analysis discussed in Chapter 1 and with the writings of Al-Qaradawi.[37] Yet, Christians, he argues, are conspicuous in the main for their lack of reciprocal respect shown to Islam.[38] Nevertheless, despite this apparent perception, Muslims are still encouraged to live peacefully as active citizens and to engage in dialogue with Christians in a respectful manner.[39] Siddiqui cites several verses that discuss the People of the Book; among them are *sūrat al-ʿankabūt* (29):46 and *sūrat Āl-ʿImrān* (3):64.[40] These verses acknowledge that Christians and Muslims as well as Jews have been given divine revelation, even if this revelation is understood differently.[41] The concept that God guides humanity; reveals His will, and that people need God's guidance in all spheres of life is a concept that is a growing source of contention for Muslims wishing to embrace modernity and the West.[42]

In comparison to Al-Qaradawi, and Siddiqui, Ramadan's use of the appellation People of the Book is reserved primarily for interreligious dialogue. In *To Be A European Muslim: A Study of Islamic Sources in the European Context*, the appellation People of the Book is used only once. On this occasion, the reference is to the Biblical Joseph, the son of Jacob,

---

37 Siddiqui, *Christian-Muslim Dialogue*, 49. Henceforth, *Christian-Muslim Dialogue*.
38 Ibid., xiii, 35–6, 59, 195. Siddiqui notes a negative opinion of Islam is not only the legacy of western Christian contact but is also carries forward into secular society.
39 Ramadan, *Western Muslims*, 43, 53, 73, 95, 124, 56.
40 *Sūrah āl-ʿImrān* (3):64 is the key verse for the *Common Word* initiative.
41 Siddiqui, *Christian-Muslim Dialogue*, 57–8; Ramadan, *Western Muslims*, 19.
42 Siddiqui, *Christian-Muslim Dialogue*, 58.

working for the King of Egypt, who was "not from the People of the Book".[43] The analogy here is between the polytheist king and European society. In *Islam, the West and the Challenges of Modernity*, henceforth *Challenges of Modernity*, the term appears three times in relation to dialogue and co-operation in reforming society. In *Western Muslims and The Future of Islam*, henceforth *Western Muslims*, Ramadan's use of the term appears more frequently as a means of identifying Christians as potential partners in dialogue and social reform. Throughout *Western Muslims* he discusses how Muslims living in the West need to chart their own future independent of outside influences, based on faithfulness to the universal principles of Islam applied for all intents and purposes in secular society.[44] Use of the term People of the Book is reserved for specific conversation dealing with religious forms of dialogue.[45]

Farid Esack's use of the term People of the Book is more nuanced. In *Qur'an, Liberation & Pluralism; An Islamic Perspective of Interreligious Solidarity Against Oppression*, he demonstrates not only an awareness of traditional critical understanding of the term, but also highlights what he sees as the need to rethink relationships with categories of believers.[46] This sense of the intrinsic value of the other is present in Esack's other works including *Muslims Engaging the Other and the Humanum*, as well as *On Being A Muslim: Finding a Religious Path in the World Today*. Esack acknowledges that the struggle against Apartheid challenged the Muslim community in South Africa. On the one hand the regime allowed certain Muslims a privileged existence while others felt the pains of oppression.[47] Based on

---

43 Tariq Ramadan, *To Be a European Muslim: A Study of Islamic Sources in the European Context* (Leicester: The Islamic Foundation, 1999), 167. Henceforth referred to as *European Muslim*.
44 *Western Muslims*, 126, 58–61. Cf. *European Muslim*, 93–5.
45 *Western Muslims*. Cf. Chapter 9. Interreligious Dialogue 200–214.
46 Esack, *Liberation & Pluralism*, 17, 149–55. Henceforth referred to as *Liberation & Pluralism*.
47 Ibid., 4, 218 fn. 6. The contrast is made here between the lives of members of the National Youth Action, and the South African Black Scholars Association with the conservative Durban based Islamic Propagation Centre, headed by the renowned proselyte Ahmad Deedat.

traditional teachings, Esack examines the early Muslim community's integration in the town of Medina. Here he views the twinning of exiles with helpers and the inclusion of non-Muslims in the Treaty of Medina as the first steps to a "New Society" based on a fraternity of believers.[48]

Similarly, there are examples of different contextual interactions with Christians from Abyssinia and Najrān. These examples are important because Esack affirms that Muslims look to Qur'ānic literature for templates for coexistence with religious "others". In the time of Muhammad, the religious "others" were predominantly the People of the Book and therefore their examples are very important for determining relationships today.[49] However, as part of Esack's hermeneutic of liberation he notes that it is very important not to forget the historical context. The Jews and Christians today may be part of the legacy of the People of the Book known to Muhammad and the early Muslim Ummah, but they are not exactly the same and neither are the Muslims. There is a need therefore to avoid generalizations. Esack prefers to examine the contextual interactions as indicators of practices and attitudes in order to differentiate between allies today in the struggle for social justice. Relying on categories of people who lived during the time of Muhammad and who were predisposed to seeking justice may prove counterproductive given the role of Judaeo-Christian political supremacy today.[50] Citing *sūrat al-baqarah* (2):134 Esack reminds Christians and Muslims that communities cannot base their claims of moral superiority on the achievements of their forebears. "That is a community foregone; to them belongs what they earned and to you belong what you earn, and you will not be asked about what they had done".[51] The point being, the People of the Book today may have different attitudes and political interests that are incompatible with the quest for justice of their forebears.

Siddiqui and Ramadan both acknowledge the change in traditional understanding of the People of the Book from a religious perspective. The West is viewed in the context of modernity as increasingly secular,

---

48 Ibid., 150.
49 Ibid., 152; "Muslims Engaging", 533–46. Henceforth referred to as *Muslims Engaging*.
50 *Liberation & Pluralism*, 152–3.
51 Ibid., 175.

to the point where secularism exerts an influence on the expression of Christianity.[52] Hence, Christianity rather than actively engaging with modern society to explain the teachings of Christ is considered a servant of secularism.[53] Siddiqui and Ramadan write extensively concerning the secularization of the West and the challenges this has on religious pluralism. Ramadan states that people in the West are at best more likely to describe themselves as "spiritual" rather than religious. Outwardly society is religion free.[54] Siddiqui points out an interesting feature of this idea, the fact that the writings of Sayyid Qutb, a leading figure in political Islam (Muslim Brotherhood movement), berates Christians for not providing leadership in the face of the modern drive to separate religious ideals from society.[55] The lack of spiritual discipline endemic in the West, as well as the lure of consumerism, inspires Ramadan, who is himself the grandson for the founder of the Muslim Brotherhood, to warn Muslims that they need to guard their faith. In addition, through their faith, Muslims can be a bridge to other people of faith, or none, if they too are concerned about human values.[56]

For Siddiqui, the term the "West" sometimes acts as a euphemism for contemporary Christianity. Unfortunately, this simplification links western Christians with colonialism and imperialism, rather than as a people following in the footsteps of Christ.[57] One positive element of modernity is the fact that Muslims and Christians are increasingly sharing the same space as equal citizens. Muslims in the "West" are growing in confidence and no

---

52 Siddiqui, *Christian-Muslim Dialogue*, 23. Cf. Ramadan, *Western Muslims*, 32. Ramadan notes that some Muslim scholars question whether the West has forgotten God entirely. *Islam, the West and the Challenges of Modernity*, trans. Saïd Amgher (Leicester: Islamic Foundation, 2001; repr., 2009), 182. Ramadan notes that often Muslims make the mistake of confusing the West with Christianity.
53 Siddiqui, *Christian-Muslim Dialogue*, 3, 17, 51–2. Citing Gai Eaton and Ziauddin Sardar, n 8.
54 Ramadan, *Western Muslims*, 17.
55 Siddiqui, *Christian-Muslim Dialogue*, 17.
56 Ramadan, *Western Muslims*, 121–4.
57 Siddiqui, *Christian-Muslim Dialogue*, 3, 49.

longer see themselves as immigrants.⁵⁸ Therefore there is the potential and need for greater co-operation between Muslims and Christians.⁵⁹

In light of the fact that there are greater numbers of Muslims living in the West, the old designations of *dar as-salām* or *dar al–harb* are less meaningful. The West, with all its flaws, can be thought in terms of *dar al-'ahd* [Land of Agreement], *dar ash-shahādah* [Land of Witness], or even *dar al-da'wah* [Land of Mission], as the case for Mecca before the Hijra. Ultimately, there is no consensus in this area.⁶⁰ In the West therefore, Muslims are bound to accept the prevailing rule of law as citizens as long as they are free to practise their own faith.⁶¹ If the laws of society interfere with the practices of Islam then Muslims, he argues, should act as conscientious objectors.⁶²

This leads Ramadan to call Muslims based in the West to rethink *fiqh al-aqalliyyāt*, the [law/jurisprudence of the minorities].⁶³ He fervently believes Muslims in the West need to respectfully become independent from eastern Muslims intellectually, politically and economically. They need to develop their own ability to independently assess the needs of Muslims living in the West by remaining faithful to the principles of Islam, aware of the "need of Him" but developing their own personality in their own context.⁶⁴ In this regard Ramadan discusses the work of Al-Qaradawi, who views Muslims living in the West as strangers in "other societies" rather than at home.⁶⁵ Alternatively, Ramadan is confident that Western Muslims can participate in society as equal citizens and co-operate with

---

58   Ibid., 199. The point is made that Muslims have played an important, but neglected role in Europe's History.
59   Ibid., 20. As identified by the first Muslims-Christian Convocation, Bhamdoun, Lebanon, 1954.
60   Ibid., 64–6, 70–2, 195.
61   Ramadan, *European Muslim*, 173.
62   *Western Muslims*, 174. For instance for *ribā*, charging, or paying interest. Cf. 94, *alam al-harb* 176. *European Muslim*, 34, 176.
63   *Western Muslims*, 6.
64   Ibid., 6–7. Cf. *European Muslim*, 221.
65   *Western Muslims*, 53, fn. 52.

"others", that share similar values.⁶⁶ In this regard Ramadan is quite visionary, since he encourages Western Muslims to use their influence to effect social justice by bearing witness to Islam and creating a bridge with other concerned people.⁶⁷

A fundamental tool for negotiating the balance of life for Western Muslims between *darūra* [necessity], and *rukhas* [exemptions], is the activity to understand the *al-muamalāt* [the social teachings] of the Qur'ān in their particular context, in order to discern the universal principles from within their historical context.⁶⁸ This is achieved through the application of *'ilm usūl al-fiqh* [the science of the fundamental laws], in order to gain *ijtihād*, a critical interpretation of verses from the Qur'ān and of *hadīths* dealing with the subject.⁶⁹ The rules governing *ijtihād*, as explained by Ramadan, are in keeping with those examined in Chapter 1. As an illustration of early use of *ijtihād*, Ramadan draws upon the example of Mu'ādh; the companion of Muhammad sent to govern Yemen while Yemen was still a Christian country. Mu'ādh needed to rely on his own intellect in a new environment where seeking answers to life's questions may not be clear.⁷⁰

Esack does not seem to view the march to secularism with the same degree of trepidation. In fact, the material examined here suggests that Esack is far more willing to engage in a spirit of solidarity with secularists to work on issues traditionally regarded as taboo by mainstream Muslim clerics. For instance, while speaking in a general sense, Esack describes the makeup of the activists involved in the international solidarity movement as comprising People of the Book, feminists, trade unionists, liberals, LGBT, environmentalists and others that might have Apartheid "as just one of a number of social-ideological forces that they believed dehumanized people, and had to be relentlessly opposed".⁷¹ These are areas where Esack

---

66   Ibid., 4–7, 169–99.
67   Ibid., 123–24. In fact Part II of *Western Muslims* concerns Muslims reforming Western society.
68   Ibid., 43, 54–5.
69   Ibid., 21–22, 43–48.
70   Ibid., 43. Cf. *European Muslim*, 82–3.
71   Esack, *Liberation & Pluralism*, 239–40.

believes faith based movements need to challenge traditional ideologies held by conservatives.⁷² He further notes that the future of progressive Islam, at least in a South African context, will be shaped by contempt as well as a reverence for religion, since religion was a tool of the oppressor that justified racial discrimination and other forms of oppression.⁷³ The liberation of South Africa came about by all types of people engaged in a struggle whereby all people would be fully human and fully alive, as Esack says, drawing upon a Quaker adage, "that of God in all of us", would be respected.⁷⁴ In fact, in pursuit of liberation, Esack seems to imply that he is willing to tolerate a degree of immorality in the short term, in order to bring secularists closer to God in the long term.⁷⁵

New Sharī'ah *Discourse and the People of the Book*

Dhimmitude and *Sharī'ah* are two highly emotive topics that come under the heading of "Protected Citizens". Siddiqui points out interestingly that neither word is found in the Qur'ān. Protected citizenship is an area that the followers of Muhammad developed after the death of Muhammad and during the early military conquests.⁷⁶ Siddiqui defines *Sharī'ah* as "the way". The objectives of *Sharī'ah*, *maqasid al-shari'ah*, is theoretically clear, but in practice quite vague, "to promote the public good", or as Ramadan would say, *al-maslaha* [the common good].⁷⁷ The purpose of *Sharī'ah* is

---

72 Ibid., Cf. 6–15.
73 <http://www.britannica.com/EBchecked/topic/174603/Dutch-Reformed-Church>: Up until 1986 the Afrikaans Nederduitse Gereformeerde Kerk (NGK) followed a Biblical justification for Apartheid.
74 Esack, *Liberation & Pluralism*, 251.
75 Ibid., 197–203. <http://aliciapatterson.org/stories/south-africa's-gay-imam-and-his-disciple> accessed 10 April 2015.
76 Siddiqui, *Christian-Muslim Dialogue*, 64.
77 Ibid., 62. Ramadan, *Western Muslims*, 38–43. Cf. *European Muslim*, 76–85.

not just to give legal guidance, but guidance for all aspects of life.[78] Citing Al-Ghazali the purpose of *Sharī'ah* is "to promote the welfare of the people, which lies in safeguarding faith, their life, their intellect, their posterity and their wealth. Whatever ensures the safeguarding of these five serves public interest and is desirable".[79] Ramadan also lists quite similar objectives of *Sharī'ah* as *istislāh* [to seek the common good].[80] The objectives allow for a great deal of compromise in light of *al-wāqi'* [the state of the world]. The practice might change but the universal principles remain the same.[81]

In contrast to Siddiqui, Esack notes that variants of the word *Sharī'ah* appear three times in the Qur'ān along with the word *minhāj* [a clear path].[82] In keeping with Esack's hermeneutics of liberation, he points out that the Qur'ān is a comprehensive guide against injustice.[83] Therefore *Sharī'ah* should be something that guides society. He explains the etymology of *Sharī'ah* and *minhāj* as concerning a path leading to water. While engaging in exegetical investigation, Esack examines the possibility that through verses like *sūrat al-mā'idah* (5):48 and to a lesser extent *sūrat al-hajj* (22):67, that concern the People of the Book, there could be more than one *Sharī'ah* or *minhāj* acceptable to God, even after the arrival of Muhammad. He approaches this examination by considering whether the context of *sūrat al-mā'idah* (5):48 with its emphasis on competing in good works, implies that the communities in question were contemporary, that is, coexisting in Medina, or whether they are communities that passed away along with their abrogated *Sharī'ah*. While outlining that exegesis of Al-Tabari and al-Razi, both of which accept the latter explanation, Esack opts to side with Rida, since Esack considers the literal interpretation of the verse with its inclusive implications more conducive to reason. What use, he surmises, is a competition for good works for communities that are not contemporary and unaware of their theological differences?

78 *Western Muslims*, 32, 34.
79 Siddiqui, *Christian-Muslim Dialogue*, 62.
80 Ramadan, *Western Muslims*, 38.
81 Ibid., 37. *European Muslim*, 234.
82 Esack, *Liberation & Pluralism*, 169. Cf. "Muslims Engaging", 543.
83 *Liberation & Pluralism*, 106.

Underpinning this plurality of *Sharīʿah* is a reconsideration of some traditional terms like *islām*, submission, in relation to *dīn* [religion]; *imān* [faith], *muʾmin* [believer] and *kufr* [disbelief], in light of working together for social justice. During the early years of Islam these terms described personal qualities, only gradually did they come to refer to groups, "bordering on ethnic characteristics".[84] The nuanced meaning and use of the terms are examined in Chapter 4 of *Liberation and Pluralism*.[85] For instance Esack employs critical analysis, beginning with *sūrat Āl-ʿImrān* (3):19 which deals extensively with the People of the Book, to demonstrate that traditionally the word *islām* is used in the Qurʾān as both a noun, denoting the community of Muhammad, or the emerging reified Islam, as well as a verb, describing the very personal act of submitting one's life to God.[86] Understanding *islām* as a personal act, once again allows for a plurality of *Sharīʿah*.[87] The important feature of plurality is that each community strives to do good works.[88]

The application of *dhimmī* status for minorities within a Muslim country has always been situational, including the areas of *zakāt* and *jizyah*. Siddiqui quotes Fazlur Rahman who says, "Muslim jurists in the early centuries of Islam conceived of *jizyah* as a tax imposed upon the Peoples of the Book in lieu of military service, because these communities could not be expected to join Muslims in *jihād*".[89] In the same text Rahman, like Al-Qaradawi above, notes that during the caliphate of ʿUmar ibn al-Khattab some (Christian) tribes in Syria refused to pay *jizyah* because they considered the tax humiliating. As a form of compromise, ʿUmar requested the tribes pay *zakāt*.[90]

The implementation of *Sharīʿah* in countries undergoing Islamization or the application of *Sharīʿah* is the cause of fear amongst Christians in

---

84 Ibid., 115. For further discussion of the generic use of the terms *kufr*, *islām* and *fitra* see Ramadan, *European Muslim*, 67.
85 Esack, *Liberation & Pluralism*, 126–44.
86 Ibid., 126.
87 Ibid., 132.
88 Ibid., 166–72.
89 Siddiqui, *Christian-Muslim Dialogue*, 64.
90 Ibid.

countries like Nigeria, Pakistan and Sudan.[91] In spite of these difficult cases, Siddiqui elaborates on the possibilities of Muslims and Christians working together to make *Sharī'ah* more amenable to both communities, since there are no fixed rules for what will make society a better place.[92] This includes the rights of Christians and other minority religions to practice *da'wah* [invitation/mission]. Siddiqui notes that there is a world of difference between the *da'wah* of dialogue and the *da'wah* of evangelization.[93] In a very inspiring and enlightened way Siddiqui expects that Christians will try to convert Muslims to Christ, since spreading the message of Christ is part of the Great Commission. However, this need not be formal conversion, but through dialogue people may convert from their previous position towards an understanding and acceptance of the other.[94]

Modernity and the Changing Nature of Dialogue with Christians

Modernity's penchant for the secular provides an opportunity for dialogue and co-operation for Muslims and Christians. Yet, historically, Muslims have regrettably often experienced Christianity in the forms of colonialism, imperialism and aggressive missionaries, who sought to divide and conquer Muslims and demonstrated scant regard for the Qur'ān and Muhammad.[95] Therefore Muslims have reason to question if dialogue is a gesture to build

---

91 Ibid., 63, 69; Esack, "Muslims Engaging", 529. The suffering of Christians in Pakistan has greatly affected the world-view of Esack.
92 Siddiqui, *Christian-Muslim Dialogue*, 62, 196. Siddiqui notes that there are Muslim scholars, like Usman Bugaje, that feel *Sharī'ah* is a highly developed area with less room for manoeuvre.
93 Ibid., 194.
94 Ibid., 76.
95 Ibid., 23–4, 54–55, 59. Following the air of reconciliation brought on by *Nostra Aetate*, Muhammad Hamidullah wrote on behalf of Muslims in France to Pope John XXIII to "officially disavow and declare annulled the [Church's] past unjustifiable resolutions of former Councils, Synods and other writings of anti-Islamic character". This is a mistake repeated by Pope Benedict in Regensburg 2006. "Inter-Faith Relations in Britain since 1970-an Assessment", *Exchange* 39, no. 3 (2010): 242.

bridges and reconcile past grievances, or merely a rebranding of the evangelical missionary project, especially when coming from Western countries.[96]

In *Christian-Muslim Dialogue* Siddiqui demonstrates an awareness of the differences between Christian creedal communities with a concise overview of the development within both the World Council of Churches and the Roman Catholic Church encyclicals concerning the challenges of dialogue with Islam.[97] Accordingly, reconciliatory shoots began to appear following the international evangelical Edinburgh Conference of 1910, the Jerusalem Conference of 1928 and the Tambaram missionary conference of 1938. Here Protestant missionaries from a spiritual perspective, recognized and affirmed the values of other faiths, including the need to understand other faiths and cultures from a first-hand perspective. In addition, from a social or political perspective, the missionaries perceived the need of people of all faiths to confront the growing threats of communism and secularism together.[98] Since then, the idea has developed, that dialogue with Muslims and other non-Christians is essential. Yet segments within both the Catholic and Protestant confessions struggle to find a balance between responding to the call to "make disciples of all nations" and the need to enter into dialogue.[99]

Given the fact that neither mainstream Protestants, as represented by the World Council of Churches, nor the official encyclicals of the Roman Catholic Church are admittedly free from the desire to convert Muslims to Christ, what attitude can Muslims possibly adopt towards dialogue? Siddiqui answers this question in very practical terms. For some Muslims dialogue is not necessary.[100] There are verses in the Qur'ān that support the idea that Islam is complete and that Christians cannot be taken as friends or protectors.[101] The history of conflict between Muslims and Christians certainly attests to the fact that Muslims have much to be apprehensive

---

96 *Christian-Muslim Dialogue*, 50–5; Ramadan, *Western Muslims*, 201.
97 Siddiqui, *Christian-Muslim Dialogue*. Cf. Chapters 1 and 2.
98 Ibid., 24–26.
99 Ibid., 5, 32, 35, 38, 57.
100 "Since 1970", 250.
101 *Christian-Muslim Dialogue*, 51. Citing *sūrat al-māʾidah* (5):51.

about.[102] Nevertheless, Siddiqui offers various definitions of dialogue that demonstrate the benefits including inspiring words from A. Z. Abedin, "A dialogue is a process wherein people with diverse faith backgrounds come together and recognising each other's confessional identity and integrity, join hands in equality and respect to resolve a common and mutually perceived threat to all".[103]

For Ramadan, Western societies' religious pluralism makes mutual knowledge essential.[104] A challenge for dialogue today is to move the dialogue from the specialist, who may or may not reflect the views of their coreligionists, to ordinary believers and those with more closed opinions. The role of the specialist is to bring others with more traditional views from within their communities along a path towards increased understanding of the other. Thus new horizons may open up for living together in mutual respect and providing better means of resolving conflicts that may arise.[105] Ramadan excels in his explanation of how diversity is part of God's plan. Citing from a cluster of verses, Ramadan explains that if it had been God's will, all people would have believed the same, that diversity of religion, culture and race are intended to test us.[106] In fact in *Challenges of Modernity* Ramadan's use of the term People of the Book is explicitly linked to striving together for the common good. This point is made clear by way of *sūrat al-mā'idah* (5):68, "People of the Book, you do not stand on anything, until you perform the Torah and the Gospel, and what was sent down to you from your Lord".[107] This is a very important verse. Through this verse Ramadan seems to accept a salvific potential for both the Torah and Gospel that also encourages People of the Book to follow the guidance

---

102 "Since 1970", 247. Dialogue can be seen as a political tool of a state against terrorism.
103 *Christian-Muslim Dialogue*, 57, 56–60. Cf. *The Role of Believers in Promoting Mutual Trust and Community* prepared for the Muslim-Christian Colloquium organized by the World Council of Churches in 1987.
104 Ramadan, *Western Muslims*, 200.
105 Ibid., 200–1.
106 Ibid., 202–3. Citing extracts from *sūrat al-an'ām* (6): 35; *sūrah Yunus* (10):29; *sūrat al-mā'idah* (5):48; *sūrat al-baqarah* (2): 251, 256; *sūrat al-hajj* (22):40; *sūrah al-hujurat* (49):13. *European Muslim*, 230. Citing *sūrat al-hujurāt* (49):13.
107 *Challenges of Modernity*, 188. *sūrat al-mā'idah* (5):68.

given to them. He sees the role of the Torah, Gospel and Qur'ān as tempering and refining how "we" understand our own sacred texts and God.[108]

Further evidence of critical analysis is employed to explain difficult verses that are cited by literalists, as reasons for not entering into dialogue. Ramadan states that difficult texts are frequently cited out of context. Those that declare all the People of the Book are guilty of *kufr*, or that say their religions are no longer acceptable after Islam, citing *sūrat Āl-'Imrān* (3):19 and (3):85, assume only inane interpretations of these verses. Such interpretations of difficult verses can reduce dialogue to simply *da'wah*, or proselytism; that is an invitation to accept Islam and nothing more. Purely literal readings however, deny the possibility of interpretations that seek to extract the universal message from the specific context and apply the lesson to new contexts.[109]

In essence, dialogue should be about mutual understanding towards reducing the reasons for potential conflict.[110] Dialogue should lead to *ma'rūf* [promoting good] and *munkar* eradicating [evil].[111] Siddiqui notes that with verses that promote dialogue, while revisiting *sūrat Āl-'Imrān* 3:64 and *sūrat al-'ankabūt* 29:46, God is central and "God is the prime motivator in dialogue".[112] Ramadan, like Siddiqui, cites the same verses to demonstrate the need for mutual respect for critical analysis.[113] Through dialogue it becomes possible to reinvigorate society, to allow God back into social discourse.[114] For Ramadan, "Interreligious dialogue should be a meeting of 'witnesses' who are seeking to live their faiths, to share their convictions, and to engage with one another for a more humane, more just world, closer to what God expects of humanity".[115]

---

108   *Western Muslims*, 202–4. Ramadan cites two verses also cited by Siddiqui that utilizes the term People of the Book, *sūrat imran* (3):64 *and sūrat al-'ankabūt* (29):46.
109   Ibid., 205–6.
110   Siddiqui, "Since 1970", 241–2. Here the Race Relations Act could assume the goodwill of the participants in spite of deep suspicions.
111   *Christian-Muslim Dialogue*, 76.
112   Ibid., 58.
113   Ramadan, *Western Muslims*, 202–3.
114   Siddiqui, *Christian-Muslim Dialogue*, 58–9.
115   Ramadan, *Western Muslims*, 208. Cf. Siddiqui, *Christian-Muslim Dialogue*, 60.

In addition, Ramadan offers practical rules for dialogue. He says there should be respect for the legitimacy of each other's convictions. There should be greater appreciation for how other people interpret their own tradition and not what we want them to say. People should be free to ask any question and there should be greater self-criticism of the meanings of texts.[116] Moving beyond dialogue, there is a need to motivate religious people to take part in practical engagement. Ramadan suggests that religiously minded people need to find a civil role to counter "postmodernism" that he says, seems to wish to deny any legitimacy to all references to a universal ethic.[117]

Esack sees a more immediate need for dialogue culminating in political co-operation. In *Liberation & Pluralism* he calls for a hermeneutics of liberation that includes dialogue with the People of the Book and others that is in keeping with Christian liberation theology.[118] The hermeneutics of liberation presents a need-based approach that chooses to confront difficult texts in order to understand "the subsumed meanings" while appropriating new meanings.[119] The hermeneutics of liberation facilitates a discourse with others, since the re-appropriation of interpretations that exclude Muslim co-operation with non-Muslims faces stern challenges of orthodoxy without orthopraxis.[120] Behind the hermeneutics of liberation the choice is simple, to support, or not, the poor and oppressed in society and those who struggle for liberation. In defence of this argument Esack cites the exegetical work of Rida, who chides those who claim to be Muslim, yet do not act in the cause of justice, saying they are in effect, only *ethnic* Muslims.[121]

In *Muslims Engaging* Esack describes different types of dialogue where Muslims might relate to the other.[122] Addressing issues relating to postmodernity is the genre of dialogue called, "The Other as Self and Spiritual

---

116 Ramadan, *Western Muslims*, 210–11.
117 Ibid., 212.
118 Esack, *Liberation & Pluralism*, 14, 72, 198, 201, 02. Esack frequently cites the works of Gustavo Gutierrez as well as Leonardo and Clodovis Boff.
119 Ibid., 115, 18.
120 Ibid., 185.
121 Ibid., 215.
122 "Muslims Engaging", 530–4.

Partner". Here the dialogue is a source of mutual spiritual enrichment against the backdrop of Western society's push to marginalize belief in God. Nonetheless, Esack notes that this form of dialogue seldom engages with the structures of injustice.[123] Moving from the spiritual to the practical is the genre of engagement referred to as, "The Other As Self and Comrade". This form of engagement is more concerned with a *liberative praxis* that intends to create a world with greater socioeconomic as well as gender justice. Through verses like *sūrat al-baqarah* (2):62, *sūrat al-māʾidah* (5):48 Esack provides the exegetic groundwork for accepting at least some of the People of the Book as potential allies. This is based on the idea that the Qurʾān acknowledges "some people" among the People of the Book as believing in one God and who fill their lives with good deeds.[124] Taking the logic of deeds further, Esack notes the struggle against Apartheid and other injustice creates its own definition of who is *muʾmin* and who is *kāfir*.[125]

A Common Word Initiative

In October 2006, thirty-eight Muslim scholars wrote an open letter to Pope Benedict XVI in response to comments made in his Regensburg address.[126]

---

123 Ibid., 534.
124 Ibid., 541–6.
125 Ibid., 544–5. *On Being a Muslim*, 151–2. In a very practical sense Esack relates an early experience of solidarity his family experienced with a Christian neighbour, Mrs Batista. Through her *islām* Esack realized the need to reassess the meaning of many Islamic terms in light of changed contexts.
126 David Gibson, "Pope Benedict Xvi's Regensburg Lecture on Islam Gets a Second Look in the Wake of Islamic State" (2014). Cf. <https://www.ncronline.org/news/world/regensburg-redux-was-pope-benedict-xvi-right-about-islam>. The precise initiate of the Common Word is more nuanced then presented here. Although Pope Benedict's Regensburg was a factor there were other factors in train like the Amman Message of 2005 that made the call to dialogue inevitable. *A Common Word between Us and You*, 5-Year Anniversary Edition (Amman: The Royal Aal Al-Bayt Institute for Islamic Thought (MABDA), 2012), 17. Cf. Pope Benedict, "Faith, Reason and the University Memories and Reflections", in *Libreria Editrice Vaticana* (Libreria Editrice Vaticana, 2006).

This open letter went largely unanswered.[127] The following year 138 Muslim scholars wrote again to Pope Benedict and other Christian leaders calling for peace and understanding between Muslims and Christians.

The letter known as *A Common Word Between Us and You* states that, the basis for peace and understanding already exists between the two faiths. Both faiths are built upon the common principles of love of God and love of neighbour. These principles provide the common ground on which Muslims and Christians should come together. The basic premise of this document outlined the fact that Muslims and Christians together make up more than 55 per cent of the world's population. Without peace between Muslim and Christians there cannot be meaningful peace in the world.[128] The title of the *Open Letter* comes from *sūrat Āl-'Imrān* (3):64 where it says,

> Say, O people of the Scripture (Book) Come to a common word between us and you: that we shall worship none but God, and that we shall ascribe no partner to Him, and that none of us shall take others for lords beside God. And if they turn away, then say: Bear witness that we are they who have surrendered (unto Him).[129]

People of Scripture is a variation on the translation of *ahl al-kitāb* as *People of the Book*.[130] The historical context of the verse is discussed in Chapter 2. In brief, this verse pertains to the visit from an official delegation of Najrān Christians to Muhammad. Having discussed their theological differences, the delegation made clear that they were willing to submit politically to Muhammad, but intended nonetheless, to remain Christian.

The *Open Letter* is significant for a number of reasons. One of the weaknesses of interfaith dialogue for Muslims is that they do not have a

---

127 *A Common Word between Us and You*, 16. In fact the Vatican may have only responded positively after other Christian Churches accepted the ACW invitation, 33. For a genesis of the *Common Word* see 131–134.
128 38 Muslim Scholars, "An Open Letter and Call from Muslim Religious Leaders To:", in *A Common Word* (The Royal Aal al-Bayt Institute for Islamic Thought, Jordan, 2007), 2. Henceforth referred to as the *Open Letter. A Common Word between Us and You*, 251.
129 "An Open Letter and Call from Muslim Religious Leaders To:", 13–4.
130 Alterative translations of *sūrat Āl-'Imrān* (3):64 using "People", rather than "Scripture", are found for instance in The Presidency of the Islamic Researches and IFTA, *The Holy Qur'ān*, 159.

centralized authority to support any resolutions that might present themselves from discussions. With the endorsement of 138 leading scholars, Islam is responding with as broad an authoritative voice as possible.[131] In addition, since the *Open Letter's* publication, hundreds more Muslim and Christian scholars have added their weight to the message.

In line with traditional Islamic exegetics, the *Open Letter's* message draws upon more than thirty Qur'ānic verses, including verses *sūrat an-Nisā'* (4):171 *and sūrat al-mā'idah* (5):48, some *hadīth* and more than twenty verses from the Old and New Testaments to demonstrate the fundamental commonality between Christianity and Islam. This demonstration of commonality does not diminish points of departure, but rather, calls upon Christians to see the wider picture. One of the most profound statements reiterates the fact that in spite of their theological differences, "Muslims, Christians and Jews should be free to each follow what God commanded them", further insisting that there is no compulsion in religion.[132]

Muslims state unequivocally in the *Open Letter* that neither they, nor Islam are against Christians. Drawing upon seemingly contradictory verses from the Synoptic Gospels, one question Muslims pose relates to a concern raised earlier by Siddiqui, namely, that although Muslims recognize Jesus, why then are Christians so demeaning of Islam? Matthew 12:30 suggest that those who are not with Jesus are against him. The *Open Letter* cites, however, the commentary offered by *Blessed Theophylact* that this refers to demons and not people. Therefore, given that *sūrat an-Nisā'* (4):171 states that Jesus is the Messiah and that both Mark 9:40 and Luke 9:50 allow for those who are not opposed to Jesus to be considered "on the side" of Jesus, Muslims invite Christians to consider them as "not against and thus for them, in accordance with Jesus Christ's words".[133]

---

131 *A Common Word between Us and You*, 12, 251. Three points that make *A Common Word* significant include its grounding in scripture, the acceptance of theological differences and the participation of high ranking religious leaders. 40–41.
132 Scholars, "An Open Letter and Call from Muslim Religious Leaders To:", 14. *A Common Word between Us and You*, 19.
133 "An Open Letter and Call from Muslim Religious Leaders To:", 14–15.

Conclusions

The work of Al-Qaradawi acts as a classic juxtaposed in contrast to the voices of Siddiqui, Esack, and Ramadan. Their voices reflect the gradual shift in authority in Islam away from the Middle East to the places of residence of Muslims worldwide. In keeping with traditional *tafsīr*, they affirm that whether Muslims form the majority of society, or minority, they are encouraged to form good relations with the People of the Book.

The modern Islamic scholars develop their understanding of the People of the Book further. Each scholar employs *tafsīr* in order to lay the foundation for discerning the subsumed meaning of the Qur'ān in light of modern context. For Siddiqui, the British model of migration and dialogue uncovers the disparity between Christians and Muslims whereby Islam affords the People of the Book respect, based on the origins of their teaching. Unfortunately, he perceives little reciprocation from Christians. This attitude can be seen throughout the history of Christian imperialism and mission that continues even with secularization. In addition, Christians today are more likely to act as the mouthpiece of secular values than promote the teachings of Christ. Nevertheless, Siddiqui encourages Muslims to engage respectfully with the People of the Book for reasons of faith and for the betterment of society.

Each of the modern scholars discusses the treatment of non-Muslims in Muslims majority countries. Siddiqui elaborates on the implications of *Shari'ah* and *dhimmī*. He notes that the application of *Shari'ah* is simply to improve society. Siddiqui points out that Christians theologically have a right as People of the Book, to contribute to the process of governance. In spite of the broad spectrum of coexistence between Muslims and the People of the Book, Siddiqui accepts that witnessing to the Gospel is a requirement of Christianity. However, the goal of dialogue and *da'wah* need not be formal conversion, but may result in a positive change in understandings of the religious other. Most importantly, "God is the prime motivator in dialogue".

Ramadan suggests a poetic image of continually returning to the source for guidance when negotiating the present. He states that Western Muslims need to differentiate between what is necessary and what is open for discussion. A fundamental tool for finding the balance in life between *darūra*, necessity and *rukhas*, exemptions, is found in understanding the social teachings of the Qur'ān in their particular context. Ramadan's use of the term People of the Book is in keeping with Al-Qaradawi and Siddiqui even if employed with greater reserve. He encourages Christians to follow their religion, citing *sūrat al-mā'idah* (5):68. Ramadan sees the role of the Torah, Gospels and Qur'ān as refining how "we" understand our own sacred texts and God. Ramadan, like Siddiqui, sees People of the Book as potential partners. He councils against simplistic interpretations of difficult verses that label People of the Book as *kuffār* like *sūrat Āl-'Imran* (3):19 and (3):85. He contends that closer examination of the context of these verses helps identify the root issues concerned and their universal trajectory. This trajectory includes Muslims and the People of the Book working together to counter the secularization of society.

Esack is far more willing to challenge the claims of those who declare that they are believers based solely on their declaration of Islam, or Christianity. Esack ventures the idea that the People of the Book just happened to be the "religious other" that Muhammad came into contact with. Still, their willingness, or not, to coexist with Islam in the days of Muhammad provides a template for interaction with "believers" to this day. Through the lens of a hermeneutic of liberation, other less conventional social groups may in fact better serve the aims of a just society than the traditional People of the Book. In this regard Esack is willing to cooperate with people advocating for social justice who are nontheists and unconventional on issues of *zinā* [fornication], ostensibly with the intent through contact of encouraging the promotion of religious values.

If further proof were needed to underline the importance of *ahl al-kitāb* as a tool for advancing relations between Muslims and Christians then Pope Benedict XVI's address at the University of Regensburg could not have been better gauged. The *Common Word* open letter epitomizes the importance Muslims place on Qur'ānic understanding of *ahl al-kitāb* for coexistence with the religious other. The large support garnered throughout the Muslims world to speak with one voice and to call upon the teachings of *sūrat Āl-'Imran* (3):64 to remind Christians that Muslims respect Christianity and wish to be seen as on the side of Jesus, the Christ and Messiah speaks volumes. More will follow on this subject in the next chapter.

CHAPTER 5

Contemporary Muslim-Christian Engagement with the People of the Book

Introduction

Since the *Common Word* initiative there have been many interfaith conferences around the world.[1] This chapter examines a few post-*Common Word* texts by one Muslim and three Christian scholars to see how they use the term People of the Book in theological, social and political spheres.

The scholars examined are well aware of the meaning and significance of the term *ahl al-kitāb*. There is an acceptance of the value that it affords, but also awareness of its limitations. For this reason some scholars suggest alternatives, or develop the term beyond its traditional use, not as a means of setting the term aside, but as a way of building on the strength of the appellation in order to bring Muslims and Christian closer together.

From People of the Book to People of the Word (Daniel A. Madigan)

The first scholar examined in this section is Daniel A. Madigan. Madigan is an Australian Jesuit based in Georgetown University, Washington, DC. He has a keen interest in interfaith dialogue especially in issues relating

---

1 Volf, Talal, and Yarrington, *A Common Word between Us and You*. Cf. 13–15, 104–118 and responses 22–46. In addition see also Declarations from Marrakesh in 2016 and Al-Azhar in 2017.

to coexistence and mutual respect between Muslims and Christians. He is an avid speaker and has published many books and articles relating to these topics, including a commentary on the *A Common Word* initiative.[2]

In *People of the Word: Reading John with a Muslim* (2007) Madigan appreciates the appellation *ahl al-kitāb* and its potential to inspire interfaith dialogue. Madigan translates *ahl al-kitāb* as *People of Scripture*, just as in the *Common Word*.[3] He notes that the use of this appellation presents both opportunities and obstacles for Muslim-Christian dialogue. On the one hand the term offers Christians, as well as Jews, what he refers to as a special status within Islam that may be called upon to engage in dialogue with Muslims. On the other hand, the term implies a certain polemic, whereby according to Islam, Jews and Christians have somehow corrupted the revelation entrusted to them, which Madigan maintains can inhibit dialogue. Further, the term *ahl al-kitāb* potentially obscures the fact that as Madigan asserts, "Jesus is not simply the bringer of the Word, but that he himself *is* the Word and message".[4] For this reason he suggests entering into dialogue with Muslims as the *People of the Word*.[5] Madigan contends that this term is appropriate since Muslims and Christians both recognize the presence and expression of the divine Word, albeit in the text of the Qur'ān and the person of Jesus respectfully.[6] Consequently, John's Gospel, with its highly developed theology of the Word, is an ideal catalyst for Muslims and Christians to begin a dialogue towards better understanding of each other.[7]

Through his commentary on the prologue of John's Gospel Madigan demonstrates the profundity of John's understanding of the incarnation

---

[2] Daniel Madigan, "A Common Word between Us and You: Some Initial Reflections", *Thinking Faith: The Online Jesuit Journal*, no. January (2008): 1–6.

[3] *Jms (2): Resonating with the Word*, vol. 2, *John Main Seminar* (Elmhurst College Chicago2014). Here the term scripture is preferred since "scripture functions in ways differently from most books".

[4] "People of the Word: Reading John with a Muslim" *Review and Expositor* 104, no. Winter (2007): 91–3.

[5] Ibid., 81, 91–3. The *People of the Word*, meaning for Christians the Word-made-Flesh.

[6] Ibid., 92.

[7] Ibid., 82.

of Jesus from and within Jewish tradition, to the Word's universal *kerygma*.[8] Madigan notes that John's Gospel begins with a phrase that brings the reader back to Genesis, *wa-yomer* [and He said ...] This phrase occurs eleven times in the first thirty verses of Genesis, affirming that it is through God's speaking that God realizes creation.[9] Therefore John's Gospel makes clear that the "Word" of God is a very powerful "something".[10] It is in fact the "Word" of God that comes to the prophets.[11]

Madigan, citing Daniel Boyarin, devotes considerable effort to examining how the use of the term "word" or *logos* in John's Gospel might be considered within the first century drift in Judaism from an understating of God's Word, as an *amar* [verb], in Hebrew, to *memra* [a noun], in Aramaic.[12] Here, God's Word is increasingly thought of as *deuteros theos* [second God].[13] Within the Greek-speaking Jewish world of Philo emerged a *logos* theology that Boyarin compares with John's use of *logos*, increasingly seen as in relationship with God, as an attribute, or a form of binitarianism, or even a hypostasis.[14] In fact Boyarin, citing Hannah and Niehoff, who both cite Philo, identify an Aristotelian description of an uncreated divine Word, yet not identical to God, as found in Deuteronomy 5, or more appropriately, in John, "What God was the Word was ..."[15]

Following an intricate examination of the beginning of John's Gospel Madigan establishes the foundation for drawing parallels with Islamic theology. John's Gospel expresses the relationship between God and the "Word" as, *pros ton theon* [was with God].[16] *Pros*, implies a movement towards God, not simply beside God. Madigan explains the phrase *kai*

---

8   Ibid., 82, 83, 92.
9   Ibid., 83.
10 Ibid., 84.
11 Ibid.
12 Daniel Boyarin, "The Gospel of the Memra: Jewish Binitarianism and the Prologue to John", *The Harvard Theological Review* 94, no. 3 (2001): 243–84. Cf. discussion of *Memra* 246, 252–261.
13 Ibid., 249–52. This drift from verb to noun occurs in spite of rabbinic opposition.
14 Madigan, "People of the Word", 84–6.
15 Boyarin, "Gospel of the Memra", 249–50.
16 Madigan, "People of the Word", 84.

theos en ha logos [and a god was logos], states that the logos is divine.[17] The phrase implies that "God is not reducible to the Word, yet the Word is no less divine than is God", this is reminiscent to the description offered by Abū Qurrah in the third chapter.[18] From here Madigan makes the link with *memra* as the aspect of the divine that is in relationship with humanity. It is through the *memra* that God creates, reveals and saves.[19] Madigan examines how in Islam the speech, or Word of God, *kalām Allah*, is understood as an essential attribute, *sifa dhātiyya*. The Word of God acts in a manner reminiscent to Genesis, "God said ... and it was so".[20] Hence for Judaism, Christianity and Islam the Word of God is an essential aspect of faith. For instance, in *sūrat al-baqarah* (2):117 "The originator of the heavens and the earth when He determines something, just says to it, 'Be' and it is".[21] He notes the similarities between the Islamic tradition with John's prologue, where the divine attribute of *kalām* is described as, "neither identical with God nor other than God".[22] A translation of the Greek into English renders John's opening verse, "In the beginning was the Word, and the Word was with God and the Word was God".[23]

In Islam, as in Christianity, *kalām*, the Word is an eternal attribute of the divine. In John verse 2, the Word existed in relationship with God in the beginning unlike anything created. The Word is not a possession, neither is it a part of God, since God is not divisible by parts. Further Madigan notes that just as with Judaism, Muslims and Christians face the challenge of how to appropriately express the relationship between the *kalām* of God

17 Ibid.
18 Ibid., 85.
19 Ibid.
20 Ibid., 85–6.
21 Ibid., 86.
22 Madigan does not provide a source for his comment. However, Al-Nasafi's Islamic Creed offers a rendition of this formula. Cf. Austin P. Evans, *A Commentary on the Creed of Islam: Sa'd Al-Dīn Al Taftāzāni on the Creed of Najm Al-Dīn Al-Nasafi*, ed. Austin P. Evans, trans. Earl Edgar Evan, vol. XLIII, Records of Civilization Sources and Studies (New York: Oxford University Press, 1950), 49, 58.
23 *The Holy Bible: English Standard Version*, 1056.

and God.[24] The dilemma expressed by Madigan is very similar in tone to the debates of the ninth to twelfth centuries examined previously.

Through John 1:4–5 Madigan compares the Word with *life*, *light* and *darkness*. These verses state, using the pronoun "him and it" for the Word, that "In him was life, and the life was the light of men. The light shines in the darkness, and the darkness has not overcome it". Most importantly Madigan demonstrates that in the Qur'ān God undertakes these activities. "That [God] He may bring you forth from darkness to light", *sūrat al-ahzāb* (33):43; "God is the light of the heavens and the earth ... Light upon light. God guides to His light whom He will" *sūrat an-nūr* (24):35. In addition, just as with John's Gospel, the darkness is no match for the light, as in *sūrat ar-rad* (16):13 and *sūrat fātir* (35):20.

There are other points of commonality that involve the role of the prophets bringing the message of God's light into the world. John the Baptist (John verses 6–8), as Moses and Muhammad, bore witness to the light.[25] This harbingering of the light into the world has two points of commonality: The Light of God and the reception of the light. The prophets throughout history have acted as vehicles of God's word, inviting humanity toward the light of God, which is constantly attempting to reconnect with humanity, or restore humanity's relationship with God. More often than not, as the Qur'ān reminds the reader, the reception is disbelief, ingratitude, *kufr*.[26] For John's Gospel those who accept the Word become "children of God".[27] Madigan notes that this concept can be divisive. However, he also notes (like Rashid Rida in the first chapter) that the word "child" can imply metaphorical closeness, as with the Arabic use of *ibn* for [son] rather than *walad* [son] with its more biological connotations.[28]

John 1:14 introduces two contentious terms: "only begotten" and "father". Although these terms are obvious points of contention within Islam, they may similarly be treated as expressions of faith rather than

---

24 Madigan, "People of the Word", 86–87.
25 Ibid., 87–8.
26 Ibid., 88–9.
27 Ibid., 89.
28 Ibid.

literal truths. Interestingly, Madigan suggest that John's, *hōs monogenous para patros* [as of a father's only son], probably does not intend the same sense that the phrase will come to have in later generations.[29] Nevertheless, Madigan recommends that the phrase "begotten" is retained as a Christian attempt to express the relationship between God's Word and God's self. Christians imply, Madigan posits, to communicate the point that God's Word and self, share the same nature. The term "begotten" has fairly obvious limits as an analogy since a parent and a child have two different natures. What Christians wish to express is the relationship between the Word and God's self is very similar to the Islamic description of an eternal divine attribute discussed above, or God's eternal self-expression, *kalām nafsī*.[30] Consequently Madigan boldly suggests that rather than defending a creedal position, Christians should invite Muslims to work with Christians to grapple with the theological challenge to express the relationship between God and his Word. As Madigan posits,

> We are both confronted with the double necessity of recognizing that the Word has its origin in God, but also that it is not originated in the way anything else is. In this way, we learn the limits of traditional theological language, or perhaps better, the metaphoric and analytical nature of that language. Muslims also learn that Christians have not fallen back into a pagan belief in gods who beget other gods.[31]

Through *People of the Word: Reading John with a Muslim* Madigan pioneers a faithful alternative to *ahl al-kitāb* as a basis for entering into dialogue with Muslims. As People of the Word, Muslims, Christians and Jews may explore the perhaps indescribable unity of God's Word and God's self. Although the remit of the article is decisively theological the ramifications are potentially far more profound, since dialogue leads to understanding, and through mutual understanding to better social and political relations. Rather than pit our scripture, which only obtains its importance because the believing Christian community has judged that the words of scripture

---

29 Ibid., 90.
30 Ibid., 91. This term bears a very strong resemblance to Sulaymān's *qah-emah binafisha*, God's self-existing substance examined in the previous chapter.
31 Ibid.

put us in touch with Christ, against their scripture, Madigan suggests a closer examination of the *Word* behind the text, the subject of the text, and our experience of the Word-made-Flesh.[32]

Madigan in his 2008 response to the *Common Word* document further clarifies some points raised above. He notes the motivation behind the writing of the *Common Word* is the realization that peace, even the existence of humanity, depends on the two largest religions in the world reaching not only a political détente, but theological common ground as well.[33] Muslims see this common ground between the *ahl al-kitāb* in the joint commands to love God and to love neighbour. He suggests that *A Common Word* is in keeping with the attempts of the Vatican's *Nostra Aetate*, "the bracketing of differences in order to work together for justice and peace in the world".[34] As such *A Common Word* is in keeping with the Amman project that seeks by weight of authoritative voice, to reclaim the position assumed by extremist voices. Therefore the audience of *A Common Word* includes not only Christian leaders, but also Islamic leaders.

As laudable as the *A Common Word* endeavour is, Madigan questions whether Christians should (in the air of communality) accept the reduction of Christian faith to a few verses from Leviticus and Deuteronomy as a summation of faith. In explanation, Madigan elucidates, Jesus' response in the Gospel to the greatest commands are invariably responses to trick questions.[35] Rather than accept the premise that our commonality is based on "the love of God", meaning humanity's obligatory love of the creator, we should acknowledge that God is the source of this love. The implications are then that God loves us, therefore we should love God and neighbour as explicated in 1 John 4:10, John 15:9 and 13:34. This focus on God loving the sinner regardless of fault or failure as the basis for loving our neighbour, although present in Islam, is crucially absent from the *A Common Word* document.[36]

---

32 Ibid., 93.
33 "Some Initial Reflections", 1–6.
34 Ibid., 2.
35 Ibid., 3. Citing Matthew 22:35; Luke 10:25 and Mark 12:34.
36 Ibid., 3–4. For example see *sūrat al-mā'idah* (5):54, or *sūrat al-mumtahanah* (60):7.

One final concern involves the terms of acceptance. Madigan notes that Muslim have one pre-condition to friendship with Christians. This pre-condition is found in *sūrat al-mumtahanah* (60):8: "so long as they do not wage war against Muslims on account of their religion, oppress them and drive them out of their homes".[37] The verse clearly challenges the foreign policy of many nations and the tacit support of Christians worldwide. However, Madigan does not believe this pre-condition has to be an impediment to the larger goal of both *A Common Word* and *Nostra Aetate;* an appeal to common elements of our respective faiths with the need to move beyond theory to praxis. Subsequently, Madigan sees the necessity to go beyond talk of loving God and neighbour to a dialogue of mutual repentance, and of *mea culpa*.[38]

Lover of Islam, Believing in Jesus (Paolo Dall'Oglio)

The next text examined is by Paolo Dall'Oglio. He was an Italian Jesuit who lived in Syria for more than thirty years until his presumed death in 2013.[39] In his book, *Amoureux de l'Islam, Croyant en Jésus* [*In Love with Islam, Believing in Jesus*] Dall'Oglio gives a fascinating insight into the heart and mind of a man who dedicated his life to building bridges between Muslims and Christians.[40] The stated goal of *Amoureux de l'Islam* [*In Love with*

---

37 Ibid., 5.
38 Ibid. On other occasions refers to the next *Common Word, mea culpa.* Cf. *Jms 2014 (01): A Word in Common* vol. 1, *John Main Seminar* (Elmhurst College Chicago: World Community of Christian Meditation 2014).
39 Fr Paolo Dall'Oglio is a victim of the Syrian civil war. He was kidnapped 29 July 2013. Cf.: <http://www.ibtimes.co.uk/islamic-state-syria-father-paolo-dalloglio-alive-raqqa-according-isis-defector-1525076> and <http://www.thedailybeast.com/articles/2016/02/29/the-mysterious-fate-of-the-dissident-italian-priest-snatched-by-isis.html> accessed 8 May 2016.
40 Paolo Dall'Oglio, *Amoureux De L'islam, Croyant En Jésus* trans. d'Églantine Gabaix-Hailé, 1st edn (Paris: Les Éditions l'Atelier, Éditions Ouvriès, 2009). Henceforth referred to as *Amoureux De L'islam*.

Islam] is to present Islam as a religion with a wealth of values capable of nourishing our emerging global society.[41] Here Dall'Oglio offers interesting insights into the Patriarch Abraham, the Incarnation, the Crucifixion, the prophethood of Muhammad and the syncretism of faiths.

Dall'Oglio formed part of a religious community in Syria based in Deir Mar Moussa the Abyssinian, an ancient monastery dating back to the sixth century. Below the Altar window are the remains of a salutation that could easily have come from the Qur'ān, "In the name of God the Most Merciful and Compassionate".[42] Before the civil war the monastery acted as a centre for interfaith dialogue.[43] The community that lived and worshiped there chose the name *al-Khalil*, the Friend of God, the Biblical and Qur'ānic title for the patriarch Abraham. There the hospitality of Abraham was more than just symbolic.[44] Those who visited joined in the daily contemplative Syriac monastic life of prayer, learned about Islam and Arabic.[45] Dall'Oglio hoped Mar Moussa would provide a template for other Christian Churches in Muslims lands.[46]

Dall'Oglio expressed his knowledge of the term *ahl al-kitāb* in the second chapter, *Ma relation à l'Islam* [*My Relation to Islam*]. He candidly portrayed his admiration for Islam, describing his temptation to convert as a young Jesuit following Friday prayers in a mosque in Bosra. In the book he defines his relationship with Islam as dual membership that finds its source in Christ and a Church in motion.[47] Dall'Oglio's use of the term *ahl al-kitāb* is limited. He identifies Islam as a religion that has always respected other religions. This tolerance, he says, "is based on knowledge of the fact that God established these communities".[48]

---

41 Ibid., 170–1.
42 Ibid., 14.
43 Guyonne de Montjou, *Mar Moussa, Un Monastère, Un Homme, Un Désert* (Paris: Albin Michel, 2006), 23–25.
44 Dall'Oglio, *Amoureux De L'islam*, 19, 174.
45 Ibid., 21–8.
46 Ibid., 30.
47 Ibid., 31–2. In fact he tells the young Imam that he has been a *Muslim* since birth, echoing the response of the historical Christians of Najrān to the call to Islam while staying with the Muhammad.
48 Ibid., 44.

Islamic tolerance for *ahl al-kitāb* is in contrast to the historical Church that Dall'Oglio describes as imperialistic and totalitarian. Throughout *Amoureux de l'Islam* Dall'Oglio expresses his understanding of the term *ahl al-kitāb*. For instance in Chapter 3 of *Une Église de l'Islam* [A Church of Islam], he discusses three Qur'ānic verses that mention the People of the Book in relation to the primacy of God as judge of mankind and their deeds.[49] Other times under the subheading of "*Bon voisinage en dépit de la discrimination*" [Good neighbours in spite of discrimination], he discusses the unequal rights in marriage whereby a Muslim man can marry a Christian woman, but a Christian man cannot marry a Muslim woman without changing his religion.[50] Therefore it is safe to say that the concept of *ahl al-kitāb* is an important part of Dall'Oglio's unarticulated knowledge of Islam, but is not a concept he chooses to employ to promote dialogue and improve relations. In fact, he employs alternative terms like "*Peuple de Dieu*" [People of God] and "*Peuple de Prophètes*" [People of the Prophets] just as often.[51] Unfortunately, there is not enough information given to discern if Dall'Oglio's reluctance to use the term *ahl al-kitāb* is due to its limitation, as with Daniel Madigan, or if it is because his audience is primarily western Christian and therefore explaining the concept to westerners would entail a separate discussion in itself. To promote dialogue and better relations Dall'Oglio opts for dialogue in a framework of modern, evolving pluralist society using a plethora of means.[52] Although *Amoureux de l'Islam* primarily presents theological arguments there are immense social and political ramifications interwoven throughout.

---

49   Ibid., 52. *Sūrat al-baqarah* 2:62, Cf. discussed in Chapter 1; *sūrat al-māʾidah* 5:69; and *sūrat al-ḥajj* 22:17.
50   Ibid., 53–4. The right for a Muslim man to marry a woman from the People of the Book is intended to promote better relations between Muslims and Christians, but the right still implies the superiority of Islam over Christianity as the perfected religion.
51   Ibid., 138–9. Cf. People of God Conference. 144. People of the Prophets offered by Christian de Chergé.
52   Ibid., 54. Examples of subtle cultural discrimination cited by Dall'Oglio against Muslims by the West include the prominence of Christian heritage, dietary laws, and dress, even the calendar.

Social Inculturation and the Sacrament of Good Neighbours

Dall'Oglio describes Arabic culture as his adopted culture.[53] It should come as no surprise then that inculturation is an important feature of Dall'Oglio's mission; enabling the witness of the Gospel to the host culture. Examples of inculturation include carpets on the floor of the church, removing shoes before prayer and adoption of the Syriac Rite and Arabic as the liturgical language. Most importantly inculturation encourages Muslims and Christians to engage in daily life in a way that brings out the best of each religion.[54] The practice of hospitality and Dall'Oglio's desire to inculturate the Church and message of Christ within an otherwise Muslim society rely primarily on the basic Qur'ānic acceptance of Christians as *ahl al-kitāb*.[55]

Yet, inculturation does not imply absorption or reduction or mixing of core values, but rather a Church that is willing to exist lovingly and harmoniously amongst Muslims.[56] In fact Dall'Oglio aspires to transform the Church in order to "*aller vers*" [move towards] Islam.[57] He draws inspiration from Fr Matteo Ricci's work in China during the sixteenth century. Since, as John Paul II notes, Fr Matteo Ricci encouraged the Church to be Chinese with the Chinese.[58] Dall'Oglio thus tries to be as close to Islamic culture and beliefs as he can.[59] Through greater empathy, Christians in the Middle East are able to trust the work of the Spirit, "leave it to God alone" with regard to difficult theological questions concerning, for example, the prophethood of Muhammad.[60]

Within the framework of inculturation, Dall'Oglio discusses the issue of conversion. Dall'Oglio believes Muslims and Christians should be free to

---

53 Ibid., 22.
54 Ibid., 66, 79.
55 Ibid., 169–70.
56 Ibid., 49–68, 169–70.
57 Ibid., 30, 49. This Church for Islam is in contrast to an Islamo-Christian Church discussed here.
58 Ibid., 80. In addition Dall'Oglio mentions 1 Corinthians 9:20–23.
59 Ibid., 33–4.
60 Ibid., 28, 81. This empathy makes Muslims part of the family of Mar Moussa.

convert if they wish.⁶¹ Yet, this present author senses that Dall'Oglio would prefer that the lines between Islam and Christianity become somewhat blurred.⁶² For instance, he prefers the word "adhesion", since, as he sees it, adhesion is to a way, whereas, conversion is from sin to God. Consequently Dall'Oglio does not desire to convert Muslims to Christianity; rather he desires to bring every soul to God.⁶³ Furthermore, while there are some Muslims who are led by the Spirit to Christ, many choose not to be baptized.⁶⁴ Conversely, there are others who are baptized as Christians, but outwardly Muslim, since it is forbidden for a Muslim to convert to Christianity.⁶⁵ Not surprisingly, these Muslim-Christians describe their experience of Jesus as saviour differently from the Jesus they experience in Islam. Some do not sense that it is necessary to believe in Christ's torture, crucifixion and death.⁶⁶ These Muslim-Christians are a natural bridge between the two faiths. He hopes they will help develop a harmony between the Qur'ān and Christian teachings.⁶⁷

Through inculturation Muslims and Christians are inevitably playing a greater role in each other's lives including occasions for prayer. Dall'Oglio identifies the opportunity of "Communal Prayer" as occasionally awkward. Nevertheless, there are times when Muslims and Christians can and do take the name of God together in praise. One way is when remembering God, *dhikr*. This remembering takes place before and after a meal or conference. Other times include reciprocal presence as guests at each other's services. Here Dall'Oglio says it is important to have pre-established boundaries. The third occasion includes spontaneous prayer, keeping in mind that, "All authentic prayer is sustained by the Spirit of God who is mysteriously present in the hearts of all men".⁶⁸

61 Ibid., 88.
62 Ibid., 139–40.
63 Ibid., 85–88. Dall'Oglio acknowledges that not every person who wishes to convert is sincere. Cf. 86.
64 Ibid., 85–6, 90, 93.
65 Ibid., 88–89, 93.
66 Ibid., 117.
67 Ibid., 90. Cf. Muslim-Christians 55–6.
68 Ibid., 91, fn. 7. Citing John Paul II.

Theological Considerations

Dall'Oglio chooses several hermeneutical devices to convey his hopes for greater understanding and harmony between Christians and Muslims. These devices do not contradict the lessons surrounding the appellation *ahl al-kitāb*. In many ways devices like returning to the faith of Abraham, the reappraisal of the prophethood of Muhammad and the hermeneutics of love compliment the nuanced issues raised by the traditional commentary of *ahl al-kitāb*.

Abraham, Hospitality and a Model of Faith

The place of Ishmael in Arab culture and Islam is both ethnic and symbolic.[69] God's fulfilment of the promises made to the patriarch Abraham potentially plays a major unifying role, according to Dall'Oglio. This is a different approach than the approach taken by many Christians who look for deficiencies in Islamic perceptions of Biblical themes.[70] In Islam, Abraham is also the "Friend of God", where God takes the initiative and offers his alliance. Abraham is a model of faith and patriarch of the Arabs through his son Ishmael. Therefore, through Muhammad and the revelation of the Qur'ān, the circuit of the three prayers of Abraham is complete.[71] Dall'Oglio contends that understanding the role of Abraham in Islam is the key for Christians trying to understand Islam.[72] To this end Dall'Oglio examines the question, in what way is it possible to speak of an Abrahamic ascendance of Islam, or create a Judeo-Christian Islamic community of Abraham.

This trajectory views God's promises to Abraham as running parallel to promises made to Isaac. Dall'Oglio is not trying to erase or minimize the differences, but would like Christians to consider that God did not

---

69   Louis Massignon draws spiritual strength through contemplation of the anguish that must have been experienced by Abraham, Isaac, Hagar and Ishmael. Ibid., 76.
70   Ibid., 72–73. For example, the lack of discussion of the Messianic promise, whereas in Islam the Alliance is loyalty to God only.
71   Ibid., 39–40, 131.
72   Ibid., 69.

abandon Ishmael and Hagar, nor did He chastise them.[73] Through reading the Qur'ān it is possible to appreciate that Muhammad entered into contact and engaged with the Bible at a moment in time. Through the Qur'ān Christians can discover that Islam is the inheritance of the promises made by God to Abraham regarding his son Ishmael.[74] This theme is discussed further in Chapter 4 of *Amoureux de l'Islam* where Dall'Oglio challenges Christians who are interested only in Sarah and not the fate of Hagar and Ishmael, since they were sent to wander the desert like displaced people.

Although Vatican II highlights some of the common ground between Islam and Christianity, for Dall'Oglio the authenticity of Islam is found in the conscience of Muslims. For instance Lumen Gentium 16 speaks of the faith of Abraham, monotheism, the experience of Divine Mercy and similar eschatology. There are, however, differences. In Islam the centre of experience is with Muhammad. The Messianic promises found in the Bible are absent. For Islam the theme is loyalty to God alone. For Dall'Oglio this represents a deepening of the theology of history and of existence. This enlargement of salvation through Islam is the work of the Holy Spirit. Dall'Oglio explains, however, that this view is not a challenge to the Church's essential understanding of the salvific role of the divine through the person of Jesus Christ. The role of Christ is as a source of faith that remains open to each person, in all places and all times.[75]

Challenging Traditional Positions

A major theme of *Amoureux de l'Islam* concerns the degree to which Christians are willing to accept the mission of Muhammad. For non-Muslims familiar with Islam this question is easier to answer than it is for the Church due to its traditional and dogmatic position.[76] Historically however, the first Christians that came into contact with Muhammad could not

---

73 Ibid., 74. Citing an opinion given by Cardinal Carlo Mario Martini. Cf. fn. 9.
74 Ibid., 71–2. Cf. *sūrat al-baqarah* (2):124, 126 & 128–9.
75 Ibid., 73, 110, 115. This draws upon understanding Jesus as the pre-eternal Word of God.
76 Ibid., 95.

decide whether or not he was a prophet. Dall'Oglio, aware of the historical context of Muhammad, points out that part of the problem is that the historical context includes the internal fighting amongst Christians regarding a number of heresies. For this reason perhaps, John of Damascus describes Islam as a new heresy from Arabia.[77] Dall'Oglio posits that it should be possible for Christians to accept the prophethood of Muhammad.[78] His argument is multi-pronged and includes a description of what it means to be a prophet, leading on to developments in the Church's teaching regarding re-examination of types of prophets and Biblical narratives, in addition to taking on board the results of Muhammad's mission.[79]

While examining attributes of prophets it is clear that Muhammad fulfils some of the criteria, as outlined by the Church, even if questions remain regarding other aspects. If the Qur'ān and Islam are outside the alliance with Abraham and Isaac, is there a precedent for viewing Muhammad as a non-Biblical prophet? Dall'Oglio makes the case by listing a number of well-known prophetic figures that are not part of the alliance with Abraham. These include Noah, Balaam, Job, Lemuel, and Cyrus. In addition, there are Biblical passages that call for the gift of prophecy to be extended to all peoples.[80] The Second Vatican Council allows for such a possibility and declares that the Church does not reject anything that is true in other faiths.[81] This position represents a fundamental shift in attitude from centuries of condemnation.[82] Perhaps, Dall'Oglio asserts, it is time for the Church to promote a positive image of Islam and allow for people to recognize Muhammad as a prophet without imposing acceptance.[83]

---

77 Ibid., 98, 106.
78 Ibid., 100.
79 Ibid., 95–108. Outside Church texts, Meggitt mentions that historically much of the Islamic sentiment in Europe is based on prejudice. Justin J. Meggitt, *Early Quakers and Islam: Slavery, Apocalyptic and Christian-Muslim Encounters in the Seventeenth Century*, 1st edn, 59 vols, vol. 59 (Uppsala: Swedish Science Press, 2013), 25–33.
80 Dall'Oglio, *Amoureux De L'islam*, 95–97, 165. Incidentally Isaiah 45:1 declares Cyrus (a non-Jew) God's anointed.
81 Ibid., 98, fn. 5. Referring to *Nostra Aetate*. Muhammad is not mentioned in the text.
82 Ibid., 101.
83 Ibid., 99–100.

Yet, for Christians there are serious questions concerning the acceptance of a prophet that does not recognize the incarnation of Jesus, or his crucifixion and resurrection.[84] At best, Dall'Oglio believes these issues necessitate Christians contemplate a deeper understanding of the Oneness of God, and to find ways to get beyond the Qur'ānic criticism. He relays the thoughts on the subject of the Incarnation held by an anonymous sheikh, who says that the problem with the Christian description of Jesus as the "Son of God" is that Christians do not understand that we are all children of God. Further, that all creation is "family of God" loved by God, even though man has a special status, "as viceroy of God in creation, as an eldest son to whom the father has entrusted his property".[85] In addition, Dall'Oglio discusses *sūrat Āl-'Imrān* 3:159 and Colossians 1:15–16, where he compares the similarities between Jesus and Adam as created by God's volition. Dall'Oglio considers the image of angels kneeling before Adam and Jesus. For Muslims, Adam and Jesus are created beings, favoured, but not separate. Further, humanity shares in a greater portion of Divine attributes with God than other forms of creation, such as reason. In this manner it is acceptable to assert that man is created in the image of God.[86]

Dall'Oglio devotes an entire chapter to the examination of what the crucifixion means for Muslims and Christians.[87] It is not an area where Christians and Muslims will achieve agreement. It is an area however, where we can better understand each other. For Muslims the authoritative witness to the fate of Jesus on that epic Friday is described in *sūrat an-Nisā'* (4):157–8. In these verses God elevates Jesus to himself rather than allow those who rejected faith to kill or crucify him. For Muslims Jesus will return in the future, inaugurate the resurrection and fight the anti-Christ.[88] From here Dall'Oglio explains the eschatological details are vague. It is not known whether or not Jesus is the Mahdi, or works with the Mahdi, or even if Jesus can be killed in battle by the anti-Christ. If so, Dall'Oglio asks, how

84   Ibid., 96.
85   Ibid., 125.
86   Ibid., 125–6.
87   Ibid.,
88   Ibid., 151.

is it possible that Jesus' death in battle would be glorious, but unacceptable to die on the cross?[89] For Muslims it is not necessary to believe in the suffering, death and resurrection of Christ to have faith in an afterlife, belief in the miracle of the Qur'ān is sufficient.[90]

Harmony and Syncretism

Dall'Oglio hopes that the Church will one day embark upon a hermeneutic of interpretation of the Qur'ān and prophethood of Muhammad that will lead to a greater harmonization of the Bible and the Qur'ān.[91] Dall'Oglio posits that it is important for Christians to keep in mind that Muslims are not only part of the Abrahamic tradition, but that they believe Jesus is the Messiah and wait for his return.[92] If Christians can accept Islam as at least chronologically a post-Christian community then it is possible to focus on the future where Christians as well as Muslims envision the return of Christ. Here there is a future replete with harmony for the final manifestation of Jesus and the inauguration of God's Kingdom.[93]

The future reconciliation of the Church with the Muslim world relies on the Spirit of God.[94] Dall'Oglio recognizes the Spirit of God is at work within Islam in spite of the differences between the Church and the *Ummah* that often make Islam appear to be a rival. The theological differences need to be taken as a catalyst for renewal, for reinterpretation in light of theologies of faith.[95] Dall'Oglio considers several functions of Islam in salvation history that Christians should consider. The functions include the last revelation in the Abrahamic tradition and completing the circuit of bringing the children of Ishmael back into the fold. Islam also calls people to faith against the failings of the Christian mission in the secularized West. For

---

89   Ibid., 154.
90   Ibid., 156–7.
91   Ibid., 97, 116, 34.
92   Ibid., 139.
93   Ibid., 116, 119–20. Dall'Oglio values the potential of eschatology as a unifying force much more than Evangelization.
94   Ibid., 35.
95   Ibid., 39.

Dall'Oglio this call to faith is not necessarily a call to convert to Islam as for people to reconnect with their own faith, "*car la conversion est à Dieu*" [because conversion is to God].⁹⁶

One way of learning to empathize with Muslims is to consider the results of the prophethood of Muhammad. For Dall'Oglio it is not difficult to admit that Muhammad enjoyed a relationship with God. Muhammad understood his mission was to recall people to an original truth, *fitrah*, and he amassed a large following.⁹⁷ Nevertheless, Dall'Oglio clearly states that the Grace of Christ affects all souls.⁹⁸ Christ is the Eternal Word that empowers all truth for all time.⁹⁹ Muhammad's mission includes a call to pluralism that accepts other faiths alongside Islam, namely the People of the Book. Dall'Oglio euphemistically describes this built-in pluralism as the *cross* of Muhammad.¹⁰⁰ When our spiritual experience meets their spiritual experience it might be easier to overlook the paradoxes and contradictions of our traditions, which ironically are in part responsible for our spiritual experiences, "*même par voie de contradiction et de paradoxe, notre attitude cherche un accès à une expérience spirituelle qui ne peut exister sans cette lettre à dépasser*" [even in matter of contradiction and paradox, our behaviour looks for a way to reach a spiritual experience that cannot exist without going beyond this letter].¹⁰¹

Acceptance of Muhammad as some degree of prophet and an extension of the practice of good neighbours, allows for a rereading of both the Bible and the Qur'ān in ways that open up new horizons.¹⁰² Here Muslims and Christians can remain loyal to their respective teachings yet open to viewing the text of the other as inspired and worthy of consideration.¹⁰³ As mentioned above, issues of Christian faith such as the Trinity, Incarnation

---

96   Ibid., 39–44.
97   Ibid., 112. This idea lends itself to viewing the mission of Jesus as *wali*, guardian of the truth.
98   Ibid., 129.
99   Ibid., 110.
100 Ibid., 106.
101 Ibid., 117, 20.
102 Ibid., 121–34.
103 Ibid., 106.

and Crucifixion are difficult for Muslims to accept. Questions regarding the prophethood of Muhammad are likewise difficult for Christians. Yet through greater knowledge and respect for each other, Muslims and Christians can explore alternative understandings of these issues. Failure to integrate, failure to explore each other's experience of faith is centuries old.[104] Perhaps when seeking to understand the experience of faith of the other, Muslims and Christians, can create a common language of dialogue and move beyond the dialogue of the deaf.[105] Dall'Oglio offers the historical example of St Francis who said it is possible to live amongst Muslims and remain Christian.[106]

Dall'Oglio considers the political implications of loving God and loving neighbour. One of the clearest products of inculturation is empathy and action.[107] Towards the end of *Amoureux De L'Islam* Dall'Oglio discusses his opinions regarding the state of democracy in the West, comparing the results of valueless secularization to a tyranny.[108] On one occasion Dall'Oglio cites a friend, Sheikh Yasser Hafez, concerning his observations of European politics. Sheikh Hafez notes that even though Europe likes to say it is pro-Arab, Europe always sides with the enemies of the Arabs (who are primarily Muslim). When asked about democracy Sheikh Hafez says he is disappointed with the Western model, but still considers democracy as possibly the best model, if it is tailored to suit different cultures and situations.[109] Dall'Oglio believes that Christians in this ever-increasing global society should make friends with Muslims. He says that Muslims have a lot to offer in terms of values that the West is losing. Instead of dwelling on

---

104 Ibid., 68.
105 Ibid., 142. A great example is when John Paul II while visiting a mosque cited the Qur'an.
106 Ibid., 43, 84, 128. Other examples include Louis Massignon, Charles de Foucard, and Christian de Chergé.
107 *La Rage Et La Lumière: Un Prêtre Dans La Revolution Syrienne*, trans. d'Églantine Gabaix-Hailé, 1st edn (Ivry-sur-Seine: Les Éditions l'Atelier, Éditions Ouvriès, 2013), 127.
108 *Amoureux De L'islam*, 170.
109 Ibid., 171.

past differences Muslims and Christians should focus on building a more spiritual future together.[110]

Divine Hospitality: Foundations for Interreligious Coexistence (Fadi Daou and Nayla Tabbara)

The last publication examined here is *L'hospitalité divine: L'autre dans le dialogue des théologies chrétienne et musulmane* by Fadi Daou and Nayla Tabbara, a Maronite priest and a Sunni scholar.[111] Jean-Marc Aveline states in the preface that *Divine Hospitality* introduces a new approach to interfaith dialogue, *"theologies in dialogue"*. With *theologies in dialogue* exists *"la communion spirituelle"* [Spiritual Communion] between believers of different religions where theological questions faithfully translate into terms of everyday life.[112] The strength of this approach is that it does not rely on apologetic or polemic confrontation. Rather *theologies in dialogue* encourages a growing understanding and appreciation of the religious other as a companion on a long journey. This approach promotes the idea that the religious other, without reduction or syncretism of beliefs, is genuinely part of God's plan and that *"la foi est plus un cheminement qu'une identité"*

110   Ibid. The pages of *Amoureux De L'Islam* do not offer an indication of Dall'Oglio's own political concerns. Perhaps at the time of writing the cracks in Syrian society were not yet fissures. In *La Rage et la Lumière: Un Prêtre dans la Revolution Syrienne* Dall'Oglio explains the origins of the present implications of the conflict and his aspirations for the future. Cf. *La Rage*, 45–62, 155–84.
111   Fadi Daou & Nayla Tabbara, *L'hospitalité Divine: L'autre Dans Le Dialogue Des Théologies Chrétienne Et Musulmane*, French edn (Berlin: Lit Verlag 2013). Henceforth referred to as *Divine Hospitality*. The English title of the book is *Divine Hospitality: A Christian-Muslim Conversation*. This research cites texts from both editions.
112   Ibid., 13–4. Jean-Marc Aveline is the series director of *Colloquium Salutis: Études En Science Et Théologie Des Religions*. In many ways *théologies en dialogue* is very similar to Dall'Oglio's philosophy of inculturation, divine hospitality and dialogue discussed above.

[faith is more a journey than an identity].[113] As the authors see it, theology is responsible for providing answers for religious diversity in order to promote the common good. Failure to do so is paramount to contributing to a hostile environment between people of different faiths.[114] A paradigm for this approach is found in the concept of Divine Hospitality exemplified by the patriarch Abraham.

Although there are social and political implications from this tome, its approach is primarily theological. The concept of the People of the Book is critical to *Divine Hospitality*. Tabbara expounds the Islamic understanding of the People of the Book in order to provide the theological foundation for embracing religious plurality.

Elsewhere membership of the collective People of the Book and understanding of the concept is implied without formal identification as necessarily separate from other religions. This is patently true for Daou who, although he does not use the term, considers the concept germane to the Muslim narrative of other religions. One might assume therefore that when Daou refers to Christians in an Islamic context, or the collective group of Jews, or Christians, he is well aware of how Muslims perceive the collective, that is, that the concept can be called upon to help build better relations. Daou further explains,

> That Islam recognizes the divine origin of my faith; that Islam considers Christianity being in the same category with Islam and Judaism (religions of the book); it reminds me of the importance of the word of God (the Biblical text and its holy dimension, not just moral or theological ones); that I have a role to explain to Muslims that Christians are not only "*ahl kitāb*" but also "*ahl Allah*" through the incarnated word of God.[115]

Daou promotes *theologies in dialogue* based on Christian teachings. In this way, he prepares the Christian audience for the Capernaum leap of faith from perceiving God in the other through a traditional Christological lens to recognizing that of God in other faiths as authentically part of God's plan. In his opening chapter, "Christ and the Other: Union Embracing Difference", Daou

---

113   Ibid., 14.
114   Ibid., 17, 18.
115   Fr Fadi Daou, 20 June 2015. Research question response.

sets the foundation for viewing the faith of others as something that Christ acknowledged through his interactions with people of other faiths, in spite of traditional Jewish reticence. This is demonstrated through his interaction with the Canaanite and Samaritan women as well as the Centurion.[116] Here Christ places a greater value on faith than on external practice. This aspect of faith became part of the early Church exemplified by the Apostle Peter in Acts 10:34–35. Yet, Daou acknowledges that the Church has not always been welcoming of other religions, but rather insisted, "outside the Church, no salvation".[117] Therefore for some Christians, faith as a shared journey with Muslims may require a reappraisal of values. Daou makes the point, that the basis for dialogue with people of other faiths is the realization that we are all children of God.[118] However, it is through Christ's sacrifice and the work of the Holy Spirit that all humanity benefits.[119]

Fitra and the People of the Book

The first appearance of the term People of the Book is found in Chapter 2, "The Economy of the Reminder: Islamic Perception of the History of Revelation". Here Tabbara introduces a discussion of the religious "other" found in the Qur'ān. Tabbara notes that there are verses that encourage a spirit of openness and fraternity as well as verses that foster the need to keep separate and to subjugate the religious other. In order to avoid the charge of contradiction, Tabbara reminds the reader, like Ramadan above, that knowing the context of the verses is of the utmost importance.[120] The use of the term People of the Book begins with discussion of *sūrat*

---

116   Tabbara, *L'hospitalité Divine*, 24–29.
117   Ibid., 31.
118   Ibid., 34. Citing Pastor Wesley Ariarajah.
119   Ibid., 37–42. Here Daou draws upon the teaching of *Lumen Gentium* and *Gaudium et Spes* 22:2 & 5, as well as several verses from the Gospel of John.
120   Ibid., 43.

al-baqarah (2):135. Here there are Jews and Christians who call people to join their religions in order to secure salvation. This comes in the wake of the discussion of *fitra* as innate disposition.[121] Through the discussion of *fitra* Tabbara points out differences between Islam and Christianity in relation to understanding human nature and salvation.[122]

Another shared theme concerns God sending or guiding all people. In Islam this refers to messengers. This idea is emphasized with the concept of *dhikr* [remembrance], that all communities have received God's message as a reminder, as noted in several verses including *sūrat Fāṭir* (35):24. Most importantly, Tabbara comments that some of the messengers are more easily recognized than others. Thus, the way is open for Muslims to keep an open mind as to who is sent to call people to believe in God and act justly, since the call to believe in God and act justly is for all people regardless of religion.[123] Tabbara defends this argument through examination of verses *sūrat ar-Raḥmān* (55):7–9; *sūrat al-māʾidah* (5):48; *sūrat Luqmān* (31):28 and *sūrat al-mutaffifīn* (83):1–3. Here the onus is on humanity to strive in faith and good works as a response to God's natural calling.[124]

The Faith of Abraham is Inclusive Islām

Tabbara examines two ways in which Abraham responds to God. These are through *fitra*, and through revelation. In pre-Islamic times and throughout the Qurʾān the faith of Abraham is regarded as an example for mankind. Those that followed the pure faith of Abraham were called the *hunafāʾ*.[125] Like Esack and Ramadan above, Tabbara notes that the Qurʾān uses *islām*

---

121   Ibid., 45–49. Cf. *Divine Hospitality: A Christian-Muslim Conversation* [L'hospitalité divine: L'autre dans le dialogue des théologies chrétienne et musulmane], trans. Alan J. Amos (Geneva: World Council of Churches, 2017), 32. *sūrat al-aʿrāf* (7):172. According to the Sufi Scholar Tirmidhi, *fitra* is the divine anointing, *sibhga*, of all humanity.

122   *L'hospitalité Divine*, 48. For instance the fact that Islam does not subscribe to the concept of original sin and that man only needs to repent and return to original *fitra* for his sins in order to be forgiven.

123   Ibid., 48–50, 52.

124   Ibid., 52–3.

125   This subject is extensively covered in this dissertation's chapter concerning *al-jāhiliyya*.

and *Muslim* as terms to refer to those who follow God in the broader sense.[126] This logic is then applied to *sūrat Āl-'Imrān* (3):19, which states that the religion before God is *islām*. Tabbara challenges the medieval interpretation of the verse that refers to a reified *islām* rather than the state of faith of a believer. For Tabbara the *sense large* of *islām* represents "the way", the spiritual path, followed by all the prophets and individuals. They are called *Muslims* since they placed their trust in God and submitted to Him.[127]

In Chapter 3, *Covenants and Revelations*, Daou discusses different types of alliances between God and man. There is the alliance with Adam. Here God is like a parent. Man, however, refuses to take responsibility and brings disorder into the world. This alliance is followed with a renewed alliance with Noah, where even though man continues to disobey God, God still hopes for a new life for man.[128] With Hosea God's relationship with humanity is like a fiancée. The results of God's love for humanity are peace and reward in heaven for those who are faithful. Yet, the revelation of God is love for all humanity and knowledge of God. Through the alliance with Abraham, the universal invitation to a relationship with God is expanded. In Genesis 12:2–3 God promises to bless all people. Through the example of the faith of Abraham and his relationship with Melchizedek, Daou demonstrates that God's alliance with Abraham is not exclusive to other forms of grace in the world. All people are "people of God".[129] This love is exemplified by God's promise and relationship with Hagar and Ishmael. Here even though Hagar is cast away from Abraham's household the Angel of God comforts her and announces God's plans for Ishmael.[130]

The common feature of these prophetic alliances is that they are external as well as internal, with the emphasis on a personal relationship with God.[131] Through Moses and the revelation of the Ten Commandments

---

126 Tabbara, *L'hospitalité Divine*, 56. Cf. *sūrat al baqarah* (2):135 or *sūrat an-Nisā'* 4:125.
127 Ibid., 56–58.
128 Ibid., 63–4. Cf. Genesis 6:1–21 and 9:9–10.
129 Ibid., 67–8. Cf. John Paul II, *Slavorum Apostoli*, 1985, fn. 19.
130 Ibid., 68. Cf. Genesis 16:13. This is a slight variation of Dall'Oglio's revision of the blessings bestowed on Hagar and Ishmael.
131 Ibid., 69.

the People of God are required to uphold a moral standard as their part of the alliance. God's alliances are permanent.[132] Salvation in history is not linear. Salvation does not pass from one revelation to the next replacing the former.[133] This point is crucial to Daou's defence of the universality of the mission of Jesus as God's eternal word in contrast to the Islamic concept of abrogation.

In addition to recognizing that both Judaism and Christianity share a common heritage with the faith of Abraham, Daou acknowledges that Islam also follows the faith of Abraham and believes in the same God. This pronouncement is clear in *Lumen Gentium* 16.[134] For Daou Islam is the closest to the faith of Abraham, even closer than Judaism and Christianity, since both Judaism and Christianity contain new revelations; they develop the faith of Abraham, whereas Islam heralds a return to the faith of Abraham. This is why Abraham represents the model of faith, while in Judaism and Christianity Abraham is the Father of Faith.[135] Daou asks what are the implications of Christians accepting Islam as the new branch on the Abrahamic tree of salvation? He recalls that for Christian de Chergé the joy is accepting Muslims as fellow believers and finding God in their religion and life, with all the questions and perhaps not too many definitive answers. *"J'apprends à mieux découvrir les solidarités et même les complicités d'aujourd'hui, y compris celles de la foi, à ne pas figer l'autre dans l'idée que je m'en fais, que mon Église peut-être m'en a transmis, ni même dans ce qu'il peut dire de lui actuellement, majoritairement"* [I am learning in order to discover better the identities and even the complicities of today, including those of faith, not to fix on the other the idea of faith that I form for myself, which my Church perhaps has transmitted to me, nor even what the Church may actually be able to say about it from a majority viewpoint].[136] Most importantly he states that

---

132 Ibid., 69–72. Cf. *Lumen Gentium* 16 and *Nostra Aetate*, 4. This is a rejection of earlier Church teaching regarding replacement theory.
133 Ibid., 74.
134 Ibid.
135 Ibid., 75. Daou sees this in Hanafism.
136 Ibid., 76; *Divine Hospitality*, 51. From Christian de Chergé, *L'invincible espérance*, 171.

the experience of solidarity with dialogue produces the best environment for interreligious dialogue as well as for reassessing Christian faith.[137]

However, there are quite varying ideas of just how Islam fits into the Abrahamic spectrum.[138] Daou suggests Islam is not "son" of the promise like Judaism and Christianity, but is "son" of an alliance as described in Genesis 17:18–20. Islam affirms and revitalizes the religion of Abraham as well as bringing its own revelation with the *Sunnah* of Muhammad.[139] Daou points out that this revelation brings with it challenges as to how it views the status and message of Jesus Christ as well as the fullness of his revelation. Fortunately, these issues do not need to divide Muslims and Christians. He refers to *sūrat al-mā'idah* (5):48 as an example of how Muslims and the People of the Book can live together in spite of their differences. In a spirit of Abrahamic fraternity, Muslims and Christians should learn to appreciate the differences between the two faiths, just as most people can recognize the work of the Spirit of God in the lives of Mother Teresa, Gandhi, or Badsha Khan.[140]

In fact, Daou, like Dall'Oglio, posits that it is possible for Christians without complaisance, or compromise of their fundamental values, to afford the Qur'ān as well as Muhammad a degree of recognition as divinely inspired. This follows from the Christian concept of Salvation History, where Islam is seen in the mystery of the light of Jesus as the universal saviour and in the fullness of the revelation of God for humanity. An important detail that Daou wishes to assert is that this recognition challenges the Islamic idea that the Qur'ān in some way takes on a greater importance than Jesus due to chronology, or abrogation, since Daou argues the importance of Jesus is eschatological. In this view Muhammad's prophethood is

---

137 *L'hospitalité Divine*, 76–77. This idea is supported by *Ad Gentes, Decree on the Missionary Activity of the Church*, 22.
138 Ibid., 77–79. Daou examines the opinion of two renowned Lebanese Maronite scholars, Fr Michel Hayek (d. 2005) and Fr Youakim Moubarac (d.1995). These scholars offer different opinions regarding the place of Ishmael and Islam within the various alliances discussed above.
139 Ibid., 81–2.
140 Ibid., 83–5.

within the alliance of Abraham. However, for Daou, unlike Dall'Oglio, the Qur'ān is not the uncreated word of God, but the Qur'ān can function as a revelation, or *dhikr*, a reminder, for Christians when it is consistent with the teachings of Abraham. By accepting a limited authenticity for Islam he hopes Muslims will reciprocate by considering the Torah and Gospel as a sort of ancient Testament to the Qur'ān.[141]

Indeed, Tabbara ventures that Muslims should also consider the scriptures of the People of the Book as a form of *dhikr*. In support Tabbara cites a number of verses including *sūrat al-anbiyā'* (21):7, *sūrat Yūnus* (10):94 and *sūrat al-mā'idah* (5):44–47.[142] Where there are differences between the Qur'ān and the respective texts, she hopes that these differences will be considered matters of interpretation and not *taḥrīf* [falsification of the text], since, the Qur'ān sees itself as confirming the scriptures that came before it. Muslims should therefore study the scriptures in order to understand the Qur'ān better.[143] Further, Tabbara notes that the Qur'ān mentions that there are People of the Book who accept the revelation given to Muslims as well as their own revelation.[144] Ultimately, the Qur'ān does not differentiate between *mu'minūn*, believers; they are *muslim* whether they are followers of Muhammad or People of the Book.[145]

Jesus Is the Son of God and Muhammad Is a Prophet

For Daou and for Christians it is through Jesus that the fullness of God is known.[146] Yet Jesus is not the founder of a new religion, but the founder of the new alliance with all creation as described in 1 Corinthians 15:28 and Colossians 2:9. Through Jesus God speaks, not as a prophet but as the "son"

---

141   Ibid., 85–8, fn. 34. Dall'Oglio, *Amoureux De L'islam*, 147.
142   Tabbara, *L'hospitalité Divine*, 167–8. *Sūrat al-mā'idah* (5):44–47 reflects Jesus' teachings regarding the expiation of sins.
143   Ibid., 168–70. There are errors here listing *sūrat al-mā'idah* (5):57 instead of (5):47 and (5):60, instead of (5):50. Cf. Genèvieve Gobillot discussion in *Chréstiens Face à l'islam*. 163 and Gabriel Said Reynolds in *The Qur'an and its Biblical Subtext*. Cf. fn. 10, 11 & 12.
144   Ibid., 170. The verse incorrectly listed above as *sūrat Āl-'Imrān* (3):119 instead of (3):199.
145   Ibid., 171–2. This opinion is partially based on the work of Fred Donner. Cf. fn. 18.
146   Ibid., 91.

who is heir to all things. For these reasons Christians do not accept that there is a new revelation that is greater. Christ is the Alpha and the Omega of history.[147] However, citing the work of Jacques Dupuis, Daou makes the point that this does not prevent the self-revelation through other prophets and other religions. Without attempting to unravel the theological challenges presented by the seeming contradictory beliefs held by Islam and Christianity regarding the role of Jesus, Daou presents the prophethood of Muhammad in line with the universal gift of prophesy following Pentecost found in Acts 2:17.[148] Further, Daou shifts the focus to recognizing the accomplishments of the prophets and the *One* through whom the prophets are fulfilled. Ultimately, in light of the universal mission of Christ, the role of the Church is to help bridge the gap between other faiths.[149]

Evolution of the Relationship with the People of the Book

In the fourth chapter, *Islam and Other Religions*, Tabbara discusses the People of the Book through the study of a number of Qur'ānic verses. Citing Aziz Esmail, Tabbara examines the different phases of revelation as well as the context that contributes to the emerging Qur'ānic position regarding not only the People of the Book, but also polytheists.[150] Unlike most Qur'ānic scholars, Tabbara divides the phases of revelation into three, not two. These are the Meccan phase, beginning with the first revelation, the Medinan phase following the migration of Muhammad and a third phase beginning with the triumphant return to Mecca before Muhammad's death in 632 CE. Viewed in a thematic and chronological order, Tabbara

---

147 Ibid., 89–90.
148 Ibid., 90–1. Daou notes that the International Theological Commission supports this idea. Cf. fn. 37.
149 Ibid., 91–97.
150 Ibid., 102. Aziz Esmail interestingly views the Qur'ān as a running commentary and response set in the context and environment of the Hijaz.

presents an evolution of theological understanding of the religious other generally overlooked in Qur'ānic studies.[151]

In the first Meccan phase, approximately 609–622 CE, Islam faces persecution. Discussions concerning the People of the Book are characterized predominantly by Biblical narrative and reference to previous patriarchs and prophets. While direct contact is with Meccan pagans, prophetic religions are viewed as one community of faith with the Muslims, as exemplified by *sūrat al-mu'minūn* (23):52–53. However, by the end of the period there is greater direct contact with People of the Book. This is characterized by an emphasis on the common points of faith between Muslims and People of the Book as expressed in *sūrat al-'ankabūt* (29):46.

In the second phase, the Medinan phase, there is further direct dialogue and acceptance of living individuals and communities from among the People of the Book. Tabbara notes in *sūrat al-baqarah* (2):62 faith and good works are upheld as meriting salvation.[152] An important feature of the period is the call to the People of the Book to join with Muhammad and his followers to form a single faith community. In this wider community Muslims and the People of the Book are required to believe in all the prophets and patriarchs, Jews must accept Jesus as the Messiah, and Christians must relinquish belief in Jesus as God's incarnation and son.[153]

Through *sūrat al-baqarah* (2):75 Tabbara further addresses the charge of *tahrīf*. She notes different interpretations of the verse championed by two highly respected scholars, Muhammad ibn Jarir Tabari (d. *c.* 922 CE) and 'Ali b. Sahl Rabban al-Tabari (d. *c.* 855 CE). Both scholars accept multiple understandings of the text and context. The issue of *tahrīf*, she contends, developed because Muslims did not find verses in the Bible referring to Muhammad as successor of Jesus and prophets such as posited by the Qur'ān. Yet Rabban al-Tabari makes the point that just as Christians discovered new meanings in the ancient Jewish texts after experiencing Jesus, so too Muslims discovered new meanings in the Gospel in light of Muhammad. An important distinction is that Christians adopted the Jewish texts as their own while Muslims

---

151   Ibid., 123.
152   Ibid., 104–6.
153   Ibid., 104.

have thus far refrained from embracing the Torah and Gospel as theirs.[154] The reason for this omission lies in part with the importance Muslims place on the chronology of revelation. However, in spite of the greater importance Muslims place on the Qur'ān and in spite of the fact that the historical Jews and Christians of the time did not accept Muhammad as a prophet, the Qur'ān continues to define the measure of faith in terms of belief in one God, belief in the Last Day and the importance of performing good works, not membership of a religious community *per se*.[155] In fact, following the meeting with the delegation of Christians from Najrān, Muhammad, through the revelation of *sūrat Āl-'Imrān* (3):64 invites People of the Book to compromise, and to a "common word".[156]

Tabbara, like other scholars above, notes that criticism of the People of the Book is constrained to personalities and never to the collective. In fact, the Qur'ān never forgets that there are believers amongst the People of the Book and most importantly that the collective are never called *kuffār*. Disagreements with the People of the Book generally can be divided into three categories concerning dogma, ethics and political contexts. Tabbara asserts that those who apply the term *kuffār* to the People of the Book are tampering with the meaning of the Qur'ān.[157] Nevertheless, Tabbara maintains that the failure of the historical People of the Book to embrace the early community of Muslims largely contributed to the development of Islam as an autonomous religious community. She continues that during this phase the tensions between Muslims and the Jews of Medina deteriorated to the point of enmity and wars, and it is in this period that she places *sūrat at-tawbah* (9):29, that heralds the great cry of *jihad* against the People of the Book, while considering some traditional accounts as to the circumstances surrounding the revelation of the verse as historically questionable.[158]

---

154   Ibid., 107–8, 61. Cf. Abdelmajid Charfi, *La pensée islamique, rupture et fidélité*, Paris, Albin Michel, 2008, 193–4.
155   Ibid., 109, 13, 23.
156   Ibid., 111.
157   Ibid., 113–5.
158   Ibid., 118–9. Cf. Safiur-Rahman Al-Mubarakpuri, *The Sealed Nectar (Ar-Raheeq Al-Makhtum)*, 2002 edn (Riyadh: Darussalam, 2002; repr., 2002), 495–510. It is

During the latter period of the Medinan phase, strong theological differences emerge between the faiths. *Sūrat an-Nisā'* 4):171 refutes the incarnation of Christ and the concept of the Trinity. *Sūrat al-mā'idah* (5):116 refutes that Jesus ever demanded that people should pray to him or his mother. *Sūrat at-tawbah* (9):30 accuses Christian of declaring Jesus the Son of God and the Jews of declaring that Uzayr is a Son of God. Two very interesting verses that Tabbara identifies from this period are *sūrat an-Nisā'* (4):156–9 *and sūrat Āl-'Imrān* (3):55. Both these verses concern the crucifixion of Jesus. In *sūrat an-Nisā'* (4):156–9 the Jews are said to sully the reputation of Mary and boast that they killed Jesus. Tabbara focuses on verse 159 that says, "And there is none of the People of the Book but must believe in him before his death; And on the Day of Judgment he will be a witness against them".[159] This verse, she says, is certainly one that could use greater exploration. Sūrat Āl-'Imrān (3):55 concerns the crucifixion of Jesus and the issue of whether he died on the cross. The traditional debate centres round the meaning of *mutawaffika*, and whether or not the word in this context implies the death of Jesus. Tabbara suggests that the earliest exegetes accepted the possibility that Jesus may have died briefly on the cross.[160]

The third phase of revelation concerns the return of the prophet to Mecca. Tabbara notes a distinctive change in the relationship with the People of the Book and other communities at this time. Here there is even accommodation for polytheists, as in the time of Abraham, so long as there is mutual respect.[161] At this time the inclusive nature of Islam comes to the

---

noteworthy that the cause of the battle and subsequent verse may concern the killing of one of Muhammad's emissaries. Apparently, the Byzantine army, seeing the strong position of the Muslim Army, fled the city leaving the residents defenceless.

159 Tabbara, *L'hospitalité Divine*, 122. English translation from The Presidency of the Islamic Researches and IFTA, *The Holy Qur'ān*, 268.

160 Tabbara, *L'hospitalité Divine*, 121–2. Citing Tabari *Tafsir* III, 289. Al-Tabarī, "L'exégèse" Vol 1:166. Suggests that God gave Jesus' image to another. Yet, Tabbara notes that the theory that Jesus was somehow switched or saved from death is not in the Qur'ān, but is a later exegetical concept.

161 Tabbara, *L'hospitalité Divine*, 124. Cf. The evolution of the relationship with polytheists from *sūrat al-kafirun* (109):1–6 to *sūrat at-tawubah* (9):28 to *sūrah al-Mumtahinah* (60):4–9.

fore. Tabbara makes the point that this nuanced change in the relationship with the religious other is often neglected in most Islamic studies.[162]

For People of the Book interested in interfaith relations the third phase of revelation provides the context of some of the most heartening verses in the Qur'ān. Tabbara discusses several verses from *sūrat al-mā'idah*, as well as from *sūrat al-hujurāt, sūrat al-hajj, sūrat Āl-'Imrān* and *sūrat Luqmān*. These verses promote the idea that God calls all humanity to return to Him, no one that devotes their life to God and performs good works need fear.[163] Most importantly, religious diversity is portrayed as part of God's plan.[164] This theme is expressed in many verses, including *sūrat al-hujurāt* (49):13, where the Qur'ān employs the phrase, "O mankind!" And reminds all humanity of their common heritage through Adam and Eve. In addition, *sūrat al-mā'idah* (5):64 refutes Jewish claims that God's hands are tied, that salvation blessings are reserved for them, while stating that God's hands are open and He bestows blessings where He wills.[165]

In support of religious diversity Tabbara cites *sūrat al-mā'idah* (5):68–9. She states that Mahmoud Ayoub considers these verses the most important in the Qur'ān concerning other religions.[166] These verses challenge the People of the Book to follow the revelation given to them by their Lord. Here the Qur'ān clearly acknowledges the merit of the Torah, Gospel and other revelations as well as the necessity to put faith to practice. There are differences between the faiths, yet, as noted with *sūrat al-mā'idah* (5):48, the differences should do no more than challenge people to strive to better serve God. Tabbara notes, "*The Muslims with the People of the Book are therefore invited to live together under the shadow of the divine generosity and hospitality, accepting one another, and adoring themselves with generosity and hospitality in the image of their one God*".[167]

---

162 Ibid., 123. The most important Qur'ānic chapters for this period are from *sūrat al-mā'idah* and *al-hajj*.
163 Ibid., 124–33.
164 Ibid., 137.
165 Ibid., 126–7.
166 Ibid., 129.
167 *Divine Hospitality*, 101. Cf. *L'hospitalité Divine*, 131.

The People of the Book and Beyond

In the process of placing the finishing touches on their arguments for accepting the religious other as part of God's plan Tabbara and Daou expand the concept of Divine Hospitality to include all people of conscience. In the fifth chapter Daou outlines the teachings of the Catholic Church regarding other faiths and their potential for salvation. Here Daou cites one of the most inclusive, if not ethereal elements of *Nostra Aetate*. This is that the Catholic Church does not reject what is true and good in other religions. This statement is supported by two verses from the New Testament Mark 10:17–18 and John 14:6. The first simply states that Jesus challenged a person who called him good, saying that only the Father is good. Therefore all that is human is in need of God's guidance. In the second verse Jesus proclaims, "I am the way and the truth and the life. No one comes to the Father except through me".[168] This verse is often used to express the exclusiveness of Christian faith. However, Daou, like Dall'Oglio, uses the verse in an inclusivist manner to assert that the eternal word of God is not absent from other religions, even if there are differences in their understanding of God.[169]

Daou recognizes that there is a difference between religion and faith. Religions may contain flaws, but a person's faith in God is separate. Daou humorously likens the idea that other religions are bereft of salvific merit to the Church's historical views on Copernicus. He further draws upon the words of John Paul II, "all authentic prayer is sustained by the Holy Spirit who is mysteriously present in the heart of each person".[170] The fact that God accepts other religions is evidenced above with the examples of the Centurion, the Canaanite and the Samaritan women. It seems that the criteria for salvation is simple: other religions must be consistent with God's design for love and salvation.[171]

---

168 *L'hospitalité Divine*, 139. The English translation of the verse is from the ESV, 2007.
169 Ibid., 139–40. Here Daou draws upon the teachings of *Lumen Gentium* and *Redemptoris Missio* for support.
170 *Divine Hospitality*, 111–2. Cf. *Lumen Gentium*. 62.
171 *L'hospitalité Divine*, 143.

Daou notes that other religions are a positive challenge for the Church. It is necessary to recognize the spiritual experiences of others as religious virtues and that the Spirit of God blows where it wills. The message of John Paul II in *Redemptoris Missio* 56 states that other religions contain signs of the presence of Christ and the actions of the Spirit. The Qur'ān also contains examples of Christian devotion. In fact, if we keep open minds, Daou posits, it is possible to see that "the presence of the other is the voice of God in our life".[172] Ultimately the question is, what is the purpose of the differences? Daou maintains that we need to allow other religions a role in our theology. This avoids two pitfalls. The first is that by learning of their spiritual experience we avoid locking the other religion into a question of whether or not the other has divine status. The second reflects the need to appreciate the gifts that God bestows on other faiths. Understanding other faiths helps avoid naïve stereotypes. What is required is a theology that chooses to accompany the other through life.[173]

This is the essence of *theologies in dialogue*. It concerns having the spiritual maturity to accept that no religion has a monopoly on God, or the truth. Both Islam and Christianity share a universal mission in spite of their differences. Just as each individual is on a spiritual journey, so too are Muslims and Christians. Christians cannot abandon their mission to spread the good news of Christ. Yet Christians need to understand that the mission of the Church is not different from God's. God is the final destination of faith, not the Church. God desires the salvation of all humanity, and the institution of His Kingdom on earth. The Church is the servant of God's mission. The Church must be ever mindful that the Spirit of God "*souffle où il veut*" [blows where it wills].[174] It is interesting to consider, Daou reflects, that neither Jesus nor the Gospel ever called for people to change their religion. Rather the call is to follow God's way.[175]

For Daou one of the mysteries of salvation is when Christians can recognize the work of God in the religion of others without losing faith in

---

172 Ibid., 143–4. Daou highlights the examples of Sufis and Christian Monastic life.
173 Ibid., 143–6.
174 Ibid., 146–153. Dall'Oglio also makes this point.
175 Ibid., 154.

their own and its role in God's design.[176] He posits that Christians today need to learn how to live with respect for religious diversity, a diversity that has its foundation with the love of God for mankind and respect for human freedom. The dialogue is not just between the interlocutors but also with God present.[177] By engaging or living in fellowship with Muslims, Christians will find a spiritual solidarity that is based on witness. It is necessary to take a step of faith beyond, perhaps, a purely academic interest, to appreciate the religious other in spiritual communion, despite our differences, as on the day when we all stand before God.[178]

Tabbara advocates accepting the authenticity of the beliefs of the religious other, especially the People of the Book. However, as reflected in the words of Mahmoud Ayoub, history demonstrates that the lessons of the Gospel and Qur'ān that promote the universality of love and mercy are too often transformed into narrow dogma in order to exclude others.[179] Interestingly, Tabbara makes the point that the idea that Islamic law abrogates the laws of the People of the Book has never received universal acceptance. Tabbara confirms that the promises of salvation made to the People of the Book, stand alongside the revelation of the Qur'ān.[180]

Consequently, if religious diversity and cultural pluralism are part of God's plan for salvation, what role is left for Islamic Mission, *da'wah*? Tabbara sees the role of Islam to call people to God in a similar manner as Daou. For support Tabbara calls upon *sūrat fussilat* (41):33 that states, "Who is better in speech than one who calls (men) to Allah, works righteousness, and says, 'I am of those who bow in Islam'".[181] Thus, from the perspective of plurality, Tabbara asserts Muslims are not required to call people to convert

---

176   Ibid., 155–6.
177   Ibid., 156, fn. 18.
178   Ibid., 158–9, fn. 25. A rough paraphrase of the sentiment expressed by Christian de Chargé.
179   Ibid., 161, fn. 1. Verses like *sūrat al-baqarah* (2):62 and *sūrat al-maidah* (5):69 affirm that those who believe and fill their lives with good deeds need not fear the Day of Judgement, are pushed aside by restrictive interpretations.
180   Ibid., 161–2.
181   Ibid., 161–5. The Qur'ān translation is from The Presidency of the Islamic Researches and IFTA, *The Holy Qur'ān*, 1463.

to Islam *per se*, but to call people to God. A prime example for mankind is found in the life of Abraham explained in *sūrat al-mumtaḥanah* 60:4. Abraham faithfully follows God and separates from his father's community, but rather than live in enmity, says to his father that he will pray for him that he will be forgiven for his transgressions.[182] In addition there is the example of Muhammad and his community as expressed in *sūrat al-baqarah* (2):143 to be a witness before all mankind. The Qur'ān teaches Muslims to accept religious diversity as God's will and to allow God to be the final arbitrator concerning the issues that divide believers of different religions.[183] This point is made quite clear by the famous mystique Hallaj, who sees each religion as necessarily contributing to the whole of God's revelation.[184]

Hospitality Among the Community of Believers

For Daou and Tabbara *spiritual communion* is not just a dream. In our increasingly intertwined world we need to reappraise how we view the religious other, how our worldview makes space for all peoples. Daou, in his conclusions, boldly declares that God is greater than the mission of Christ and his disciples. He says, quoting John 14:2 "that in my Father's house there are many rooms … " Perhaps there is a temptation to create a worldview that allows us to reduce God to what we can understand, who we perceive to be good and who is worthy of salvation. However, the Divine Hospitality envisions a world where not only are there many rooms, but all are made to feel welcome.[185]

Similarly, Tabbara reminds the reader that one of the divine attributes of God is, *al-wāsi'* [the Vast]. God is beyond limits in mercy and knowledge.

---

182 Tabbara, *L'hospitalité Divine*, 165.
183 Ibid., 168. For instance *sūrat al-mā'idah* (5): 44–7 and (5):48.
184 Ibid., 163. "*J'ai réfléchi sur les religions en m'appliquant á les comprendre, et j'ai trouvé qu'elles étaient un seul tronc á ramifications nombreuses. Ne demande donc pas á l'homme d'adopter une religion, car elle le détournerait du tronc unique et sûr …*".
185 Ibid., 179–80. For Daou, where the believers are made mutually welcome, there is God.

Al-Ghazali, on the subject of divine attributes, says that through faith, believing Muslims can cultivate space internally for God and His attributes.[186] Tabbara notes that this is not unrelated to Divine Hospitality. In this way the believing Muslim cultivates hospitality in his heart, a place for God where the vastness of God enlarges our capacity to know and love God. Tabbara cites a beautiful *hadīth* on this subject that says, "Not my earth, nor my sky can contain me, only the heart of my adoring believer can contain me".[187] Through this hospitality a space is made for love and knowledge of others.

Tabbara ends by recalling the theme of *A Common Word*: love of God and love of neighbour. Through Divine Hospitality, the other's fears, thoughts and comprehension of their relationship with the world and with the Divine becomes part of our spiritual being, in spite of, and in respect of, our differences. The Divine within necessitates changes in our perspective, enlarges our compassion and comprehension, leaving behind the comforts of our own community to move towards and with the other.[188]

Conclusions

Inspired by the *Common Word* Christians and Muslims have continued to meet and exchange ideas relating to the social and theological challenges and opportunities as believers *vis-à-vis* modern society. Some Christian scholars are sensitive to the limitations and theological implications of *ahl al-kitāb*. They prefer to draw on more nuanced terms like *People of Faith*, *People of the Word*, *People of God*, *Children of Abraham*, or *People of the Prophets* in order to create what they consider to be a more equitable basis for dialogue.

---

186   Ibid., 181, Cf. fn. 1.
187   Ibid., 181–2, Cf. fn. 2.
188   Ibid., 182–3. Here Abraham defends the people of Lot.

Madigan acknowledges that the term *ahl al-kitāb* affords Christians and Jews a special status in Islam. Intrinsic with this status however, are certain limitations that insist that Christians have in some way falsified their revelation. As a result, Madigan considers the term *ahl al-kitāb* limiting. He suggests that Muslims and Christians should focus on what they have in common as *People of the Word*. As People of the Word, Muslims and Christians share a common task of discerning the relationship between God and his Word. Muslims, Christians and Jews respect that through God's Word, *wa-yomer/kun fa yakūn* ... things happen.

Interestingly, Madigan discusses the idea that Christians through the use of *only begotten* and *father* are trying to express the relationship between God and his Word. These expressions indicate that God and his Word share the same nature; the Word is not God's creation, but is his self-expression, *kalām nafsī*. Most profoundly, Madigan suggests avoiding the polemic by novel means. By not defending the Christian creedal tenets of begetting and fatherhood Muslims are invited to explore other means of defining the relationship between God and His Word together with Christians. What Madigan is trying to avoid is limiting the perception of Christians as *ahl al-kitāb* to people who are preoccupied with the Gospel books. Another limitation that Madigan draws attention to is the fact that for Christians, Jesus is more than a prophet with a message. Jesus is the message, God's Word incarnate.

From a socio-political perspective Madigan draws attention to the importance of Muslims and Christians living in peace. Madigan seems to find the condition, set out in *sūrat al-mumtahanah* (60):8, whereby Christians do not attack Muslims, as challenging and suggests that Muslims and Christians both need to begin a dialogue of repentance. However, in this air of *mea culpa*, Madigan regretfully refrains from outlining any practical steps to demonstrate how this could be advanced. Perhaps a way forward might be for Christian leaders to be seen to be more critical of military adventurism.

From an enculturated Middle Eastern perspective Dall'Oglio acknowledges that the People of the Book are to be respected since God established these communities. He contrasts this ideal with the totalitarian and imperialist attitude of his Roman Catholic Church. In spite of Dall'Oglio's admiration for the term he is not averse to pointing out its shortcomings, that is, with regard to marriage and conversion. For these reasons Dall'Oglio employs more neutral terms like *People of the Prophets*, or *People of God*, or even calling on the merits of citizenship in modern evolving pluralist society to foster an environment whereby civil rights can be used to counter the apparent inequalities he sees in the implementation of Islamic teachings.

As a missionary Dall'Oglio is ahead of his time. On the one hand, he wishes to inculturate the Church towards Islam in order to make the Church more accessible to Muslims. His philosophy aspires to bring the daily lives of Muslims and Christians closer together so that they can bear witness and come to a better understanding of one another. On the other hand, he encourages Christians to read the Qur'ān as an inspired text through the hermeneutics of interpretation. His idea of conversion is not conventional. Like Siddiqui, he wishes to refrain from formal conversion and is quite content for Muslims and Christians to move towards each other in rather vague terms, as perhaps reflected in his own circumstance. Furthermore, he does not see the traditional understandings of the cross and crucifixion as issues worth labouring over for Muslims who come to encounter Christ. Dall'Oglio is quite content that these Muslims act as a bridge between the two faiths with their new perspective.

Dall'Oglio, like Daou and Tabbara, encourages Muslims and Christians to re-examine the Biblical personages of Abraham, Hagar and Ishmael to witness that in their stories lies a rich means of understanding Islam as the fulfilment of promises made to Abraham as the model of faith. Hagar and Ishmael's relationship with God is blessed. God never abandoned or chastised them. They have a role to play in bringing the children of Ishmael back into the fold. Tabbara identifies the faith of Abraham as simple return to *fitra*, thereby linking submission, *islām* to all believers regardless of whether they follow Muhammad or not. They, we, are all *Muslim* in the non-reified sense.

Dall'Oglio and Daou both advocate that Christians should accept Muhammad as a prophet. In so doing they do not outline a rigid argument of how this should be reasoned, but rather advocate that the Church should promote a positive image of Islam and Muhammad as perhaps, an ex-Biblical prophet. This is a challenge for Christians since Muhammad taught against many tenets of Christian faith. Nevertheless, there are areas of commonality that are often overlooked that might otherwise provide opportunities for greater understanding. For example, Muslims believe that Jesus is the Messiah and anticipate his return at the end of time to manifest God's Kingdom. With regard to the crucifixion of Jesus, Tabbara insists that there has never been consensus concerning the death of Jesus. Yet arguing over the crucifixion detracts from the fact that the Qur'ān states that all mankind must come to believe in Jesus. This is an area Tabbara says is in need of further common exploration.

From a socio-political perspective, for a church moving towards Islam and for Christians learning to share their lives with Muslims there are important implications. On the positive side, Dall'Oglio, like Siddiqui and Ramadan in the previous chapter, sees that Christians striving to keep religion relevant in society will find ready allies with Muslims. Their stalwart faith in contrast with the secularization of Christianity is perhaps a foreshadowing of things to come. Just as Siddiqui pointed out earlier, however, the West in general often projects an anti-Islamic bias that it is reluctant to admit. This bias is discernible during times of conflict when European nations side with "other" nations pursuing political agendas. This is an area that will challenge Christians to choose between political pragmatism and spiritual solidarity.

Divine Hospitality encourages Muslims and Christians through the practice of *theologies in dialogue* to understand from their own tradition that God's plan of salvation includes the religious other. *Theologies in dialogue* encourages better understanding of the religious other as two people sharing a long journey. This concept shares much with Dall'Oglio's *In Love with Islam*. Daou understands the concept of the People of the Book, but he does not rely on it to promote better understanding of Islam by Christians. This he develops through the teachings of Christ, through the theological teachings of his own creedal tradition and through terms that encompass the religious other like *People of God*.

By considering how Jesus interacted with the Samaritan and Canaanite women, as well as the Centurion, Daou presents to Christians, that for Jesus, faith in God is more important than membership of the "correct" religion. Examining the teachings of the church regarding the different types of alliances between man and God, the way is open for Christians to make a leap of faith and accept, like Muslims, that religious diversity is part of God's plan. Like Dall'Oglio, Daou asserts that all humanity benefits from the sacrifice of Christ regardless of if they are Christian or not. In this regard, God's promises of salvation are not linear, whereby one set of promises abrogate the former. Daou, like Dall'Oglio, maintains that through greater familiarity with Muslims, Christians should be able to recognize and respect their faith for what it is.

Tabbara, like Ramadan, makes the point that reading the Bible and Torah may inspire Muslims to attain a deeper appreciation of their own faith. She suggests Muslims consider that the traditional accusations of falsification are primarily down to interpretation and not within the texts themselves. Her exploration of the evolution of the relationship between Islam and the People of the Book through a close examination of the stages of revelation of the Qur'ān highlights an interesting trajectory. She identifies three phases that progress from a call to unity refusing diversity, to a tense acceptance of diversity as a fact, to a final stage where she calls on scholars to consider that diversity is accepted as ordained by God. One of the most important points she makes concerns the use of the term, *kuffār*. She astutely observes that the term is reserved for individuals and not to the collective, except in the case of the polytheists who were fighting the early Muslims.

Both Daou and Tabbara expand the concept of *theologies in dialogue* to explain that even some exclusivist verses can be accepted as including the religious other. Daou, through examination of *Nostra Aetate* and *Redemptoris Missio* suggest a new understanding of John 14:6 whereby all who believe and follow their conscience are accepted as following in the way of Christ. This is true even if people believe differently since religions may be flawed but not faith. The eternal Word of God is not absent from other religions. In fact Daou sees the role of the Church much like Dall'Oglio, as a servant of God, calling people to faith, not to the Church as the final destination. For Tabbara exclusivist verses like *sūrat Āl-'Imrān* (3):19 can include all people of faith since submission to God, that is to the source of life, is the same for all faiths. Moreover, the revelation of the People of the Book remains salvific alongside the revelation of the Qur'ān. She feels Muslims are required to encourage all people to move closer to God, because conversion is to God, not necessarily to Islam *per se*.

Through *theologies in dialogue* Muslims and Christians, as well as all other people, can experience *spiritual communion*. Here the religious other and their faith becomes our companion through life. Christians and Muslims need to take this bold step towards each other to ensure that they have correct knoweldge of the other, letting the other's faith have a voice in each other's theology so that people can avoid naïve and dangerous stereotypes. For both Muslims and Christians this is a difficult challenge, but one that people of faith must rise to. Today, more than ever, the world needs people of faith to create a narrative that respects all people.

Conclusions: Challenges and Opportunities

The Qur'ānic representation of Christians and Christianity provides ample opportunities and challenges for interfaith dialogue and religious plurality. Nevertheless, their representation through the Qur'ān and traditional commentary is epistemologically insufficient for comparative theological purposes. This is due to the fact that the traditional commentary does not adequately describe the nuanced Christian self-understanding. Therefore, their study requires significant expansion into nascent socio-cultural, historical and interreligious theological terrains. Combining these approaches contributes to a more comprehensive understanding of Christians and Christianity depicted in the Qur'ān and an appreciation for the potential the concept of the People of the Book offers for contemporary Muslim-Christian dialogue and religious plurality.

The science of *tafsīr* offers Christians an opportunity to engage with Muslims using an authoritative system of discourse. Understanding how *tafsīr* works opens up opportunities for understanding the complexities involved in the science of interpretation, appreciating the accepted variance of opinion from the earliest days of Islam. Expanding knowledge of the *asbāb an-nuzūl*, especially the social and anthropological context of the Qur'ān, strengthens the science of *tafsīr*.

The research presented here confirms the existence of a theoretical construct concerning Christians and Christianity identified by McAuliffe. This theoretical construct is a composite reflection of the facts. The theoretical construct is open to challenge on the basis that it does not distinguish between Christian denominational creedal formulae, their reformulation or clarifications. Although this research concurs with McAuliffe concerning the general thrust of the theoretical construct, its findings part company with McAuliffe with regard to the salvific value of Christianity. Al-Tabari, from the classical period, and Rida, Esack and Tabbara from the modern era, challenge the idea that without acceptance of the prophethood of Muhammad the deeds of Christians, the People of the Book, or anyone else are unacceptable since they do not conform to the message of Islam. Through the *tafsīr* of *sūrat al-baqarah* (2):62 al-Tabari and Rida reflect the possibility that letting one's life speak is more important than membership to a religious community, including reified Islam. "God has not specified the wage of righteous action together with faith for some of His creatures rather than others".[1] In support Rida cites *sūrat an-Nisā'* (4):123–4, "Not your desires, nor those of the People of the Book … If any do deeds of righteousness … and have faith, they will enter heaven, and not the least injustice will be done to them".[2]

Another challenge is the social and historical pre-Islamic Arabia, the broad *asbāb an-nuzūl* of the Qur'ān examined in the second chapter. This is an area that would benefit from in-depth research since the *sabab an-nuzūl* of any verse is a formal aspect of *tafsīr* that is not very well understood. In fact, the people of pre-Islamic Arabia, by and large, remain something of a mystery to the modern scholar of inter-faith relations. Information provided in a typical exegesis may give the names and communities involved, in the context of the revelation of a verse, but this information hardly does justice to the complexities of the individuals and cultures concerned. Their reaction to the revelation of the Qur'ān is at least in part a product of their place and time.

An important aspect of the culture of pre-Islamic Arabia is the narrative that connects it with Biblical entities like Shem, Abraham and Moses. Hence the concept of monotheism is not strange or new, but part of the story of these disparate people. Most importantly, especially for tribes around Mecca, is the connection with Abraham, Hagar and Ishmael. Their story weaves in and out of the narrative found in Genesis and tends to be overlooked by most Christians and Jews as an unimportant subnarrative to the story of Abraham's relationship with Isaac and his descendents. Dall'Oglio, Daou and Tabbara, however, discuss the potential of their narrative as one that might help build a bridge between the People of the Book and Islam.

The Jews of the Hijaz, as well as the Jews of Himyar, proselytized as the indigenous alternative to Christianity. They expected a messiah of sorts,

---

[1] Al-Tabarī, *Tafsīr Al-Tabarī*, Vol. 1:359, 64.
[2] Rida, *Tafsir Al-Manar*, Vol. 1–2:278.

Conclusions: Challenges and Opportunities

with whom the community of Medina often threatened their enemies. In fact, several of the tribes living in and around Medina made sure they were on good terms with Muhammad before his *hijra* to Yathrib, just in case he became an implement of wrath for the birthright Jews. Unfortunately, good relations between the new *ummat al-mu'minīn* and the Jews of Medina were not to be.

The would-be leader of Yathrib, Ibn Ubayy, and the other tribal leaders did not seem to know what to make of Muhammad's mission to replace the traditional alliances in favour of his Treaty of Medina. The influence an expected Messiah might have had on their willingness to accept Muhammad is an area open to further research, as is the unwillingness of the Jews of the Hijaz to engage with, or seek the support from, Jews outside of Arabia when relations soured with Muhammad.

The Christians of Ethiopia are one of the most important communities in the development of early Islam. Faith in the God of Abraham in Ethiopia and the Axum Empire can be traced back to the Queen of Sheba. Christianity in Abyssinia arrived in waves from as early as Philip and the Ethiopian eunuch. According to the exegetes, the Christians of Abyssinia, under the leadership of Ashama ibn Abjar, could not have provided a greater contrast to the Jews of Medina. They epitomize the exemplary Qur'ānic Christians discussed in *sūrat al-mā'idah* (5):82, who follow God's guidance from revelation to revelation and recognize the truth when they hear it. Even when they fail to convert to Islam, Muslims anticipate better relations with them. Consequently, Abyssinia earned the reputation of *dār al-hiyād*, the realm of neutrality and received Muhammad's command, *utruku al-habasha mā tarakūkum*, "Until the Abyssinians attack you, do not attack them". This guidance is similar to that echoed in *sūrat al-mumtahanah* (60):8 found in *A Common Word*. Interestingly, since Ethiopians are strong Trinitarians, the basis for good relations would appear to be the willingness of the people to respect each other and the mutual security it afforded, rather than any substantial theological commonality, thus leaving the way open for future communities to adopt their model of coexistence.

The third chapter considers how post-conquest Christians of the Levant adapted to the challenges of the Islamization of their culture and to accusations from the traditional Qur'ānic commentary of "excesses" in religion discussed in Chapter 1. The Islamization of the culture and the emergence of Arabic as the *lingua franca* inspired Christians to rethink how they expressed their faith, since the now dominant culture found the theological expressions of Sonship, Incarnation and Trinity heretical.

From as early as the latter half of the eighth century, during the first Abbasid century, Christian scholars began to write in Arabic. The emerging literature first attempted to strengthen the resolve of the indigenous Christians, many of whom began to convert to Islam. The second genre of literature sought to defend the tenets of Christian faith more directly. The earliest existing text of this genre is the anonymous *On the Triune Nature of God*. Its blend of Biblical and Qur'ānic verse attempted to demonstrate the soundness of Christian beliefs; "Ye have said that ye believe in God and His Word and the Holy Ghost, so do not reproach us, O men! That we believe in God and His Word and His Spirit: and we worship God in His Word and His Spirit, one God and one Lord and one creator".[3]

Around the time that Christian scholars began to write in Arabic, Muslims scholars developed a profound interest in the Greek translation movement. An important by-product of the translation movement is the science of theological dialogue, *'ilm al-kalām*. *'Ilm al-kalām* enabled Muslims and Christians to apply Greek philosophical methods of reasoning to discuss concepts of faith, just as Islamic scholars from the Mu'tazilite and Ashrite traditions sought to consider the implications of absolute *tawhīd* vis-a-vis God's Divine attributes, *sifāt Allah*. Christians also began to define God according to His attributes, as found in the *al-asmā al-husnā*, the Divine Names. These Divine attributes, Christians argued, could be reduced to three primary hypostases of existence, *mawjūd*, living, *hayy* and speaking *nātiq*.

The three Arabic-speaking Christian scholars examined here, Abū Qurrah, Sulaymān ibn Hasan al-Ghazzī and Paul of Antioch, lived in different places and times. It is difficult to say to what degree their theological defences of Christianity reflect their social and political context, but this surely had an influence. Each author's defence touches on their experience of faith. This experiential defence is an area for future research. Although each author demonstrates

---

[3] Anonymous, *An Arabic Version*, VII, 6.

knowledge of Islam, they do not directly address the science of *tafsīr*, which remains far more authoritative for Muslims seeking to remain credible within their own community than the application of Greek reasoning. Yet, without a doubt, *'ilm al-kalām* represents an important chapter in Muslim/Christian relations. Here a common project provided a neutral language from which to engage in sincere discourse concerning contentious issues that modern interlocutors would do well to examine closely, even if other modes of commonality like citizenship and human rights may now be to the fore.

Chapters 4 and 5 examine contemporary usage of the term *ahl al-kitāb*. For Muslims scholars, interaction with Christians in all facets of life is still based on the traditional understanding of the term. Christians, as People of the Book, remain an integral part of the Islamic narrative. The Muslim scholars examined in these chapters accept the authority of *tafsīr* even if they argue, like Esack, that the present state of the world is so far removed from the *asbāb an-nuzūl* that terms like *Muslim, belief, Christian* and *kāfir* need to be reappraised in order to be faithful to the subsumed historical meanings of the terms. In this sense the voices of Siddiqui, Esack, Ramadan and Tabbara reflect the gradual shift in authority in Islam into new contexts, wherever Muslims reside today.

So, what are the lessons for today's world? Of primary importance for Christians is the need to recognize that the science of *tafsīr* remains authoritative in spite of the presence of other important catalysts for dialogue, including philosophical reasoning, alternative terms to "People of the Book", or secular debates regarding human rights and citizenship. These alternatives, though important in their own right, miss the opportunity to progress together as fellow believers, each striving to understand themselves and the religious other better, as on a faith journey through life and in service to God. Further, the alternatives discussed above lack the theological authority found in *tafsīr*. Therefore, it is this author's opinion that attempting to coax Muslims away from *tafsīr* is counterproductive. It would be better for Christians to embrace *tafsīr* so that when difficult theological issues are discussed Christians are not asking their Muslim counterparts to be less Muslim, no more than Christians should be expected to be less Christian.

Since religion today is largely deterritorialized, especially amongst developed nations, has the time not come to take bold steps towards each other? From among the scholars examined, it appears that conversion in the literal sense is not a high expectation. From Siddiqui to Tabbara, Madigan to Daou the common denominator appears to be better understanding, respect for the beliefs of others and co-operation on social issues of mutual concern. Perhaps unexpectedly, the strongest criticism of Christianity in the twenty-first century is not related to belief in Jesus as the Son of God, the Incarnation, or the Crucifixion and Resurrection, but rather poignantly, that Christians need to bear witness to Christ.

Dall'Oglio offers a model of inculturation to bring Christians in the Middle East closer to Muslims. This is an excellent model whereby the example of the Hospitality of Abraham inspires greater contact and co-operation between Muslims and Christians, as well as revisits the importance of the overlooked healing narrative of Hagar and Ishmael. In the West Christianity, *vers Islam* would of course take a different shape. Any change in direction will require a paradigm shift in recognition of the religious other and their sacred text as integral to our theological and spiritual future. The Faith of Abraham is a three-volume set, with each text an essential component of the whole. This shift in understanding requires strategies that will bring Muslims and Christians closer together. Daou and Tabbara offer *theologies in dialogue*. This method of life and dialogue provides a promising model for the future. It represents a huge challenge to the way in which people receive their religious education concerning the religious other, whereby the religion of the other is presented as sufficient for salvation on its own merits and offering its own wisdom for those seeking God's guidance.

In light of the *Common Word* document and the willingness of Muslims to be seen as on the side of Jesus and not against him, perhaps Christians could reciprocate by boldly expressing in some way that they accept Muhmmad and the Qur'ān are divinely inspired.[4] Perhaps Christians could suggest that they wish to be considered like those of historical Abyssinia or referred to in *sūrat al-maidah* 5:82, *sūrat Āl-'Imrān* (3):199 and *sūrat al-qasa* (28):52–5. This is something both Muslims and Christians will need to resolve in the coming generations. The scholars have stated that the

---

4 In reference to Mark 9:40 and Luke 9:50.

common goal of both Islam and Christiaity is to call people to God, and in so doing come closer to accepting each other in a new covenant of believers. This concept revisits the missed opportunity offered by Muhammad to the People of the Book centuries ago.

Part of the problem is that the shared journey may not provide any definitive answers to questions which separate Muslims and Christians. Perhaps Madagan's suggestion that Christians sharing theological problems with their Muslim counterparts is the solution, not just for the relationship between God and his Word, but also *tahrīf* and the requirement for all to believe in Jesus, without expecting definitive answers soon.

To conclude, I would like to share a reflection on a blending of two well known stories, The Road to Emmuas and Muhammad's Night Journey. The story begins with the two disciples travelling along the road; This time one of the disciples is a Christian and the other a Muslim. On the way they discuss important theological matters involving prophethood, messiahship, crucifixion, resurrection, prayer, salvation, faith and works.

Along the way the disciples are joined by two strangers who overhear their conversation, listen intently, and offer advice regarding the interpretation of scripture. As they approached the Emmaus, the strangers continued on as if they were going farther. But the Disciples urged them strongly, "Stay with us, for it is nearly evening; the day is almost over". So the strangers remained with them.

When they were seated at the table, one of the strangers took the bread, gave thanks, broke the bread and shared it with the others. Then the disciples' eyes were opened and they recognized the strangers. Now around them at the table they could see the Angel Gabriel, the prophets Adam, Abraham, Moses, Aaron, Joseph, Idris and many more. The disciples were frightened and yet overjoyed.

They had many questions and hoped they would finally have some answers regarding matters on which they disputed. When at last the disciples paused for a response, Jesus and Muhammad looked at each other, then turned to the disciples and said, "For you these matters are dificult. Yet, for God the solution is quite simple".

Glossary

ad-darūriyyāt, الضروريات the imperative, necessity. The vital ones, as in, the vital ones. Excuses the forbidden ones. When everything is forbidden everything is allowed.

adhān, أذان call to prayer.

adrakū Muhammad, أدركوا into the time of Muhammad. They knew, they got to know.

ahl adh-dhimma, أهل الذمّه protected people.

ahl al-injīl, أهل الإنجيل People of the Gospel, found in 5:47 (only ever used once).

ahl al-kitāb, أهل الكتاب the People of the Book, and the collective Arabic name for Christians, Jews, Sabians and Zoroastrians.

ahl an-nār, أهل النار People of the Fire, those destined to go to hell.

ajruhum, اجرهم their reward.

aliyá (Hebrew) Return to the Promised Land.

al-'urf, العرف a custom.

'amal, عمل he makes, an action.

ām al-fīl, عام الفيل Year of the Elephant. Around 570 CE. The year the Christians of Najrān marched on Mecca. The year Muhammad was born.

amānū, آمنوا found in "those who believed", or a true belief.

ansār, أنصار helpers. Protectors of Muhammad.

aqānīm, اقانيم hypostasis.

'arad, عرض accident.

asab al-tha'r, اصب الثار revenge duty.

'asabiyyah, عصبية the law of cohesiveness of the nomadic tribe.

ashbāb al-ukhdūd, اصحاب الاخدود People of the Trench.

ashrāf, اشراف more noble, i.e. Aristotelian, see David Thomas, Syrian Christians 212.

aslamā, أسلم submitted to God.

aslamāh, أسلمة Islamicization, or Islamification, the process of a culture becoming more Islamic.

asmā allāh al-husnā, أسماء الله الحسنى the Beautiful Names of God.

āya, آيه a sign or verse, i.e. Jesus was a sign, a phrase or sentence from the Qur'an.

Bahīrā, the name of a monk who recognized Muhammad as a prophet when he was just a child.

Beta Israel, (Ge'ez), name for Jews of Ethiopia.

Bid'a, bid'ah, بدعة heretical exegesis. A bad idea or introduction of a poor practice.

Bilād ash-Sham, بلاد الشام Greater Syria.

dār ad-da'wa دار الدعوه "house of invitation". Where Islam is newly introduced to a country, or just prior to its arrival, as in *al-jāhiliyya* Arabia.

dār al-'ahd, دار العهد war-free zone. *dār al-harb*, دار الحرب house/abode of war.

dār al-hiyād, دار الحياد realm of neutrality.

dār al-islām, دار الاسلام abode of Islam.

dār ash-shahāda, دار الشهادة abode of testimony. Land of Witness.

dār al-tā'ah, دار الطاعة land of obedience to God.

Da'wah, دعوة invitation, as to religious conversion.

deuteros theos (Greek) a second lesser God, a hypostasis like entity.

dhālika al-kitāb, ذلك الكتب that Book, as opposed to *hādhā al-kitāb*, this Book.

dhāt, الذات *essence of God.*

dhikr, ذكر recollection

dhimmī, ذمّي a person from the People of the Book entitled to protection under Islamic law.

dīn, دين religion.

dīwān, ديوان poetry collection of a spiritual or inspirational nature.

diyyah, ديّة blood money, retribution.

falashas (Ge'ez) meaning exiles or strangers, referring to Jews who did not convert to Christianity.

fard 'ayn فرض عين personal responsibility.

farid kifya, فرض كفايه collective responsibility.

fatwa, فتوى legal ruling. Fatawa, pl.

fiqh, الفقه Islamic law and jurisprudence.

fiqh al-aqalliyyāt, فقه الأقليات the law of the minorities.

fiqh al-aqalliyyāt al-muslima, فقه الأقليات المسلمة the religious law of Muslim minorities. *fiqh al-muwāzanāt*, فقه الموازنات or applying a juristic preference to strike a balance in order to weigh the pros and cons of a certain thing in view of an existing situation.

firqa, فرقة, *firaq* pl. فرق a sect/sects.

fitrah, فطرة instinctual nature, Tariq Ramadan, *fitra*, nature, of a newborn child as an example of a *Muslim*.

galut (Hebrew) Diaspora

ghazw, غزو invasion, plunder.

ghiyār, الغيار "the law of differentiation".

gebr/gäbr, (*Ge'ez, or* Amharic) slave, or servant, is used as a prefix to a name in a manner similar to *Abd*-name, or عبد الله, servant of God before an Arabic name.

ghuluw fi ad-dīn, غلو في الدين excesses in the religion.

hāda, هاد repented.

hadīth, حديث sayings of the prophet, usually concerning the interpretation of the Qur'ān of some aspect of Islam.

hāfiz, حافظ a person who can recite the Qur'ān by heart.

hāja, حَاجَة need.

Hajj, الحج Pilgrimage to Mecca.

hāla istithnā'iyya, حاله استثنائيه exceptional situation.

hanīf, حنيف pl. *hunafā* حنفاء pure monotheism as practised by Abraham, also to revert.

Hasan al-Bannā, حسن البنا founder of the Muslim brotherhood, grandfather of Tariq Ramadan.

al-hawāriyyūn, الحواريون the disciples of Jesus.

hayy, حي alive, *hayāh*, حياة life.

hegira or *hijra*, هجْرَة the name given to Muhammad's migration from Mecca to Medina. *al-hijiyyah*, الحجيّه necessary complimentary, الحاجيات.

hōs monogenous para patros, (Greek) as of a father's only son.

hulūl, حالول indwelling of the divine, similar to *sakina* السكينة.

ibād, اباد a pre-Islamic Christian.

ihsān, إحسان a beautiful word meaning the constant striving for perfection, minimizing pain and conflict. *al-ihsan*, used by Tariq Ramadan for excellence, not forgetting God (*Western Muslims*, 79), similar to continuous prayer.

ijāra, الإجارة traditional tribal protection.

Ijmā', إجماع consensus.

ijtihād, اجتهاد independent reasoning, not to be undertaken in religious contexts by non-scholars. See *mujtahid* مجتهد below.

Ikhwān, الإخوان Muslim brotherhood.

'ilm, علم knowledge.

'ilm usūl al-fiqh, علم أصول الفقه the science of the fundamental laws.

imān, إيمان faith, belief.

imitizāj, امتزاج mingling of the divine with the human.

In hoc signo vinces, (Latin) "under this sign you will conquer".

injīl, الإنجيل Gospel, Bible.

Insān, الإنسان human being, humanity.

Inshallah, إن الله شاء essentially meaning "God willing". The word has myriad uses.

Isa, عيسى Jesus

ishārāt, اشارات hinting at a meaning, suggesting a meaning rather than exactly defining.

islām, الإسلام submission to God.

istislāh, استصلاح to seek the common good or *maslaha* صلحة public interest.

isnād اسناد chain of transmission.

ittakhadha li-nafsihi, اتخذ لنفسه to take to oneself.

al-jāhiliyya, الجاهلية the Time of Ignorance.

al-jahl, الجهل ignorance.

Jacobites, Syrian Orthodox Christians.

jawhar, جوهر similar to *ousia* (Greek) substance, essence.

jizyah, جزية a tax paid by the People of the Book in lieu of military service in Muslim countries.

jism, جسم body.

Al-jum'ah al hazīnah, الجمعة الحزينة Good Friday.

Juz', جزء a section, chapter or part of the Qur'ān. pl. *ajzā'*, أجزاء The Qur'ān is divided by 30 *ajzā'* and 114 *sūrah*.

kāfir, كافر unbeliever, *kuffār* pl. كفار

kalām, الكلام (dialogue), speech.

kalām nafsī, كلام نفسي God's eternal self-expression.

Glossary

kenosis, in Christian theology, *kenosis* (from the Greek word for emptiness κένωσις, is the "self-emptying" of one's own will and becoming entirely receptive to God's divine will.

Keturah, קטורה (Hebrew) incense. According to Parash 25:1 this is the name given to Hagar when she remarried Abraham.

Khalaqa, خلق to create, *akhluqu*, اخلق create, *takhluqu*, تخلق you create.

Al-khalīl, الخليل friend, as in friend of God.

khamr, خمر alcohol.

Kharāj, الخراج agricultural tax.

kitāb, كتاب book.

kufr, كافر disbelief.

lā ilāha illa Allāh, لا إله إلا الله There is no god, but God.

latīf, لطيف subtle.

libs al-aghiyār, لبس الغيار distinctive dress, policy of differentiation between Muslims and the People of *the Book*.

Logos, λόγος (Greek) reason and word. Acting reasonably (σὺν λόγῳ)

Ma'ānī, معاني referents, having to do with divine attributes.

Madhhab, مذهب name for a school of *fiqh*/jurisprudence.

Majūs, مجوس (Zoroastrian).

mansūkh, المنسوخ abrogated.

maqāsid, مقاصد objective (s) مقصد pl. Usually referring to the purpose of Islamic law.

ma'rūf, معروف that which sound human nature regards as good. As opposed to *munkar*, منكر which sound human nature rejects as evil.

masālik, مسلك caravan trails, king's road.

al-masīh, المسيح *masīhī* the Messiah, Jesus.

Al-Masjid an-Nabawī, المسجد النبوي the Mosque of the Prophet in Medina.

Maslaha, مصلحة the common good.

mawlā, مولى non-Muslim individuals gradually become adopted into an Arab Muslim tribe and eventually convert, thus escaping *dhimmī* status.

mawlūd, مولود begotten.

mawjūd, موجود existing.

menahhemana, in Aramaic, *paráklētos* in Greek, comforter, consoler

mihrāb, محراب a small semicircular area that indicates qibla, direction of Muslim prayer.

millet, مِلَّة the system of governing the People of the Book as *dhimmī*.
minbar, منبر pulpit for Friday prayers.
minhāj, منهج a pathway, like *sharī'ah* as a path to God, God's way.
Mu'āhid, معاهد a *dhimmī*, or pagan that entered into treaty with Muslims after a war, their lives must be protected as *dhimmī*.
Mu'allaqāt, معلقة pre-Islamic poetry.
al-muamalāt, المعاملات the social teachings of the Qur'ān.
mubāhala, مباهلة mutual invocation, or the ordeal of fire with regard to the delegation of Najrān or the introduction of Judaism to Himyar.
mufassir, مفسر *mufassirūn*, scholar(s) مفسرون.
Muhājir, مهاجر emigrant, refugee.
Muhājirūn, مهاجرون those who emigrated with Muhammad from Mecca to Medina.
Muhaymin, المهيمن guardian, *muhayminan*, المهيمنه meaning guardian over.
muhdth, محدث originator.
muhkam, محكم firmly established meaning. Holding one meaning that is clear and does not need interpretation.
muhkamāt, محكمات easy to interpret, a very clear verse.
mujtahid, مجتهد independent thinker. One who does deductive reasoning. Mujtahid fi al-maddhab, مجتهد في المذهب a particular school of religious thought, with Islamic jurisprudence, may differ within its boundaries.
mujtahid fi-ashl-shar', مجتهد في الشرح a person not obliged or permitted to follow an existing authoritative *madhhab*, i.e. allowed to think independently.
mu'min, مؤمن *mu'minūn*, مؤمنون true believers meaning.
munāfiqūn, المنافقون hypocrites, those who profess belief or allegiance, but do not keep their word.
munahhamanā, a Syriac word that means Muhammad, in Greek, *paraklētos* (Paraclete) according to Ibn Ishāq, *sīra*.
Muqatta'āt, مقاطع الحروف These letters form part of the fourteen mysterious that precede several chapters of the Qur'an.
Murīid مُريد disciples.
Mushaf, مصحف early written copies of Qur'ān from oral tradition.
mushrik, مشرك those who associate partners with God. *Muslimūn* مسلمون Muslims, singular مسلم

mutakallim, متكلم a person that engages in *kalām*, theological debate or dialogue. The one who speaks, the good speaker.

mutakallimūn, متكلمون plural of *mutakallim*. The one who can speak, public debater of theological issues.

mutashābihāt, متشابهات difficult to interpret.

mutawaffika, متوفيك cause to die, Cf. (3):55 "I will take your soul and cause you to die ..."

Najāshī, النجاشي the title given to the Abyssinian king.

Najrān, نجران historical town in Southwest Arabia.

nasārā, النصارى *al-nasārā*, *(sing. nasārī)* Christian.

nasab, النسب descendancy, referring to blood ties.

naskh, نسخ abrogation, replace.

Nāsirah, الناصرة Nazareth.

An-nāsirī, الناصري Christian.

Nāsirīyūn, ناصريون Nazerene, possible name for Christians.

nātiq, ناطق rational speaking, as written by Sulayman ibn Hasan al-Ghazzi. Modern Arabic منطقي.

Nestorians, Church of the East.

An-niyya, النيّة intentions, Tariq.

Nussāk, نساك general ascetics.

qadīm, قديم primordial.

Qashīda, قصيدة poem.

Qaswā, قسوا the name of Muhammad's favourite camel.

al-Qayūm, القيوم The self-existing.

qebat (Ge'ez) fully unified through the Holy Spirit.

qibla, قبلة direction of Mecca.

qissīsīn, قسّيسين priests *rahbān*, رحبان monk, *rahbāniyya*, الرهبنة monasticism.

qist, قسط equity, as in equal share, *al-muqsit*, المقسط The Equitable, *a name of God*.

Qur'ān, القرآن Qur'ānic, Qur'ān.

Rābi'a al-Adawiyya, رابعة العدوية *name of a famous soufi woman*.

Ar-Rahman, الرحمن the Beneficent.

rasm, رسم bare consonant form of word, i.e., no *teshkeel*. تَشْكِيل or diacritical markings (*harakāt* الحركات or short vowels, *tashkīl* are supplementary

diacritical consonant markings consonant for "forming". *i'jām*, إِعْجَام consonant forming).
Rasūl, الرسول sing or الأنبياء prophet, or messenger.
ra'y, رأي personal opinion with regard to exegesis.
ribā, الربا interest.
risālah, رسالة letter, mission, epistle, tractate, bill or statement, e.g., Paul of Antioch's Letter
to a Muslim Friend.
rūh, رُوح spirit (brill).
saba'a, صبأ convert.
sabab an-nuzūl سبب النزول occasion of revelation, plural the *asbāb an-nuzūl*, اسباب النزول
Sābi'ūn, الصابئة considered a religion of the People of the Book.
sakinah, سكينة (calmness and tranquillity) for instance, Sheikh Khalid Sallabi describes the experiences of *sakinah* he felt at a Quaker Meeting for Worship. Cf. *Sufi Sakinah*.
salaf سلف righteous ancestors.
salafi, السلفي righteous ancestors, conservative, radical Islamists.
sālihūn, صالحون righteous.
sa'lūk, صعلوك tribal outcast.
shahādah, الشهادة Islamic testimony of faith.
Shari'ah, الشريعة laws, road, way, path to God.
shari'at al-'adl, شريعة العدل Sharia Justice.
shari'at al-fadl, شريعة الفضل law of grace.
Shiloh, שילה (Hebrew) a messianic figure that the Jews of the Hijaz anticipated.
הליש אבי יב רע (Hebrew) "until the *Messiah* to whom the kingdom belongs comes".
shirk, mushriks, شرك, مشرك associating partners with God and a person who associates partners with God.
shubbiha lahum, شُبِّهَ لَهُمْ so it appeared to them …
shubhah, شبهة obscure misguided argument, usually against Islam by Christians, Jews or atheists.
sibhga, صبغة divine anointing, the hue given by God to life.
sifa dhātiyya, صافه ذاتية divine attributes.

Glossary

sifāt Allah, صفات الله God's attributes.

sīra, السيرة Biography of Muhammad.

Sost Ledat (Ge'ez) an adoptionist theory describing the nature of Jesus.

sunnah, السنّة the way or the example, *sunnah al-nabi*, سنّة النبي the way of the prophet.

sūrah, or *sūrat* سورة a passage from the Qur'an, plural suwar. There are 114 sūrah, سُوَر and thirty ajzā', أجزاء (parts or chapters) in the Qur'an.

Ta'āruf تعارف knowing each other, used in 49:13, relating to co-operating for the common good.

tabī'a, طبيعه natural, normal occurrence.

tābī'a, تابعة or تابع followers, as in the students from the second generation of followers.

tābi'ūn, تابعون the second generation of Islamic scholars and students of the companions.

tafsīr, تفسير *tafāsīr*, التفاسير exegesis of Qur'ān or hadīth.

tajassud, التجسُّد incarnation.

at-tajsīm, التجسيم anthropomorphism.

tahrīf, تحريف scriptural falsification.

tahsīniyyāt, تحسينيات and *kamaliyyāt*, كماليات enhancing and perfecting.

takfīr, تكفير declaring Muslims to be outside Islam.

taqarrub, تقرب (from قرب) nearness, peaceful co-operation, community, from قرب.

taqlīd تقليد uncritical allegiance, imitating a tradition, or the solid foundations of the application of the means of exegesis. *Taqlīd* is sometimes used in this book in place of the modern sociological term *altanshi'ah al-ijtimā'iyyah* التنشئة الاجتماعية socialization or social conditioning.

taqwā, تقوى consciousness of God.

tasdīq, تصديق affirmation of the truth of God's existence, dedication to what God expects people to do and opposition to what God forbids.

tashkīl, تَشْكِيل orthographic markings, or diacritic annotation, usually referring to vowels.

tashrīd, تشرّيد deterrence (from Abi Bakf Naji's *The Management of Savagery*, *idarat at- tawahhush*).

Tawahedo (Ge'ez) Union, as described the nature of Jesus subsumed in the Divine.

tawhīd, توحيد the oneness of God.
ta'wīl, تأويل interpretation including esoteric meaning.
at-taysīr fī al-fatwā wat-tabshīr fī al-da'wa", التيسير في الفتوى والتبشير في الدعوة (facilitation in issuing *fatwā*s and promoting Islam through proselytizing).
teshuvah תשובה (Hebrew) repentance.
thālith الثالوث *thalātha*, trinity, three.
theotokos (Greek) Mother of God.
Tsadkan (Ge'ez) the righteous ones.
ummat al-mu'minīn أمة المؤمنين the community of believers of Muhammad.
ummatan ummatan, أُمَّةً أُمَّةً community by community.
ummatan wasata أُمَّةً وَسَطًا a middle nation or a balanced nation.
ummatun muqtasidatun, أُمَّةٌ مُقْتَصِدَةٌ a balanced people. The one who saves. They do not waste.
uqnūm, أقنوم in one hypostasis, i.e. two natures in one hypostasis
usūl, أصول fundamentals of religion.
usūl al-fiqh, أصول الفقه law and jurisprudence.
al-wahi al-qur'āni, الوحي القرآني inlibration, revelation of the Qur'an.
al-walā' wa'l barā', الولاء والبراء loyalty and disavowal. Loyalty to things that please God and disavowal and opposition to things that displease God.
wali, ولي guardian.
al-wāqi', الواقع current state of affairs, context.
wasatī, wasatiyya وسطي وسطيّة systematic and liberal interpretation of Islamic regulation governing the life of Muslim minorities that seeks to preserve Islamic identity and facilitate Islamization of the West, as opposed to Salafi interpretation of regulations.
al-wāsi', الواسع the vast, an attribute or divine name.
Wa-yomer, (Hebrew) "and He said ..."
wujūd, وجود existence, existing, being.
wahdat al-wujūd, وحدة الوجود, unity of being, unity of existence.
yahūd, اليهودي a Jew.
Yahūda (Judah) the eldest son of the Prophet Yaqub (Jacob).
Zabūr, زبور referring to the Book revealed to David, Psalms.
zakāt, زكاة tax for the poor.
zinā, زِنَا this term is used to discuss sexual relations outside of marriage in various forms.

Bibliography

Abboud, Tony. *Al-Kindi: The Father of Arab Philosphy*. Great Muslim Philosphers and Scientists of the Middle Ages. Edited by Munir A. Shaikh. New York: Rosen, 2006.
'Abdil-Wahhaab, Muhammad bin. *An Explanation of Aspects of the Days of Ignorance* [in English/Arabic]. Translated by Isma'eel Alarcon. New York: Sanatech, 2005.
Abu-Munshar, Maher Y. *Islamic Jerusalem and Its Christians: A History of Tolerance and Tensions*. London: I. B. Tauris, 2013.
Adamson, Peter. *Al-Kindī*. Great Medieval Thinkers. Edited by Brian Davies. Vol. 8. NewYork: Oxford University Press, 2007.
Al-Azami, M. M. *The History of the Qur'anic Text: A Comparative Study with the Old and New Testaments*. Leicester: UK Islamic Academy, 2003.
Al-Bukharī, Muhammed Ibn Ismael. *The Translation of the Meaning of Sahih Al-Bukharī* Translated by Dr Muhammad Muhsin Khan. Riyadh: Darussalam, 1997.
Al-Khudrawi, Deeb. *A Dictionary of Islamic Terms, Arabic-English*. Translated by Diane Humaidh Deeb Al-Khudrawi. Damascus-Beirut: Al Yamamah, 1995.
Al-Mubarakpuri, Safiur-Rahman. *The Sealed Nectar (Ar-Raheeq Al-Makhtum)*. 2002 edn. Riyadh: Darussalam, 2002. 1979.
Al-Qaradawi, Yusuf. *The Lawful and the Prohibited in Islam (Al- Al-Halāl Wal Harām Fil Islam)* [in English] [Al-Halal Al-haram Fil-Islam]. Translated by M. Moinuddin Siddiqui Kamal El-Helbawy, Syed Shuky. Edited by Ahmad Zaki Hammad. 2nd edn. London: Shorouk International Limited, 1985. American Trust Publications
_____. *Non Muslims in the Islamic Society* [غير المسلمين في المجتمع الاسلامي]. Translated by Khalil Muhammad Hamad Sayed Mahboob Ali Shah. Indianapolis: American Trust Publications, 1985.
Al-Tabarī, Abū Ja'far Muhammad B. Jarīr. *The Commentary on the Qur'ān* [Jāmi al-Bayān 'an ta'wīl āy al-Qur'ān]. Edited by L. J. Cooper. Oxford: Oxford University Press; Hakim Investment Holdings (M. E.) Limited, 1987.
_____. "L'exégèse Du Saint Coran". In *L'Exégèse*, 1600: Dar Al-Kotob Al-Limiyah, 2009.
Anatolios, Khalid. *Athanasius: The Coherance of His Thought*. New York: Routledge, 1998.

Anonymous. *An Arabic Version of the Acts of the Apostles and the Seven Catholic Epistles*. Translated by Gibson. Studia Sinaitica Edited by Margaret Dunlop Gibson. 1st edn. Vol. VII. Piscataway, NJ: Gorgias Press, 2003.

Arberry, A. J. *The Seven Odes: The First Chapter in Arabic Literature*. London: George Allen & Unwin Ltd, 1957.

As-Sallaabee, Ali Muhammad. *The Biography of Abu Bakr as-Siddeeq* [Sira Abu Bakr As-Sideeq]. Translated by Faisal Shafeeq. Riyadh: Darussalam, 2007.

———. *The Noble Life of the Prophet, Peace Be Upon Him*. Translated by Faisal Shafeeq. 3 vols. Riyadh: Dar-us-Salam, 2005.

As-Sallabi, Ali Muhammad. *The Biography of Uthman Ibn Affan Dhun-Noorayn*. Translated by Nasir Khattab. Riyadh: Maktaba Dar-us-Salam, 2007.

Asbridge, Thomas. "Talking to the Enemy: The Role and Purpose of Negotiations between Saladin and Richard the Lionheart During the Third Crusade". *Journal of Medieval History* 39, no. 3 (2013): 275–96.

Baalbaki, Dr Rohi. "Al-Mawrid". In *A Modern Arabic-English Dictionary*. Beirut: Dar El-Ilm Lilmalayin, 2007.

"Babylonian Talmud: Kethuboth". In *Hebrew-English Edition Of The Babylonian Talmud*, edited by B. A. Rabbi Dr I. Epstein, PhD, D. Lit. London: Soncino Press, 1971.

Bamyeh, Mohammed A. *The Social Origins of Islam: Mind, Economy, Discourse*. Minneapolis: University of Minnesota Press, 1999.

Barber, Malcom C. "The Challenge of State Building in the Twelfth Century: The Crusader States in Palestine and Syria". In *The Stenton Lecture 2008*, edited by Dr Rebecca Rist, 1–20. Reading: University of Reading, 2009.

Barnes, Timothy D. *Athanasius and Constantius: Theology and Politics in the Constantinian Empire*. Cambridge, MA: Harvard University Press, 1993.

Bayfield, Tony, Alan Race, and Ataullah Siddiqui, eds. *Beyond the Dysfunctional Family: Jews, Christians and Muslims in Dialogue with Each Other and with Britain*. London The Manor House Abrahamic Dialogue Group, 2012.

Beaumont, Mark. *Christology in Dialogue with Muslims: A Critical Analysis of Christian Presentations of Christ for Muslims from the Ninth and Twentieth Centuries*. Regnum Studies in Mission. Edited by Kwame Bediako, Gillian Bediako, Hwa Yung, C. B. Samuel, Chris Sugden and Doug Regnum Eugene: Wipf and Stock Publishers, 2011. doi:6/7/2011. 2005.

Bell, Richard. *The Origin of Islam in Its Christian Environment; the Gunning Lectures, Edinburgh University, 1925*. Islam and the Muslim World. Edited by Jon Ralph Willis. 2nd edn. Vol. 10. Edinburgh & London: Frank Cass and Company Limited by arrangement with Macmillan and Co. Ltd, 1925. 1968. 1926.

Benedict, Pope. "Faith, Reason and the University Memories and Reflections". In *Libreria Editrice Vaticana*, 6: Libreria Editrice Vaticana, 2006.
Berg, Herbert. *The Development of Exegesis in Early Islam*. Richmond, Surrey: Curzon Press, 2000.
Binns, John. "Theological Education in the Ethiopian Orthodox Church". *The Journal of Adult Theological Education* 2, no. 2 (2005): 103–13.
Bokser, B. M. "Messianism, the Exodus Pattern, and Early Rabbinic Judaism". In *The Messiah: Developments in Earliest Judaism and Christianity*, edited by James H. Charlesworth, 239–58. Minneapolis, MN: Fortress Press, 1992.
Bousquet, G. H. "Some Critical and Sociological Remarks on the Arab Conquest and the Theories Proposed on This". Translated by Philip Simpson. In *The Expansion of the Early Islamic State*, edited by Fred M. Donner. The Formation of the Islamic World, 15–21. Hants: Ashgate Publishing Limited, 2007.
Boyarin, Daniel. "The Gospel of the Memra: Jewish Binitarianism and the Prologue to John". *The Harvard Theological Review* 94, no. 3 (July 2001): 243–84.
Brown, Jonathan A. C. "The Problem of Literary and Historical Sources". *Arab Studies Quarterly* 25, no. 3 (2003).
Brown, Raymond E., Joseph A. Fitzyer, and Roland E. Murphy, eds. *The Jerome Biblical Commentary*. 2 vols. Englewood Cliffs, NJ: Prentice-Hall, 1968.
Budge, E. A. Wallis. *The Kebra Nagast: The Queen of Sheba and Her Only Son Menyelek* [in Ethiopic] [Kebra Nagast]. Translated by E. A. Wallis Budge. London: Forgotten Books, 2007. 2007. 1932.
Bulliet, Richard W. *Conversion to Islam in the Medieval Period*. Cambridge, MA: Harvard University Press, 1979.
Byron, Gay L. "Manuscripts, Meanings, and (Re)Membering: Ethiopian Women in Early Christianity". *Journal of Religious Thought* 59/60, no. 1 (January 2006): 83–99.
Caetani, Leone. "The Art of War of the Arabs, and the Supposed Religious Fervour of the Arab Conquerors". Translated by Gwendolin Goldbloom. In *The Expansion of the Early Islamic State*, edited by Fred M Donner. The Formation of the Islamic World, 1–7. Hants: Ashgate Publishing Limited, 2007.
Caskel, Werner. "The Bedouinization of Arabia". In *The Arabs and Arabia on the Eve of Islam*, edited by F. E. Peters. The Formation of the Classical Islamic World, 34–44. Aldershot, Hampshire: Ashgate Publishing Limited, 1999.
Cohen, Jack. *The Reunion of Isaac and Ishmael*. New York: Mosaic Press, 1987.
Conrad, Lawrence. "Ibn Butlān in Bilad Al-Shām: The Career of a Travelling Christian Physician". In *Syrian Christians Unser Islam: The First Thousand Years*, edited by David Thomas, 131–58. Leiden: Brill, 2001.

Cragg, Kenneth. *The Arab Christian: A History of the Middle East*. London: Mowbary, 1994.
Crowley, Roger W. *Ethiopian Biblical Interpretation: A Study in Exegetical Tradition and Hermeutics*. University of Cambridge Oriental Piblications. Vol. 38, Cambridge: Cambridge University Press, 1988.
Dall'Oglio, Paolo. *Amoureux De L'islam, Croyant En Jésus* Translated by d'Églantine Gabaix-Hailé. 1st edn. Paris: Les Éditions l'Atelier, Éditions Ouvriès, 2009.
———. *La Rage Et La Lumière: Un Prêtre Dans La Revolution Syrienne* [in French]. Translated by d'Églantine Gabaix-Hailé. 1st edn. Ivry-sur-Seine: Les Éditions l'Atelier, Éditions Ouvriès, 2013.
Dana, Nissim. *The Druze in the Middle East: Their Faith, Leadership, Identity and Status*. Brighton: Sussex Academic Press, 2003.
Daou, Fr Fadi. 20 June 2015. Private correspondence in response to a research question.
Dick, Ignace. "Samonas De Gaza Ou Sulaïmān Al-Gazzi: Évêque Melchite De Gaza Xie Siècle". [In French]. *Proche Orient Chrétien* no. 29 (1980 1980): 175–8.
Doane, Thomas William. *Bible Myths and Parallels in Other Religions: Being a Comparison of the Old and New Testament Myths and Miracles with Those of Heathen Nations of Antiquity Considering Also Their Origin and Meaning*. Edited by J. W. Bouton. 4th edn. New York: The Truth Seeking Company, 1882.
Donner, Fred M. *Muhammad and the Believers: At the Origins of Islam*. Cambridge, MA: The Belknap Press of Harvard University Press, 2010.
Durant, Will. *The Age of Faith. The Story of Civilization*. 11 vols. Vol. 4. New York: MJF Books, 1950. Simon & Schuster Inc.
Eckstein, Zvi, and Maristella Botticini. "From Farmers to Merchants, Conversions and Diaspora: Human Capital and Jewish History". *Journal of the European Economic Association* 5, no. 5 (2007): 885–926.
Edelby, Néophytos. *Sulaimān Al-Gazzī: Xe-Xie Siècles*. Patrimoine Arabe Chrétien. Edited by Mgr Néophytos Edelby and P. Kh. Samir S. J. Rome: Pontificio Istituto Orientale, 1984.
Efrati, Rabbi Binyamin. *"Sh'ma B'ni" a Treasury of Stories and Lessons from the Weekly Parashah* [in Hebrew] [Otzar HaTorah LaYeled]. Translated by Rabbi Yaakov Yosef Iskowitz. Edited by C. D. Sklar. 2005 edn. Jerusalem: Feldheim Publishers, 2005. 1975.
Erlich, Haggai. *Ethiopia and the Middle East*. Boulder, CO: Lynne Reinner Publishers, 1994.
Esack, Farid. "Muslims Engaging the Other and the Humanum". *Emory International Law Review* 14, no. 2 (2000): 529–69.
———. *On Being a Muslim: Finding a Religious Path in the World Today*. Oxford: Oneworld, 2002.

_____. *Qur'an, Liberation & Pluralism; an Islamic Perspective of Interreligious Solidarity against Oppression*. 2002 edn. Oxford: Oneworld, 1997.
Evans, Austin P. *A Commentary on the Creed of Islam: Sa'd Al-Dīn Al Taftāzāni on the Creed of Najm Al-Dīn Al-Nasafī*. Translated by Earl Edgar Evan. Records of Civilization Sources and Studies. Edited by Austin P. Evans Vol. XLIII, New York: Oxford University Press, 1950.
Finneran, Niall. "Hermits, Saints, and Snakes: The Archaeology of the Early Ethiopian Monastery in Wider Context". *International Journal of African Historical Studies* 45, no. 2 (2012): 247–71.
Firestone, Reuven. "Holy War in Modern Judaism? "Mitzvah War" and the Problem of the "Three Vows". *Journal of the American Academy of Religion* Vol. 74, No. 4 (December 2006): 954–82.
_____. *Journeys in Holy Lands: The Evolution of the Abraham-Ishmael Legends in Islamic Exegesis*. Albany: University of New York Press, 1990.
Ford, F. Peter. "Christian-Muslim Relations in Ethiopia: A Checkered Past, a Challenging Future". *Reformed Review*, Spring (January 2007): 1–14.
Frank, Richard M. "Attribute, Attribution, and Being: Three Islamic Views". In *Classical Islamic Theology: The Ash'arites*, edited by Dimitri Gutas, 258–78. Aldershot, Hampshire: Ashgate, 2008.
_____. *Beings and Their Attributes*. Albany: State University of New York Press, 1978.
_____. "Hearing and Saying What Is Said". In *Classical Islamic Theology: The Ash'arites*, edited by Dimitri Gutas, 1–14. Aldershot, Hampshire: Ashgate, 2008.
_____. "Science of Kalām". In *Classical Islamic Theology: The Ash'arites*, edited by Dimitri Gutas. Aldershot, Hampshire: Ashgate, 2008.
Frumkin, Amos, Roi Porat, and Hanan Eshel. "Finds from the Bar Kokhba Revolt, from Two Caves at En Gedi". *Palestine Exploration Quarterly* 139, no. 1 (2007): 35–53.
Gafni, Isaiah M. *Land, Center and Diaspora: Jewish Constructs in Late Antiquity*. Journal for the Study of the Pseudepigrapha. Edited by Lester L. Grabbe James H. Charlesworth Vol. 21, Sheffield: Sheffield Academic Press Supplement Series, 1997.
Geisler, Norman L., and Abdul Saleeb. *Answering Islam: The Cresent in Light of the Cross*. 2nd edn. Grand Rapids, MI: Baker Books, 2006.
Gibbon, E. *The History of the Decline & Fall of the Roman Empire*. London: Penguin, 1994.
Gibson, David. "Pope Benedict Xvi's Regensburg Lecture on Islam Gets a Second Look in the Wake of Islamic State". 2014.
Gil, Moshe. *A History of Palestine, 634–1099* [Erets Yisra'el ba-tekufah ha-Muslemit ha-rishonah (638–1099)]. Translated by Mrs Ethel Broido. Vol. 1. Cambridge: Cambridge University Press, 1993. Tel Aviv University 1983.

_____. "The Origin of the Jews of Yathrib". In *The Arabs and Arabia on the Eve of Islam*, edited by F. E. Peters. The Formation of the Classical Islamic World, 145–66. Aldershot, Hampshire: Ashgate Publishing Limited, 1999.

Gilliot, Claude. "Creation of a Fixed Text". In *The Cambridge Companion to the Qur'an*, edited by Jane Dammen McAuliffe, 41–58. New York: Cambridge University Press, 2008.

Ginzberg, Louis. "The Legends of the Jews". In *The Legends of the Jews*, edited by Boaz Cohen. London: John Hopkins University Press, 1998.

_____. *The Legends of the Jews* [in German]. Translated by Henrietta Szold. 6th edn. Philidelphia, PA: The Jewish Publication Society Of America, 1909.

Grafton, David D. "The Identity and Witness of Arab Pre-Islamic Arab Christianity: The Arabic Language and the Bible". *Hervormde Teologiese Studies* 70, no. 1 (2014): 1–8.

Griffith, Sidney H. *The Bible in Arabic: The Scriptures of the "People of the Book"*. Jews, Christians, and Muslims from the Ancient to the Modern World. Edited by William Chester Jordan and Peter Schäfer Michael Cook. Princeton, NJ: Princeton University Press, 2013.

_____. "Christian Lore and the Arabic Qur'ān: The 'Companions of the Cave' in Surat Al-Kahf and in Syriac Christian Tradition". In *The Qur'ān in Its Historical Context*, edited by Gabriel Said Reynolds, 109–38. Abingdon, Oxon: Routledge, 2008.

_____. "Christian Theology in Islamic Terms". In *Thinking the Divine in Interreligious Encounter*, edited by Norbert Hintersteiner and François Bousquet, 147–74. Amsterdam: Rodopi, 2012.

_____. *The Church in the Shadow of the Mosque: Christians and Muslims in the World of Islam*. Princeton, NJ: Princeton University Press, 2008.

_____. "Comparative Religion in the Apologetics of the First Christian Arabic Theologians". In *The Beginnings of Christian Theology in Arabic: Muslim-Christian Encounters in the Early Islamic Period*, 63–87. Hampshire, Burlington: Ashgate Publishing Limited, 2002.

_____. "Faith and Reason in Christian Kalām: Theodore Abū Qurrah on Discerning the True Religion". In *Christian Arabic Apologetics During the Abbasad Period (750–1258)*, edited by Samir Khalil Samir and Jørgen S. Nielsen. Leiden: Brill, 1994.

_____. "The Melkites and the Muslims: The Qur'ān, Christology, and Arab Orthodoxy". *Al-Qantara* XXXIII 2, no. July-September (2012): 413–43.

_____. "The Monks of Palestine and the Growth of Christian Literature in Arabic". *The Muslim World* 78, no. 1 (1988): 28.

_____. "Muslim and Church Councils; the Apology of Theodore Abu Qurrah". In *The Beginnings of Christian Theology in Arabic: Muslim-Christian Encounters in the Early Islamic Period*, 270–99. Hampshire, Burlington: Ashgate Publishing Limited, 2002.

_____. "Paul of Antioch". In *The Orthodox Church in the Arab World, 700–1700: An Anthology of Sources*, edited by Samuel Noble & Alexander Treiger, 216–35. DeKalb: Northern Illinois Press, 2014.

Gutas, Dimitri. *Greek Thought, Arabic Culture: The Graeco-Arabic Translation Movement in Baghdad and Early 'Abbāsid Society (2nd-4th/8th-10th Centuries)*. London: Routledge, 1998.

Haddād, Gibrīl Fouād. *The Four Imams and Their Schools*. London: Muslim Academic Trust, 2007.

Harduf, David Mendel. *Rabbinic Exegesis of Biblical Names and Narratives (in the Talmud and Midrash)*. 2nd edn. Willowdale: Beit Ra'if Publishing, 2002.

Hassan, Dr Farooq. "Re-Examining the Possibility of Peaceful Co-Existence of Muslims and Non-Muslims in the West Based on the Abyssinian Model ". *Interdisciplinary Journal of Contemporary Research in Business* 3, , no. 11 (March 2012): 869–80.

Heijer, Johannes Den. "Apologetic Elements in Coptic-Arabic Historiography: The Life of Afrahām Ibn Zur'ah, 62nd Patriarch of Alexandria". In *Christian Arabic Apologetics During the Abbasad Period (750–1258)*, edited by Samir Khalil Samir and Jørgen S. Nielsen. Christian Arabic Apologetics During the Abbasad Period (750–1258): Brill, 1994.

Henze, Paul B. *Layers of Time: A History of Ethiopia*. New York: Palgrave, 2000.

Hiestand, Gerald. "Not 'Just Forgiven:' How Athanasius Overcomes the under-Realised Eschatology of Evangelicalism". *Evangelical Quarterly* 84, no. 1 (2012): 47–66.

The Holy Bible: English Standard Version. Wheaton, IL: Good News Publishers, 2001

Holy Bible, from the Ancient Eastern Text [in English from Aramaic of Peshitta]. Translated by George M. Lamsa. New York: Harper One, 1933. A. J. Holman Co.

Hoyland, Robert. *Seeing Islam as Others Saw It: A Survey and Evaluation of Christian, Jewish and Zoroastrian Writings on Early Islam*. Vol. 13. Princeton, NJ: Darwin Press, 1997.

Ibn Kathīr, Al Hafiz. *Tafsīr Al-Qur'ān Al-Azīm* [in English] [Al-Misbah Al-Munir fi Tahdhib Tafsir Ibn Kathir]. Translated by Jalal Abualrub. Tafsīr Ibn Kathīr (Abridged) Edited by Shaykh Safi Ur Rahman Al-Mubarakpuri. 10 vols. Riyadh: Darussalam, 2003.

Ireland, Islamic Cultural Centre. "Fatwas of European Council for Fatwa and Research". edited by Said Fares Al-Falah Foundation. Cairo: Islamic Inc., 2002.

Ishāq, Ibn. *The Life of Muhammad, a Translation of Ibn Ishāq's Sirat Rasul Allah* [Sirat Rasul allah]. Translated by Alfred Guillaume. 22nd edn. Karachi: Ameena Saiyid, Oxford University Press, 2009. 1967. 1955.

Janine Di Giovanni, Conor Gaffey, Lara Adoumie, Stav Ziv. "The New Exodus: After Years of Slow and Steady Decline Christians Are Being Driven from the Middle East by Isis". *Newsweek Global* 164, no. 13 (03/04/2015 2015): 10.

Johns, Chris. *Valley of Life, Africa's Great Rift*. Charlottesville, VA: Thomas-Grant, 1991.

Juynbol, G. H. A. *Studies on the Origins and Uses of Islamic Hadih*. Aldershot, Hampshire: Variorum, 1996.

Kaegi, Walter E. "Initial Byzantine Reactions to the Arab Conquest". In *The Expansion of the Early Islamic State*, edited by Fred M. Donner. The Formation of the Classical Islamic World, 113–23. Hants: Ashgate Publishing Limited, 2007.

Kaplan, Steven. "Dominance and Diversity: Kingship, Ethnicity, and Christianity in Orthodox Ethiopia". *Church History and Religious Culture* 89, no. 1–3 (2009): 291–305.

Katsh, Abraham I. *Judaism in Islām*. New York: New York University Press & Bloch Publishing Company, 1954.

Katz, Joseph, and Ben Abrahamson. "The Persian Conquest of Jerusalem in 614ce Compared with Islamic Conquest of 638ce: Its Messianic Nature and the Role of the Jewish Exilarch". *Alsadiqin: the Committee for Historical Research in Islam and Judaism Copyright* (1954).

Khaalid, Khaalad Muhammad. *Men around the Messenger* [in English] [rajil hwul al rasul]. Translated by Sheikh Muhammad Mustapha Gemeiah Al Azhar Administration. Edited by Aelfwine Acelas Mischler. El-Mansoura: Dar Al-Manarah, 2003.

Khaldûn, Ibn. *The Muqaddimah: An Introduction to History* [The Muqaddimah]. Translated by Franz Rosenthal. Vol. 1. Princeton, NJ: Princeton University Press, 2005. 1969. 1967.

Khalidi, Tarif. *Arabic Historical Thought in the Classic Period*. Cambridge: Cambridge University Press, 1996. 1994.

———. *The Muslim Jesus: Sayings and Stories in Islamic Literature*. Convergences. 12 vols. Cambridge, MA: Harvard University Press, 2001.

Khalifé, Élie. "Notice Sur Un Manuscript Du Poète Arabe Chrétien Sulaimān Ibn Hasan Al Gazzi". *Parole de l'Orient* 2 (1966 1966): 159–62.

Khoury, Adel Theodore. *Les Théologiens Byzantins et L'islam*. Paris: Beatrice-Nauwelaerts, 1969.

Khoury, Paul. *Paul D'antioche: Évêque Melkite De Sidon (XIIe S.)* [in French]. Translated by Paul Khoury. Vol. XXIV. Beyrouth: Imprimerie Catholique, 1964.

Kimball, Richard L. "An Exploration of the Concept of Messiah through Judaism, Christianity and Islam". St Andrews: St Mary's College, School of Divinity, University of St Andrews, 2008.

Kister, M. J. "The Seven Odes". In *Studies in Jāhiliyya and Early Islam*, edited by M. J. Kister. Variorum Collected Studies Series; C S 123, 27–36. London: Variorum, 1980.

———. *Society and Religion from Jāhiliyya to Islam*. Collect Studies Series; Cs327. Aldershot, Hampshire: Variorum, Gower Publishing Group, 1990.

Korotayev, Andrey. "Apologia for 'the Sabaean Cultural-Political Area'". *Bulletin of the Oriental and African Studies, University of London* 57, no. 3 (1994): 469–74.

Kukkonen, Taneli. "Al-Ghazālī on the Signification of Names". *Vivarium* 48 (2010 2010): 55–74.

Kung, Hans. *Islam: Past Present and Future*. Translated by John Bowden. 1st edn. Oxford: Oneworld Publications, 2007.

La Spisa, Paolo. *I Trattati Teologici Di Sulaymān Ibn Hasan Al-Ghazzī, Tomus 52* [in Italian and Arabic]. Translated by Paolo La Spisa. Corpus Scriptorum Christianorum Orientalium. Vol. 648, Tomus 52. Louvain: In Aedibus Peeters, 2013.

———. *I Trattati Teologici Di Sulaymān Ibn Hasan Al-Ghazzī, Tomus 53* [in Italian]. Corpus Scriptorum Christianorum Orientalium. Vol. 649, Tomus 53. Louvain: In Aedibus Peeters, 2013.

La Spisa, Paolo, and Johannes Den Heijer. "La Migration Du Savoir Entre Les Communautés; Le Cas De La Littérature Arabe Chrétienne". [In French]. *Res Antiquae* 7 (2010): 63–72.

Lamoreaux, John C. "Theodore Abu Qurra". In *The Orthodox Church in the Arab World, 700–1700: An Anthology of Sources*, edited by Samuel Noble & Alexander Treiger, 60–89. DeKalb: Northern Illinois Press, 2014.

———. *Theodore Abū Qurrah*. Translated by John C. Lamoreaux. Vol. 1, Provo, UT: Bringham Young University Press, 2005.

Lassner, Jacob. *Jews, Christians, and the Abode of Islam: Modern Scholarship, Medieval Realities*. Chicago & London: University of Chicago Press, 2012.

Lecker, Michael. "The Conversion of Himyar to Judaism and the Jewish Banū Hadl of Medina". In *Jews and Arabs in Pre-and Early Islamic Arabia*, 129–36. Aldershot, Hampshire: Ashgate Publishing Limited, 1998.

———. "A Note on Early Marriage Links between Qurashis and Jewish Women". In *Jews and Arabs in Pre-and Early Islamic Arabia*, edited by Michael Lecker, 17–39. Aldershot, Hampshire: Ashgate Publishing Limited, 1998.

———. "Zayd B Thābit: 'A Jew with Two Sidelocks' Judaism and Literacy in Pre-Islamic Medina (Yathrib)". *Journal of Near Eastern Studies* 56, No. 4 (1997): 14.

Lewis, Bernard. *The Jews of Islam*. Princeton, NJ: Princeton University Press, 1984.

Lilie, Ralph-Johannes. *Byzantium and the Crusader States 1096–1204* [Byzanz und die Kreuzfahrerstaaten]. Translated by J. C. Morris and Jean E. Ridings. Poikila Byzantina. Edited by Wilhelm Fink Verlag. Oxford: Clarendon Press, 1993. 1988. 1981.

Lindberg, David C. *The Beginnings of Western Science: The European Scientific Tradition in Philosophical, Religious, and Institutional Context, Prehistory to A. D. 1450*. 2nd edn. Chicago: University of Chicago Press, 2007. 1992.

Lings, Martin. *Muhammad, His Life Based on the Earliest Sources*. India: Allen & Unwin, 1983.

Maalouf, Amin. *The Crusades through Arab Eyes* [in English] [Les croisades vues par les Arabes]. Translated by Amin Maalouf. London: Al Saqi Books, 1984. 1983.

McAuliffe, Jane Dammen. *Qur'ānic Christians: An Analysis of Classical and Modern Exegesis* New York: Cambridge University Press, 1991.

Madigan, Daniel. "A Common Word between Us and You: Some Initial Reflections". *Thinking Faith: The Online Jesuit Journal*, no. January (18 January 2008): 6.

———. *Jms 2014 (01): A Word in Common* vol. 1, *John Main Seminar* Elmhurst College Chicago: World Community of Christian Meditation 2014.

———. *Jms (2): Resonating with the Word*, vol. 2, *John Main Seminar* Elmhurst College Chicago, 2014.

———. "People of the Word: Reading John with a Muslim". *Review and Expositor* 104, Winter (2007): 14.

Marcus, Harold G. *A History of Ethiopia*. Berkeley: University of California Press, 1994.

Margoliouth, D S. *The Relations between Arabs and Israelites Prior to the Rise of Islam*. The Schweich Lectures 1921. London: Oxford University Press, 1924.

Martin, Jugie A. "Une Nouvelle Invention À Mettre Au Compte De Constantin Palaeocappa: Samonas De Gaza Et Son Dialogue Sur L'eucharistie". *Miscellanea Giovanni Mercati* III (1946): 342–59.

Martinez, Florentino Garcia. *Hagar in Targum Pseudo-Jonathan*. Leiden: Brill, 2011.

Mazuz, Hagai. "Massacre in Medina". *Segula: The Jewish Journal Through History*, no. 3 (2010): 28–39. Meggitt, Justin J. *Early Quakers and Islam: Slavery, Apocalyptic and Christian-Muslim Encounters in the Seventeenth Century* [in English]. 1st edn. 59 vols. Vol. 59, Uppsala: Swedish Science Press, 2013.

Moberg, Axel. *The Book of the Himyarites; Fragments of a Hitherto Unknown Syriac Work*. Translated by Axel Moberg. Skrifter Utgivna Av Kungl. Humanistiska Vetenskapssamfundet I Lund. Edited by Axel Moberg Vol. VII. Leipzig: Lund, C. W. K. Gleerup, 1924.

Montjou, Guyonne de. *Mar Moussa, Un Monastère, Un Homme, Un Désert*. Paris: Albin Michel, 2006.

Moreen, Vera B. "Ish[H]Ma'iliyat: A Judeo-Persian Account of the Building of the Ka'ba". In *Judaism And Islam Boundaries, Communication And Interaction: Essays in Honor of William M. Brinner*, edited by John L. Hayes Benjamin H. Hary, Fred Astren. Leiden: Brill, 2000.

Mourad, Suleiman A. "Christians and Christianity in the Sira of Muhammad". In *Christian-Muslim Relations: A Bibliographical History*, edited by David Thomas, Barbara Roggema, Juan Pedro Monferrer Sala, Johannes Pahlitzsch, Mark Swanson, Herman Teule and John Tolan, 57–71. Leiden: Brill, 2009.

Muhibbu-Din, M. A. "Ahl Al-Kitab and Religious Minorities in the Islamic State: Historical Context and Contemporary Challenges". [In English]. *Journal of Muslim Minority Affairs* 20, no. 1 (2000): 16.

Muir, William, K. C. S. I. , L L. D. *The Apology of Al Kindy: Written at the Court of Al Māmūn, (A. H. 215, A. D. 830) in Defence of Christianity against Islam*. Charleston: Bibliolife, 2014. Bibliolife LLC. Smith, Elder & Co., 15 Waterloo Place, London, 1882.

Mujahid, Ibn Jabr. *Tafsir Mujahid Ibn Jabr* [in Arabic]. Edited by Dr Muhammad Abdul-Salam Abu Al-Neel. 1st edn. Medina Nasr, Cairo, Egypt: Dar Al Fiqr, Modern Islamic Ideology, 102h.

Mujahid, ibn Jabr Abu al-Hajjaj al-Makhzumi. *Tafsir Mujahid* [in Arabic]. Translated by Sumia Bel Haj. Edited by Abd al Rhman Tahir al-Surati. sponsored by Emir of Qatar, Sheikh Khalif Ibn Hamad Al Thani edn. Islamabad, Pakistan: Islamic Research Center, Islamabad, 1976.

Mumayiz, Ibrahim. "Imru' Al-Qays and Byzantium". *Journal of Arabic Literature* XXXVI, no. 2 (2005): 135–51.

⸺. *Society, Religion and Poetry in Pre-Islamic Arabia*. Translated by Arabic Translators International. Edited by Ahmed Allaithy & Abied Alsulaiman. Antwerp-Apeldoorn: Garant, 2010.

Munt, Harry. "Writing the History of an Arabian Holy City: Ibn Zabāla and the First Local History of Medina". *Arabica*, no. 59 (January 2012): 1–34.

Murad, Abdal Hakim. "Understanding the Four Madhhabs: The Facts About Ijtihad and Taqlid". In *The Muslim Academic Trust*, edited by The Muslim Academic Trust. London: The Muslim Academic Trust, 2012.

Nau, François. *Les Arabes Chrétiens De Mésopotamie Et De Syrie Du Viie Au Viiie Siècle* [in French]. Cahiers De La Société Asiatique. Vol. 1. Paris: Imprimerie Nationale, 1933.

Nicolle, David. *The Fourth Crusade 1202–04: The Betrayal of Byzantium*. 1st edn. Oxford: Osprey Publishing, 2011.

⸺. *Historical Atlas of the Islamic World*. London: Mercury Books, 2004. Thalamus Publishing.

Noble, Samuel. "Sulayman Al-Ghazzi". In *The Orthodox Church in the Arab World, 700–1700: An Anthology of Sources*, edited by Samuel Noble & Alexander Treiger. The Orthodox Christian Series, 160–70. DeKalb: Northern Illinois Press, 2014.

―――. "Sulaymān Al-Ghazzī" In *Christian-Muslim Relations: A Bibliographical History*, edited by David Thomas and Alex Mallet, 617–23. Leiden: Brill, 2010.

Novenson, Matthew V. "Why Does R. Akiba Acclaim Bar Kokhba as Messiah?". *Journal of the Study of Judaism*, no. 40 (2009): 551–72.

Parrinder, Geoffrey. *Jesus in the Qur'an* [in English]. Oxford: Oneworld Publications, 2003. 1965.

Phillips, Jonathan. "The Fourth Crusade and the Sack of Constantinople". *History Today* 5, no. 54 (2004): 21–8.

The Presidency of the Islamic Researches, and IFTA. *The Holy Qur'ān: English Translation of the Meanings and Commentary*. Translated by Ustadh Abdullah Yusuf Ali. Al-Madinah Al-Munawarah, Saudi Arabia: King Fahd Holy Qur'an Printing Complex, 1989.

Qutb, Sayyid. *Milestone*. USA: SIME, 2005

Rabkin, Yakov M. *A Threat from Within: A Century of Jewish Opposition to Zionism* [in English/French] [Au nom de la Torah, Une histoire de l'opposition juive au sionisme]. Translated by Fred A. Reed. Edited by Brenda Conroy. Black Point, Nova Scotia: Fernwood, 2006.

Ramadan, Tariq. *Islam, the West and the Challenges of Modernity*. Translated by Saïd Amgher. Leicester: Islamic Foundation, 2001. 2009. 2001.

―――. *The Messenger, the Meanings of the Life of Muhammad*. London: Penguin, 2007.

―――. *To Be a European Muslim: A Study of Islamic Sources in the European Context*. Leicester: The Islamic Foundation, 1999.

―――. *Western Muslims and the Future of Islam*. New York: Oxford University Press, 2004.

Rashid, Qasim. "A Muslim's Ramadan Message to Isis: You Don't Speak for Islam". In *Huff Post*, Religion: Huffington Post, 2014.

Renard, John. *Islam and Christianity: Theological Themes in Comparative Perspective*. Berkeley: University of California Press, 2011.

Reston, James. *Warrior's of God: Richard the Lionheart and Saladin in the Third Crusade*. London: Faber & Faber Ltd, 2001.

Ricks, Thomas W. *Early Arabic Christian Contributions to Trinitarian Theology: The Development of the Doctrine of the Trinity in an Isamic Milieu* Emerging Scholars. 1st edn. Minneapolis, MN: Fortress Press, 2013.

Rida, Rashid. *Al Manar* [in Arabic]. Translated by Abdul Haseeb. Tafsir Al-Manar. 1990 edn. 7 vols: The General Egyptian Foundation of the Book, 1990.

Romeny, Bas ter Haar. "Athanasius in Syriac". *Church History and Religious Culture* 90, no. 2–3 (2010): 33.
Rose, Rosalie Rakow & Lynda J. *Sana'a City of Contrast*. Burke: Tandem Publishers, 1981.
Saleeb, Norman L. Geisler and Abdul. *Answering Islam*. 2nd edn. Grand Rapids, MI: Baker Books, 2006. 1993.
Samir, Samir Khalil. *111 Questions on Islam, on Islam and the West* [Cento Demande Sull'Islam: Intervista a Samir Khalil Samir]. Translated by Claudia Castellani. Edited by Wafik Nasry. San Francisco, CA: Ignatius Press, 2008. 2002.
———. "Le Commentaire De Tabari Sur Coran 2/62 Et La Question Du Salut Des Non-Musulmans". [In French]. *Annali: Istituto Orientale de Napoli* 40, no. 30 (1980): 555–617.
———. "The Prophet Muhammad as Seen by Timothy I and Some Other Arab Christian Authors". In *Syrian Christians under Islam: The First Thousand Years*, edited by David Thomas, 75–106. Leiden: Brill, 2001.
Schochet, Jacob Immanuel. *Mashiach: The Principles of Mashich and the Messianic Era in Jewish Law and Tradition*. New York: S. I. E., 1991.
Scholars, 38 Muslim. "An Open Letter and Call from Muslim Religious Leaders To:". In *A Common Word*, 1–29: The Royal Aal al-Bayt Institute for Islamic Thought, Jordan, 2007.
Sebeos. *The Armenian History Attributed to Sebeos*. Translated by R. W. Thomson. Vol. 31, Liverpool: Liverpool University Press, 1999.
Sellassie, Sergew Hable. *Ancient and Medieval Ethiopian History to 1270*. Addis Ababa: United Printers, 1972.
Shakir, M H. "Concordance of the Qur'ān: Extracted from the M. H. Shakir Translation of the Qur'ān". In *Concordance of the Qur'ān: Extracted from the M. H. Shakir Translation of the Qur'ān*. New York: Tahrike Tarsile Qur'an, Inc., 2005.
Shepherd, Michael B. "Targums, the New Testament, and Biblical Theology of the Messiah". *Journal of the Evangelical Theological Society* 51/1, no. March 2008 (2008): 45–58.
Siddiqui, Ataullah. *Christian-Muslim Dialogue in the Twentieth Century*. 1st edn. London: MacMillan Press Ltd, 1997.
———. "Inter-Faith Relations in Britain since 1970-an Assessment". *Exchange* 39, no. 3 (2010): 236–50.
Slade, Darren M. "Arabia Haeresium Ferax (Arabia Bearer of Heresies)". *American Theological Inquiry (online)* 7, 1 January 2015 (01 November 2016): 11.
Smart, Ninian. *The Phenomenon of Christianity*. London: Collins, 1979.
Smith, M. A. *From Christ to Constantine*. Leicester: Inter-Varsity Press, 1976.

Stark, Rodney. *The Rise of Christianity: How the Obscure, Marginal Jesus Movement Became the Dominant Religious Force in the Western World in a Few Centuries*. 2nd edn. San Franscisco, CA: Harper Collins, 1997. Princeton University Press, 1996.

Starr, Joshua. *The Jews in the Byzantine Empire 641–1204*. Texte Und Forschungen Zur Byzantinisch-Neugriechischen Philologie. Edited by Nikos A. Bees. Hants: Gregg International Publishers Limited, 1969. 1939.

Stetkevych, Suzanne Pinckney. *The Mute Immortals Speak*. Ithaca, NY: Cornell University Press, 1993.

Stevenson, J., and W. H. C. Frend, eds. *A New Eusebius: Documents Illistrative of the History of the Church to A. D. 37*. 7th edn. London: S. P. C. K., 1957.

Subhani, Ayatullah Ja'far. *Introduction to the Science of Tafseer of the Qur'an* [Tafsir-e-Sahih-e-Ayat-e-Mushkile-Qur'an]. Translated by Saleem Bhimji. Middlesex, England: The Islamic Education Board of the Federation of KSIMC, 2006. Tafsir-e-Sahih-e-Ayat-e-Mushkile-Qur'an, The correct Exegesis of the Difficult Verses of the Qur'an.

Suermann, Harald. "Sulaymān Al-Gazzī, Évêque Melchite De Gaza (XIe Siècle): Sur Les Maronites". [In French]. *Parole de l'Orient* 21 (1996): 189–98.

Swanson, Mark N. "An Apology for the Christian Faith". In *The Orthodox Church in the Arab World, 700–1700: An Anthology of Sources*, edited by Samuel Noble & Alexander Treiger. The Orthodox Christian Series, 40–59. DeKalb: Northern Illinois Press, 2014.

Tabbara, Nayla, & Fadi Daou. *Divine Hospitality: A Christian-Muslim Conversation* [in English] [L'hospitalité divine: L'autre dans le dialogue des théologies chrétienne et musulmane]. Translated by Alan J. Amos. Geneva: World Council of Churches, 2017. L'hospitalité divine: L'autre dans le dialogue des théologies chrétienne et musulmane.

———. *L'hospitalité Divine: L'autre Dans Le Dialogue Des Théologies Chrétienne Et Musulmane* [in French]. French edn. Berlin: Lit Verlag 2013.

Thomas, David. "Idealism and Intransigence: A Christian-Muslim Encounter in Early Mumluk Times". *Mamlūk Studies Review* 13, no. 2 (2009): 19.

———. "Paul of Antioch's Letter to a Muslim Friend and the Letter from Cyprus". In *Syrian Christians under Islam: The First Thousan Years*, edited by David Thomas, 203–21. Leiden: Brill, 2001.

Tibi, Bassam. "The Worldview of Sunni Arab Fundamentalists: Attitudes Towards Modern Science and Technology". In *Fundamentalisms and Society: Reclaiming the Sciences, the Family, and Education*, edited by R. Scott Appleby Martin E. Marty. The Fundamentalism Project, 602. Chicago: University of Chicago Press, 1997.

Torrey, Charles Cutler. *The Jewish Foundation of Islam*. The Hilda Stich Stroock Lectures. New York: Bloch Publishing Co., 1933.
Trimingham, Spencer J. *Christianity among the Arabs in Pre-Islamic Times*. Beirut: Libraire Du Liban, 1990.
Vaglieri, Laura Veccia. "The Patriarchal and Umayyad Caliphates". In *The Cambridge History of Islam*, edited by P. M. Holt, Ann K S Lambton and Bernard Lewis. The Central Islamic Lands from Pre-Islamic Times to the First World War. Cambridge: Cambridge University Press, 1995.
Volf, Miroslav, Prince Ghazi bin Muhammad Bin Talal, and Melissa Yarrington, eds. *A Common Word between Us and You*. 5-Year Anniversary Edition, vol. 20. Amman: The Royal Aal Al-Bayt Institute for Islamic Thought (MABDA), 2012.
Zegeye, Abebe. "The Construction of the Beta Israel Identity". *Social Identities* 10, no. 5 (2004): 589–618.
Zoba, Wendy Murray. "Guardians of the Lost Ark: Ethiopia's Christians Stake Their Identity on Being Heirs of Solomon and Keepers of His Treasure". *Christianity Today* 43, no. 7 (14 June 1999): 6.

Index

Aaron 36, 285
Abbasid 5 n6, 144, 151, 154, 159, 282
Abduh, Muhammad 24
Abedin, A. Z., 228
Abraham 37, 45, 53, 75, 78–82, 96, 110, 125, 149, 166–7, 245, 249–51, 253, 257, 259–63, 267, 272–5, 280–1, 284–5, 289, 291, 298, 301, 304
Abreha, General, 131–4
abrogation 21, 31, 45, 47, 50–2, 68, contemporary use 216, 224, 261–2, 293
Tāriq al-Hākim, Abū ʿAlī Mansūr, Caliph, *see* Al-Hākim bi-Amr Allah, 177
as Mad Caliph 177, 212
Abū Hāritha, ʿAuf ibn 92
Abū Harithā, Bishop, 135–6, 142
Abyssinia 4, 20–1, 60–3, 66, 69–70, 73–5, 110–16, 119–20, 123–4, 126, 128–9, 131–6, 139–41, 204, 219, 245, 281, 284, 293, 303
Adam 37–8, 38, 73, 137, 156, 252, 260, 268, 285
Aedisius 115
ʿAffān, ʿUthmān ibn 145
ahl al-dhimmi 211–12
ahl al-injīl 287
ahl al-nar, People of the Fire, 22, 287
Ahmad, Imam 17, 48,
ahruf 13
Aishah 46
ajruhum 24, 287
Aksum, 113–15, 128
Alexandria 43, 62, 116, 181
Ali, Abdullah Yusuf 20, 21, 33, 47, 58

aliyá 102, 287
al-wahi al-qurʾāni, see inlibration
al-walāʾ waʾl barāʾ 296
ām al-fīl, see Year of the Elephant
Amalkites 278
ansār 26, 51, 103, 107, 125, 287
anthropomorphism, 45, 165 n114, 199, 200, 295
Anūshīrwan 89
apartheid 218, 222, 223 n73, 231
Aqabah,105 n131
aqānīm, see hypostasis
ʿarīd 198, 287 accident, *see* ʿarīd
Arianism 116, 128
Ariat, general 132
Aristotle 45, 155, 162
asab al-thaʾr, see revenge duty
asbāb an-nuzūl, 4, 22, 111, 279, 280, 283, 294
Ashama ibn Abjar, King 4, 60, 113, 119–20, 123, 140, 281, 293
People of the Trench, 128, 287
ashrāf, 287 more noble
aslamā, submitted to God, 22, 287
asmā allāh al-husnā, see the Beautiful Names of God
as-Sahrastānī 157
As-Samit, Ubadah ibn 48 n160, 57
Athanasius, Patriarch 116–19, 128
at-tajsīm, see anthropomorphism
ʿAus ibn Hāritha ibn Laʾm, 92–4
Aveline, Jean-Marc 256
Axum Empire 115 n181, 128, 281
al-Ayham 136
Ayoub, Mahmoud 268, 271
Ayyūb, Abu 103, 107

Babylonian Talmud 101–2, 298
Baghdad 5 n6
Bahīrā 106, 288
Bakr, Abu 12, 16, 46, 110, 145, 148 n23
Balaam 251
Bani al-Haritha 56, 92
Bani an-Nadr 56
Bani Awf bin al-Khazraj 57
Bani Aws 56, 107
Bani Jasm 56
Bani Malik 107
Bani Qaynuqa 56–7
Bani Quraydah 56
Bani Sa'dah 56
Bani Tha'laba 56
Banū Asad 89–90, 108
Banū Auf 107
Banū Bakr 85–6
Banū Fugayn Harīth ben Malik 133
Banū Khazraj 108, 109
Banū Māsika 100
Banū Murra 133 n264
Banū Nadir 109
Banū Qaynuqa 109
Banū Taghlib 84–7
Bar Kokhba 97, 101, 301, 308
bayt al-hikma 155
Beautiful Names, 5, 179 n174, 197, 202, 288
Bedouin 82–4, 99–100, 110
Benedict XVI, Pope 231, 235
Beta Israel 116, 288
Bethel 166
Bosra 245
Buhaisa 93–6
al-Bukharī, Muhammad b 15, 16, 18, 38, 125
Byzantine 5, 90, 96, 101, 110, 114, 118, 135–6, 140, 144, 146, 147, 162, 187, 202

Caleb, Ellā-Asbehā 131–2
Canaanites 60
Cappadocia 116
Chalcedonian 116, 144, 146, 149–50, 159, 161–2
Cheikho, Lewis 85 n44, 92, 176
Christ 36–8, 45, 111, 128, 130, 162, 165, 167–8, 172, 174, 177, 186, 198, 203
  challenges and opportunities 284
  Chapter 5 conclusions 275–7
  contemporary Christian use 243, 245, 247–8, 250, 253–4
  contemporary Muslim use 220, 226, 233, 234, 235
  in relation to Divine Hospitality 257–8, 262, 264, 267, 270, 272 267
  see also Jesus and Messiah
citizenship 6, 223, 275, 283
Common Word 139, 231–5, 237
Companions of Muhammad 4, 15
consensus see *Ijmā'*
Constantine 43, 45, 145
Constantinople 133, 187
Coptic 40 n120, 62, 118, 150, 181 n186, 215
Council of Nicea 143
Courbage, Yousef 150
crucifixion 34, 123, 199
  contemporary discussion 245, 248, 252, 255, 267, 275, 276, 284–5
Cush 114
Cyprus 185 n211, 186
Cyrus, Christian emperor 62–3
Cyrus of Persia 36, 251

Daesh 212
Ad-Dahhak 52
dār ad-da'wa, 288
dār ul-'ahd, 221, 288
dār al-harb, house/abode of war 288
dār al-hiyād, realm of neutrality 112, 281, 288

Index 315

dār al-islām, 288
dār ash-shahāda 221, 288
Day of Judgement 95, 211, 267
Day of Resurrection 17, 24, 59, 195, 211
de Chergé, Christian 261
De virtutibus animae 162
Deir Mar Moussa 245
deuteros theos 239, 288
Dhāt 288
dhikr 248, 259, 263, 288
Dick, Ignace 178
dhimmī, 148, 202, 211, 212, 225, 234, 288, 291, 292
dhimmitude 148, 223
Dhū al-Yamīnayn Tāhir b. al-Husayn 162
Dhubyān 92, 95
divine attributes 152, 157, 159, 172–3, 175, 182, 197, 202
  contemporary usage 252, 273, 282
  glossary 291, 294, 295
divorce 93, 215, 216
Dīwān 175, 288
diyyah, *see* retribution
Donner, Fred 147, 148–9
Dublin 209, 315
Duma 99
Dupuis, Jacques 264

ecumenical 149
Edessa 161
Edinburgh Conference 227
Egypt 44–5, 65, 81, 116, 118, 128
  contemporary use 209, 214, 216, 218
Elias of Nisibis 186
Ellā-Asbehā 131
Eretz Yisrael 78
Esack, Farid 216, 218–9, 222–6, 230–1, 234–5, 259, 279, 283
Esmail, Aziz 264
Ethiopia 111–9, 125, 128, 281, 288
European Council for Fatwa Research 209

Evangelical 100, 227
Ezanas 115–6

Falashas 116, 288
Farasān 129
Fargues, Philippe 150
farid kifya 288
al-Farisi, Salman 22–3, 68
Fatwa 209, 288, 296
Faymiyūn 127
fiqh 15, 288, 291
fiqh al-aqalliyyāt 221, 288
fiqh al-aqalliyyāt al-muslima 289
fiqh al-muwāzanāt 289
firqa 289
fitrah 28, 254, 289
fornication 235
Frankish provinces 187
Friedman 150
Frumentius 115–6, 128

Gabra Masqal 117
Gabriel 12, 38–9, 285
Galut, (Hebrew) Diaspora 102, 289
Gandhi 262
Al-Ghazali, Imam 32, 224, 273
Al-Ghazzi, Sulayman ibn Hasan 5, 144, 160
  comparison with Paul of Antioch and Abū Qurrah 196, 203
  Conclusions 282
  ideas of 175–85
ghazw 89, 99, 289
ghiyār, see libs al-aghiyār
Ghuluw fī ad-dīn 289
Gil, Moshe 100–1 n115, 3 n126, 146–9 n27
Girgashites 78
Gebr/gäbr, (*Ge 'ez, or* Amharic) 122 n219, 289
Great Commission 152, 180–2, 193, 226
Griffith, Sidney H., 158, 162
Grigentius, Bishop 131–3, 135

Habsa, daughter of Hayyān 130–1, 141
hāda, 25, 289
hadīth 13–20, 145
   Abyssinia 122 n219, 124 n222, 141
   Al-Baqarah (2):62 22, 26, 28, 31
   Common Word 233
   Glossary 289, 295
   an-Nisā' (4):171 34, 35, 38, 46
   al-mā'idah (5):48 46, 51, 54–5, 56
   al-mā'idah (5):82–3 60, 61, 63
   pre-Islamic Arabia 74
   Qaradawi 211, 216 n34
   Ramadan 222
   Tabbara 273
Hadramawt 132
hāfiz 289
Hāfiz, Imam 125
Hafsah 12
Hagar 78–81
   Abū Qurrah 166
   Dall'Oglio 249–50, 275
   Daou 260, 275
   Conclusions 280, 284
   Glossary 291
hāja 289
Hajar, 'Aws b 91
Hajj, Pilgrimage to Mecca 105, 289
l'Hakam, Abu, also known as Abu Jahl 75
Hallaj 280
al-Hamadhānī, 'Abd al-Jabbār 160
Hanīf, pl. hunafā' 259, 289
al-Hārith, King 86
al-Hārith, son of King Imr al-Qais 88
Al-Hārith, son of 'Auf ibn Abū Hāritha 92–6
Harrān 162
Hasan al-Bannā 289
Hatib bin Abi Balta'ah 62, 70
al-Hawāriyyūn 289
Hayy, alive, *hayāh*, life, 159, 197, 282, 289
Hayyān 130

Hebron 81
Heraclius, Emperor 62, 135, 147, 149
hifz 13
Hijaz 59, 62, 75
   challenges and opportunities 280
   Glossary 294
   Jews of 96–111 n161, 140
   Paul of Antioch 190
   Tabbara 264 n150
   transition of faith 124
al-Hijiyyah 289
Al-Hijr 98
hijra 21, 119, 135 281, 289
Himyar, Jews of 75, 81, 98, 101, 124, 125, 280
   Christianity 127–35
   deputation to Najrān 135, 141, 149, 292
Hind, (daughter of Muhalhil Ibn Rabī'a) 84–5
   King 'Abn Ibn Hind 86–7
Hind, 'Amr Ibn 86, 87
Hittites 78
Holy Land 59, 65, 102, 150, 186
Holy Spirit 33, 39–44
   Abū Qurrah, 161, 165, 167–75
   challenges and opportunities 282
   Dall'Oglio 250
   Daou 258, 269
   Ethiopian views on 118
   Glossary 293
   Paul of Antioch 189, 192–4, 196–8
   Sulaymān 180, 182–4
   as Trinity 152–3
Horites 78
Hosea 165, 260
Hōs monogenous para patros 242, 289
house of invitation, see *dār ad-da'wa*,
house of Israel, see *Beta Israel*
Hoyland 150
Hubaysh 156
Hudhayfa b. Badr 92
hulūl 289

Index

Hunayn Ibn Isḥāq 155–6
hypocrites 57, 109, 292
hypostasis, 159, 287

Ibād 289
Ibn Abbas, *tafsīr* 15–16
   Al-Baqarah (2):62 26, 30, 31
   an-Nisā' (4):171 35
   al-māʾidah (5):48 48–9, 50, 51, 54
   al-māʾidah (5):82–3 60–3, 67
Ibn Abi Hatim 51, 55
ibn Abi Rabah, Ata
Ibn al-Nadīm
Ibn Isḥāq, Muhammad (historian) 81,
   104, 119, 125, 127, 133, 136, 292
Ibn Juraij 26, 27
Ibn Kathir 2, 14
   al-baqarah (2):62 20–1, 24–6, 28,
      30–1, 34
   al-māʾidah (5):48 48–9, 51–2--4
   al-māʾidah (5):82–3 59–61, 64, 67, 69
   an-Nisā' (4):171 38, 39–40, 44
   pre-Islamic Arabia 104 n127, 108, 125,
      137 n282
Ibn al-Khattab 17–18, 91, 145, 212 n14,
   213, 225
Ibn al-Nu'man Qatadah 26, 28, 50, 53, 61
Ibn Saluba 54, 108
Ibn Ubayy 104, 281
Ibn Zaid 28
Idris 285
Ihsān 52, 70, 289
Ijāra 86, 290
Ijmāʾ 212, 221, 276, 290
Ijtihād 17, 32, 53, 157, 188, 189, 222, 290
Ikhwān 290
Ikhtiyār 13, 121, 185
ʿilm 290
ʿilm al-kalām, 5, 156–8, 203, 240, 282–3, 290
ʿilm uṣūl al-fiqh 222, 290
imān 23, 225, 290

imitizāj 290
In hoc signo vinces 145, 290
incarnation 143–4
   Abū Qurrah 162, 175
   challenges and opportunities 282, 284
   Chapter 3 conclusions 203–4
   Dall'Oglio 245, 252, 254
   early Christian Arabic 152, 157
   al-Ghazzī 178, 179
   Glossary 295
   Madigan 238
   Paul of Antioch 186, 189, 193, 196,
      197–8
   Tabbara 265, 267
   three Arabic-speaking Christian
      scholars 160
India 113, 154
injīl 50, 61, 287, 290
inlibration, 73, 193, 296
insān 290
Ireland 264
Isa 35, 38, 40, 43–4, 61, 290
ʿĪsā ibn Sabīr al-Murdār 160
Isaac 79–81, 166–7, 249, 251, 280
Isḥāq, Abu 49
Isḥāq, Ibn 81, 101 n117, 104, 119, 120 n210,
   125, 127, 133, 135 n273, 136, 292
Ishmael 78–82, 125
   contemporary considerations 249–50,
      253, 260, 262 n138, 275, 280, 284
Islamic State, *see* Daesh
Isnād 15
Istislāh 224, 290

Jabr, Mujahid ibn 2, 16
   Al-Baqarah (2):62 22, 23, 27–8, 30
   Chapter 1 conclusions 67
   al-māʾidah (5):48 47, 50
   al-māʾidah (5):82–3 58, 60
   an-Nisā' (4):171 34
Jacob 26, 166–7, 217, 296

Jacobites 44, 111, 142 n289, 261, 290
Ja'far ibn Abī Ṭālib 60, 120–1
al-Jāhiliyya 3, 4, 55, 65, 69
    beyond *al-Jāhiliyya* 73–7, 91–2, 96, 99, 107–10, 124–5, 135, 137, 139, 140
    Glossary 288
al-Jahl 75, 141, 197, 290
Jaifar bin al-Jalandi 62
Jawhar 182, 200, 290
    Chapter 3 conclusions 203–4
    al-Ghazzī 179–85
    Glossary 290
    Madigan 242 n30
    Paul of Antioch, 196–7, 200
    as substance 119
Jesus, Abyssinia 111, 117–19
    al-baqarah (2):62 26, 30
    A Common Word 233, 235
    Challenges and Opportunities 284–5
    Chapter 1 conclusions 68–70
    Chapter 3 conclusions 203–4
    Chapter 5 conclusions 274, 276
    Dall'Oglio 244, 248, 250, 252, 253, 254 n97
    Daou 261–2, 262–4, 269, 270
    deputation from Najrān 135–7
    Glossary 288, 289, 290, 291, 295
    Ja'far's defence 121–2
    Madigan 238–9, 243
    mā'idah (5):48 48, 53
    al-mā'idah (5):82–3 61–7 67–70
    an-Nisā' (4):171 33–46, 48
    Paul of Antioch 190, 193–6, 198–9, 201
    post-conquest 143–4
    Qaradawi 215–16
    Abū Qurrah 161–2, 165, 168, 169 n136, 172, 174, 175
    Sulaymān Al-Ghazzi 177, 185
    Tabbara 265, 267, 269
    tafsīr 19
    Triune Nature of God 152–3
    see also Christ, Messiah
Jerusalem iv, 5, 96 n89
    Jerusalem Conference 227
    Jews of the Hijaz 97, 105
    Qaradawi 213
    sectarian contrast 135 n272, 140, 146–7, 149
    Treaty of Ramla 187
Jews *al-baqarah* (2):62 25–8, 29–30
    Abū Qurrah 171, 192
    challenges and opportunities 280–1
    children of Abraham 78–9 n14, n17, 81–2 n27
    Chapter 1 conclusions 67, 70
    Chapter 1 introduction 5
    Chapter 2 conclusions 140–2
    Chapter 3 conclusions 201–2
    Chapter 5 conclusions 274
    contemporary use 217, 219, 233, 238, 242
    Divine Hospitality 257, 259, 265–7
    Glossary 287, 288, 294
    Hijaz 96–111
    Himyar region 125, 129, 133, 138
    al-mā'idah (5):82–3 54–7
    al-mā'idah (5):82–3 58–9, 62, 65
    an-Nisā' (4):171 34–5, 36
    post-conquest 146–7, 148–50
    pre-Islamic Arabia 74–5, 77
Jibril, *see* Gabriel
Jizyah 19, 28, 147, 211–13, 225
Job 192, 251
John Paul II, Pope 247, 255 n105, 270
Joseph, son of Jacob 81, 166, 217, 285,
al-Jum'ah al hazīnah 290
Jubayr bin Nufayr 46
Judaism 27, 54, 81, 96, 100
    Abyssinia 111, 114–17 n195
    Chapter 2 conclusions 140–1
    contemporary use 239–40, 257, 261–2

expectations of Messiah 101–4 n127
Glossary 292
Himyar region 124–6, 128, 138
Muhammad in Medina 110
Judea 97, 161, 166
Jundishur 22
Justinian 90

Ka'b bin Asad 54, 108
Ka'bah 80–1, 133–4, 290
Kāfir 2, 24, 231, 283, 291
Kalām nafsī, 274, 290
Kalb, tribe of 22
Kaleb, King 117
Kebra Nagast, 74, 117
Kedar, prophet of 82
Ketene, Robert de 188
Keturah 79 n14, 80–1, 291
Khaibar 98, 144 n5
khalaqa 291
Khalid b. Zayd 103
Al-Khalīl, *see* Hebron
Khamr, *see* wine
Khan, Badsha 262
kharāj 291
Khārija ibn Sinān 92–6
Al-Khattāb, Umar ibn 145, 212–13, 225
Khoury 188
Kinda, tribe of 88–9, 156
Al-Kindī, Abū Yusūf Ya'qūb b. Ishāq 156
'Umar b Al-Kittab 12
Koloe 113
kufr 225, 229, 291
Kulthūm, 'Amru Ibn 85, 88
Kulthūm Ibn Malīk 85
al-kutub al-sittah 15

Lailā, mother of 'Amru Ibn Kulthūm 85, 87
Lakhmid kingdom 89–90
Lakhnī'a Dhū Shanātir 126, 141
Lamoreaux, John C., 160

latīf 181, 198, 200, 203, 291,
    see also subtle substance
Lecker, Michael 98 n107, 100, 125 n227, 141
Lemuel 251
Levant
    challenges and opportunities 281
    Chapter 1 introduction 4–5
    Chapter 2 conclusions 140, 143 n1
    post-conquest 145, 148, 150, 161, 187, 201–2, 205
LGBT 222
libs al-aghiyār 178, 289, 291
Lings, Martin 120, 122 n219, 123 n221, 134, 135 n272
Logos 239–40, 291
Lumen Gentium 250, 258 n119, 261, 269 n169

Ma'ānī 291
McAuliffe, Jane Dammen 15, 19, 60, 68, 279
Machpelah 81
Madhhab 291, 292,
Madigan, Daniel A., 6, 237–46, 274, 284
Magi,
Al-Mahdi 155, 252
Mahoza 97
Majūs, 28, 291
Makeda of Sheba (Queen of Sheba), 114, 117 n195, 125, 136, 281
Maluf, I., 176
Mansūkh, *see* abrogation
Al-Mansur, Caliph 154
Maqāsid 223, 291
Mar Sabas 161
Mar Zutra 97
Ma'rūf 229
Mary
    Arabic-speaking Christian response 190, 193–4, 198, 201

Biblical Abyssinia 115, 121–2
contemporary use 267
deputation from Najrān 137
Tafsīr 34, 36, 38, 39, 41, 43, 49
see also Maryam
Maryam 35, 38, 40, 61, 121, 194, 199
see also Mary
masālik 291
al-Masīh, Abd 136, 138
Masjid an-Nabawī 291
al-maslaha 223, 291
Masruk 134
Mas'ūd, Abdullah b. 99
Mawlā 291
Mawlūd 291
Mawjūd 159, 282, 291
Mecca 21, 22, 28, 60, 80–1, 99
   at the beginning of Islam 105, 112, 119, 120, 125 n228, 132–4
   contemporary use 221, 264–5, 267, 280
   Glossary 287, 289, 292, 293
   origins of 80–1
   pre-Islamic importance 99
Medina *al-baqarah* (2):62 20–1, 22
   Challenges and Opportunities 281
   conclusions chapter (1) 70
   conclusions chapter (2) 139–41
   contemporary use 219, 224, 264–7
   delegation from Najrān 137
   expectations of a Messiah 104
   Himyar Region 125, 132
   Jews of the Hijaz 97
   al-mā'idah (5):48 46, 54, 56
   al-mā'idah (5):82–3 60
   an-Nisā' (4):171 33
   post-conquest 148
   relationship with Muhammad 105–11
   social historical context 75 78 n13
Melkite Church 42–3, 111, 142 n289, 159, 160, 176, 178 n173, 180 n177
menahhemana 40–1, 70–1, 291, 292

Mesopotamia 28, 161, 162
Messiah
   Arab-speaking Christian 152, 161, 179–80, 185, 193–4, 197–9, 204
   contemporary use 233, 235, 253, 265, 276, 280–1
   early Islamic Arabia 101–3, 105, 111, 119, 137
   Glossary 294
   al-Masīh 36, 40, 191, 291
   tafsīr 27, 34–5, 36–8, 42, 45, 61, 62–3, 69–70
   see also Christ, Jesus
Michael I, Patriarch of Antioch 160
Midian, Tribe of 82
Mihrāb 291
Millet 292
Minbar 292
Minhāj 224
al-Misri, Abu Salih 63
Mokhār 129
Moldova 187
Moses 17, 26, 45, 51, 53, 62
   Abū Qurrah 164–5, 167, 171
   contemporary use 241, 260, 280, 285
   Paul of Antioch 192, 193, 200, 203
   pre-Islamic importance 78, 81–2, 114
Mosul 22, 28
Mother Teresa 262
mu'āhid 292
mu'allaqāt 83, 92, 96, 292
al-Muamalāt 222, 292
Mubāhala 125, 138, 292
Mufassir, mufassirūn, 21, 23 n50, 50, 292
muhājir 104, 107, 292
muhājirūn, see muhājir
Muhalhil Ibn Rabī'a 84
muhaymin 47, 49–50, 69, 292
muhdth 182, 292
muhkam 30, 67, 137, 292
muhkamāt 137, 292

Mujahid, Abu Bakr b. 13
Mujtahid 290, 292
Mujtahid fi al-maddhab 292
Mujtahid fi-ashl-shar' 292
Mumayiz, Ibrahim 91,
Mu'min 24, 47, 225, 231, 263, 292
Munāfiqūn, see hypocrites
Al-Mundhir III 89, 131
Muqatta'āt 21,191, 292
Murīid 292
Mushrik 292, 294
Mushaf 13, 292
Muslim Brotherhood 107, 209, 220, 290
Muslimūn 76, 292
Mutakallimūn, 152, 160, 293
Mutashābihāt 137 n281, 293
Mutawaffika 267, 293
Mu'tazilite 157, 160, 202, 282
Al-Muttalib, Abdul 134

al-Naishapuri, Muslim b. Hajjaj 16
Najāshī, *see* Ashama ibn Abjar, King 60, 113, 119–20, 123, 140, 281, 293
Najrān
    Chapter 2 conclusions 139, 141, 142
    contemporary use 245, 266
    deputation of 135, 138, 144, 148, 180 n179, 213, 232
    Glossary 287, 292, 293
    post-conquest 148, 219
    pre-Islamic Arabia 75, 114, 127, 129–30, 149
nasab 293
nasārā 26–7 293
naskh, see abrogation
Nāsira 26, 293
    see also Nazareth
an-nāsirī 26, 27, 293
nāsirīyūn 26, 293
Nasrallah, Mgr J., 176–8
nātiq, 159, 197, 282, 293

Negus, see Ashama ibn Abjar, King
Nehemiah ben Hushiel, Exilarch 97, 105, 109 n155
Neoplatonic 156–7
Nestorians, as Church of the East 44, 142 n289, 161, 162, 293
Nicene 116
Niehoff 239
Nigeria 226
An-Niyya 293
Noah 53, 104, n127, 114, 125, 166, 251, 260
Nostra Aetate 226 n95, 243–4, 269, 277
Nufayl 133–4
nussāk 293

Omar b. al-Khattab 17–8, 91, 145, 213, 215
oral tradition, *see suhuf*

Pakistan 226
Palestine 90, 97, 98, 124 n223, 143 n1, 147–9, 151, 161
Paradise 31–26, 38
Paraclete 33, 40–1, 65, 67, 69–70, 111, 123, 153, 292
Paráklētos 40, 291, 292
Paran 79
Paul of Antioch 5, 144, 160, 165, 185–201, 203–4
    conclusions 282
    Glossary 294
People of the Scripture 28, 34, 64, 139, 232, 238
People of the Word 237–9, 241–33, 273, 274
Persian 5, 15
    early Islam 96, 97, 101, 105
    influence in southern Arabian Peninsula 114, 128 n240, 135, 140
    post-conquest Levant 147, 149, 155, 202
Petra 110
Philo 239

Plato, 45
  see also Neoplatonic
polytheists 21, 28, 59, 62, 264, 267, 277
Protestant 215, 227

qadīm 182, 293
Qahtān 103
al-Qais, Imr 84, 88, 89–91, 156
al-Qais', Imr 84, 88–91, 156
Al-Qaradawi, Yusuf 6, 213–17, 221, 225, 234, 235
qashīda 83–4, 293
Qaswā 107, 293
Qatadah 26, 28, 50, 53, 61
Qaylah, sons of, 106
Qays, Shas bin 54, 108
'Qays ibn Zuhayr 92
al-Qayūm 197, 293
qebat 118, 293
qibla 291, 293
qissīsīn 60, 293
qist 293
Quaker 223, 251 n79, 294
Qubā 106
Qubādh 89
Quraysh 13, 95, 104, 106, 120, 133
Qurrah, Theodore Abū 5, 136 n247, 144
  challenges and ppportunities 282
  comparison with Madigan 240
  comparison with Sulaymān al-Ghazzī and Paul of Antioch 179, 182, 185, 189, 192, 193, 203–4
  ideas of 159–75
Qutb, Sayyid 76–7, 220
Ata bin Abi Rabah 61

Rabbanan d'Aggadta 74, 78–9
Ramadan, Tariq 6, 216–30, 234–5, 258–9, 276–7
Ar-Rahman 293
Rahmānist 98

rasm 293
rasūl 37, 294
ra'y 16, 294
realm of neutrality, see dār al-hiyād
recitation, see Ikhtiyār
Redemptoris Missio 269 n169, 170, 277
Regensburg 226 n95, 231, 235
Renard, Jack 207
Resurrection, 252–3, 284–5
  Day of, 17, 24, 59, 195, 211
retribution, 48, 86 n46, 89, 288
revenge duty 90, 96, 287
ribā 294
Ricci, Fr Matteo 247
Richard the Lionheart 186
Rida, Rashid 2, 11
  Al-Baqarah (2):62 24–5, 27–9, 32–3
  challenges and opportunities 279–81
  contemporary use 224, 230, 241
  al-mā'idah (5):48 50–7
  al-mā'idah (5):82–3 59, 61–2, 66–9
  an-Nisā' (4):171 36, 39–41, 44–6
  pre-Islamic Arabia 76
riddah, Wars of 12
risālah 294
Robertson, William 214
rūh 38–9, 294
ruhban 60

Saba'a 27, 294
Sabians 21, 25, 27–30, 287, 294
Sābi'ūn, see Sabians
Sabta 114
Sahabah 15–16
  Jubayr, Sa'id b. 63
Suhaylī 100
Sahih Bukharī 16, 18, 79 n14, 80 n20, 122 n219, 125
Sahih Muslim 16
sakinah 75, 294
Salaam, Abdullah ibn 100

Index 323

Salaf 16, 294
Salafi 2, 6, 294, 296
Sālihūn 294
Salool, Abdullah bin Ubay bin 57
Sa'lūk 88, 294
Samaria 97
Samau'āl ben Ādiyā 90
Samhūdī 100, 103
Ubadah ibn As-Samit 57
Sana'a 99, 133 n261
Sarah 79–81, 166, 250
Satan 33
Sbath, Paul 176
Seba 114
Sellasie, Sergew Hable 123 n221, 131 n254, 133
shahādah 149, 294
sharī'ah 214, 224, 225
Sharī'at al-'adl 294
Sharī'at al-fadl 294
Shiloh 102–3, 294
Shirk, 42, 68, 69, 141–2, 178, 294
shubhah 294
shubbiha lahum, see crucifixion
sibhga 259 n121, 294
Siddiqui, Ataullah 6, 216, 217, 219–20, 223–9, 233
    challenges and opportunites 283–4
    Chapter -4 conclusions 234–5
    contemporary use 275, 276
Sidon 143 n1, 185, 187
sifa dhātiyya 240, 294
sifāt Allah, 157, 159, 295
Siméon the Younger 186
Sinai, Mount 164
Socotra, island of 135
Sodom, 126, 167
Sost Ledat 118, 295
Spain 154
substance
    Chapter 3 conclusions 203–4

    as employed by al-Ghazzī 179–85
    as employed by Madigan 242 n30
    as employed by Paul of Antioch, 196–7, 200
    Glossary 290, 291
    in reference to the Ethiopian Orthodox Church 119
    as subtle substance 181, 198, 203, 291
Sudan 226
Al-Suddi 22, 28, 50
Sufyan Ath Thawri 16, 49
suhuf 12
Sumuyafa' 'Aswa' 131
Sunnah al-nabi 14, 295
Surya, Abdullah bin 54, 108
Swiss 6, 216
Syriac 111, 118, 144, 150, 155, 161, 183
    contemporary use 245, 247
    Glossary 292

Ta'āruf, 295
al-Tabari, Rabban 265
Al-Tabari, *Tafsīr* 2, 15
    Al-Baqarah (2):62 23, 25, 26, 27, 28, 29, 30, 31
    Chapter 1 conclusions 67
    contemporary use 224, 279, 280
    al-mā'idah (5):48 48, 49, 50, 51, 52, 53, 54, 55, 56
    al-mā'idah (5):82–3 59, 60, 61, 63, 64
    an-Nisā' (4):171 34, 36, 37, 38, 41, 42
    pre-Islamic Arabia 76, 123 n220, 133, n264
Tabbara, Nayla
    challenges and opportunities 279–80, 283–4
    contemporary use 256–60, 263–9, 271–3, 275–7
    introduction 6–7
tabī'a, 295
tābi'ūn 16, 295

Tabuk 98
Taghlib 84–7, 129, 147, 212 n14
tajassud, see incarnation
at-Tajsīm 199, 295
Taḥrīf 263, 265, 285, 295
Tahsīniyyāt 295
Taiy, tribe of 92
Takfīr 295
Tahawwadathu 100
Taima 90
Talhah, Ali bin Abi 50
Talmud 97, 101–2, 110
At-Tamimi 49
taqarrub 295
taqlīd 17, 32, 54, 62, 68, 195
taqwā 49, 69, 295
tasdīq 295
tashkīl 13, 37 n105, 293, 295
tashrīd 295
tawahedo 101, 117–18, 295
tawḥīd 35, 41–2, 65, 67–9, 157, 178
    challenges and opportunities 282
    Chapter 3 conclusions, 202
    Glossary 296
Tayma 98
Ta'wīl 137 n281, 296
Teshuvah 80, 296
Thābit, Zaid Ibn 12–13, 99
Thalātha aqānīm 159
Ath-Thawri, Sufyan 16, 49
Theotokos 136 n277, 296
Tibān As'ad Abū Karīb 81, 103–4, 107, 125
Torah *Al-Baqarah* 25–6
    Abū Qurrah 164
    Chapter 1 conclusions 69
    Chapter 3 conclusions 203
    children of Abraham 79 n17
    contemporary use 228, 229, 235, 263, 266
    Jews of Hijaz 98, 99–100, 101
    Jews of Medina 110

al-mā'idah (5):48 47–50, 51–3, 55
al-mā'idah (5):82–3 63
an-Nisā' 35
Paul of Antioch 190, 268, 277
Treaty of Ramla 187
Trimingham, J. Spencer
    Christians of Abyssinia 114 n171, 115 n181
    Himyar Region 125 n277, 126 n231, 127 n234, 130 n248
    pre-Islamic culture 83 n32, 110
Tripoli 187
Treaty of Medina 139, 148, 219, 281
Tsadkan 118, 296
Tubba, *see* Tibān As'ad Abū Karīb
Tyre 187

Uhud 152
Ukaz 99
'Umar, Covenant of 147, 213,
ummat al-mu'minīn 57, 104, 145, 281, 296
ummatan wasata 296
ummatun muqtasidatun 296
Umayyad Dynasty 83, 148, 215 n31
Unaiza 88–9
uqnūm 296
Urban II, Pope 186
usūl 290, 296
usūl al-fiqh (law and jurisprudence) 296
Uthman, Caliph 13, 99, 145

waḥdat al-wujūd 296
Wahhaab, 'Abdil 73, 76, 77, 297
wali 254 n97, 296
al-wāqi' 224, 296
war-free zone, *see dār al-'ahd*
wasatī 296
al-wāsi' 272, 296
wa-yomer 239, 274, 296
wine 90, 113, 177, 178, 212, 291

Index

World Council of Churches 227, 228 n103, 259 n121
wujūd 296

Vatican II 250
Vienna 188

Yahūda 26, 296
Yaksum, son of General Abreha 134
Yamamah, Battle of 12
Yasser Hafez, Sheikh 255
Yathrib, 22, 81, 82 n27, 96–104, 281
    see also Medina

Yazan, Sayf b. Dhū 135
Year of the Elephant 133, 142, 287
Yūsuf Dhū Nuwās 97, 104–5, 126, 128–33, 141

Zabūr 28, 296
Zafār 114 n171, 128 n240, 129–31, 132
zakāt 212, 225, 296
Zinā 235, 296
Zoroastrian, *see* Majūs
Zuhair Ibn Abu Salmā 84, 91
Zur'a Dhū Nuwās 126

Index of Qur'ānic verses

sūrat al-baqarah
(2):8 25
(2):61 24
(2):62 2, 20, 24, 67, 68, 191, 231, 231 n49, 280
(2):75 19
(2):117 240
(2):120 19
(2):125 80
(2):127 80
(2):135 259, 260 n126
(2):143 67, 272
(2):253 39
(2):255 197
(2):256 213

sūrat Āl-'Imrān
(3):7 21
(3):18 137, 138, 229, 260, 277
(3):19 229, 260, 311
(3):24 137
(3):31 137
(3):45 137
(3):47 49, 137
(3):49 137
(3):55 35 n97, 267
(3):59 38 n109, 43 n130, 137
(3):60–63 138
(3):64 138, 217, 229, 232, 266
(3):71 19, 46 n161
(3):79 138
(3):85 30, 31, 190 n234, 229
(3):154 75
(3):199 52 n176, 64, 263 n144, 284

sūrat an-Nisā'
(4):123–124 32, 280
(4):156–159 267
(4):157–8 252
(4):171 2, 20, 33, 34, 38 n109, 68, 143, 152, 174, 194, 204, 233, 267

sūrat al-mā'idah
(5):4 46 n152
(5):5 19
(5):45 48, 108, 137
(5):46 48
(5):47 49, 263, 287
(5):48 2, 20, 31, 46, 49, 62, 69, 161, 231, 233, 259, 262, 272
(5):49 54, 55, 108, 137
(5):50 55, 75, 108, 263
(5):66 20
(5):75 19, 40,
(5):82 2, 20, 58, 70, 109, 111, 192, 281, 284
(5):83 58, 60, 64
(5):110 153
(5):111 39
(5):112–115 196
(5):116 43, 267

sūrat al-an'ām
(6):101 194, 198

sūrat at-tawbah
(9):29 19, 266
(9):30 267
(9):31 19, 35

sūrat Yunus
(10):62 31
(10):94 263

sūrat Hūd
(11):118 212

sūrat an-nahl
(16):2 39

sūrat al-isrā'
(17):107 49
(17):110 197

sūrat Maryam
(19):16–21 121
(19):16–34 38
(19):34 194

sūrat al-anbiya'
(21):7 263
(21):91 39

sūrat al-ahqāf
(46):12 18

sūrat al-hajj
(22):40 19

sūrat al-mu'minūn
(23):7–9 57
(23):52–53 265

sūrat an-nūr
(24):35 241

sūrat al-qasas
(28):52–55 64, 112, 284

sūrat al-'ankabūt
(29):46 19, 191, 217, 229

sūrat Luqmān
(31):28 259

sūrah as-sajdah
(32):8–9 39

sūrat al-ahzāb
(33):33 75
(33):43 241

sūrat saba'
(34):15–19 104

sūrat fātir
(35):20 241
(35):24 259

sūrat Ghāfir
(40):7–8 190

sūrat fussilat
(41):30 31

sūrat ash-Shūra
(42):13 53
(42):15 213
(42):51 194, 198
(42):52 39

sūrat l-dukhān
(44):37 104

sūrat al-fath
(48):26 75

sūrat al-hujurāt
(49):13 295

sūrat ar-Rahmān
(55):7–9 259

Index

sūrat al-ḥadīd
(57):25 191
(57):27 61

sūrat al-mumtaḥanah
(60):4, 272
(60):4–9 153
(60):7 243
(60):8 244, 281

sūrat aṣ-ṣaff
(61):14 26

sūrat at-taḥrīm
(66):12 193

sūrat al-muṭaffifīn
(83):1–3 259

sūrat al-balad
(90):1–3 194, 198
(90):4 153

STUDIES IN THEOLOGY SOCIETY AND CULTURE

Religious and theological reflection has often been confined to the realm of the private, the personal or the Church. In Europe this restriction of religion and theology can be traced back to the Enlightenment and has had long-lasting and pernicious consequences for the understanding of religious faith and society. On the one hand, there has been a rise in religious fundamentalisms around the globe, while, on the other hand, so-called advanced societies are constructed mainly along economic, pragmatic and rationalistic lines. Added to this is the reality that religious faith is increasingly lived out in pluralistic and multi-faith contexts with all the challenges and opportunities this offers to denominational religion.

This series explores what it means to be 'religious' in such contexts. It invites scholarly contributions to themes including patterns of secularisation, postmodern challenges to religion, and the relation of faith and culture. From a theological perspective it seeks constructive re-interpretations of traditional Christian topics – including God, creation, salvation, Christology, ecclesiology, etc. – in a way that makes them more credible for today. It also welcomes studies on religion and science, and on theology and the arts.

The series publishes monographs, comparative studies, interdisciplinary projects, conference proceedings and edited books. It attracts well-researched, especially interdisciplinary, studies which open new approaches to religion or focus on interesting case studies. The language of the series is English. Book proposals should be emailed to any, or all, of the following:

SERIES EDITORS:

- Dr Judith Gruber, Research professor, Leuven University
- Dr Norbert Hintersteiner, University of Münster (norbert.hintersteiner@uni-muenster.de)
- Dr Declan Marmion, St Patrick's College, Maynooth (Declan.Marmion@spcm.ie)
- Dr Gesa Thiessen, Trinity College, The University of Dublin (gesa.thiessen@tcd.ie)

Vol. 1   Patrick Claffey and Joe Egan (eds):
         Movement or Moment? Assessing Liberation Theology Forty Years after Medellín.
         276 pages. 2009. ISBN 978-3-03911-991-2.

Vol. 2   Declan Marmion and Gesa Thiessen (eds):
         Trinity and Salvation: Theological, Spiritual and Aesthetic Perspectives.
         197 pages. 2009. ISBN 978-3-03911-969-1.

Vol. 3   Pádraic Conway and Fáinche Ryan (eds):
         Karl Rahner: Theologian for the Twenty-first Century.
         265 pages. 2010. ISBN 978-3-0343-0127-5.

Vol. 4   Declan O'Byrne:
         Spirit Christology and Trinity in the Theology of David Coffey.
         274 pages. 2010. ISBN 978-3-0343-0191-6.

Vol. 5   Joe Egan:
         From Misery to Hope: Encountering God in the Abyss of Suffering.
         384 pages. 2010. ISBN 978-3-0343-0234-0.

Vol. 6   Gideon Goosen:
         Hyphenated Christians: Towards a Better Understanding of Dual Religious
         Belonging.
         190 pages. 2011. ISBN 978-3-0343-0701-7.

Vol. 7   Jean Lee:
         The Two Pillars of the Market: A Paradigm for Dialogue between Theology
         and Economics.
         301 pages. 2011. ISBN 978-3-0343-0700-0.

Vol. 8   Stephen Butler Murray:
         Reclaiming Divine Wrath: A History of a Christian Doctrine and Its Interpretation.
         315 pages. 2011. ISBN 978-3-0343-0703-1.

Vol. 9   Kieran Flynn:
         Islam in the West: Iraqi Shi'i Communities in Transition and Dialogue.
         269 pages. 2013. ISBN 978-3-0343-0905-9.

Vol. 10 Patrick Claffey, Joe Egan and Marie Keenan (eds):
         Broken Faith: Why Hope Matters.
         323 pages. 2013. ISBN 978-3-0343-0997-4.

Vol. 11 Leah E. Robinson:
         Embodied Peacebuilding: Reconciliation as Practical Theology.
         293 pages. 2015. ISBN 978-3-0343-1858-7.

Vol. 12   Dermot A. Lane (ed.):
         Vatican II in Ireland, Fifty Years On: Essays in Honour of Pádraic Conway.
         421 pages. 2015. ISBN 978-3-0343-1874-7.

Vol. 13   Wilfred Asampambila Agana:
         "Succeed Here and in Eternity": The Prosperity Gospel in Ghana.
         379 pages. 2016. ISBN 978-3-0343-1932-4.

Vol. 14   Richard Lawrence Kimball:
         The People of the Book (ahl al-kitāb): A Comparative Theological Exploration
         342 pages. 2019. ISBN 978-1-78874-268-9.